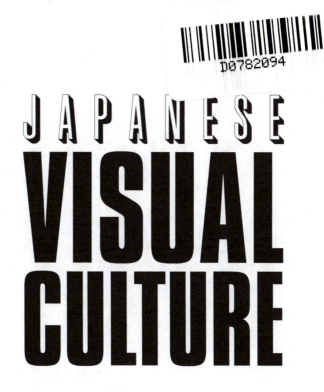

JAPANESE
VISUAL
CULTURE

JAPANESE VISUAL CULTURE

Explorations in the World of Manga and Anime

Edited by Mark W. MacWilliams

Foreword by Frederik L. Schodt

An East Gate Book

Routledge
Taylor & Francis Group

LONDON AND NEW YORK

An East Gate Book

First published 2008 by M.E. Sharpe

Published 2015 by Routledge
2 Park Square, Milton Park, Abingdon, Oxon OX14 4RN
711 Third Avenue, New York, NY 10017, USA

Routledge is an imprint of the Taylor & Francis Group, an informa business

Published with support from the Japan Foundation

Library of Congress Cataloging-in-Publication Data

Macwilliams, Mark Wheeler, 1952–
 Japanese visual culture : explorations in the world of manga and anime / edited by
Mark W. MacWilliams.
   p. cm.
Includes bibliographical references and index.
 ISBN 978-0-7656-1601-2 (cloth : alk. paper)—ISBN 978-0-7656-1602-9 (pbk. : alk. paper)
 1. Comic books, strips, etc.—Japan—History and criticism. 2. Animated films—Japan—
History and criticism. I. Title.

NC1764.5.J3M33 2008
741.5'952—dc22   2007025425

ISBN 13: 9780765616029 (pbk)
ISBN 13: 9780765616012 (hbk)

Contents

Foreword
Japan's New Visual Culture

By September 4, 2006, it was clear to me that manga had truly conquered North America. That week, the *New Yorker* magazine featured on its cover a cartoon titled "Back to Cool," showing an average American teenager slouching back to school, his brain depicted as an enlarged map divided into zones of interest. There, along with MySpace, Video iPod, PS3, Snoop Dogg, Algebra, and YouTube, was a large zone labeled "Manga." There was no translation of the word, of course, and—with the market for English versions of both manga and anime now estimated to be in the billions of dollars—who would need one?

I never dreamed that manga and anime would become so popular outside of Japan. I personally became interested in manga, especially, back in 1970, when I was an undergraduate Asian Studies major attending a university in Tokyo and trying to learn Japanese. I noticed that my fellow Japanese students seemed to be spending far more time reading giant weekly manga magazines than they did cracking their textbooks, and it did not take me long to become hooked, too. Manga were fabulous entertainment, and I could easily rationalize reading them as a way to learn Japanese.

In the process I also eventually discovered that manga are much more; they are an open window onto the Japanese id, a view—not necessarily of reality itself—but of a culture's aspirations, dreams, nightmares, fantasies, and fetishes. As is often noted, Japan is a culture where the difference between public and private realities, and appearance and reality, is often great. In this context, for non-Japanese trying to fathom what is really going on, both manga and—to a lesser extent—anime can be an immense aid in bridging the disconnect. It is especially true because Japan is today one of the only countries in the world where "comic books" have become a full-fledged medium of expression, on par with novels and films, and read by what often seems to be everyone.

At the time, the idea of going to graduate school was not particularly appealing to me, but I can recall at one point vaguely and naively thinking that—if I failed to find anything else suitable—perhaps I could someday do research on manga at a university in America. It seemed like a wonderful way to counter what then sometimes seemed to be an overemphasis in academia on the more formal aspects of Japanese culture—in effect, to use manga as a tool to understand what was really going on. But I had no idea of how to implement this idea, and it remained a fantasy.

I went on to become an interpreter, translator, and occasional writer, and I managed to continue my interest in manga in other ways. Around 1977, in the belief that more people outside of Japan should know about manga, some friends and I began translating a few of the better-known ones. But it was still an era in which most Americans had never tried sushi and knew little about Japan, especially its popular culture. I soon realized that it was too early for manga to be read or accepted in the United States, at least, so I therefore set out to write a book that would introduce the manga phenomenon to non-Japanese. This became my first book, *Manga! Manga! The World of Japanese Comics* (1983). The main idea was to draw people's attention to an interesting social phenomenon and—if possible—encourage them to read manga.

When I finished my manuscript I had a good-natured argument on the phone with my editor, Peter Goodman, about the title. I wanted to use *Japanese Comics: The New Visual Culture*. He wanted something more "pop," and advocated for *Manga! Manga!* in the main title. I was afraid that by putting "manga" in the title that the book would be filed next to "manganese" in library card catalogs (which were of course then the main way people located books), or that most people in bookstores would think the book I had slaved over so long had something to do with Italian cooking.

My book never sold many copies, but eventually the manga/anime phenomenon in Japan itself became so huge that the rest of the world could not ignore it. Fans mushroomed in other Asian countries, then in Europe, and finally in North America, where in the last two decades they have exploded in number. It is energetic fans who have proselytized on behalf of their favorite stories and characters, and pushed for greater acceptance of the material they enjoy, encouraging reluctant publishers to expand their lists and include translated manga, or pushing broadcasters to devote more time to anime shows. The reasons for the popularity of manga and anime in North America are varied and complex, but probably can best be summarized by saying that manga and anime are great fun, and also demonstrate the true potential of comics and animation—both of which were first developed in North America but were later neglected and ghettoized as entertainment for juveniles or emotionally immature adults.

As young American fans of manga and anime moved from high school into college, and kept reading manga and watching anime, it was inevitable that more and more of them would to want to study and write about the object of their interest. And in this they were aided by major changes both in American higher education and in Japan. Just as translated manga and anime became more popular, at universities the study of pop culture, once regarded as frivolous, also became more legitimate and eventually even fashionable. A similar trend also appeared in Japan, as intellectuals who had once pooh-poohed the importance of indigenous pop culture started to take manga and anime much more seriously, and began publishing more and more works of criticism.

I first noticed that American undergraduates were writing papers about manga and anime around 1990. Not too long after that, candidates for master's degrees also began writing about them. Now, there are even doctoral candidates writing about manga, and tenured professors who specialize in either manga, anime, or both.

I have had the opportunity to see many research papers written in English about manga and anime. In the early years, it is true that some were compromised by over-enthusiasm on the part of their authors, who were occasionally working outside of their language or cultural skill set and lacked access to reference materials from Japan. And sometimes the writing of early scholars was infected by the same postmodern fads that have infected all liberal arts education, as manifested in overuse of garbled terms such as "postmodern," "concomitantly," "deconstruction," "commodification," "fetishization," and my all-time favorite, "global phallic hegemony."

But a few years back that all began to change. There is some serious and highly *useful* writing on manga and anime being done today in English, and this book is a smorgasbord of some of the best work, done by some of the best scholars in the field. Many of the topics are dear to my own heart. There are chapters on the use of cartoons and comics throughout different periods of Japanese history, including the Russo-Japanese war of 1904–1905, or the Aum Shinrikyō cult of the 1990s. Individual creators such as Osamu Tezuka and Satoshi Kon are examined, and the development of *shōjo*, or girls' manga, is explored. In the process we can see how the study of manga—and anime—can help illuminate aspects of a society that otherwise might remain opaque. And these explorations hint at the ways in which manga and anime were long destined to become such a huge social phenomenon. Kudos, therefore, to the authors, the editor, and the publisher of this delightful work.

Frederik L. Schodt
September 14, 2006

A Note on Language

In Japan, people's names are usually written with the family name first and the given name last. However, as this book is written not just for Japan specialists but also for a more general audience, I have listed Japanese names in the usual English order: given name first and family name last.

Japanese words are generally italicized in English text (e.g., *yume*, *namida*). An exception is made for words that are used repeatedly in a chapter; such words are italicized and defined the first time they are used (e.g., *enka*, *anime*), and thereafter printed in roman type (enka, anime). A "long sign" (macron) over a vowel in a Japanese name or word indicates that the sound of the vowel is sustained; thus the difference in pronunciation between *koi* (love) and *kōi* (an act of kind intentions, or goodwill).

In Japanese titles that include "borrowed" English words I have generally used the Japanese phoneticized spelling followed by the standard English spellings of those words in parentheses, thus *Yūkan kurabu* (Yūkan Club).

A Note on Language

JAPANESE
VISUAL
CULTURE

Introduction

MARK W. MacWILLIAMS

Reading *manga* (comic books and graphic novels) and watching *anime* (animation) is a significant part of daily life for millions of Japanese. Japan's literacy, newspaper circulation, and TV viewing rates are among the world's highest, and its mass media (*masu komi*) creates an environment that is replete with stories. Modern Japan is what Michel de Certeau describes as a "recited society" where people walk "all day long through a forest of narratives from journalism, advertising, and television, narrativities that still find time as [people are] getting ready for bed to slip a few final messages under the portals of sleep" (1984, 186). Japan is also what Susan Sontag refers to as an "image world," since much of Japanese mass media is involved in producing and consuming images, at a time when they have "extraordinary powers to determine [people's] demands on reality and are themselves coveted substitutes for firsthand experience . . ." (Sontag 2003, 80). The animated images that flicker across the screen and fill the pages of comic magazines and books are a major source of the stories that not only Japanese, but also an increasingly global audience, consume today.

An example of the ubiquity of manga and anime can be seen in Machiko Hasegawa's (1920–1992) famous *Sazae-san. Sazae-san* became a fixture in postwar Japanese life after it first debuted as a four-panel comic strip in the *Asahi shimbun* in 1946. The newspaper serialization ended in 1974, but Fuji TV's animated version has appeared every Sunday since 1969, making it the longest-running TV series in Japan. The show is a nostalgic throwback to an earlier and simpler age; it features a young suburban housewife who lives with her in-laws in a traditional three-generation Japanese household, occasionally enjoys wearing a kimono, and never uses a cell phone, a personal computer, or an MP3 player. And yet, Sazae Isono is also a modern middle-class woman whose house is filled with the latest electronic domestic appliances, courtesy of Toshiba, the show's longtime corporate sponsor. The weekly episodes are sprinkled with lighthearted humor about the everyday trials and tribulations of an ordinary Japanese family (Lee 2000, 189–190). As one fan puts it, "we see their life go through each season's transition with a smile" (Mari 2004).

Sazae-san generates consistently solid ratings, making it a family-oriented TV staple. In the last week of November 2006, for instance, it was Fuji TV's top-rated weekly show with a 20.9 percent market share, and it has achieved an almost ritualistic status among Japanese viewers. Those who habitually watch it can suffer from that grievous Sunday-evening malady known as *Sazae-san* syndrome, the depression that sets in when the show's final credits roll, signifying the end of the weekend (Mari 2004). *Sazae-san* is a good example of how manga and anime occupy an important place in everyday Japanese life as forms of entertainment.

However, classics like *Sazae-san* are only a small part of an immense narrative universe. There are thousands of manga, anime, and computer games that avid fans, known as *otaku,* said to number about 2.4 million in Japan and spend over 2.5 billion dollars a year on these products, enjoy (Makino 2007). One realizes this by going to Mandarake, the large manga emporium in Shibuya in downtown Tokyo. It is overwhelming to first view the tens of thousands of brightly colored manga volumes packed in the rows and rows of bookshelves that stretch out before you. This same experience is also available virtually. Just typing in "manga" and "anime" on the Google search engine, for example, yields 180,700,000 hits, close to what you would get for *eiga* (movies) at 201,000,000. One of the interesting Web sites that will turn up on such an Internet search is the *Anime News Network* (www.animenewsnetwork.com). This key electronic source for information on new anime releases lists over 4,354 anime titles, ranging from TV specials and series to OVAs (original video animation) with provocative titles like *Death Note, Samurai X: Trust and Betrayal,* and *Fullmetal Alchemist* to full-length movies, such as Hayao Miyazaki's Academy award-winning *Spirited Away* (2001). Where does one begin to explore what for some might seem a dauntingly vast and exotic world of Japanese comic, graphic, and animated art? Who are the artists? What kinds of stories do they create, and why do so many people find them so entertaining?

In recent years, a growing number of works in English have appeared to address these questions. These range from introductory works geared for a popular audience to more sophisticated scholarly studies. Important books on manga include Frederik Schodt's *Manga!Manga! The World of Japanese Comics* (1983) and *Dreamland Japan: Writings on Modern Manga* (1996), Sharon Kinsella's *Adult Manga* (2000), Paul Gravett's *Manga: Sixty Years of Japanese Comics* (2004), Jaqueline Berndt and Steffi Richter's *Reading Manga: Local and Global Perceptions of Japanese Comics* (2006), and, most recently, Frederik Schodt's *Astro Boy Essays: Osamu Tezuka, Mighty Atom, and the Manga/Anime Revolution* (2007). In the case of anime, several books are also worth mentioning: Antonia Levi's *Samurai from Outer Space: Understanding Japanese Animation* (1996), Gilles Poitras's *The Anime Companion: What's Japanese about Japanese Animation* (1999), Helen McCarthy's *Hayao Miyazaki: Master of Japanese Animation* (1999), Patrick Drazen's *Anime Explosion: The What? Why? and Wow! of Japanese Animation* (2002), and Susan Napier's *Anime from Akira to Howl's Moving Castle: Experiencing Contemporary Japanese Animation* (2005). In addition, several anthologies on Japanese popular culture include important studies of manga and anime, such as John Whittier Treat's *Contemporary Japan and Popular Culture* (1996), Timothy Craig's *Japan Pop! Inside the World of Japanese Popular Culture* (2000), John Lent's *Illustrating Asia* (2001), Timothy Craig and Richard

King's *Global Goes Local: Popular Culture in Asia* (2002), and, most recently, Steven Brown's *Cinema Anime* (2006).

This recent surge in publishing is partly a response to manga and anime's increasing popularity among Western fans. As Toshiya Ueno has noted, "If people once asked, 'What is ZEN?' now they ask, 'What is otaku?' In the past, it was Japan's high culture, such as Zen Buddhism and the fine arts, that was the object of the Western obsession for things Japanese. This derives from early connoisseurs such as Ernst Fenollosa, who popularized the idea that Japanese art displayed a "carefully nurtured refinement" that gave "deep insight into the secrets of the East" (Chisolm 1963, 96). These refined spiritual sensibilities seemed exotic to those, like Fenollosa, who envisaged the West as a culture mired in a crass materialism. But today, the elegant geisha strolling in a tranquil tea garden has been replaced by a saucer-eyed, super-sexy heroine in a post-apocalyptic dystopian landscape. Fenollosa would have been appalled, dismissing this aesthetic as supremely low culture, but it now reigns supreme. Manga and anime are not fine arts on display in a museum; they are popular art forms created by an industrialized, corporate, capitalistic culture found on TV, in the movie theater, at the local bookstore, or in manga cafes (*manga kissa*). That being said, however, both media have gained artistic recognition as exemplified by the new museums dedicated to their exhibition, such as the Osamu Tezuka Manga Museum in Takarazuka, northwest of Osaka, the Studio Ghibli Museum in Mitaka near Tokyo, and the new Kyoto Intenational Manga Museum.

Manga and anime attract fans, both Japanese and Western, not because of any Eastern mystical sense of harmony with nature, but because of what Jean Marie Bouissou has called their "aesthetic of excess, conflict, imbalance, and overt sensuality." They are especially appealing because they are "pure pleasure commodities," inexpensive forms of entertainment that are to be enjoyed (2006, 149–155; Berndt 2001, 351). However, this does not mean that they are nothing more than cheap thrills, created to escape from the pressures of the real world. Most would agree with manga expert Frederik Schodt that they also have the power to express people's hopes and fears. They are mediascapes of dreamscapes, "where stressed-out modern urbanites daily work out their neuroses and frustrations. Viewed in their totality, the phenomenal number of stories produced is like the constant chatter of the collective unconscious, an articulation of a dream world" (1996, 31; see also Napier 2005, 73–74). We must explore these dream worlds found within manga and anime.

The present volume, *Japanese Visual Culture: Explorations in the World of Manga and Anime,* attempts to do just this. This essay collection was originally inspired by panel presentations at the Seventh Annual Asian Studies Conference at Sophia University in Tokyo, 2003. Over the next few years, I became acquainted with an international coterie of researchers studying in this area, some of whom have contributed to this volume. All of the essays in this book presume that manga and anime are important to study for two reasons: first, they are a key part of contemporary Japanese mass visual culture, and second, they play an increasingly important role in the global mediascape of electronic and print media that is shaping the collective imaginations, experiences, and feelings of people throughout the world.

Manga and Anime as Contemporary Japanese Visual Culture

Manga and anime share a mixed or hybrid nature. First, they both blend the visual and the verbal into a unified whole, manga via a synthesis of text and images and anime through dialogue in cinematic live action (Carrier 2000, 69). Second, both are cultural hybrids originating from Japan's contact with the modern West. Both are inspired by Western styles of visual culture while drawing upon Japan's venerable tradition of caricature and sequential art (Craig 2000, 7; Nakamura 2003, 10). Third, as forms of contemporary art, they ultimately dissolve what some envisage as an impermeable line between high and low art; these days it is impossible to dismiss the finest examples of manga and anime as somehow inferior to what is lauded as the "fine arts" (Berndt 2001, 352). Fourth, they are also integrally part of a "mixed media" of entertainment that constitutes an important marketing niche in Japan's increasingly globalized culture industry. By "mixed media," I refer to a phenomenon of contemporary markets in which a single corporate conglomerate dominates by producing and distributing a wide variety of media products to its consumers (Iwabuchi 2002, 456; Ito 2003–2004, 31–32).

A good example of this is Yoshi's popular manga version of his novel, *Deep Love* (*Ayu no monogatari*), the tragic story of a Tokyo teenage prostitute named Ayu, who finds love despite her nightmare life of rape, STDs, and anorexia of which she ultimately dies. The novel, which reads like a Harlequin romance geared for a female young adult audience, first premiered on Bandai's wireless network as a cell-phone novel in 2001. Although originally a piece of "mobile literature," it spawned a multimedia industry as a feature-length movie, a TV series, a successful two-volume manga version in 2003–2004, and, most recently, a new comic about Ayu's pet, Pao, who might be euthanized at the dog pound if no one saves him (Wired News 2007). More typically, manga inspire the media mix, with spinoffs into anime, novels, video games and other consumer goods, as in the case of Tsugumi Oda's recent mega-hit manga, *Death Note*. What is important to note here is the multimedia synergy that exists between manga and anime: manga are the source for over 90 percent of anime (Trautlein 2006).

Manga and Anime as Mass Art

Manga and anime are important examples of what philosopher Noël Carroll has called mass art. By "mass art," Carroll means the TV shows and movies that are consumed by millions. Calling these "popular culture" is misleading, Carroll argues, because it is ahistorical; mass art refers to forms of art that have emerged recently in urban, industrial, capitalistic society. This art, which is reproduced and distributed by mechanical and digital reproduction technologies, is intentionally designed to attract a mass audience. As such, it is different from avant-garde art since the key to its success is accessibility which is exoteric rather than esoteric, for the average consumer rather than the connoisseur, and often reflects rather than transgresses conventional tastes (1998, 184–186). Carroll takes as his example comic books and popular movies that tell their stories through pictures. Any child is able to recognize what a picture represents if she already knows the real-world object that is being referenced. Recognizing that Bugs Bunny is a rabbit, though a strange one, requires no further abstruse study in "code, language, or any special procedure of inference other than simple object recognition" (1998, 192). To enjoy them, all the consumer needs is a conventional everyday knowledge about the modern world.

This is particularly true for manga and anime. Even if you cannot read the speech balloons in manga or understand the dialogue in anime, you can still get the gist through the sequence of images that advance the story. Comic book theorist Scott McCloud defines comic art as the consecutive arrangement of images in order to communicate information as well as elicit aesthetic, emotional, and cognitive responses in their audiences (1993, 9). In manga, as in anime, it is the flow of images that is key. According to Aarnoud Rommens, the storytelling relies upon an "analytical montage," by which he means that a sequence of images scatters the narrative action over several frames through a flexible page layout rather than having one picture/text to represent one story event. Moreover, by adopting a style of having different "camera angles," fading in and out, and so on—manga can mimic a cinematic style by creating a seamless visual continuum that turns the act of reading into a scanning of images (2000, 1–3). Since manga contain less text than Western comics, they are extremely easy to read, with reader-viewers consuming a 320-page comic book in twenty minutes, or scanning a page every 3.75 seconds (Schodt 1996, 26). Anime, of course, does this too, replicating cinematic techniques in the flow of its cels to create an animated narrative for its audience.

Osamu Tezuka's great manga masterpiece *Hi no tori* (*The Phoenix*) provides an interesting illustration of the use of sequenced images without relying on much text to advance the plot. On one page, Tezuka draws a set of portraits of the famous Japanese emperor Keiko. He does this to create multiple perspectives, transforming him from an august monarch into an object of ridicule through a sequence of distortions—from a likeness of Adolf Hitler to a Piccasso-esque work of abstract expressionism into a series of unflattering caricatures. The montage is in fact a sequence of portraits that a group of fawning artists have drawn to try to capture the pompous emperor. It sets the scene because they have been showing him their work in an attempt to impress the moody monarch. This page of paintings is cleverly crafted to make a key point—that the true likeness of Keiko, as a buffoon and a tyrant, was never transmitted through the official sanitized histories. Here, the sequence of images does not advance the plot temporally, but it does, through its biting satire, set the stage for the story that follows. While "reading" this montage requires a certain level of cultural sophistication, even the Picasso, although avant garde, is a readily recognizable piece of pop culture for Tezuka's older fans.

But while manga and anime are easily intelligible, how do they function as mass entertainment? Critics often dismiss mass art as kitsch. Theodor Adorno, for example, argues that it is best understood as a commodity produced by a monolithic "culture industry." Since it is explicitly designed for the sole purpose of maximizing profits,

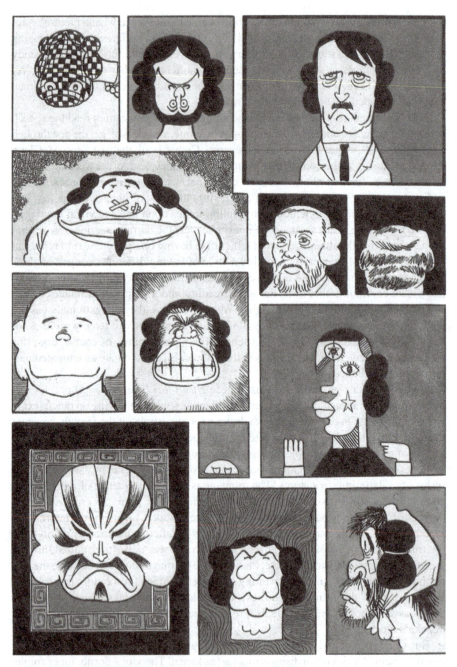

Emperor Keiko's portrait broken down into a pastiche of caricatures.
(Copyright Tezuka Productions)

mass art maximizes its appeal to the lowest common denominator. While reinforcing the values of the capitalist system that produces it, it dulls the mind with monotonous, formulaic "mechanical standardization" that frees people "from thought and negation." Mass art fills people's leisure time with fanciful and escapist fantasies based upon the feel-good but "decayed romanticism" of bourgeois ideology. It also encourages a spirit of passivity by encouraging consumers to conform to the status quo, unlike genuine art, which intellectually engages them to reflect critically on their lives in a way that may lead to revolutionary social change (Carroll 1998, 72–76; Adorno 1991, 11, 67; Witkin 2003, 138).

Carroll rejects this kind of critique as a caricature of what mass art really is and how the public experiences it. Yes, manga and anime are a big business, with major publishers like Kōdansha and Shōgakukan and major production studios like Gainax and Studio Ghibli deeply involved in the industry. However, manga and anime are anything but homogeneous in style, content, characterization, themes, or meanings, as they are aimed at different subcultures, age levels, and genders, and produced within ever-changing social-historical contexts. Moreover, the fantasies they evoke are not homogeneous either; they do not uniformly convey any master narrative or transcendent system of capitalistic values to their audiences. As anthropologist Mizuko Ito aptly describes, manga and anime, along with their "media mix" of TV series, video games, and character goods, create "a highly distributed and pervasive imaginary that spans multiple material forms, an imaginary that is massive, but not mass" in Adorno's pejorative sense of the term (2003–2004, 34).

That is not to say that consumer capitalism and commodity fetishism are wholly absent as a subtext or a deliberately crafted marketing strategy in manga and anime franchises. A good example is *Sailor Moon,* the hugely popular manga and anime series that debuted in 1992. *Sailor Moon*'s schoolgirl hero, Usagi Tsukino, is also the quintessential teenage consumer whose magical power comes from the accessories she acquires—her jewelry, her makeup, and her magic prism. The show was an instant cash cow for the Japanese toy company Bandai, which sold over 400 million dollars worth of merchandise over a two-year period (Grigsby 1998). *Sailor Moon* characters are also trademarked, enabling their use as brand names from apparel to frozen foods. This type of commodification through product licensing has been part of cartooning from the very beginning; anyone who ever owned a pair of Buster Brown shoes, "one of the world's best-known children's shoe brands" according to their advertisements, might or might not know that the name comes from Richard Outcault's famous *Buster Brown* American comic strip of 1902. In Japan, manga characters like Sailor Moon or Tezuka's Astro Boy are invariably stars in the image-based advertising that is pervasive today (Gordon 1998, 37–38).

In other cases, it is the story rather than character licensing that has marketing power. The currently popular manga series *Kami no shizuku* (Drops of God), for example, is a mystery story that also introduces European wines to its readers. The writers, Yuko and Shin Kobayashi, who happen to love wine, select the bottles that appear in their episodes based upon their own careful research into moderately priced but delicious wines. The result is that, although the series does not have any vintners as sponsors, sales of featured wines appearing in the manga have jumped thirty percent in Japan since the series first came out (Hardach 2007).

Recently, the Subaru car company has taken the commodification of the media to new heights with their new ten-million-dollar ad campaign for the 2008 Impreza WRX. Their Web site (Subaru.com/legend) features three commercials that make up a "three-part epic series," entitled "The Legend is Reborn." The three thirty-second anime are about a man who lives "in a land of forbidden secrets" (Japan) who discovers "the key to his destiny" (the car) and "attracts an admirer along the way" (a new sexy girl friend). The episodes blend real-life film footage of the speeding car with fantasy landscapes that are reminiscent of manga and anime stories. Episode two, "The Meeting," for example, takes place with the car speeding through a futuristic urban cityscape evocative of scenes from movies such as *The Fast and the Furious: Tokyo Drift, Blade Runner,* and anime hits such as *Ghost in the Shell* (Elliot, 2007). Here it is the story format as well as the slick hyperreal anime graphics that sell Subaru's cars to their young adult market. In other words, manga, anime and marketing usually mix.

Yes, manga and anime are formulaic, but that does not mean they lack expressive power or depth. They rely on easily comprehensible schema of representation, clear plots, and the reader/viewers' easy identification with the stories' characters. Stock plots and stylistic conventions are powerful modes of communication because audiences can quickly learn their codes through repeated exposure. Here familiarity does not breed contempt, but rather facilitates intelligibility. The stories can also arouse powerful emotions such as horror, sexual desire, or suspense in the audience.

A case in point us Hideaki Anno's renowned *Shinseiki ebangerion* (Neon Genesis Evangelion, 1995), a postapocalyptic tale set in 2015 about special children who captain gigantic bio-machines called Evas to fight against Angels, mysterious beings from outer space bent on destroying not only Tokyo-3 but all humankind. Over the twenty-six episodes of the original TV series, Shinji Ikari, the main character, and the other children pilots face off every week against a new numbered angel, which they eventually defeat through teamwork. Anyone familiar with Japanese children's TV programming from the 1980s and 1990s knows this is a formulaic plot of heroes piloting mecha versus monster. And yet, Anno uses the old formula to explore all sorts of disturbingly new questions, particularly Shinji's dysfunctional relationship with his cold and distant father, who, as head of a UN special agency called Nerv, is preoccupied defending the earth against the destructive angels. The episodes present an unstintingly dark portrait of childhood loneliness in a broken society where dad is always working—a depiction that would strike a nerve for any child growing up in 1990s Japan before the collapse of the bubble economy.

Yes, manga and anime are deliberately designed for easy enjoyment, but that does not mean they are palliatives for people seeking relief from the tedium of daily life. Rather than just serving up fantasy escapes from the real world, they are potentially a source for political, ethical, or existential critical reflection. This is possible because they offer "new resources and disciplines for the construction of imagined selves and imagined worlds," and also provide a "staging ground for action and not only escape" (Appadurai 1996, 3, 7; Treat 1993, 365–366; Ito 2003–2004). One example that comes to mind is the work of manga artist Jōji Akiyama, whose classic *Zeni geba* (Money Crazy, 1970), is a story about an evil capitalist named Futaro who, after a miserable childhood, decides he will do anything for money. Futaro is so obsessed by power through profit that it ultimately drives him insane. Akiyama's manga is anything but a paean for the spirit of capitalism, and, as an unsparingly harsh critique of "mad money," Akiyama's work provokes readers to question the dominant corporate system with its obsessive materialism and casual disregard of human values.

Manga, Anime, and Mass-Media Technologies

Carroll's second characteristic of mass art is that it is intimately connected to the spread of modern industrial mass-media technologies. He is referring here to the "mass delivery systems" capable of spreading content to multiple sites simultaneously (1998, 202). Comic strips are a case in point. In the West, comics first appeared when rising literacy rates made them attractive for newspapers appealing to a newly literate audience (Carrier 2000, 108). When the first American comic strip, Richard Outcault's "Yellow Kid," made its debut in the *New York World* in 1895–1896, its serialization dramatically increased the Joseph Pulitzer newspaper's circulation (Gordon 1998, 14). From 1895 to 1901, Outcault, along with other popular artists of the time, adapted existing visual technologies of word balloons, image sequences, and panel design to develop the basic comic strip conventions familiar today (Carrier 2000, 108). Comic strips quickly became a fixture of American print media, appearing in over eighty-three city papers in fifty locations by 1908. By the 1920s, comics such as Outcault's famous *Buster Brown* in the *New York Herald* were read by millions, becoming part of everyday American life (Gordon 1998, 37). Through newspapers and magazines, comics became the new icons of national culture, visual symbols that America's "imagined community" shared.

What about the case of Japanese comic strips? They developed as the new Western media culture rapidly flowed into Japan at the end of the nineteenth century. For example, one of the founding fathers of Japanese manga, Rakuten Kitazawa (1876–1955), initially studied Western-style caricature, particularly Outcault's work and Rudolph Dirk's (1977–1968) *The Kazenjammer Kids,* which first appeared in 1897 in the "American Humorist," the Sunday supplement of the *New York Journal.* As early as 1902, Kitazawa began publishing his own in the Sunday *Jiji manga* (comic strips), a section in Yukichi Fukuzawa's widely circulated newspaper, *Jiji shimpō.* Another early manga artist, Ippei Okamoto (1886–1948), whose political cartoons first appeared in *Asahi shimbun* in 1912, became deeply influenced by American Sunday funnies such as George McManus's *Bringing Up Father,* a serial that also was published in Japanese newspapers (Okamoto 2991, 207). By 1917, Okamoto published his own cartoon serial, "Cinematic Novel: The Woman with One Hundred Faces" (*Eiga shōsetsu: onna hyakumensō*) in the magazine *Fujokai* (Woman's World) (Isao 2001, 137).

My point is that the rapid proliferation of new print technologies coincided with the spread of new visual genres in Japan. Political cartoons, comic strips, and cartoon series, Western genres associated with newspapers and magazines, proliferated in Japan as it developed into a modern industrialized nation-state. As such, they served as important new sources of Japanese collective identity. A similar process also occurred in the case of Japanese anime (see McDonald 2006, 76–77).

Both the manga and anime industries, therefore, are local Japanese manifestations of a globalized "mediascape" for the mass circulation of images, originally through newspapers, magazines, and comic books, but now also through the electronic media of video games, the Internet, and cell phones (Appadurai 1996, 35). In the latter case, with over two-thirds of Japanese (over eighty million people) owning cell phones, "mobile manga and anime" represents the latest means of distributing content online through companies such as Softbank Creative Corporation, Sony Pictures Entertainment, Bandai Networks, the publisher Shinchōsha, and NTT Solmare Corporation. NTT Solmare, for example, is a leading distributor, with over three million manga downloaded in March 2006 alone, often by commuters who find that viewing the liquid crystal displays of their cell phone is more convenient than carrying a bulky book or magazine (Sato 2006; J-CAST 2006; Taylor, 2006).

The Mass Audience for Manga and Anime

Carroll's third characteristic of mass art is that it reaches a huge audience. One milestone certainly had to be Osamu Tezuka's debut work, *New Treasure Island* (*Shinta-karajima*), written in 1947. Tezuka published it as a "red book" (*akahon*), a cheaply made comic for children that had evolved from newspaper comic strips of the 1930s. It was a perfect format for Tezuka's innovative style and was an astonishing hit, selling between 400,000 and 800,000 copies and marking the advent of the story manga boom in Japan so indicative of the postwar period (Schodt 1983, 62).

This period also witnessed a phenomenal growth of weekly and monthly manga magazines, such as *Nakayoshi* (Best Friend, a monthly magazine for girls founded in 1954, circulation in 2006, 418,500) and weekly magazines like *Shūkan shōnen magajin* (Weekly Boys' Magazine, founded in 1959, circulation in 2006, 2,839,792). The manga magazine market came of age in the 1970s and 1980s, by developing into adult niche markets as the readership grew older but still enjoyed the medium. Some examples include Shōgakukan's weekly *Biggu komikku supiritsu* (Big Comic Spirits, circulation in 2006, 394,042), first published in 1980 and targeted toward young salarymen in their twenties, and romance-oriented women's comics like Shūeisha's *Young You,* first published in 1986, discontinued in 2005, and now replaced by its sister publications *YOU* (circulation in 2006, 202,750), *Office YOU* (circulation in 2006, 120,000), and *Kōrasu* (*Chorus,* circulation in 2006, 164,583), all geared toward young adult women. Some notable milestones in the expanding market of magazines include the 1988 New Year's special edition of *Shūkan shōnen jampu* (Weekly Boys' Jump), which was purchased by 70 percent of all boys between the ages of ten and fifteen. Although it reached its peak of circulation at 6.53 million copies in 1995, this manga magazine, with 2.78 million in circulation today, is still the largest weekly in Japan (Kumagai 1996, 74). By the 1990s the manga industry had twelve magazines with a circulation of one million or more and over fifty at the 150 thousand level (Kinsella 1999, 567).

The numbers for manga published in book form (*tankōbon*) are equally impressive. To give but one example, Tsugumi Oba's recent hit manga, *Death Note,* which originally ran over 108 episodes in *Shūkan shōnen jampu* from December 2003 until May 2006, had sold over eighteen million copies as an eleven-volume series by June 2006 (Mainichi Newspapers 2006). Overall, the manga industry occupies a commanding position in the print media market, making up 22.5 percent of total sales of books and magazines sold in Japan in 2004 with 37.2 percent of the total volumes sold. Despite eleven years of declining sales, domestic Japanese manga sales totaled 481 billion yen in 2006.[1]

The same can be said for Japanese anime. Along with the exponential growth of household TV sets in the 1950s, animated features became part of regular TV programming. It was Tezuka, again, who helped lead the way with his manga series *Tetsuwan Atomu (Astro Boy),* which became the first TV anime in 1963 and was soon dubbed and exported abroad (Morton 2003, 243). Despite a recent slip in DVD sales, the Japanese domestic anime market remains strong, worth over twenty-seven billion dollars (Krikke 2006, 15). On Japanese TV currently, over eighty anime shows reach tens of millions of consumers each week. It is clear that the manga and anime culture industries are a powerful presence in Japanese mass media today. All this shows that almost every Japanese person is a consumer (at least at some point in life) irrespective of age, gender, education, and social class. Manga and anime are part of mainstream Japanese pop culture.

The Globalization of Manga and Anime

Manga and anime are an increasingly important part of the global culture industry. These pop cultural exports, along with Japanese fashion, pop music, and TV dramas, are now avidly consumed not only throughout much of Asia, but also in Europe and North America. Toshiya Ueno argues that the Western interest in otaku culture springs from new currents in globalization and information capitalism. When Disney held the international monopoly on entertainment, "globalization" was synonymous with "Americanization"; however, what Ueno calls "Japanimation" is now a dominant transnational economic and cultural force, a part of the larger global flow of Japanese popular culture. This is apparent in such divergent areas as sushi restaurants, karaoke bars, Hello Kitty merchandise, and the latest episode of *Inuyasha* on the U.S. cable Cartoon Network (Ueno 2002, Moeran 2004, 1). According to Koichi Iwabuchi, this new global "J-cult" flow comes from a relatively small number of transnational media conglomerates (2002, 457). A good example is Bandai Visual, a pioneer on the Japanese animation scene that was founded in 1983. In 2005, Bandai established its own subsidiary, Bandai Visual USA, to integrate its domestic and international operations. It now distributes its extensive catalog of anime through independent American companies like Image Entertainment and Geneon Entertainment. The result is evident at any entertainment store, where walls are stocked full of anime for purchase.

Anime were first introduced on American television with Osamu Tezuka's *Atom Boy* in 1963 and *Speed Racer* in 1967. With the introduction of the videocassette in the 1980s, American fans had direct access to anime imports. Today, the market has evolved from its original niche of college males into a rapidly growing market, with teenage and young adult girls and boys making up a major segment of the consumer demographics (Trautlein 2006). In 2003, anime was a five-billion-dollar business, over three times the value of Japanese steel exports to the United States. This market is now growing rapidly; the Japan External Trade Organization (JETRO) reports that Japanese anime DVD exports to the United States have increased dramatically from 2.1 million units in 2000 to 12 million units in 2005, possibly because of the sexually explicit content of pornographic anime, which have become big sellers (Hongo 2006). According to the Japan Information Network, Japan's export market is approaching over 60 billion dollars, with 60 percent of all cartoon shows on TV throughout the world made in Japan (Krikke 2006, 15).

The overseas market for manga reveals a similar trend. In the case of the U.S., since 1999, manga sales have taken off, mainly because the popularity of anime paved the way for manga that served as their source of inspiration (Trautlein 2006). Publishers such as Viz Media, TokyoPop, and Darkhorse have shown exponential growth. Viz Media, a pioneer distributor with over twenty years experience, began by selling a small number of pamphlet comics. By 2007, Viz was the American distributor of two of the largest manga publishing houses in Japan, Shūeisha and Shōgakukan. Viz publishes the English language edition of Shūeisha's flagship manga magazine, *Shonen Jump* (2007 U.S. circulation, 180,000) as well as over 350 graphic novels, including best-sellers like *Naruto* and *Death Note* (Cha 2007). Another sign that manga has become part of mainstream American culture is the fact that trade book publishers like Del Ray (via Random House) and Penguin, as well as American comic book companies like DC Comics, have entered the business, brokering licensing agreements with Japanese companies for content in order to produce their own titles (Reid 2007a, 2007b). Total sales of manga books in the United States have grown from 7.8 million in 2005 to 9.5 million in 2006, a 22 percent increase (Phillips 2007). Overall, 44 percent of all graphic novels sold at bookstores or comic shops are manga (*Publishers Weekly* 2007). Sales revenue at the retail level has grown dramatically from 60 million in 2002 to an estimated 170 to 200 million dollars in 2006 (*Publisher's Weekly* 2007; see also Webb 2006). Recently, I was surprised to find a manga section that matched the science fiction collection in size at a local Barnes and Noble store in a Fayetteville, North Carolina mall—not a place where I thought I would find Japanese manga. And if you want to buy Viz Media's top selling English version of *Naruto,* all you have to do is go to your local Walmart, which is good evidence that manga is becoming a mass-market phenomenon in America.

Another sign of how anime and manga have become mainstream in the United States are the many conventions and local clubs that have proliferated in recent years. Anime- and manga-related conventions regularly occur throughout the United States; the Yaoi-Con in Millbrae, California, the New York Comic Con, Baltimore's Otakon, and Anaheim's Anime Expo, which was held across from Disneyland and attracted a record 41,000 visitors (Schou 2006), were all held in 2006. On a local level, even my little local library in Canton, New York, has two manga/anime clubs, one for children and another for the over-thirteen young adult set. The image of Japan for American youth today is not Pearl Harbor, kamikaze pilots or Japan's traditional "classical" culture, but *Naruto, Cowboy Bebop,* and *Ranma 1/2.*

Are Manga and Anime "Japanese" or Culturally Odorless?

Some see manga and anime's global popularity as evidence of the distinctive "expressive strength" of Japanese artists (Allison 2006, 224–225). Finding national identity through culture has a long history in Japan. It first arose in the early twentieth century as a response to the challenges of modernization and Westernization. "Japaneseness" became identified with high cultural symbols like Zen, the tea ceremony, and *ukiyo-e* prints. In the 1980s, Honda Civics and Sony Walkmans were added to the mix as potent new symbols of Japan's superior high-tech industrial power. But with the collapse of the bubble economy in the early 1990s, and as Japanese companies began aggressively to market J-Cult worldwide, software began to replace the fine arts and high-tech hardware as the newest icons of Japanese identity—what Iwabuchi and others refer to as "soft nationalism." (Iwabuchi 2002, 451, 459; Nakamura 2003, 1–2).

How do manga, anime, and video games express a Japanese "soft nationalism"? Partly, it has to do with Japan's quest for a "cultural uniqueness" in contrast to foreign nations, a national soul-searching about what it means to be Japanese (*Nihonjin-ron*) that began in the 1980s. In 1994, the connection between manga, anime, and nationalism came to the forefront over the *Lion King* controversy. At that time, several Japanese comic artists and fans accused Disney of stealing the story from Osamu Tezuka's famous comic, *Janguru taitei* (literally, the Jungle Emperor, known in the United States as *Kimba the White Lion*), which became a rallying point of national pride (Kuwahara 1997, 44). Since then, the Japanese government has pushed for Japanimation's official status as one of Japan's key cultural exports (Kinsella 2000, 91–93). Officials, like the self-acknowledged manga fan Foreign Minister Taro Aso, tout Japan's global media culture as an effective tool of diplomacy. "Soft power" is just as valuable as "hard power to boost Japan's brand image," because it reflects "Japanese sensitivities and way of thinking."

A good example of Japanese soft nationalism in action is the popular TV anime, *Captain Tsubasa*, which, renamed as *Captain Majed* and dubbed in Arabic, has been widely popular throughout the Middle East ever since it first aired there in the 1990s. The series, named as one of the top 100 TV animated series of all time by *Animage,* one of the most respected anime magazines in Japan, is about a boy, Ozora Tsubasa, who dreams of becoming a great soccer player. Since the Iraq war, the Japan Foundation made broadcasting the new 2001–2002 series on Iraqi national TV one of the key priorities of its cultural diplomacy. Coinciding with its broadcast, Japanese coalition forces working on economic cooperation projects obtained permission from Shūeisha Inc. to put Captain Tsubasa stickers on their supply trucks (*The Daily Yomiuri* 2006a). The reason for this was simple, according to a Japanese Foreign Ministry official from the cultural exchange section: "We believe children, who will shape the future of Iraq, will be filled with dreams and hopes by watching the show, and boost pro-Japanese sentiment even more" (*The Daily Yomiuri* 2006b). In effect, Captain Tsubasa as "Captain Majed" became an important part of the Japanese government's public relations campaign to propagandize its reconstruction efforts. He became a symbol of the bright future Japan was helping to create for Iraqi youth who love soccer just like the Japanese do (Massankay 2006).

Here, Japanimation is used as a cipher of Japanese identity. For some, *Captain Tsubasa* communicates Japan's true spirit as a peace-loving, soccer-playing foreign power who sincerely acts for the good of the Iraqi people. Any Iraqi can understand this by simply tuning into the show. It works to convey Japan's "brand image" to non-Japanese consumers, who assimilate *Captain Tsubasa* into their positive conception of Japan. Manga and anime, therefore, offer their own Orientalist iconography "in the complicit exoticisation of Japan" (Berndt and Richter 2006, 207).

On the other hand, Iwabuchi and others point to "ambivalence" at the heart of this "soft nationalism." Japanimation is, after all, deliberately produced for transnational mass consumption. Many would agree that, as J-cult becomes increasingly global, it becomes difficult to discern any cultural distinctiveness because "it at once articulates both the universal appeal of Japanese cultural products and the disappearance of any perceptible 'Japaneseness'" (2002, 456). For instance, Iraqis who view *Captain Tsubasa* as *Captain Majed* may not explicitly identify its connection to Japanese culture. The show may not trumpet Japaneseness in the way that McDonalds and Disney seem to trumpet Americanness, since Captain Tsubasa's identity is fluid enough to get an Arabic name unlike Ronald McDonald or Donald Duck (Moeran 2004, 8). As such, Japanimation in this and other examples seems "culturally odorless" (*mukokuseki*), by which Iwabuchi means "racially, ethnically and culturally unembedded and or erasing national/cultural characteristics" (2002, 455).

Another good example of J-cult's cultural odorlessness is Shirō Masumune's recent computer-generated imagery (CGI) anime, *Appleseed* (*Appurshiido*, 2004). Set in the year 2131 C.E., it is a postapocalyptic story about a woman warrior-for-hire named Deunan Knute. Its scenes, such as "Battle in the City," unfold in a utopian city called Olympus, which is controlled by a supercomputer named Gaia. While some of *Appleseed*'s characters have Japanese-sounding names, like Hitomi and Yoshitsune, others are named after figures in Greek mythology, like Athena and Hades. *Appleseed*'s pastiche of Japanese and Greek names of persons, places and even gods (for instance, Gaia is the ancient Greek goddess of the earth) supports John W. Treat's point that "[I]t is now impossible to write or even conceive of 'Japanese' popular culture without involving much of the rest of the world . . ." (1996, 13). It can be argued further that *Appleseed*'s cultural references, though diverse, are also superficial, since there is little about the characters or the landscape that is identifiably Japanese—or ancient Greek for that matter. Iwabuchi concludes that key to the global success of Japanese anime and manga is that "they leave their use-value to consumer tastes and cultural traditions outside Japan" (2002, 463), allowing themselves to be appropriated according to local preferences (see Allison 2006, 192–233). *Appleseed* is culturally odorless, with nothing to keep it from being consumed globally.

Cultural odorlessness also extends to the media themselves. Manga and anime are no longer solely the provenance of Japanese artists. In the case of manga, this has already happened in Asia with, for example, the development of Manhwa, a homegrown version of manga in Korea. In the United States, this process of indigenization of the media is just beginning. An example is the new Japanese-style comic *The Adventures of CG,* which was first published in the August 2005 issue of *CosmoGIRL!* This serialized manga, a collaboration with TokyoPop, features a "spunky every-girl hipster," an Ohio State college sophomore named CG who is living in Tokyo. While CG's face is drawn according to manga conventions with oversized eyes, her story is about an American coed during her semester abroad. The artist, Svetlana Chmakova designed CG's character to appeal to *CosmoGIRL!* readers (Memmott 2005).

Such original English language (OEL) manga are increasingly being sold in book format as well. The online comic *Megatokyo* (www.megatokyo.com), by popular American Web comic manga artist Fred Gallagher, for example, is now being published by CMX/DC comics (Agular 2007). TokyoPop has released twenty-eight OEL titles in 2005 and planned to double the amount in 2006 (Cha and Reid 2005). Viz Media's vice president of publishing Alvin Lu sees increasingly a "greater convergence of what we call 'comics' and what we call 'manga.' I don't know how long using these terms [as separate categories] will be applicable . . ." (Cha 2007). TokyoPop's editorial director Jeremy Ross agrees with this, adding that manga is now an "internationalized style of visual storytelling that transcends national origin. We've seen the globalization of manga taking place" (Cha and Reid 2005).

The Approach and Scope of This Book

Given manga and anime's globalization, we must avoid essentializing the themes, content, and aesthetic qualities of manga and anime as indicative of a uniquely distinctive Japanese culture (Berndt and Richter 2006, 7, 205). Toshiya Ueno, for example, is highly critical of some analyses that fall into this trap by overplaying manga and anime's cultural specificity. Some academic studies fall too readily into the trap of parroting the soft nationalism discussed earlier by concluding that certain key features, themes, or ideas present in manga and anime reflect an underlying quintessential Japaneseness. Ueno finds fault with Antonia Levi's book *Samurai from Outer Space: Understanding Japanese Animation,* for this reason. He argues that Levi errs with her overly facile interpretations of anime, which she bases upon timeless and eternal Japanese themes like "the Shinto love of nature" and "the spirit of *bushidō*." Such an approach, Ueno argues, is overly reductionistic, and lapses, in the final analysis, into a crass Orientalism (2002, 98).

It is important then not to fall into the interpretative trap of Orientalism, whether it comes from Western fantasies of Japan as the exotic other or indigenous Japanese fantasies inspired by soft nationalism. On the other hand, it is also important to avoid assuming that since manga and anime are part of the global mediascape, they are invariably culturally odorless. The authors in this book eschew both interpretative extremes by taking three different approaches.

The first approach highlights the specific historical period and social contexts in which manga and anime are produced and then discusses how the works are discursive responses to those times. The goal is not only to learn about when they were produced, but how their production and consumption created identifiable communities of senti-ment. Yulia Mikhailova's essay, "Intellectuals, Cartoons, and Nationalism during the Russo-Japanese War," takes such an approach. Mikhailova carefully examines the origin of political cartoons and their particular ideological uses during Japan's first major conflict with a foreign Great Power. Mikhailova's essay is typical of others in this volume that show how these materials were often intended for Japanese rather than transnational circulation. As such, they have a "cultural odor" that both reflects and refracts the ideas, issues, and conflicts that were central to the social, political, and cultural realities of the time in which they were produced. Their very success depended on whether they, in fact, appealed to their predominantly Japanese reader-ship. This kind of interpretative approach is fairly typical of many academic studies on Japanese pop culture (see, for example, Craig 2000, 12; Ogi 2003; Grigsby 1998; Allen and Ingulsrud 2003, etc.).

A second approach analyzes how manga and anime "move from one social arena to another, and circulate in and across cultures . . ." (Sturken and Cartwright 2001, 6). Mizuki Takahashi, for example, in "Opening the Closed World of Shōjo Manga," traces the history of generic conventions of girls' manga as they developed over time from the pre- to postwar periods. Lee Makela's chapter "From *Metropolis* to *Metoroporisu:* The Changing Role of the Robot in Japanese and Western Cinema," also examines the circulation of images cross-culturally, in particular, how the robot image moves from Fritz Lang's famous 1927 movie masterpiece to the manga world of Osamu Tezuka and, finally, to the 2001 anime version of those stories by Rintaro and Katsuhiro Ōtomo.

A third approach treats manga and anime as new media for constructing identity. According to John W. Treat, what makes popular culture so powerful is that it is "ac-tively constitutive of experience rather than passively reflective of it," and therefore provides "myriad ways in which modern people experience what makes them 'modern' or even 'people'" (1996, 6–7). In some cases, the artists see their medium as the mes-sage, a way of reconstructing their own sense of self, whether it is a localized notion of Japaneseness or a dislocated transnational identity in a postmodern globalized database world. Several essays in this volume, such as Shiro Yoshioka's "Heart of Japaneseness: History and Nostalgia in Hayao Miyazaki's *Spirited Away*," carefully examine how artists use these media for their own ideological purposes. The ambitious goal of this volume, then, is to offer a selective survey of the discursive practices, historical development, and generic richness of the vast field of manga and anime.

Japanese Visual Culture: Explorations in the World of Manga and Anime begins with two chapters that give a general historical and thematic overview of both media. Kinko Ito's "Manga in Japanese History" briefly surveys the history of manga from its genesis in premodern Japan to the newer subgenres, such as *redikomi* (Japanese ladies' comics) and sexually explicit fare known as *yaoi* or *shōnen ai* (BL, or boys' love comics). Ito argues that the power of manga is tied to its versatility; it can offer political and social commentary, educate, socialize, and create fantasy worlds to escape or reflect upon everyday life. Similarly, Gilles Poitras's "Contemporary Anime in Japanese Pop Culture" explores the rise of anime in postwar Japan. His essay clearly distinguishes anime from early Western animation in terms of emotional content, visual conventions, and cinematic effects.

The rest of this book covers a selection of major artists, genres, and themes in manga and anime studies. Chapters 3 and 4 focus on the towering figure in the world of Japanimation, "the god of comics" Osamu Tezuka. In Chapter 3, "Characters, Themes, and Narrative Patterns in the Manga of Osamu Tezuka," Susanne Phillips surveys Tezuka's career, which confirms that he was one of the most prolific and important Japanese artists of the twentieth century. In particular, she shows how Tezuka evolved as an artist, changing his narrative and pictorial styles to meet the new needs of his readership as well as to suit his own maturing aesthetic tastes. Phillips's essay questions the standard manga histories that sometimes praise Tezuka too simplistically as "*the* founder of modern manga." While Tezuka was a major trendsetter, he, in turn, was deeply influenced by other artists, and of course Western comics. Phillips's analysis frees us from uncritically lapsing into the widespread ideological nationalistic view that has elevated Tezuka into one of its preeminent icons of Japaneseness.

This project of recontextualizing Tezuka's work within the global flow of media culture and Japanese pop culture continues in Chapter 4, "From *Metropolis* to *Metoroporisu:* The Changing Role of the Robot in Japanese and Western Cinema." In his essay, Lee Makela examines how Tezuka's manga artistry was not only deeply influenced by Western cinema, but, in turn, influenced Japanese anime. Makela would accept Mark Gilson's observation that "[m]ost people's imagery of robots comes from the world of fantasy" (1998, 367). However, the key question is how this fantasy object becomes a global signifier for a host of issues, ideas, and meanings and transmogrifies as it moves through an increasingly globalized popular culture. Tezuka's 1949–1951 *Metoroporisu* was a reworking of the basic idea behind Fritz Lang's 1927 classic film *Metropolis*. A half-century later, Tezuka's robot tale was the inspiration for Rintaro and Katsuhiro Ōtomo's 2001 famous anime of the same name. Makela argues that by juxtaposing Lang's film with Tezuka's and Rintaro and Ōtomo's reworkings we can gain some basic insights into different Western and Japanese artists' understandings of "the soul in the machine."

Chapters 5 and 6 study *shōjo* (girls) manga. This genre, originally written for teenage girls, is largely neglected by critics, particularly in the West, where comic books were, until just recently, considered a boy's preserve. Like *shōnen* (boys) manga, shōjo manga developed in the postwar period. Originally pioneered by male artists, the genre developed after new women artists took over the field, writing stories that appealed to a wide range of readers, including adult women. Since the end of the 1970s, shōjo manga have proliferated into a complex number of subgenres including science fiction, fantasy, boys' romance, and ladies' comics, the latter specialty niche marketed to young women office workers and housewives (Thorn 2004). Since the late 1990s, these manga have had an impact on the global market as well, with adolescent girls, for example, now making up 60 percent of the readership in the United States (Trautlein 2006; Camper 2006). Another sign of shōjo manga's growing international popularity is the Japan Information and Culture Center's recent exhibit, "Shojo Manga! Girl Power! Girls' Comics from Japan," in Washington, D.C. (January 29–March 16, 2007).

In Chapter 5, "Opening the Closed World of Shōjo Manga," Mizuki Takahashi explores the historical roots of this form of cartooning by tracing its origin to prewar girls magazines. Takahashi shows how young women's magazines and novels offered "idealized images of girlhood." What makes shōjo manga distinctive is their use of pictures rather than plots or story lines to express powerfully the inner psyche of their heroines.

In Chapter 6, "Situating the *Shōjo* in *Shōjo Manga*: Teenage Girls, Romance Comics, and Contemporary Japanese Culture," Deborah Shamoon concentrates on the development of the genre since the 1970s, especially such recent examples as Kiriko Nananan's *blue* (1996). Shamoon argues that it is more useful to see such works "as part of a continuing process of generic experimentation and innovation" than as a static form. While shōjo manga in the classic works of the 1970s are defined by an "aesthetic of sameness" that highlights formulaic features, such as layering panels and cloud-like and flowery dreamy backgrounds, since the 1990s the genre has changed significantly. Artists like Nananan have abandoned the earlier aesthetic style for an "aesthetic of flatness" characterized by closed rectangular panels, stark backgrounds, and a tendency to obscure the characters' faces and eyes. Both Takahashi's and Shamoon's essays show the complexities behind the historical and artistic evolution of this major manga genre.

Another important theme in manga and anime is Japan's wartime past. In Chapter 7, Yulia Mikhailova discusses early newspaper cartooning in Japan, a genre that combined cartoon picture styles from the premodern period with caricature techniques imported from the West. Mikhailova shows how famous Japanese political cartoonists during the Russo-Japanese War (1904–1905) were instrumental in forging an "imagined community," whipping up Japanese nationalistic sentiment through their graphic caricatures of the enemy "other." By closely analyzing the political cartoons from the period, Mikhailova concludes that they were as "important as the railroads and postal system in the making of modern Japan."

Eldad Nakar continues to explore the connection between war manga, Japanese identity, and nationalism in Chapter 8, "Framing Manga: On Narratives of the Second World War in Japanese Manga, 1957–1977." Nakar is especially interested in how society shapes people's memories of World War II. By surveying a large number of examples from this genre, Nakar identifies two different "hegemonic" war narratives that developed in the postwar period—those that emphasize Japan's aerial war as a heroic struggle against an implacable but craven enemy, and the later works that are harshly critical of the horrors of war. He concludes that these mass-produced manga, designed primarily to entertain boys, reflect disparate but deeply felt collective moods about the war, which reflect changes in sentiment over time.

Both Mikhailova's and Nakar's essays underscore the fact that, as Arjun Appadurai has described it, "imagination is a social practice." Political cartoons and war manga are not escapist fantasies from the real world, nor are they ruminations of an elite class that are irrelevant for ordinary people. Manga, instead, are examples of a field of social practice that redefines reality through a process of a "negotiation" between individual artists, their readers, and their increasingly "globally defined fields of possibilities." As Appadurai notes, "[t]his unleashing of the imagination links the play of pastiche . . . to the terror and coercion of states and their competitors" (1996, 31).

The key topic of the next three chapters is the tie between manga, anime, and religion in Japan. Manga and anime can transform reality as well as simply reflecting it. As Stuart Hoover has recently observed, the complex interplay between mass media and religion is particularly important in this regard since "religion operates in the integration of experience, identity and meaning" just as media does, shaping a sense of self and community in everyday life (2001, 147).

In Chapter 9, Richard Gardner looks at religion, mass media, and identity in his "Aum Shinrikyō and a Panic About Manga and Anime." Aum is the religious movement responsible for the sarin nerve gas attacks on the Tokyo subway system in 1995. Gardner is interested in how Aum members and their critics describe the role of manga and anime in shaping Aum's eschatological vision of the end of the world as well as the events leading up to Aum's terrorist attack. As it turns out, both Aum and Japanese cultural commentators were highly critical of the dangerous effects of mass media, technology, and virtual reality on human life. Did apocalyptic manga inspire violent visions for Aum members, as well as for the generation of Japanese growing up at the end of the millennium? Was mass media the means used by evil forces to brainwash humanity and control the world? This is the debate between Aum and its detractors over the meaning of mass media.

Chapters 10 and 11 examine specific examples of manga and anime that draw upon traditional religion in order to wrestle with the question of contemporary identity. Raj Pandey's "Medieval Genealogies of Manga and Anime Horror," focuses on the popular horror-manga artist Hideshi Hino. His Kafkaesque tales, like *Hatsuka Nezumi* (White Mouse), which are marketed to teenage girls and boys, have recently attracted new fans in the United States after being translated into English. Pandey asserts that it is wrong to categorize Hino's horror manga as a Japanese version of the Western horror genre. While Hino's gruesome spectacles of bodily mutilation and disintegration are fascinating postmodern evocations of the "decentering and dispersal of subjectivity," Pandey argues that Hino's expression of postmodernism is heavily indebted to the traditional pictorial styles of Japanese medieval hell scroll paintings that offer a profoundly Buddhist spiritual vision.

In Chapter 11, "The Utopian 'Power to Live': The Significance of the Miyazaki Phenomenon," Hiroshi Yamanaka reveals the spiritual dimension of Miyazaki's hit anime *Spirited Away*. While it enjoyed only modest success internationally, the anime was a huge box-office hit in Japan. Yamanaka argues that the film's popularity came from its ability to provide "psychological healing to those Japanese people suffering from an identity crisis." Like Pandey, Yamanaka argues that Japanese religion is a powerful source of inspiration. Yet, Yamanaka's point is that the *kami*-like spiritual beings in *Spirited Away* are not awe-inspiring divinities (*kami*) of traditional folk religion so much as lovable and friendly characters that express Miyazaki's own optimistic view that there are positive forces in the world. Miyazaki's faith also actively contests the more chauvinistic forms of Japanese nationalism.

Chapters 12 and 13 deal with another key theme in manga and anime: nostalgia for a lost past. Such a longing, as Pickering and Keightley have recently noted, is endemic to modern life. It can be couched either as a conservative reactionary form of "social amnesia," or an escapist fantasy in reaction to "the velocity and vertigo of modern temporality" (2006, 923). However, Pickering and Keightley also see a third, more positive, form of nostalgia that "attempts a form of dialogue with the past and recognizes the values of continuities in counterpart to what is fleeting, transitory and contingent" (923). In other words, nostalgia can have a critical and subversive potential in some cases.

This third form of nostalgia is exactly what Shiro Yoshioka and Melek Ortabasi find in their studies of the anime of Hayao Miyazaki and Satoshi Kon respectively. In Chapter 12, "Heart of Japaneseness: History and Nostalgia in Hayao Miyazaki's *Spirited Away*," Yoshioka observes that Miyazaki created an imaginary link between Japan's past and present. But after the horrors of World War II, Miyazaki was disgusted by the exceptionalistic myth of the Japanese nation-state that fostered what he saw as a dangerous form of nostalgia glorifying Japan's imperial past. According to Yoshioka, Miyazaki constructs a notion of Japanese identity that is cosmopolitan, culturally diverse, and protean.

Nostalgia is conceived quite differently in Satoshi Kon's 2001 anime *Millennium Actress* (*Sennen joyū*). It is another case of a film well regarded in Japan that did poorly at the U.S. box office. In Chapter 13, "National History as Otaku Fantasy: Satoshi Kon's *Millennium Actress*," Melek Ortabasi argues that Kon's "movie about movies" is a nostalgia film in a way that is very different from Miyazaki's films. While Kon's film pays tribute to the modern golden age of Japanese cinema from the 1930s to the 1960s, it does not dish up heartwarming nostalgia, nor does it present an idealized history of modern Japan as revealed in the actress-idol Chiyoko's recollections of her life on screen and off. Instead, the story is a fantasy of Genya, the idol-obsessed fan in the movie for whom Chiyoko is his desired object. Here, the otaku of *Millennium Actress* is not the typical negative mass-media stereotype of the passive introvert, or deviant antisocial threat, or lost soul whose life is lived in a fragmentary "depthless present" of hyper-reality. Instead, he is the embodiment of the new Japanese otaku subculture that practices "consumption as production," and symbolizes new possibilities for Japanese identity. This kind of otaku nostalgia is a positive one—productive rather than passive in the sense that it is "potentially democratic, opening up new spaces for the articulation of the past and acting as a mode of assimilating this to the rapidly changing modern environment" (Pickering and Keightley 2006, 923).

Chapter 14 concludes the book with a theoretical and methodological critique of Western academic studies. In "Considering Manga Discourse: Location, Ambiguity, Historicity," Jaqueline Berndt offers a wide-ranging critique of "manga discourse," which she defines as the ways social institutions, the mass media, and the academic world understand manga and its social relevance. The essays in this volume are all examples of this discourse, and, therefore, should be read in light of Berndt's criticisms.

Berndt judges that such studies often suffer from "methodological blind spots." For example, she notes the widespread tendency to treat them as "mirrors of Japanese culture." She observes that scholars often fall prey to a version of what might be called a "natural attitude" by assuming that these texts resurrect an immutable given from the real world beyond them. Their fault does not lie in some mistaken faith that Japanimation somehow duplicates the world. Few today would be so naive as to think that "Life does not mean, Life is; and the degree to which the image, aspiring to the realm of pure Being, is mixed with meaning, with narrative, with discourse, is the degree to which it has been adulterated . . ." (Evans and Hall 1999, 25). Mostly, the problem is that critics overemphasize the fact that manga and anime are meaningful. First, they often uncritically assume a homogeneous audience, and prefer making interpretations that concentrate on narrative analysis and identifying key themes. As a result, their studies are often biased toward story manga rather than genres that deemphasize plot and are "less centered on thematic content," and favor their own rather that the audience's discourse on the media. Second, these critics ignore "the history and present variety of animation in Japan" as well as the unique conditions of Japan's culture industry, its own patterns of publication, distribution, and consumption. Berndt cautions that we must take into account Japan's own highly successful culture industry that has its own unique patterns of publication, distribution, and consumption.

To delve into Berndt's point more deeply, taking a particular example proves useful. How, for example, should we interpret *yaoi*/BL(or boys' love) manga? One has to first recognize that not everyone reads this type of manga. It caters not to some generalized inchoate "Japanese audience," but rather to a particular niche market of readers. Some of them describe themselves as *fujoshi*, a pun literally meaning "rotten girl" but also a homonym for woman. Any study of this subgenre must understand who its audience is, and how it goes about consuming it. Moreover, *fujoshi*-centric works, in fact, have almost no plot to speak of with episodes that seem designed primarily to feature prominently pretty-boys (*bishōnen*) in homoerotic scenes (Comi Press 2006). Why do artists create such romances about gay men? Who is reading this subgenre and why is it so popular that it merits its own separate aisle containing hundreds of titles at the manga annex at Kinokuniya's bookstore in Shinjuku? Doing plot analyses or looking only for thematic interpretations may miss the point of *yaoi* manga. Such an approach certainly ignores the myriad ways pop culture is consumed in Japan.

Berndt also contests the fact that manga discourse inclines toward emphasizing the close connection between manga as a medium and as a uniquely Japanese premodern pictorial art. Such a view ignores the real "historical ambiguity inherent in manga" and the rich cultural hybridity that has made it fluid and dynamic as a medium to the present day. Here, Berndt is more interested in how a discourse that traces manga back to premodern picture scrolls, for example, "in itself establishes traditions." In this respect, she might be critical not only of Ito's seamless history of manga in Chapter 1, but also Pandey's account of the genealogy of Hideshi's Hino's horror manga in Chapter 10.

To conclude, echoing Paul Ricouer's famous comment about symbolism, I think that the essays in this volume show us how manga and anime "give rise to thought." What we should make of these two forms of Japanese mass art is a question of our historical moment as they evolve in the rapidly changing global mediascape and marketplace. It is my hope that this volume adds in no small way to the ongoing academic discussion.

Like other books, this one was made possible through the help and encouragement of many people. In particular, I would like to express my gratitude to the National Endowment of the Humanities and my home institution, St. Lawrence University, both of which did much to support my own initial research. My university also provided several small grants that helped pay for copyright permissions for many of the images reproduced here. This book also benefited from the generosity of the Japan Foundation, which helped support the publication expenses so that I could make this book on manga and anime visual as well as verbal.

Many people have also graciously contributed their time, ideas, and emotional support throughout ebb and flow of the publication process. I want to give my thanks to Fred Schodt, Thomas Rimer, Brian Ruppert, the Chi-Anime Club of the University of Chicago, Timothy Craig, Matt Thorn, Maureen Donovan, Kate Wildman Nakai, Lynne Riggs, Joyce Sheridan, Manabu Watanabe, and Minoru Kotoku of Tezuka Productions, who graciously permitted the use of Tezuka's *Astro Boy* image for the cover of this book. I am especially grateful to my companion Patrice LeClerc for all that she did to assist, encourage, and inspire me along the way. My kids, Zel, Ziven, Zoe, and Zia were often part of the audience as I watched a ton of anime over the years—we all had lots of fun doing this together. Throughout the challenges of editing and obtaining copyright permissions, I am enormously indebted to Victoria Esposito-Shea, who scrutinized my occasionally clumsy prose, and Masako Takei, who professionally navigated me through the complex process of securing permission to use the wonderful artwork that graces this book's pages. My appreciation also goes to the journal *Japanese Studies*, for allowing permission to use a revised version of Rajyashree Pandey's essay in this volume, and the *Journal of Popular Culture* for allowing a revised version of Kinko Ito's essay. My heartfelt thanks also goes out to the many artists, editors, and other copyright holders whose generosity of spirit made illustrating this volume possible. There are just too many of you to mention here.

Lastly, I would like to thank the editors at M.E. Sharpe, particularly Patty Loo, Makiko Parsons, and managing editor Angela Piliouras, who have shepherded this project through its various metamorphoses, for their good advice and constant willingness to help as well as their patience with an editor (me!) who was constantly distracted given his full-time teaching load. My deep respect also goes to all the contributors to this volume, whose willingness to work with me was deeply appreciated as I edited, rewrote, and wrestled with the content of their essays. I feel fortunate to have had a hand in putting their insightful work in these pages. Throughout the editorial process, I gained a precious education that I would have never received without their stimulating intellectual forays into material that was often new to me. It is my hope that those who read their essays will be as inspired as I am to delve further into this topic that has fascinated me, and continues to do so, both as a fan and a scholar.

Note

1. Many reasons have been given for declining manga magazine sales in Japan, such as the lower birthrate, the economic downturn, the sharp decrease in neighborhood bookstores, the increasing popularity of computer games, the preference of consumers to read manga in book format, and the rise of new media like the Internet and cell phones (Sato and Sakanari 2007; Shuppan Kagaku Kenkyūjo 2005, 246).

1
Manga in Japanese History
KINKO ITO

Manga, or Japanese comics, have traditionally been a significant part of Japanese popular culture. However, Japanese comics do not exist in a vacuum; they are closely connected to Japanese history and culture, including such areas as politics, economy, family, religion, and gender. Therefore, they reflect both the reality of Japanese society and the myths, beliefs, and fantasies that Japanese have about themselves, their culture, and the world. The history of manga shows how they reflect and shape Japanese society and how they came to be what they are today.

Antecedents of Manga in Premodern Japan

Manga has a very long history in Japan that begins with caricature. The Japanese word *fūshi* (caricature) refers to criticizing or slandering the defects and shortcomings of society or of particular people. The word *fūshi-e* or "caricature pictures" refers to witty and sarcastic pictures that carry out this function (Shinmura 1991, 214). For example, Hōryūji temple was built in 607 and was rebuilt in the eighth century after a fire. In 1935, caricatures of people, animals, and "grossly exaggerated phalli" were found on the backs of planks in the ceiling of the temple (Schodt 1988, 28). Another temple, Tōshōdaiji, also has ancient caricatures suggesting that exaggerating features for humorous effect was a popular pastime (Kawasaki 1996, 8).

The most famous early caricature that many scholars consider a prototype of the manga form is Bishop Toba's (1053–1140) *Chōjū giga* (The Animal Scrolls). This work is a four-volume monochrome picture scroll (*emakimono*) of humorous brush-and-ink drawings of birds and animals. The scrolls show frogs, hares, monkeys, and foxes parodying the decadent lifestyle of the upper class. In one of the pictures, a frog is wearing a priest's vestments and holds prayer beads and sutras while other "priests" are losing at gambling or playing strip poker.

Later picture scrolls take a more serious treatment of the subject of religion, such as the *Gaki zōshi* (Hungry Ghost Scrolls), drawn in the middle of the twelfth century, and the *Jigoku zōshi* (Hell Scrolls), painted at the end of the twelfth century. Both

**An *Ōtsu-e* (Ōtsu picture) of an ogre chanting a Buddhist sutra *(oni no nembutsu)*,
typically sold to travelers during the Tokugawa period.**
(Reproduced with permission from the Kawasaki City Museum)

Gaki zōshi and *Jigoku zōshi* instruct pictorially the Buddhist notion of transmigration
in the six realms of existence. The *Gaki zōshi* depicts the realm of the *pretas* (hungry
ghosts) who are suffering from hunger, and the *Jigoku zōshi* realistically shows the
fearful realm of hell to be avoided at all cost (Shinmura 1991). *Jigoku-e*, or "hell pictures" used caricature, but the intent was to teach children basic Buddhist doctrines
and ethics by showing scenes from hell. These "hell pictures" became very popular
during the Tokugawa period; much like today's informational manga (*jōhō manga*),
they used pictures with accompanying manga for instructive rather than comedic
purposes (Shimizu 2002). Unlike today's mass-oriented manga, however, medieval
emakimono were seen by only a handful of elites, such as "the clergy, the aristocracy,
and the powerful warrior families" (Schodt 1988, 32).

With the Tokugawa period (1603–1867), woodblock-printing technology allowed a
wide variety of caricatures and picture stories to be produced for commoner audiences.
The town of Ōtsu near Kyoto sold *Ōtsu-e* (Ōtsu Pictures) to travelers who were on
the main road from Kyoto to the north in the mid-seventeenth century. Ōtsu-e started
as simple Buddhist-inspired folk art for prayer, printed using a crude and primitive
process that was available to ordinary people (Kawasaki 1996, 10; Shinmura 1991,

329). Since the Tokugawa government was actively persecuting Christians, many people purchased Ōtsu-e to have a proof that they were not heretics. These pictures grew in popularity and developed themes that were secular, satirical, and sometimes scandalous, appealing to the many travelers along the Tōkaidō highway, who purchased them as souvenirs (Shimizu 1991, 23).

Toba-e pictures, witty and comical caricatures from everyday life, appeared in Kyoto during the Hōei period (1704–1711). The name Toba-e suggests that they were considered to be in the tradition of Bishop Toba; during the eighteenth century, their publication in Osaka marked the beginning of a commercial publishing industry that was based on woodblock-printing technology. In the succeeding centuries, Toba-e spread from Osaka to Kyoto, then Nagoya, and finally to Edo (today's Tokyo).

From the Genroku period (1688–1704) to the Kyōhō period (1716–1736), *akahon* also became very popular. Akahon literally means "a red book" with a red front cover. Akahon is one example of a popular and lowbrow genre called *kusazōshi* that were commonly referred to as "red books," "black books" (*kurohon*), "blue books" (*aohon*), or "combined volumes" (*gōkan*), based on the color of the cover and the specific method of bookbinding.

Akahon were picture books based on classic fairy and folk tales such as "The Peach Boy," "The Battles of the Monkey and the Crabs," "The Sparrow's Tongue," "Click-Clack Mountain," and "How the Old Man Lost His Wren." There were also smaller versions of akahon called *akakohon* or "small red books," and *hinahon* (dolls' books). Later, akahon evolved into picture books for adults consisting mostly of pictures with little text. Both Toba-e and akahon became popular commodities, whether they were hand-drawn or woodblock printed (Shinmura 1991).

Schodt (1991) sees modern manga as the direct descendant of *kibyōshi* and *ukiyo-e*. Kibyōshi (yellow-jacket books) like the red, black, and blue books that preceded them, developed from children's picture books. Kibyōshi, which mocked conventional mores through humor, jokes, satire, and cartoons, were often published as a series of monochrome paintings with captions. *Kinkin sensei eiga no yume* (Mr. Kinkin's Dream of Prosperity), written by the humorous poet and ukiyo-e painter Harumachi Koikawa (1744–1789), was a groundbreaking work. In the story, Mr. Kinbei (his nickname in the story is Kinkin), standing before the store front of Awamochiya, daydreams that he gets adopted by the rich Izumiya family and attains the height of prosperity. He leads a fast life but eventually gets kicked out of his adopted family (Shinmura 1991, 701, 843).

Ukiyo-e (pictures of the floating world) is a genre of folk illustrations that were especially popular among the urban merchant class during the Tokugawa period. Early ukiyo-e were painted, but it was woodblock printing that made them truly popular in the late seventeenth century. The most common ukiyo-e feature actors, famous beauties, and sumo wrestlers as well as landscapes, birds, and historical themes.

In 1765, Harunobu Suzuki started multicolor woodblock printing, marking the beginning of the golden age of ukiyo-e color prints (Reischauer 1990; Schodt 1988; Shinmura 1991). Katsushika Hokusai (1760–1849), born in Edo in 1760, excelled in sketches and dynamic compositions in the ukiyo-e style. Hokusai's ukiyo-e masterpieces include multicolored woodblock prints of flowers and birds, "The Thirtysix Sceneries of Mt. Fuji," illustrations for novels, and other original paintings and drawings of beauties and samurai. Hokusai's *Furyū odoke hyakku,* a series of about a dozen woodprints, was drawn in the Toba-e style. The characters had extremely long and slim hands, limbs, and legs to give the readers a sense of dynamic action. Hokusai published his fifteen-volume *Hokusai manga* between 1814 and 1878. While this work did not use the Toba-e style, it did use caricature to criticize social conditions after the Tempō period (1830–1844), which was characterized by famine, a rise in prices, and peasants' riots. Hokusai was the first to coin the term manga, and his book became a bestseller.

Manga started to permeate people's everyday lives along with *giga ukiyo-e* (funny or playful picture ukiyo-e) and illustrated newspapers. In 1867, the last year of the Tokugawa shogunate, the Japanese government displayed *Hokusai manga* and other picture books at the World Exposition in Paris (Reischauer 1990, Schodt 1988, 1991; Shimizu 1991; Shinmura 1991; Yasuda 1989), a sign of how these popular picture genres were becoming increasingly accepted by the authorities as part of mainstream Japanese culture.

Other types of pictures were more controversial. *Shunga* (spring drawings) was a popular type of ukiyo-e during the Tokugawa period; these woodblock print pictures show uninhibited Japanese sexuality and erotic materials. The lovers depicted in the shunga are rarely naked. They are clad in sensuous, loose-fitting kimonos, which were supposed to heighten sexual attraction. The naked sexual organs are exaggerated and it is obvious that the focus is the sexual act itself. Ecstasy is depicted by the comments next to the picture or by the facial expressions of the lovers. Shunga depict various kinds of lovemaking, including lesbian sex (which was then considered perfectly natural), *ménage à trois,* voyeurism, female autoeroticism, male homosexuality, and bestiality. Shunga also served as sex manuals for brides-to-be (Wilson 1989; Shirakura 2002). The kind of erotic caricature apparent in the genre also appears in contemporary adult manga (Ito 1994, 1995, 2002).

While the Tokugawa government had banned travel abroad in 1636 and Japan closed its doors to most other nations, in July 1853 the American Commodore Matthew C. Perry arrived in Japan and demanded that Japan open its ports. A tremendous amount of Western influence poured into Japan, and manga was profoundly influenced.

Charles Wirgman (1832?–1891) created and published the *Japan Punch* in Yokohama in 1862. Wirgman was a British correspondent for the *Illustrated London News* and a cartoonist who also taught oil painting to Japanese students. His cartoons depicted the tension and conflict between Japan and the West, and the *Japan Punch* continued for twenty-five years and 2,500 pages. It was popular among Western expatriates and Japanese residents alike, and is an indispensable resource for understanding the rapidly changing Japanese society at the beginning of the Meiji period (1868–1912). But it also illustrates the diffusion of Western culture into Japan (Kawasaki 1996; Schodt 1988;

The cover of Charles Wirgman's *The Japan Punch*. Note that the originally European Punch no longer appears in jester's costume, but is dressed and coiffured in traditional Japanese style.
(Reproduced with permission from the Kawasaki City Museum)

Shimizu 1991). Wirgman's cartoons show the ways in which foreign influences were assimilated to create modern manga. For example, Wirgman's cartoons often used word balloons, which many native Japanese artists, like Kyōsai Kawanabe, adapted to their own work. Kawanabe's Western-style political cartoons eventually became a staple in Japanese newspapers, such as *Nihon bōeki shimbun* (The Japan Commercial News).

Manga in Modern Japan

Up until the Taishō period (1912–1926), what we now call manga was referred to as *ponchi* (punch) and *ponchi-e* (punch picture) as well as Toba-e, Ōtsu-e, *Odoke-e, kok-keiga* (funny pictures), and *kyōga* (crazy pictures) (Shimizu 1991, 16). A French humor magazine called *Tobae,* which satirized Japanese government and society, was started in the foreign settlement in Yokohama in 1887 by Georges Ferdinand Bigot (1860–1927), a French painter. Although *Tobae* ceased publication after only three years, its style proved to be highly influential. Bigot arranged his cartoons in a narrative sequence, which (along with Wirgman's word balloons) led to modern Japanese comics (Kawasaki 1996, 80; Schodt 1988, 40; Shinmura 1991, 214; Shimizu 1991, 82–87).

Japanese manga have long been used for satire; this was particularly evident during the "freedom and people's rights movement" (*jiyū minken undō*) in the Meiji period. Taisuke Itagaki, Shōjirō Gotō, Shimpei Etō, and other political leaders, influenced by European thinkers such as Jean-Jacques Rousseau and the liberal British philosophers, formed the first political party, the Aikoku Kōtō, in 1874. Around the same time, "manga

The front cover from Fumio Nomura's *Maru maru chimbun.*
(Reproduced with permission from the Kawasaki City Museum)

journalism," which engaged in political satire, began to appear in Japanese newspapers and magazines. One early example is the *E-shimbun Nihonchi* (Picture Newspaper Japan), a magazine first published in 1874 that closely imitated the *Japan Punch.*

Groups like the Freedom and People's Rights Movement used manga to get their antigovernment message out. For example, in 1877 Fumio Nomura first published *Maru maru chimbun,* a weekly satirical magazine. *Chimbun* satirized not only the Meiji government, but also the emperor and the royal family. Since he had violated the Japanese *zanbōritsu* (slander law) and the *shimbunshi jōrei* (the press laws), Nomura soon found himself in serious trouble (Reischauer 1990; Shimizu 1991; Shinmura 1989;

Yasuda 1989), yet the controversy increased the magazine's sales. Unlike *Tobae,* which cost eighty sen per issue, *Maru maru chimbun* was only five sen per issue and thus targeted the masses (Shimizu 1991, 95). It should be noted that various technological innovations—including zinc relief and copperplate printing, lithography, metal type, and photo engraving—made such magazines possible at this time. The developing transportation infrastructure and the mail service made it possible to turn journalism into a true mass medium (Shimizu 1991, 53).

American Influence on Manga

Rakuten Kitazawa (1876–1955) and Ippei Okamoto (1886–1948) helped popularize American cartoons and comic strips. Kitazawa drew manga for *The Box of Curios,* an English-language weekly published in the foreign settlements in Japan, and was hired by the daily *Jiji shimpō* (Current Events) in 1899. Kitazawa also created *Tokyo Pakku* (Tokyo Puck) in 1905. This was the first multicolor manga magazine in Japan, and it became an instant hit. Ippei Okamoto grew up in Tokyo, where the latest Western invention, *katsudō shashin* (moving pictures), was all the rage. Okamoto was fascinated with Western cinema and drew manga that were full of cinematic expressions and images. After he joined the *Asahi shimbun* in 1912, he became a popular manga artist.

As modern manga became established in the mass media in the 1920s and 1930s, artists like Kitazawa, Okamoto, and many others visited the West. At this time, America was a center for comics and cartooning. Joseph Pulitzer's *The New World* was renowned for its *Yellow Kid* comic strips, and serialized comic strips had become a mainstay of American newspapers. Kitazawa realized that manga for children could dramatically increase newspaper subscriptions, so he started a Japanese version of *Yellow Kid* in the *Jiji shimpō*'s Sunday edition.

Manga and Political Repression

The Taishō period saw the rapid rise of parliamentary power and the leadership of party cabinets. The period was also characterized by urbanization, the emergence of a new, well-educated white-collar class, the spread of democracy, an increase in higher education, and the development of a strong industrial and business community. This liberalizing and Westernizing tendency has often been called the "Taishō Democracy."[1] This was also a time when the Japanese government regulated the content of motion pictures and other media, starting in 1925. The law gained teeth after 1931 with "thought control" police (*tokkō*) who had the power to arrest artists and editors deemed subversive because they harbored the dangerous "objective of altering the 'national essence.'" After the 1932 assassination of Prime Minister Tsuyoshi Inukai, freedom of speech, thought, and scholarship ended as communist, socialist, and liberal sympathizers were severely repressed, and some manga artists and editors were forced to recant their "dangerous thoughts."

The 1920s also saw the emergence of national manga heroes in *Shō-chan no bōken*

A scene from *Nonkina tōsan* (Easy-going Daddy) by Yutaka Asō.
(Reproduced with permission from the Kawasaki City Museum)

(The Adventures of Little Shō) by Katsuichi Kabashima and *Nonkina tōsan* (Easy-going Daddy) by Yutaka Asō. *Shō-chan no bōken* was a four-panel manga that ran in *Asahi gurafu* between 1923 and 1926. *Nonkina tōsan* appeared in *Hōchi shimbun*'s evening edition right after the Great Kanto Earthquake in September 1923. The main characters, Nontō and his buddy Taishō, are rather slow and tactless. They simply cannot adjust or adapt to the competitive urban lifestyle. The people in the Kanto area were discouraged in the aftermath of the massive earthquake. The sense of humor of Nontō and his buddy made them laugh and gave them peace of mind. The people sympathized with them and the characters in return gave them hope to keep living in a difficult time.

Manga and the War

In the 1930s, children's magazines started to include serialized comics with episodes that ran to a few dozen pages. Popular serialized comic stories were compiled and put together as deluxe hardcover volumes. The *Norakuro* (Black Stray) series by Suihō Tagawa ran in *Shōnen kurabu* (Boys' Club) from 1931 to 1941 and was compiled into ten volumes.

In this story, Norakuro, a black stray dog, joins the Imperial Army of Japan and rises from private to captain. Norakuro became a very popular mascot, reflecting the rising militarism of the time, and many *Norakuro* character goods were produced. *Bōken Dankichi* (Dankichi the Adventurer) was written by Keizō Shimada. The story, which reflects Japanese expansionism, revolves around Dankichi, a little Japanese boy who becomes king of a tropical island in the Pacific. *Bōken Dankichi* was serialized from 1933 to 1939 in *Shōnen kurabu* and eventually compiled into three hardcover volumes.

Starting with the so-called Manchurian Incident, an outbreak of war with China in 1937, Japanese totalitarian militarism escalated, and there was an international outcry against Japan. In December 1938, the Japanese government issued a book containing cartoons that had appeared in the newspapers of countries such as the United States, France, Britain, Argentina, and Canada. These cartoons criticized the Japanese invasion and depicted the Japanese as ugly aggressors. The book was distributed only among a limited segment of the government officials who needed to know how the world's other nations viewed Japan at the time (Reischauer 1990; Shimizu 1991). In August 1940, the Shin Nihon Mangaka Kyōkai (New Japan Manga Artists' Association) was established by integrating such groups as Shin Mangaha Shūdan (New Manga School Group), Sankō Manga Studio, and Shinei Manga Group. They published their first journal, *Manga,* in October 1940, and many manga depicted attacking and destroying the American and British armies. The journal printed 200,000 copies at its peak and became an important "current affairs magazine for the eyes" (Kawasaki 1996, 129–130).

After Japan went to war with the United States, the Japanese government demanded cooperation from the manga artists, who were forced to draw pro-war manga. Many artists contributed to the making of *Original Manga for Promotion of Victory in the Sacred War.* In May 1942, Rakuten Kitazawa became the head of Nihon Manga Hōkōkai, or the Japan Manga Patriotic Association, a group of artists who devoted their work to the war effort. As the war and the U.S. embargo progressed, materials such as paper became scarce, and newspapers no longer allocated space for manga. Many cartoonists were drafted and had to leave Japan for war zones, where they "created reports for the public back home, propaganda leaflets for the local populace, and leaflets to be dropped over enemy lines" (Schodt 1988, 57). Many of them also created erotic leaflets to be dropped to the Western troops in order to decrease the soldiers' morale and fighting efficiency.

A new genre of manga, *zōsan manga* (increasing production comics) also emerged during this period. As the name suggests, the manga was used to maintain and increase industrial workers' output, which was one of the government's primary concerns. In June 1944, Etsurō Katō edited and published *Kinrōseinen ga egaita zōsan mangashū* (Collection of Zōsan Manga Drawn by Working Youth). Katō had drawn the so-called "proletariat manga" or "left-wing manga" before the war, but during the war he supported the Japanese government since artists had to conform to the government's requirements or stop drawing. In 1948, three years after the unconditional surrender, Katō joined the Japanese Communist Party and drew cartoons depicting the current situation. Some manga artists sought refuge in the Japanese countryside in order to avoid metropolitan bombing attacks, and others died in air raids or from war-related wounds and diseases (Kawasaki 1996; Schodt 1988; Shimizu 1991).

Manga After World War II

In the years after the war, a number of new manga magazines were founded. These included *Manga kurabu* (Manga Club), *VAN, Kodomo manga shimbun* (Children's Manga Newspaper), *Kumanbati* (The Hornet), *Manga shōnen* (Manga Boys), *Tokyo Pakku* (Tokyo Puck), and *Kodomo manga kurabu* (Children's Manga Club). This manga boom lasted about three years. Most Japanese people at this time were hungry and poor; they were unhappy with current politics and afraid for the future. They were starving for entertainment and humor as well as for food. Manga was easily affordable, and the newly emerging civil society during the seven-year U.S. occupation provided an abundance of topics for satire.

The Allied Powers, nevertheless, gave Japanese political artists more freedom than ever before. Although the headquarters of General Douglas MacArthur's allied occupation censored some manga to ensure that they did not satirize the general, royal family members were caricatured in many manga magazines such as *Shinsō* (The Truth) and the leftist *Kumanbati*. This was the only time, aside from the nineteenth-century "Freedom and People's Rights Movement," in which the emperor and the royal family were openly satirized (Shimizu 1991).

The Korean War was a godsend to Japanese industry. It produced a big American demand for Japanese goods, and by 1951, "Japan reached almost prewar levels of production and consumption per capita" even though trade was still less than the prewar level (Hirschmeier and Yui 1975, 242). The red purge began in June 1950, and it was the children's manga that started to be energized. Many masterpieces of children's and youth manga were produced by artists such as Osamu Tezuka, Eiichi Fukui, and Shigeru Sugiura.

Osamu Tezuka, the famous so-called "God of Manga," is considered the founder of modern Japanese manga. Tezuka was born in Osaka in 1928 and lived in Takarazuka for twenty years before he moved to Tokyo. His father was a fan of movies and showed his family many films from abroad; his mother often took him to the Takarazuka Theater, which featured an all-female troupe. He was in his teens when World War II started, and after the war he became determined to teach peace and respect for life and humanity through his manga, which became his consuming passion. Tezuka is known for his humanistic themes, including the preciousness of life, and his manga are full of narratives for readers of both sexes and all ages. He received many awards, and his manga elevated comics to the level of great respectability.

Tezuka's *Shin-takarajima* (New Treasure Island), published in 1947, dazzled young readers and sold more than 400,000 copies. His comics often used cinematic techniques, such as close-ups and changing frames and points of view, which had a tremendous amount of influence on postwar manga artists. He could also "handle weighty themes and create complex characters as well as any novelist" through his manga (Schilling 1997, 263). Manga was now taken seriously as an art form to be enjoyed not only by children but also by adults (Amano 2004; Gravett 2004; Schodt 1988; Shimizu 1991; Shinmura 1991).

It was also at this time that story manga started to blossom. Popular American cartoons such as *Blondie, Crazy Cat, Popeye, Mickey Mouse and Donald Duck,* and *Superman* were translated and introduced to Japanese audiences. The people longed for the rich American lifestyle that was blessed with material goods and electronic appliances. Manga geared for children (*manga dokuhon*) and made available through rental stores (*kashiya*) or bookstores started at the end of 1954, and caused the second manga boom after World War II.

A new genre and technique of manga called *gekiga,* or "drama pictures," emerged in 1957. Manga artists such as Yoshihiro Tatsumi and Takao Saitō started to refer to their art as gekiga rather than manga because their manga read much like novels with very realistic and graphic pictures; it emphasized serious drama rather than comedy. Gekiga appealed to junior and senior high school students who had grown out of children's manga, and it later became popular among university students as its readers aged.

Sanpei Shirato's *Ninja bugeichō* (Secret Martial Arts of the Ninja) is a typical gekiga masterpiece, which was serialized between 1959 and 1962. It is like a historical novel in that it deals with various social issues, such as social stratification and the samurai class, in a feudalistic setting. At this time, the Treaty of Mutual Security and Cooperation with the United States was causing a great deal of social unrest. Japanese society was in turmoil, and university students and radicals were at the forefront of demonstrations and riots. *Ninja bugeichō* gained popularity among senior high and university students as well as adults, as its story paralleled what was going on in Japan at that time.

In March 1959, Kōdansha, one of the largest publishing companies in Japan, started to publish *Shōnen magajin* (Boys' Magazine), the first weekly comic magazine designed for boys and young adults. The magazine had a few hundred pages of manga and was primarily targeted to young males, but I also enjoyed it as a young girl. I used to spend hours reading *Shōnen magajin* and *Shōnen Sandē* (Boys' Sunday, a weekly also published by Shōgakukan) when I visited my grandparents' house where one of my male cousins lived.

Shōgakukan started publishing *Shōnen Sandē* in April 1959, only one month after *Shōnen magajin.* These two weekly magazines were not so radically different from the existing monthly manga magazines for boys, and the sales were not very good until the emergence of *Kyōjin no hoshi* (Star of the Giants, a baseball player's story) in *Shōnen magajin* in 1966 and *Ashita no Jō* (Tomorrow's Joe—a boxer's story) in 1968.

Kyōjin no hoshi was the story of Hyūma Hoshi, a boy who grew up to be a famous and successful baseball player for the Tokyo Giants. The story also featured Ittetsu

Hoshi, his Spartan father, who had also played for the Giants years before. Hyūma had to go through many tough training sessions with his father: trials of different throwing methods, defeats, and so on. In *Ashita no Jō,* Danpei Tange, an ex-boxer, finds boxing talents in Jō Yabuki, a working-class Tokyo boy who has been sent to a juvenile detention center after an incident. Tange sends Jō postcards with various boxing techniques, which Jō learns and tries. Jō gains confidence when he realizes that he is capable of winning matches. *Ashita no Jō* is a classic story manga; it ran in *Shōnen magajin* for six years and influenced everyone from children to young adults and salarymen. According to Schilling, the readers most viscerally affected by Jō were "the students who were then fighting their own passionate struggles against Japan's power structures" (1997, 26).

   The sales of *Shōnen magajin* topped 1 million in 1966, and, thanks to the popularity of *Kyōjin no hoshi* and *Ashita no Jō,* attracted even more fans. The sales of the boys' magazine exceeded 1.5 million at the end of 1968, the year *Ashita no Jō* debuted (Shimizu 1991, 190). Both *Kyōjin no hoshi* and *Ashita no Jō* are stories about hard work and perseverance as the keys to success, and their popularity could be related to the social and economic issues that were important in Japan at that time.

The 1960s and On

In The Economic White Paper of 1956, the Japanese government declared that the country was no longer in a postwar period. Japanese economic and industrial growth started to burst forth, and the people became very optimistic as the country began to catch up with the West. The 1960s saw an astonishing growth in the gross domestic product, the annual rate of which was over 10 percent over a period of ten years, and in 1964 the Olympic Games were held in Tokyo (Otsuka and Sasakibara 2001; Reischauer 1990). Gag comics started to be very popular at this time.

   Fujio Akatsuka became "the king of gag comics." Akatsuka was born in Manchuria in 1935 and returned to Japan after World War II. He began his career by drawing manga for girls' comics, but in 1962 his *Osomatsu-kun,* a manga about a sextuplet and his five brothers, became a big hit in *Bessatsu shōnen Sandē.* He has produced many unforgettable, extremely funny, and unique characters such as Baka-bon's dad, Iyami, and Nyarome. Akatsuka's characters were hilarious with their refreshingly new gags, and they became national heroes. His manga were full of fast-paced and wacky parodies that were based on sharp observations of human behavior, psychology, and the realities of life. Akatsuka's manga were made into very popular animation television programs, such as the famous *Tensai Baka-bon* (literally, "the genius idiot"), which has appeared on TV Asahi since the 1970s to popular acclaim. In this series, Baka-bon's papa is particularly zany and very funny. For example, in the theme song of the animation, he sings "The sun that rose from the West sank in the East. . . ." Akatsuka's gags often entail such total nonsense with clever wordplay and include ridiculous scenes that are humorous because they go against conventional wisdom. That is, of course, Akatsuka's major point. Baka-bon's papa, who tries to be normal but is totally irrational, shows how silly ordinary people's common-sense view of things really is.

A good example is Akatsuka's story "Baka wa Nihonsei ga ii no da" (The Best Fools are Made in Japan!), an episode of *Tensai Baka-bon* that first appeared in Kōdansha's *Shūkan shōnen magajin* (Weekly Boy's magazine) before it was published as part of a collected anthology of his work (*tankōbon*) in 1969. In this wacky tale, Fujio makes fun of Baka-bon's mother's old school friend, Non-chan, who brags constantly about her recent trip to America. Non-chan is an unbearable bore who thinks that everything American is better than what is made in Japan. She refuses to take the drink At-chan offers because it is not imported. Even her pet is an obnoxiously barking imported breed. When Baka-bon's dad meets Non-chan, he asks if her dog is another one of the old classmates, and when she barks he remarks caustically, "Wow, she barks in English!" (2000, 58–69). Akatsuka here is poking fun at Japanese who have gone overboard over Western culture at a time, in the late 1960s, when, interestingly enough, high-quality Japanese goods, like electronics and cars, were about to become American obsessions.

Regardless of their popularity, however, both the violence in gekiga and the silliness of the gag comics were attacked as bad influences on children's morale and behavior (Amano 2004; Schodt 1988).

The 1960s was also the time when certain manga started to be produced by dividing the labor between the manga writer, who is more or less like a scenario writer, and the manga artist, who draws the pictures for the story. Since many artists also hired several assistants, manga eventually became produced in the so-called "production system." This system enabled the comic magazines to be published weekly. At the end of 1966, the sales of *Shōnen magajin* topped 1 million, and in three years it surpassed 1.5 million copies.

In 1968, the magazine *Shōnen jampu* (Boys' Jump) was introduced. It featured many manga rookies, such as Gō Nagai and Hiroshi Motomiya, and became an instant hit. Nagai's *Harenchi gakuen* (Infamous School) was criticized as vulgar since it introduced overt eroticism to children and was so controversial that parents publicly burned it. Nagai depicted both male students and teachers preoccupied with catching glimpses of girls' panties or naked bodies. I still remember the days when the boys in my sixth-grade homeroom class started acting out the socially unacceptable actions of Nagai's manga protagonists in a classroom or schoolyard. When they were disciplined, the boys claimed that they were just imitating the manga.

Many parents, women's associations, and PTAs throughout Japan protested that *Shōnen jampu* was a bad influence on children (Ito 2000, 1991; Schodt 1988). In spite of these protests, *Shōnen jampu* remained very popular throughout the years. It sold over four million copies in one week in December 1984 and years later, the December 2004 issue sold over 6,530,000 copies. During this period, the average sales of the weekly magazine were 3,400,000 copies. The first volume of *Shōnen Jump* (in English translation) was published in the United States in January 2003.

Two manga magazines for adult manga maniacs were created in the 1960s. They contained not only manga, but also commentaries and criticism as well as a venue for readers to submit their own manga. By encouraging amateur artists to submit their works, they created a gateway for many to become professional manga artists. In 1964 *Garo,* which had many gekiga-type pictures, was published by Katsuichi Nagai, who was very impressed with Sanpei Shirato's gekiga. The magazine was actually created to carry Shirato's new manga, *Kamui-den (The Legend of Kamui).* Nagai gave Shirato "total editorial control, prompt payment and star billing" (Gravett 2004, 42). In January 1967, Osamu Tezuka started the monthly manga magazine *COM* for real story manga. *COM* was characterized by a touch of urban sophistication, but it went out of business by 1972. *Garo* was sold to a new owner in 1997.

From the end of 1967 to the beginning of 1968, many manga magazines for adult men were founded one after another. These included *Manga panchi* (Manga Punch), *Manga goraku* (Manga Entertainment), *Manga akushon* (Manga Action), *Biggu komikku* (Big Comic), *Yangu komikku* (Young Comic), and *Purei komikku* (Play Comic). Many similar magazines for adult men followed suit, since those readers who grew up reading boys' manga were now becoming adults. Since the 1960s, millions of manga magazines have been sold, and their animated television versions and related merchandise have also enjoyed great popularity and commercial success. Some best-selling manga used the powerful marketing ploy of being symbiotically linked to animated films and TV shows as well as character goods and toys (Gravett 2004; Ishinomori 1998; Kawasaki 1996; Mizuno 1991; Otsuka and Sasakibara 2001; Schodt 1988; Shimizu 1991).

Shōjo manga, or "girls' comics," emerged in the 1960s. *Shōjo furendo* (Girls' Friend) and *Māgaretto* (Margaret) started in 1963, and *Shōjo komikku* (Girls' Comics) in 1968. These magazines, as well as *Nakayoshi* (Good Friends), came with supplements such as cards, stickers, and paper dolls, and they became very popular among the girls who had started to recognize that they were not just children but "girls." It was the time when girls "started hating ugly stuff, boys, and dirty, violent things" and collected "cute color pens, erasers, writing boards, folders, pencil cases, notebooks, etc." (Evers 2001, 6).

The 1970s and On

When it first emerged as a new genre, shōjo manga had many stories that dealt with girls' dreams and fantasies. Interestingly enough, it was male manga artists who established this new genre. The cute heroines and beautifully drawn pictures captivated the hearts of many Japanese girls. The year 1972 was when those female shōjo manga artists who were born around 1949 started to blossom. Women manga artists now drew manga for females and they started to dominate the genre. They included such stars of the industry as Keiko Takemiya, Machiko Satonaka, Moto Hagio, Ryōko Yamagishi, and Yumiko Ōshima. Their beautifully drawn protagonists and emotion-packed scenes attracted not only young female readers but also adult males. According to Schodt, these women artists are "wealthy; their female fans are fanatically devoted; they are respected in society-at-large; and they are given almost total creative control over their work" (1988, 97). The genre of shōjo manga was expanded by female artists in the late 1960s and early 1970s. It included stories that dealt with sportswomen, epic stories, and stories based on history (Schodt 1988).

What are some classic examples of shōjo manga during this period? The Japanese volleyball team won the gold medal in the Olympic Games held in Tokyo in 1964. The success and victory of the team, nicknamed "Witches of the East," gave some artists impetus to highlight athletics in their stories, which often accented sportsmanship as a major theme. The broadcast of the live-action drama series *Sainwa V* (The Sign Is V) by TBS Television started in 1969. The drama was based on the manga of the same title written by Shirō Jinbo and drawn by Akira Mochizuki. It ran in *Shōjo furendo* from 1968 to 1970. The peak rating of "The Sign Is V" was 39.9 percent, and it became one of the most popular television series in thirty years (Clements and Tamamuro 2003, 274).

The animated television series *Attaku nambā wan* (Attack No. 1) debuted at about the same time as *Sainwa V. Attaku nambā wan* was written by Chikako Urano, a female manga artist, and serialized in the weekly *Māgaretto*, a rival manga magazine of *Shōjo furendo,* from 1968 to 1971. It is a story of Kozue Ayuhara, a volleyball player who becomes the best player in the World Championship.

The themes of *Sainwa V* and *Attaku nambā wan* include sportsmanship, friendship, injuries, fights, falling in love with the handsome male coach, competition, jealousy, dogged efforts, and any other human emotions involved in winning games. These manga were, in a sense, the girls' versions of *Kyōjin no hoshi,* and *Ashita no Jō,* which appeared in boys' comics and were also made into animated television series. I was in the sixth grade when *Sainwa V* and *Attaku nambā wan* started. Like other readers, I was exposed to the moral lessons that these manga taught while I was growing up in Japan—to persevere in any situation, and to always work hard in order to accomplish one's goals. Such stories played an important role as agents of socialization for children growing to maturity in the competitive, fast-paced world of modern Japan.

Atenshon puriizu (Attention, Please) is a story manga created by merging Itsuo Kamijō's original story and Chieko Hosokawa's drawings. It ran in *Shōjo furendo* and was made into a television drama, airing in the successful *Sainwa V*'s time slot after *Sainwa V* ended in 1970.

Atenshon puriizu was one of the very first manga that could be classified as "occupation training." It depicted modern career women who were glamorous flight attendants in uniform. The manga was originally written for girls, but the live-action television drama attracted male as well as female viewers. The story covered many aspects of the job, particularly the women's on-the-job training. The episodes taught viewers a lot about the effort it takes to master one's work as the protagonists made mistakes and learned their lessons in a real-life setting (Clements and Tamamuro 2003). This informational drama impressed upon me the importance of English as an international language; since being fluent was advantageous for the characters in the show. Many viewers including myself, began to study English very hard in order to succeed in the future. Without watching *Atenshon puriizu* at such an impressionable age, I might not have been able to write this essay in English.

Another classic example of shōjo manga during this period is Riyoko Ikeda's *Berusaiyu no bara (The Rose of Versailles)*, an epic story that dealt with the French court in the years and days leading to the French Revolution. The manga started in the weekly *Māgaretto* in 1972. The story featured three main characters: Marie Antoinette, the queen of France; Hans Axel Von Fersen, her Swedish lover; and the androgynous Oscar Francois de Jarjayes, a fictitious creation by Ikeda. Oscar was a dashing commander of guards who was actually a woman who was brought up as a boy. The series, consisting of more than 1,700 pages, was published as a set of eleven paperbacks and captivated the hearts of many Japanese girls. A friend of mine in her forties from Niigata reminisces, "I was totally absorbed with *The Rose of Versailles* when I was in senior high school. Ikeda's dramatic story, a masterpiece, with the theme of the French Revolution in the historical background, moved my heart beyond the realm of manga. I think every Japanese girl read that manga without exception in those days." All the girls in my eleventh-grade homeroom class were crazy about the story in 1974. We read it during class periods and lunch at school, on the trains and subways, and at home. The story is so captivating because it depicts the royal family, love stories and affairs, fashion, human relationships, and because the reader can learn so much about French history from reading it. The historical figures such as the king and queen of France, Maria Theresa of Austria, and the revolutionaries came to life in Ikeda's manga, and they eloquently told the readers their stories.

The popularity of Ikeda's series came to be known as the *Berubara būmu* (*Berubara* is a Japanese nickname, an abbreviation for *The Rose of Versailles,* and *būmu* is a "boom"). The boom, which started in 1975, was supported by not only girls but also by women of all ages. There are no age boundaries when it comes to love and romance. *The Rose of Versailles* was so popular that the mass media and Japanese men started to notice, and it became a social phenomenon.

The story was also made into a musical staged by the famous all-female Takarazuka Revue, which ran from 1974 to 1980, again from 1989 to 1991, and most recently in 2006. The Takarazuka company sold many records, photograph books, and posters; character goods based on both the manga characters and the Takarazuka actresses' incarnations of the characters were also popular. The story manga was also made into a live-action movie using Caucasian actors, and was shot in Versailles, France. Ikeda's other famous and popular works include *Empress Ekaterina* and *The Glory of Napoleon—Eroika.* It should be noted that Osamu Tezuka lived in Takarazuka City for twenty years and his story manga, like *Black Jack, Hi no tori (The Phoenix)*, and *Ribon no kishi (Princess Knight)*, were also adapted by the Takarazuka troupes into musicals.

Starting in the 1970s, the theme of sexuality, especially male homosexuality, was incorporated into shōjo manga. According to Ōgi, "Instead of showing a shōjo dreaming of romance with a boy, they showed boys and focused on boys' love" (2001, 151). Girls' comics that portray male heroes and their world are referred to as *yaoi,* or boys' love comics. "Yaoi" is an otaku subculture term that originated in the 1970s. It is a Japanese acronym for *yama nashi, ochi nashi, imi nashi* (no climax, no point, no meaning), and came to refer to comics with explicit homoerotic storylines. However, yaoi comics should not be considered as a niche genre made by and for gay men. Yaoi are written by and for women as well as girls. The boys' love comics offer a sharp contrast to the other type of girls' comics, which focus more on the psychology and emotion of female characters and on their development as human beings. Moto Hagio is considered a pioneer of boys' love stories characterized by adolescents' sexuality and violent emotions. Hagio's works also include philosophical themes, children, and loneliness (Amano 2004, 398–401; Gravett 2004, 88; Schilling 1997, 100–103; Schodt 1988; Shimizu 1991).

According to Aihara and Takekuma, shōjo manga reveal a changing pattern of objects of desire over the years. The first male heartthrob for young girls was "the prince" from the Takarazuka Revue. In the 1970s it became "the foreigner," a somewhat realistic and handsome Caucasian man with extremely long legs and "the captain" of a sport team. The 1980s saw the emergence of "the rebel" when "heavenly expectations in shōjo manga have come down to earth" (2001, 28–29).

Aesthetically drawn young boys have been very popular among girls and women throughout Japanese history. There are also many fans of the all-male kabuki theater and the all-female Takarazuka theater in which some of the actors play the roles of the opposite sex and wear the opposite sex's clothing. In Japan, there has been a long tradition of homosexuality and cross-dressing in theater, and it has been much more tolerated than in other countries. Popular openly gay actors, singers, writers, and commentators abound in the Japanese mass media today.

The production of Japanese comics has always revolved around men—male artists, editors, and publishers—and they reacted to yaoi comics with revulsion, which caused a sensation. The mass media criticized such stories as decadent and degenerate, using hyperbole to characterize these kinds of stories as a "violation" of manga. However, this issue of homosexuality also stimulated the industry creatively. Today, one can find many successful female artists and editors in Japan. The continuing popularity of yaoi comics also suggests that Japanese women are not shocked by gay themes.

Manga in this period also dealt with issues concerning other minorities. The Nihon Chōsen Kenkyūsho (Japan Institute of Korean Studies) protested against a manga story, *Otoko michi* (The Way of Men), that was serialized in *Shōnen Sandē* in August 1970. In this manga, Koreans and Chinese, who are ethnic minorities in Japan, were depicted negatively. They were drawn as intimidating the Japanese merchants at a black market or trying to rape Japanese women at the end of World War II. The publishers explained that they had no intention of discriminatory treatment but were forced to apologize (*Kumamoto nichinichi shimbun* 1991).

During the 1970s, general magazines read by Japanese businessmen also started to include *kyōyō* manga (academic or educational manga). This new category is referred to as "information manga," "expository manga," or "textbook manga." According to Tchiei (1998), they do not have a narrative structure and the protagonists in this genre are "applying themselves to the study of the origins of and various anecdotes about food, liquor, and annual festivals." Kyōyō manga books, which include many witty and comical drawings and explanations, are comparable to the "Beginners" series published in the United States, like *Foucault for Beginners* (1993) by Lydia Alix Fillingham.

In 1977, Hanazono University used Jōji (George) Akiyama's Tokugawa-era tale of an easygoing Samurai, *Haguregumo,* as part of its entrance examination questions, and a public university also incorporated kyōyō manga in 1984. In 1985, works by Osamu Tezuka and Sanpei Satō were also used in elementary school textbooks for the Japanese language. The publication of a book-length manga by Shōtarō Ishinomori, *Nihon keizai nyūmon* (Introduction to the Japanese Economy), followed, and was eventually translated into English as *Japan Inc.* and published by the University of California Press in 1988. A French version was published in Paris in 1989. The books soon became bestsellers, triggering the publication of many more educational manga. There are also many "educational" manga stories that provide readers with special knowledge about an occupation or a historical figure or event. They include such topics and occupations as a professional killer, surgeon, gynecologist, mahjong player, horse racer, cameraman, detective, CEO, schoolteacher, cook, fisherman, Adolf Hitler, a singing group, and a sushi chef. They all tell fascinating inside stories that the readers might not be exposed to otherwise. Informational manga have become increasingly popular. In 2004, for example, the Japanese Defense Ministry announced that, in an effort to increase readership of its densely written 450-page annual defense white paper, it planned to issue a manga version "to enhance public understanding of Japan's defense needs."

The 1980s and On

Manga gained true popularity and legitimacy as an entertainment medium in the 1980s. This manga boom exploded with skyrocketing sales. For example, *Shōnen jampu* sold 2.5 million copies in 1982, with sales increasing to more than 5 million in 1988 (Shimizu 1991, 38–39). Many new comic magazines for adults appeared, and manga automatically meant high profits. The 1980s was also the time of Japanese economic expansion, when the so-called "bubble economy" led more than 85 percent of the population to classify themselves as middle class.

Redikomi, or Japanese ladies' comics, was established as a genre for adult women in the early 1980s. It is the most recent newcomer to the manga scene. Its readers range in age from fifteen to forty-four (which, interestingly enough, roughly coincides with a woman's childbearing years). Artists for girls' comics used to retire in their late twenties and thirties, but the popularity of ladies' comics led them to continue drawing for the new adult audience. The publication of *VAL* and *FEEL* started in 1986. They contained explicitly erotic scenes, and were drawn for adult women. Such freedom of sexual expression characterized ladies' comics of the early years, and it tended to be associated with female characters. The tendency to draw more and more sexually graphic scenes escalated until the early 1990s. The themes of ladies' comic stories included falling in love, romance, mate selection, family life, female friendship, sex, and lust. More contem-

A typical scene from one of Midori Kawabata's ladies' comics *VAL* and *FEEL*.
(Copyright Midori Kawabata)

porary themes include such social, psychological, and personal issues such as divorce, domestic violence, abortion, relations with in-laws, and female diseases.

Redikomi magazines published by major publishing houses, however, have almost no pornography. Magazines such as *YOU* (published by Shūeisha), *Jour* (Futabasha), and *BE LOVE* (Kōdansha) focus more on the realities of everyday life experienced by modern housewives, office workers, and college students (Erino 1993). By the end of the 1990s, many stories from redikomi also became popular movies and television series. Today's manga is definitely a very popular and successful multimedia form of entertainment (Ito 2000, 2002).

In 1990, a sign that manga had finally become fully respectable came with the Japanese Ministry of Education's prize for manga, which officially recognized it as an artistic and cultural resource of Japan. The first award was given posthumously to Osamu Tezuka (Mizuno 1991). That same year, the animation studio Nippon Animation started production of *Chibi Maruko-chan* (Little Miss Maruko). This anime was based on Momoko Sakura's story of the same title that ran in *Ribon*, a girls' comic periodical, in 1986. Both Sakura's manga and its anime version shown on the Fuji Television Network attracted many fans of various ages. *Chibi Maruko-chan* became a national sensation and also had strong sales in collectibles and character-related merchandise.

The story revolves around a third-grade girl, Maruko, and her daily life with her family and schoolmates. It is set in an idealized version of the early 1970s, a time perceived as "the good old days" before the erosion of traditional family and community values in the competitive high-tech Japan of "examinations hell," video games, and rampant consumerism. The characters are often mischief-makers who come up with schemes for one-upmanship. They also have personal flaws, but each episode ends with the child's particular problem at home or school resolving in a happy ending. It is interesting to note that *Chibi Maruko-chan* aired in 1990 when the mass media exposed some shocking social problems that directly affected children, such as cases of student deaths from school officials' corporal punishment and classmate bullying. *Chibi Maruko-chan* provided children with a haven from the harsh reality of school life (Schilling 1997).

During the 1990s, several of Fumi Saimon's story manga were made into hit television dramas; the first was *Dōkyūsei* (Classmates), broadcast in 1989. Her *Tokyo Love Story* was broadcast by the Fuji Television Networks in 1991. *Tokyo Love Story* is a manga masterpiece that is representative of Saimon's artistry, and its four volumes sold more than 2.5 million copies. As a television drama, it was an instant smash, with a peak rating of 32.3 percent (Clements and Tamamuro 2003, 323). *Tokyo Love Story* had all the ingredients for successful television drama, known as "trendy drama," which began with *Dakishimetai* (I Want to Hug You) in 1988. Trendy drama became all the rage in the 1990s. The protagonists were in fashionable careers, wore the latest designer clothes, drove expensive cars, and lived in extremely stylish modern apartments. *Tokyo Love Story* was one of the best-loved television dramas of the 1990s, and its success was followed by many imitations.

The story revolves around Rika and her relationships, particularly with Kanchi, a new staff member at Rika's company. Rika starts to have feelings for Kanchi, but he still loves his old flame Satomi. When Satomi confesses to Kanchi that she is now living with his best friend, Ken'ichi, Kanchi is devastated by the news. At this moment of weakness, the lovelorn Kanchi is seduced by Rika after she propositions him with the words "*Ne, sekkusu shiyo*" ("Well, let's have sex!"). This begins an awkward love triangle that becomes the all-consuming interest of the drama. Rika's one-liner became famous, and led many girls to try to imitate her. Through a cartoon character, Japanese women found a way to assert their sexuality more forcefully than before.

At the end of the 1990s, manga cafés (*manga kissa*) started to appear all over Japan. For an hourly fee, fans have access to manga of various genres, including past works, and a quiet place to read them. According to Television Asahi's special on manga that was broadcast on October 15, 1999, there were about three hundred manga cafes in Tokyo alone, which had replaced karaoke establishments.

There are two major types of manga café—the coffee shop and the pay library. In the former, customers order drinks and food and can read manga for 60 to 90 minutes. In the latter, the café charges customers an hourly fee, and they can bring their own food or buy drinks. Many big cafés have as many as thirty thousand copies of manga (Asahi Shimbun 1998), and some offer services such as Internet access and CD and DVD players. Since they are usually open twenty-four hours, customers who miss their train home can stay at a manga café and get hot showers, toothbrushes, underwear, and so on.

Japanese anime rivals manga in its number of fans. There is, of course, a commercial synergy between them, with high-selling manga being made into animated films and television programs that are then exported to many other countries. In 1999, the anime *Pokémon* (an abbreviation for "pocket monster") became something of a social issue in the United States, as many preteens became addicted to the movie, television series, and trading cards. *Time* magazine even featured *Pokémon* in its November 1999 issue. Another Japanese anime, *Yu-Gi-Oh*, seems to be the next wave in the new millennium.

Since October 1999, many new TV dramas and soap operas have been based on manga characters and stories. Television networks are assured success when they see that the manga has already been very successful. Manga stories, characters, and style have also jumped to other media such as the cinema, video games, radio, and theater (*Men's Walker* 1999).

In October 2002, the first independent Japanese manga corner was exhibited at the international book fair in Frankfurt, Germany, one of the oldest and largest fairs in the world. Japanese manga have spread to France, Italy, and Spain, and in Germany two translated Japanese manga magazines are published (*Mainichi shimbun* 2002). In the United States, the last few years have witnessed anime displays in video stores and manga/graphic novel sections in many of the chain bookstores.

Manga remains ubiquitous today as a lucrative industry in Japan. There were 297 comic magazines published in 2004, and the estimated number of copies published was 1,134,000,000. One out of every three books published in Japan was a manga (*Shuppan* 2005). Manga is available online and on cell phones, even in a society that boasts one of the best literacy rates in the world. It is one of the most widespread forms of popular culture, and will surely continue to be for years to come.

Moreover, as Japanese manga and anime are increasingly exported, their cultural value is becoming further legitimized in Japan. In December 1999, the Japanese Education Ministry gave concrete expression of this acceptance by approving the application submitted by Kyoto Seika University (Kyoto, Japan) to create a School of Cartoon and Comic Art, which began operation in April 2000. It is the first such school at any four-year university in Japan (Thorn 2007). Additionally, in its 2000 White Paper on Education, the Ministry of Education also noted for the first time that manga is a very important form of contemporary communication (*Asahi shimbun* 2005). In 2002, the Association of Manga Artists and the five major manga publishers agreed to officially name November 3 Manga Day.

Manga's power is tied to its versatility as a visual medium of communication. It creates fascinating images and text that can provide political and social commentary, instruct, socialize, and entertain in any number of ways. It is also a commercial engine with the potential for economic and cultural impact—for example, by instigating fads in sports and hobbies, like the recent obsessions with tennis and the Japanese game of "Go." Some criminals have even said that they got their ideas from manga. In 1999, an ex-employee of a loan company was arrested for extortion. He coerced his client when he needed money by threatening, "Sell your kidney. I can sell it for three million yen or so. Your eye can be sold for a million yen." He got the idea from a manga called *Minami no teiō* (The King of Minami) (Ito 2000).

Manga also has the power to cause controversy. The year 2005 saw the publication of two controversial manga: *Ken Kanryū* (Hate Korean Wave) by Sharin Yamano and *Manga Chūgoku nyūmon* (Manga Introduction to China) by George Akiyama and Kō Bunyū. Both became bestsellers in Japan, and are similar because they argue that, sixty years after the end of World War II, it is time for Japan to stop apologizing and time for Korea and China to stop blaming Japan for all their problems.

What will happen to manga in the future? New technology now makes it possible to read manga on the Internet and on cell phones. One can download "electronic manga" for a fee. This offers many advantages, like conserving space and the ability to access manga virtually everywhere and at any time. They also often appear with special sound effects, and, during certain highlighted scenes, the telephone vibrates, which adds to the drama. Electronic manga appeals to those who have not read comics, and this audience may eventually purchase comic books because they liked the electronic version (*Asahi shimbun* 2005). As baby boomers who grew up reading manga get older, there surely will be a new genre of manga for the elderly. Manga is Japanese pop culture and manga is forever.

Note

1. During this period, manga artists had a sideline of making postcards that depicted the everyday life of the ordinary people, family, customs and manners, and social conditions (Kawasaki 1996, 99). These constitute interesting sociological and anthropological data on this period in Japanese history.

2

Contemporary Anime in Japanese Pop Culture
GILLES POITRAS

Let us begin with the two major definitions for anime[1]: (1) anime is simply the word used by the Japanese for all animation, without regard to its nation of origin; and (2) outside of Japan, the common use of the word anime is to refer specifically to Japanese animation. In this essay, I will use the word anime in the second manner. I will also often use the titles most commonly used in English releases for the anime I discuss.[2]

If adult Westerners with no knowledge of anime were to walk into a video store and casually browse a selection of anime box covers, they might leave the store with little impression that anime is different than the animation with which they are familiar. If they were to spend the time to take a closer look at the art and text, they would realize that anime is somewhat different than the cartoons of their youth. They might notice the lack of animal characters and the diversity of genres, and they might even be surprised to find some of the few pornographic anime that exist. If they viewed some of the titles, they might note the dramatic nature of many stories, the titles for all age groups, the lack of musicals, the scarcity of goofball slapstick comedy, and many other differences from the Western animation with which most people are well acquainted.

If they were to see *Kaubōi bappu tenkū no tobira* (*Cowboy Bebop—Knockin' on Heaven's Door*, 2001), *Metoroporisu* (*Metropolis*, 2001), *Tokyo goddofāzāsu* (*Tokyo Godfathers*, 2003) or the *Kōkaku kidōtai* (*Ghost in the Shell*, 1995) and *Kidō keisatsu Patlabor* (*Patlabor*,1989, 1993, 2002) movies in a theater, or if they were to watch bowdlerized redubbed anime on television, they would see something very different from the song-and-dance numbers, wacky antics, situation comedies, and bloodless action that are the common fare of Western animation. They would see drama, humor, action, joy, tragedy, comedy, sorrow, love, and much more.

How is anime different from Western animation, whether the familiar American products or European works? How did anime come to be such a diverse and unique

Scene showing one of the many atmospheric touches of *Patlabor 2, The Movie*, 1993.
(Reproduced with permission from Bandai Visual USA)

collection of works? To answer these questions, we need to know more about the cultural and historic origins of anime.

The History of Anime

Where did anime come from? Anime has no special origin; it comes from the same nineteenth-century roots that all animation comes from. In the Meiji era, which spanned the late nineteenth and early twentieth centuries, there was a rich flow of technical and artistic knowledge between the Japanese, European, and American cultures. Artistic theories, media, and techniques flowed among all three cultures, forever changing the arts worldwide. Animation was simply part of this phenomenon.

Pre-1960 Anime

The earliest commercial animated works were short works shown in movie theaters in addition to a main feature. The earliest of these was *Imokawa Mukuzo genkanban no maki* (Mukuzo Imokawa, the Doorman) by Oten Shimokawa, released in 1917 (Patten 2004, 369–370). It was not until 1945 that the Japanese had an animated feature film, *Momotaro umi no shinpei* (Momotaro's Divine Sea Warriors). This was funded largely by the Imperial Navy for internal propagandistic purposes, mainly to lift the spirits of Japanese children.[3] In the postwar period, the animation industry, like the film industry and Japanese society as a whole, struggled to get back on its feet. In the 1950s, freed of the censorship of the internal conservatives of the militaristic era and of the U.S. occupation forces, Japanese cinema experienced a wave of creativity that would make it world famous. In 1958, Japan's second animated feature was released, *Hakujaden* (The Legend of the White Serpent, aka Panda and the Magic Serpent). This title was to be the first of several features released by the Toei Doga Company. It would prove to be an inspiration for many who later joined the Japanese animation industry in the 1960s and 1970s, as well as proving that locally made animated features were a viable commercial product. Before this release, the only full-length animation features in Japanese theaters were from other countries, mainly the United States.

The 1960s

The largest influence on anime in the 1960s was television. With the rapid spread of this new medium in Japan, animators had a new means to sell their works. The first made-for-television series was *Otogi manga karendā* (Otogi Manga Calendar) in 1962.[4] It was a 312-episode series of three-minute educational clips discussing history. The following year saw the broadcast of the first half-hour children's series, firmly establishing the anime format in the television medium in Japan. Some of the most famous series to begin in 1963 were *Tetsuwan Atom* (*Astro Boy*), *Tetsujin 28-go* (*Gigantor*), and *8 Man* The importance of these programs lies not only with their popularity in Japan; they were also successful in overseas broadcasts. In the United States and parts of Europe these programs were among the first anime shows broadcast outside of Japan. In the case of *Astro Boy* and *Gigantor,* new versions of the original shows were also broadcast in later decades. Much of what was made in Japan at this time would be familiar to viewers elsewhere. The traditional use of anthropomorphic animals was common in anime, and animated versions of famous European fairy tales were also created. Most shows were for boys or both girls and boys, but some were targeted mainly at an audience of girls, such as *Mahōtsukai Sarii* (Little Witch Sally) in 1966.

This early period also established several genres and themes in anime. Science fiction was, and continues to be, a major genre. After all, with animation you can do some pretty fantastic things without spending huge amounts of money on sets and special effects. Two continuing themes were also established at this time. One was giant robots, with *Gigantor.* The giant robot genre gave children a chance to experience power vicariously by watching the child heroes control their robots; the viewers' own powerlessness was forgotten. This theme continues today, usually in shows with a greater degree of sophistication and an older viewing audience. The other theme, pioneered in *Astro Boy,* was the question of the defining line between the artificial and the human. Serious social issues were also present in the stories from this time. For example, *Astro Boy* creator Osamu Tezuka wrote that the issue of "robots' rights" in his story was influenced by the civil rights struggles in the United States during the 1950s and early 1960s. Also in the 1960s, *Mahōtsukai Sarii* launched the magical girl

Tetsuwan Atomu, known in the English-speaking world as Astro Boy, remains an iconic symbol of anime and manga to this day.
(Copyright Tezuka Productions)

(*mahō shōjo*) genre, which continues to be popular among viewers. Supernatural stories and Japanese historical stories also became established genres at this time.

The 1970s

The 1970s saw a rise in the number of anime aimed at middle school students as companies sought to expand the market beyond the grade school kids who had been the major consumers in the past. Powerful giant robots continued to be popular with children. In fact, toy sales were a significant barometer of the success of a giant robot show, as many shows were produced to sell a related line of toys. Toys related to popular shows were not new in Japan or the rest of the developed world. They had existed for decades in various formats. Cheap robot toys proved so popular with children that many of the anime television shows in the 1970s were simply vehicles to advertise toys modeled on the robots in the program. Often these shows were made with designs submitted by the toy companies. The use of a toy manufacturer's designs in a television show as a way to advertise the product is not limited to Japan. The American mid-1980s cartoon show *Transformers* was created for the same purpose. If the toys did not sell well, a giant robot show could be abruptly canceled, as happened with the original *Kidō senshi Gandamu* (*Mobile Suit Gundam*) TV series.

The early 1970s saw the rise of Gō Nagai as a force in anime. Nagai began his career writing children's manga, often with erotic nuances, that poked fun at respected social institutions and contained violent adventure stories. His major contribution to the giant robot genre was to place the operator in the machine in *Mazinger Z;* previously, the machines had been controlled remotely. Nagai, who had already angered some parents by pushing the barriers of good taste in his manga, now took his vision to TV in numerous popular shows. In 1972, *Debiruman* (*Devilman*) and *Majingā Z* (*Mazinger Z*), two of Nagai's most successful series, debuted. *Mazinger Z* was to be copied by a continuing series of imitative giant robot shows for the rest of the decade. Some of these shows were later rebroadcast in highly edited versions in the United States and Europe.

In 1979, Yoshiyuki Tomino created a new type of giant robot tale with the original *Mobile Suit Gundam* TV series. This took the brightly colored toy-selling vehicle of the past and transformed it into a multifaceted and highly political tale of civilians caught up in a war between space colonies and the Earth Federation. Low sales of the sponsor's toys led to a rushed ending for the series. However, rebroadcasts attracted large numbers of viewers. What had happened was that those who watched the series were often in their late teens and early twenties, too old for the cheap toys that the sponsor marketed to little children. However, they were open to buying detailed model kits, some costing as much as one hundred dollars. Marketing these to this age demographic proved very successful.

There were also less fantastic tales. *Ashita no Jō* (Tomorrow's Joe) was the tale of a young man who rose from petty thief to successful boxer. Another series was *Lupin III,* which was produced both as a TV show and feature anime. It was based on an adult manga series by an author with the unlikely pseudonym of Monkey Punch. The series featured the grandson of the fictional French thief Arsene Lupin from the novels of Maurice Leblanc. The year 1979 also saw the debut of Hayao Miyazaki as a director of animated features with *Rupan sansei Cagliostro no shiro* (*Lupin III: Castle of Cagliostro*). Miyazaki had directed some of the earlier *Lupin III* TV episodes and was now allowed to work on a larger project.

Music became a significant part of the industry in the late 1970s. Earlier recordings of anime music tended to be either 45s with two songs from a single show or LP collections of songs from a variety of children's shows. In the late 1970s, companies began to release symphonic arrangements of soundtracks. The success of single-program soundtracks rather than children's medley albums led to an increased emphasis on good music that could also be sold as recordings. Eventually it became common for a significant amount of high-quality original music to be included in a series; in fact, some television shows included so many songs and tunes that most were only heard once in the series.

The original *Gundam* TV series was followed by several sequels such as *Mobile Suit Gundam 0083 Stardust Memories* (1991), set a few years after the events of the original show.
(Reproduced with permission from Sunrise Inc.)

The 1980s

Anime continued to grow by targeting the high school and college student markets. One possible reason for this is that a large number of animators who had grown up watching anime as children were now in positions to shape the programs they were working on. Another explanation may have been the ability of many small, independent studios to produce works for television and other markets. Of course, the large volume of adult-oriented manga meant that a pool of stories existed that could be transformed into animation for older audiences. The "aging" of anime was far slower than the aging of the audience; however, works for adults were in common production by the 1990s. This is in stark contrast to American animation, which largely remains targeted to children, with the notable exception of a handful of television situation comedies for adults. Story lines continued to mature with shows like *Chōjikū yōsai Makurosu* (*Superdimensional Fortress Macross*), the 1982 science fiction series that included music as a major part of the actual story line. Another innovative science fiction series was *Sōkō kishi Botomuzu* (*Armored Trooper Votoms*); instead of giant robots, it featured robots that were much smaller, more like anthropomorphic tanks. At the same time people who had grown up regularly watching anime were entering the workforce, some as consumers, some as creators.

These new creators brought different perspectives and helped further diversify the stories being animated.

Urusei yatsura, a satirical science fantasy series that ran from 1981 to 1983, was based on a manga by a young artist named Rumiko Takahashi. The series helped launch not only Takahashi's career, but those of many of the young animators who worked on this highly popular series. *Urusei yatsura* also gave anime fandom its first major pinup girl in the character Lum, an alien princess who often wore just a tiger-striped bikini. The romantic comedy *Mezon ikkoku (Maison ikkoku),* also a story by Takahashi, ran in ninety-six episodes from 1986 through 1988 and spanned several years of the characters' lives. Another successful comedy was *Kimagure orenji rōdo* (Kimagure Orange Road), a series about a romantic triangle between three teens. For mature material there was more *Lupin III* anime as well as *Shiteii huntaa (City Hunter),* the story of a highly competent gun-for-hire who was a superbly skilled shot and an idiotic lecher around attractive women.

Hayao Miyazaki released his second animated feature in 1984, an independent project that he also wrote and directed. *Kaze no tani no Nausicaä (Nausicaä of the Valley of the Wind)* has long been considered one of the better works of anime. Miyazaki's first major masterpiece established him as a critically acclaimed director and screenwriter. The tale is rich not only with the beautiful visuals of the animation but also in dealing with issues such as environmental ethics, war, and human dignity. Miyazaki was to follow this with *Tenkū no shiro Laputa (Castle in the Sky)* in 1986, the first title from his new company Studio Ghibli.

A major development at this time was the OVA (Original Video Animation) format of straight-to-video anime that came into existence with the 1983 release of *Dallos.* OVA, sometimes referred to as OAV (Original Animation Video), was made to be released directly to video, rather than in theaters or on television. The related term "OV" refers to the similarly released live-action cinema. Such a format could not have existed before the development of the VCR, as there would have been no way for the average household to view the product. Releasing anime straight to video allows companies to target specialized markets. In some cases, OVA titles proved so popular that television or movie versions were made, so that the OVA format also became a means for testing concepts and promoting innovation. It also allowed the creation of a market for erotic anime ranging from the crudely pornographic to literary in quality.

The late 1980s saw the release of two feature films that would raise the standards for story and animation quality. Both films had plots of a complexity rarely seen in anime at the time; this, coupled with a visual richness in the animation, challenged the creators of future works. The attention to detail in the stories' environments made it seem as if one were watching a tale set in a real place. One was *Akira,* by Katsuhiro Ōtomo, who also wrote the famous manga of the same name. The other was *Oritsu uchūgun oneamisu no tsubasa (Royal Space Force—Wings of Honneamise, 1987),* the first title by an upstart group of young artists that convinced the giant toy manu-

**Cover of the program book sold at theaters during the first run of
Mamoru Oshii's movie, *Urusei Yatsura Beautiful Dreamer* (1984).**
(Reproduced with permission from Kitty Film/Shōgakukan Productions)

facturing company Bandai to underwrite a feature. They achieved this in spite of the
fact that most of them had never worked in the commercial anime industry. Within a
few years their new company, Gainax, would become a significant force in creating
anime, video games, and toys.

The 1990s

While the Japanese were economically wounded by the collapse of the bubble economy
of the 1980s, the anime market grew as people looked for cheaper entertainment alternatives; they often turned to video and television as their disposable income declined.
Anime also matured, with more titles aimed at a sophisticated adult audience and reached
a working populace that had not been a significant target audience in the past.

Gainax continued to produce excellent work. Its *Fushigi no umi no Nadia* (*Nadia,*

In Hideaki Anno and Shinji Higuchi's *Fushigi no umi no Nadia*, the hero, Nadia, discovers her true identity during the adventure she and her friends share on Captain Nemo's submarine, the *Nautilus*. (Copyright NHK/SOGOVISION)

The Secret of Blue Water, 1990–1991) TV series, loosely inspired by Jules Verne's *20,000 Leagues Under the Sea,* was produced for NHK, Japan's prestigious public television network. NHK followed with *Otaku no bideo* (*Otaku no Video*), an OVA mockumentary on Japanese science fiction fandom that also poked fun at Gainax itself. For some years after that, Gainax produced no anime; with mixed financial success, the company experimented with books, video games, and other products. In tight financial straits, Gainax still managed to find a backer and pool the funds needed to produce a new anime television series. The result was *Shinseki ebangerion* (*Neon Genesis Evangelion,* 1995), which was perhaps the most critically acclaimed anime TV series of the decade, energizing the entire industry with its large adult following. *Neon Genesis Evangelion* was a giant robot show unlike any ever made. Its complex story, set fifteen years after a cataclysm that had wiped out half of humanity, raised more questions than it answered. The characters were flawed, but struggled against tremendous odds to help save humanity from strange enemies referred to as "angels."

In another Anno hit, *Neon Genesis Evangelion,* **Rei is one of the children who
pilot the giant Evangelion bio-machines, a task impossible for an adult to do.**
(Copyright Gainax, Khara/Project Eva)

Each episode added new information concerning the past of the characters and new
adversaries for them to defeat. The series was directed and partly scripted by Hideaki
Anno, the gifted director of the *Nadia* series. Well before the twenty-sixth and final
episode aired, *Neon Genesis Evangelion* had become a major phenomenon in Japan
and a massive commercial success. The laserdisc sales set records, and over ten years
later DVD sales are still strong (Takeda 2005, 164–166). In fact, Gainax continues to
release and license *Evangelion* products at a surprising rate for a show that is over a
decade old. The show also resulted in increased TV self-censorship because it included
some risqué scenes that the networks no longer allowed. In one episode, for instance,
there is an off-camera conversation between two of the characters who are posing as
lovers in bed that was criticized as being too sexually provocative.

Other interesting television works also helped to energize the period. Two notable
series were the action- and relationship-packed *Tenkū no Esukafurōnee* (*Escaflowne,*
1996) television series, based on a girls' manga, and *Cowboy Bebop,* with its varied

soundtrack and science fiction setting. In 1997, Satoshi Kon's suspenseful master-piece *Pāfekuto burū* (*Perfect Blue*) was released to international acclaim, marking the directing debut of one of today's more cinematic animators. Satoshi Kon is an example of someone who intended to be a manga artist and ended up as a director. While creating manga, Kon worked under *Akira* creator Katsuhiro Ōtomo, another manga artist turned director, on live-action film and anime projects. In fact, it was Ōtomo who recommended Kon as the director of *Perfect Blue*. Kon has gone on to direct other critically acclaimed films, most recently, *Papurika* (*Paprika*, 2006), and even a television anime, *Mōsō Dairinin* (*Paranoia Agent*, 2004). He also works on other aspects of his anime, such as character design, which strengthens the stylistic similarities among his works.

The New Millennium

In the first few years of the twenty-first century, the technology of anime changed significantly as many in the industry shifted away from hand-painted cels to digital painting done on computers. Until recently, hand-painted animation was almost always done on transparent plastic sheets called cels. An element of the foreground, such as a person, plant, or machine, was painted on each cel. For a simple animation, such as a ball bouncing, one cel repositioned against a background might have been enough. For complex motions such as a face with the eyes, hair, and mouth moving, separate layers of cels would be used. For example, one cel would have a face painted on it without a mouth. Separate cels would be made for each position of the mouth while the character was speaking. The cel of the face was placed on a background painting, and each cel for the lips was placed on it in turn, with one or more photos taken for one or more frames in the film. Since the industry standard is twenty-four frames per second for movies, a single animated work involved thousands of cels. Currently, the initial drawings may be drawn directly on the computer by using a digital tablet or drawn by hand on paper and then scanned into a computer. In either case, the colors are later added digitally. Digital paint allows for greater control over the quality of color, enabling the harmonious mixing of cel-like two-dimensional images and three-dimensional computer-generated images.

Computer-generated anime (CGA) grew significantly and on much lower budgets than are common in the United States. The Japanese market is too small for anima-tion companies to do the expensive projects that American studios, like Pixar and DreamWorks, are able to do. Instead, the Japanese do such work on less expensive computer systems with surprisingly pleasing results. Today, a mix of digitally painted two-dimensional images and three-dimensional computer effects has become an ac-cepted technique for producing anime. Some titles that employ many three-dimensional digital techniques include *Rasuto egusairu* (*Last Exile,* 2003), *Mahō tsukai ni taisetsu na koto* (Someday's Dreamers, 2003), *Uitchi huntā robin* (*Witch Hunter Robin,* 2002), the *Kōkaku kidōtai inosensu* (*Ghost in the Shell 2 Innocence,* 2004) feature, and the *Kōkaku kidōtai Stand Alone Complex* (*Ghost in the Shell Stand Alone Complex* 1st

Chiyoko Fujiwara, the famous actress in Satoshi Kon's *Millennium Actress*, in her final role rocketing off to the moon. (Copyright 2001 CHIYOKO COMMITTEE)

and 2nd GIG, 2002, 2004) television series. Two of the best examples of mixing two- and three-dimensional animation are *Last Exile* and the *Ghost in the Shell Stand Alone Complex*. In both series, many of the vehicles are created in three dimensions, which simplifies the animation process as they make turns and other motions that would be labor-intensive in two-dimensional animation. By matching the colors for the two- and three-dimensional elements, the studios maintain a certain harmony that was not possible in the days of hand-painted cels due to the difficulty of matching colors between the two media.

Today anime is gaining more international recognition with the rapid growth of the video anime market. Titles are being shown alongside live-action works at major cinematic events worldwide. Anime became more notable after Miyazaki's *Sen to Chihiro no kamikakushi* (*Spirited Away*, 2001) won the Berlin Film Festival's Golden Bear Award in 2002 and the Oscar for Best Animated Feature Film in 2003.[5] In 2004, several anime qualified for submission for the Best Animated Feature category, including *Sennen joyū* (*Millennium Actress*, 2001) and *Tokyo Godfathers*, both directed by Satoshi Kon, but were not approved by the committee for inclusion on the ballot. Perhaps the American perception that animation is a children's medium played a role in this; certainly, it was a factor that affected the distribution of the films. Works like *Millennium Actress* and *Tokyo Godfathers*, which are aimed at sophisticated movie viewers, get a very limited release in the United States, while titles for small children (*Pokémon, Yu-Gi-Oh!*) are screened in many more theaters.

What Makes Anime Different?

Trends

I have already noted the evolution of the market over time from shows aimed at small children to anime for mature viewers of cinema. This does not mean that the younger viewers have little to watch, just that the industry has diversified in the types of products made for popular consumption. Not only has anime diversified, but the industry is also producing a much larger amount of material as a result of a larger audience.

Part of this growth was an increase in gender-specific and niche-specific genres. In the 1960s there were shows for children in general, as well as shows clearly for little girls or boys. Today that means there are also shows aimed mainly at men or women. However, there is not just gender-specific programming, as many shows can appeal to both men and women. Shows aimed at the niche markets, which are often released in OVA format, include every genre that has been made into live-action cinema.

Differences Between U.S. Cinema and Anime

Today, anime, like many Japanese live-action shows, are usually a single story rather than a series of largely disconnected episodes. Even shows that have separate stories in each episode usually tie them together with a subplot for the entire season. This was not always the case, but evolved from earlier episodic programming to become common in the 1970s. However, this also means that once the story is over, the show is over. For Japanese television, long multiyear programs are the exception; the norm is shows that last three or six months and occasionally a full year or two. This way, actors, screenplay writers, directors, and audiences get the benefit of a variety of stories on a regular basis rather than a show being good for a season or two and then dying a long, slow death by declining quality. For video releases it means that boxed sets containing the entire series are available for a reasonable price, or the show can be released as a series of individual videos over time.

Emotional Content

One of the key points of much anime is the characters' feelings. Once the audience puts aside the expectation that animation is either just for kids or just visually intriguing, and allows it to tell stories in the same manner as other media, elements like suffering or even death, including the death of innocents, is not as surprising. Requited or unrequited love, adventure, struggle, pain, and joy all can be part of a story. There is nothing that says that a particular medium has to be bound by previous genres found in it. The same variety that can be found in theater, literature, and cinema is apparent in anime. Anime is as much a work of art as other forms of entertainment. In fact, anime is a branch of cinema and has produced fine works comparable to the best live-action cinema.

There is a long tradition of feelings that play a role in Japanese literature. This is apparent from the earliest poems and historical accounts through the history of chanted epics, plays, and fiction, and feelings continue to play a significant role in modern literature, cinema, manga, and anime. The tale might be a kabuki play about lovers from different classes or siblings enacting vengeance for their parent's death. It might be the story of the solitary tribulations of an artist or a craftsman, or it may be a boys' giant robot anime show, where the characters fight with all their passion to defend their comrades and loved ones. Relationships play an especially important part in stories written for a female audience; however, some of the stories aimed at girls and women can contain as much action as any male-oriented fare. This is something that often surprises Western audiences, who are more familiar with tame fare for girls and women.

Where Do the Stories Come From? What Shapes the Tales of Anime?

The source for the stories used in the majority of anime is manga. In fact, in many ways the evolving diversity of anime follows the lead of the manga industry. The major reason for the nature of girls' and women's anime is that women play a major role in the creative side of the manga, producing a large amount of works for girls and women that are often adapted into anime. Manga's wide diversity and respectable status in Japan is a very fertile source of stories that can be adapted into anime. Sometimes this is done with little change; at other times the story is drastically rewritten and becomes a very different work of art. Two examples of anime that are very different from the original manga are *Kidō senkan Nadeshiko* (*Martian Successor Nadesico,* 1996) and the various *Ghost in the Shell* features and TV adaptations. These disparities are comparable to the differences between novels and cinematic adaptations of the same story. Relying on manga for stories is not always seen as a good thing. Director Satoshi Kon has spoken out on the importance of writing new stories rather than just adapting from manga, stating that he feels adaptation makes animation less creative than manga. Kon is determined to push the medium in new directions, and this is evident in each of his works ("Creator Profile: Satoshi Kon" 2004, 80). Other sources for both anime and manga include legend, history, novels, and even ancient plays and recited tales.

There are also traditional influences from literature that help shape the nuances of anime. For example, seasonal symbols play a major role in Japanese poetry and literature. If you see white flecks floating on the wind you may first think it is snow, but if the characters in the story are not that warmly dressed, the flakes are cherry blossoms, a symbol of spring and of the shortness of life. Life is as fleeting as a cherry blossom, flowering for a day and then falling to the ground. If the stories are set in a school, the springtime is also a clue that it is the beginning of the school year in Japan. You might see a bright day and hear the high-pitched song of the *semi,* the cicada; this tells you that the scene is in the height of the summer heat. Foods can be a seasonal clue in that certain ingredients and dishes have seasonal associations. Festivals also provide seasonal clues. Just as Christmas and Easter have seasonal associations in the West, many Japanese festivals, such as Obon, celebrated in mid-August, inform the viewer as to the time of year.

Animation Qualities and Visual Conventions

When comparing American animation to anime, it is best to compare television shows rather than theatrically released features. A single American feature can have a budget that rivals the annual budget of the entire movie industry in Japan. Many who see anime for the first time comment on certain visual qualities that strike them as different from Western animation. Shadows exist and move on faces, bodies, and objects. Vehicles may move under the shade of trees and out into the sunlight, and clouds may cast shadows on a field or even a cityscape. Hair movement is noticeable, unlike many animated works where hair is more like a helmet; at the right dramatic moment a lock may fall or a hand will move to push hair back from the face. Even hair color can be conspicuous; most Japanese have black or very dark brown hair, and a very few have deep red hair. To use precise natural hair colors would make it harder to distinguish between characters. For this reason, a character's hair may be an unnatural brown or gray. Mirroring more recent styles, hair may even be bleached or tinted. In some cases it might be very unnatural in color. Some examples of this are the green hair of the alien princess Lum in *Urusei yatsura* and the unusual colors in a highly stylized work like *Shōjo kakumei Utena* (*Revolutionary Girl Utena,* OVA 1997, movie 1999). One visual aspect noticed quickly and commented on by most viewers is the large size of characters' eyes; this is, of course, also a feature in Western animation, but for some reason it stands out. The eyes in anime are also used for subtle expressions of emotion. They may flicker as if tears are starting to form or turn dull to indicate death or diminishing of consciousness. Large eyes in many shows are also an indication of innocence. For example, in *Ranma 1/2* (OVA 1989, movies 1991, 1994), many of the young characters have large eyes. Other characters, like the adults and Kuno the upperclassman, do not. In the case of Kuno, it is because he not only lacks innocence but is also a mentally unstable and dangerous character.

Cinematic Effects

Modern cinema is another great influence on anime, and the cinema of the world often influences the visual cinematic structure and the pacing of the action. It is common for anime directors to cite influences from European, American, Chinese, or Korean cinema. This shows in the qualities of the stories told through anime. Nonlinear tales, flashbacks, foreshadowing, slow pacing, character development, and many other techniques are common in anime.

Cinematic effects included displaying a scene from different angles. It may be shown as if it were shot from an actual camera, the foreground and background may have different focal points that shift, or a stationary character or object may be circled by the point of view as though being tracked by a camera. Such effects add a visual richness to the anime, increasing the pleasure of the viewing experience. A good title to watch for many of the visual effects mentioned here is the four-episode OVA series *Taiho shichau zo! (You're Under Arrest,* 1994). Much American animation is still dominated by the early cinema model with a stationary background, as if a stationary camera were filming a stage set. A notable exception are special Halloween episodes of *The Simpsons,* which parody the visual effects of horror films.

Industrial Structure

Another factor that has influenced anime is the Japanese subcontracting and temporary worker systems. Many industries in Japan rely on subcontractors and seasonal temporary workers to do some of the production work. This gives the industry flexibility in retaining a core of highly trained workers and a pool of external labor to draw upon as needed. As the anime industry grew, subcontracting and temporary workers became part of the process. In the case of subcontracting, the credits for a particular title are likely to include a variety of companies both in Japan and other Asian nations. In fact, it is not unheard of for a small company to subcontract part of the work on their project to a larger company. One example of a company's doing work for another is Gainax's work for Studio Ghibli on *Spirited Away.* In the case of temporary workers, many move from company to company as projects end and begin. For example, in *Otaku no Video,* the great mockumentary on Japanese science fiction fandom, there is a faux interview with a "cel thief" who speaks of how the constant staff changes enable him to steal animation cels by entering studios as if he worked there. The use of temporary workers provides flexibility for established companies, enables individuals to gain skills that can land more permanent work, and enables small companies to have a source of income between major projects.

Some companies started out doing small projects and grew. GONZO is an excellent example of the way a small Japanese studio can grow and become known as an innovator in a relatively short amount of time. Founded in 1992 with a vision of expanding digital animation in Japan, the company started by making FMV (full-motion video) scenes for video-game companies and computer effects for live-action movies. In fact, GONZO was so small when it started that its members used stacks of magazines and a door to improvise a desk. Its offices were in a vacant condominium borrowed from a staff member who had recently married and moved. Today the company has modern offices and studio space and produces a steady stream of anime titles. Some GONZO titles include *Sentō yōsei Yukikaze (Yukikaze,* 2002), *Rasuto ekusairu (Last Exile,* 2003), and *Furumetaru panikku (Full Metal Panic!,* 2002) ("Inside GONZO" 2003, 20–23). For such a system to work, there has to be a large number of companies. Today there are over 400 companies, most of which are located in Tokyo (JETRO 2004). The large number of studios means that companies are often looking for different ideas to produce. This adds diversity to the industry as new markets and genres are explored, providing a healthy counter to the tendency in entertainment to simply mimic the successful. This industrial diversity also allows individuals to secure funding to produce works on their own. Many of the works of Mamoru Oshii, Satoshi Kon, and others are examples of excellent anime that is not from a major studio, but from a creative director with a group of investors and talented animators. Sometimes, several companies may be involved in a single project, such as Mamoru Oshii's *Ghost in the Shell 2: Innocence,* which was co-produced by Studio Ghibli.

International Trade

Anime is not only a product for domestic Japanese consumption. Since the early 1960s, Japan has been exporting anime for broadcast and theatrical release. In some cases anime was even made using funding from an overseas licensor. The 1965 television anime adaptation of Osamu Tezuka 's *Jungaru taitei* (literally, Jungle Emperor), known in the United States as *Kimba the White Lion,* was partly funded by NBC, enabling it to be made in color. Until recently, the distribution of anime meant television broadcasts around the world. Usually non-Japanese television broadcasts are in a reedited and redubbed format to make them more palatable for the local broadcasting industry. Since the 1980s, video has been a major medium for releasing anime into non-Japanese markets. Outside of Asia, the major market growth in the 1960s and 1970s was in Europe, especially countries like France, Italy, and Spain, and in Latin America.

The English-speaking world has been a latecomer to much of anime programming. The limited anime TV programming that existed was limited to a few shows in the 1960s and 1970s, with an increase in science fiction anime in the 1980s. The 1980s broadcasts consisted mainly of giant robot shows made in the 1970s. In North America, anime clubs played a role in spreading awareness of anime among a growing community of fans; they also helped fuel sales of early video releases. Anime clubs existed first among science fiction fans in the late 1970s, then on college campuses in the 1980s, and, by the mid-1990s, high school anime clubs were becoming common. Fans also organize numerous conventions, which can claim attendance levels from a few hundred to as high as over 20,000 for the larger weekend events. Alongside this was a growth in English-language specialty magazines and books, first among fan circles and quickly moving to professional-grade publications.

As a commercial product in the English-speaking world, anime increased in significance with the development of video technology, specifically VHS and DVD. Almost all anime in English-subtitled and redubbed versions have appeared on video rather than on television or in theaters. This can actually be seen as an advantage in that much of the spread of anime in the English-speaking world, especially in the United States, has been through a growing fan community that usually prefers its material uncut and in a subtitled format. Among fans this has also led to endless arguments over the superiority of redubbed versus subtitled shows. Fortunately, DVD has largely eliminated that issue, as almost all titles are released in both formats on the same disc. There are, however, exceptions to this. Some series are so highly edited in the spoken-English version that they result in separate redubbed and subtitled DVD releases. For example, *Cardcaptors* (2000), the redubbed version, and *Cardcaptor Sakura* (1998), the uncut subtitled version, are the same show in two very different releases. There is also a growing tendency to release some titles only in subtitled versions. These are usually titles aimed at hardcore fans or a sophisticated adult audience that is likely to see other foreign cinema and has little interest in redubbed works.

This development of the home video market for anime has grown without the major entertainment companies playing a significant role. All the major anime video companies in the United States and other English-speaking countries are either privately owned businesses or branches of Japanese companies expanding their distribution. The number of anime titles released to video by major American entertainment companies is still so small that they are almost insignificant. Major companies released five titles in 2003 while the smaller specialty companies released something like 749 videos, some only as boxed sets (AnimeONDVD.com 2003). With the growing volume of anime have come an increase in translated manga sales, art books, reference books, soundtracks, toys, and model kits, as well as burgeoning anime specialty magazine sales. In 2002 there was the formation of The Anime Network, a cable network that shows anime twenty-four hours a day, seven days a week.

Beyond Anime and Manga

Japanese cinema has long had an established viewership in the West. However, this was largely limited to either fine cinema created from the late 1940s to early 1960s or redubbed action films from the 1970s. With the growth of anime sales, the distributors started producing separate product lines for live-action cinema. With their distribution channels in place for anime, adding live-action was an easy step for them to take. In time, live-action video releases have even spread to Japanese TV dramas. In fact, some fan groups were already illegally distributing their own subtitled versions of a few live-action shows on the Internet. Novels were also translated and published by some of the anime and manga companies in the United States. Related to all of this is an increase in the distribution of graphic novels and animation from China and Korea by many of the companies that distribute Japanese products.

Anime as a Window to Japan

One facet of the growing interest in anime and manga is a growing interest in Japan. Fans want to have a greater understanding of the shows they enjoy, so they study foods, geography, history, clothing, martial arts, contemporary pop culture, etiquette, and any other aspect of Japanese society that may catch their fancy. Along with all the anime-related events, conventions may have limited-enrollment tea ceremonies, workshops on popular music, and presentations on history and other topics. The dealer's room, a must for any anime convention, will often include representatives from cultural groups and travel agents. Opening ceremonies may include *taiko* drumming, Japanese rock bands, martial arts demonstrations, or other activities.

This interest in Japan has also resulted in record enrollment in Japanese-language classes in the United States, and could be playing a role in the development of a new generation of young scholars interested in things Japanese. Ginny Parker writes in the *Wall Street Journal* that a major factor seems to be an interest in anime and other forms of Japanese popular culture (Parker 2004, A1). Modern Language Association figures show that in 2002 there were 52,238 students taking Japanese classes in institutions of higher education in the United States. This is up 21.1 percent from the last survey in 1998 (Welles 2002). And the Japan Foundation worldwide survey for 2003, which includes all types of schools, shows enrollments of 42,018 students for higher education and 140,200 for all students in the United States (Japan Foundation 2004a).

What Will the Future Bring?

What can we say about the future of anime? It is hard to predict what will come in Japan as well as the international market. Could we have predicted the dramatic growth and change in the industry in the 1980s and 1990s? The present period is one of contradictions. More shows are on the air but money is often tighter for individual programs, resulting in cost-cutting measures such as lower image counts per program. Some people feel that today there is a bubble in the anime industry that could collapse, reducing the number of studios. The only thing that can be said for sure is that there will be new works, as the worldwide market for anime is too firmly established to vanish. Given Japan's low birthrate, the industry will have to continue to expand its production of works for adults. The Japanese are very aware they will also have to increase the overseas licensing of anime products. Related to this is the possibility of changes in the animation industry worldwide as a result of anime popularity. Korea and China both have growing animation industries that are also improving in quality. If the viewing public and, more importantly, the investors become receptive to new types of animated stories, the animation industry could change dramatically. In the United States the animation industry not only has famous companies like Pixar and DreamWorks, but newer, lesser-known companies with much promise, like San Francisco's Wild Brain, whose highly talented staff will likely make its name widely known in the near future.

Postscript

I have mentioned many works in this essay. Most of these are available in English subtitled versions for the North American market; many are also available in other parts of the world. I suggest readers start viewing some of this material and explore the diversity of the anime industry. And finally, I must state that the length of this essay necessitated the exclusion of many significant titles and companies. Readers are encouraged to explore further; the books in my bibliography are one possible place to begin.

Notes

1. Researching anime in non-Japanese sources is complicated by the fact that the major non-Japanese magazines devoted to this subject are not indexed and what little material is in indexed sources is uneven or erroneous. Tracking down written materials is often best done by consulting with others. In the case of anime, the rec.arts.anime.misc Usenet newsgroup is perhaps the best forum to ask for sources on specific topics.

2. My main source for verifying title information is Clements and McCarthy (2001) and the *Anime News Network Encyclopedia*. I have also tried to limit the titles I cite to those that are available in American editions, as they would be accessible to many of the readers of this essay. Readers from non-English-speaking countries may wish to check titles in the *Anime News Network Encyclopedia*, as it attempts to include the titles used in all releases. Most of the pre-1980 titles mentioned here are not available outside of Japan. The selection also reflects some of my own biases and tastes. However, it also reflects many of the titles one should know about.

3. This title is still available on VHS from Japan as *Momotarō no shinpei* (SB-0109). See Official Website Shochiku at www.shochiku.co.jp/video/v40s/sb0109.html (accessed November 4, 2005).

4. While *Otogi Manga Calendar* (1962) was the first anime series to be broadcast, it was not the first anime broadcast. In 1960, NHK, Japan's public television network, broadcast *Mitsu no hanashi,* three anime adaptations of famous stories. (Clements and McCarthy 2001, 184).

5. The full list of awards for *Spirited Away* is most impressive. Just a few of the awards include: Best Animated Feature Film, 75th Annual Academy Awards; Best Film, 2001 Japanese Academy Awards; Golden Bear (tie), 2002 Berlin International Film Festival, and Best Animated Feature, 2002 New York Film Critics Circle Awards.

3

Characters, Themes, and Narrative Patterns in the Manga of Osamu Tezuka

SUSANNE PHILLIPPS

The legendary manga artist and anime producer Osamu Tezuka (1928–1989), known in Japan as the *manga no kamisama* or "god of Japanese comics," played a crucial role in the development of postwar manga. Active artistically for more than forty years, he left behind approximately 150,000 manuscript pages after his death. As a pioneer, he tested the narrative possibilities that word-picture combinations offer. Thus, the development of the so-called story manga *(sutorii manga)* is associated with his name.[1]

In his search for new forms of storytelling, Tezuka hearkened back to the Japanese tradition of word-picture combinations and, at the same time, introduced new pictorial elements from U.S. and European cinema. Like novelists and movie directors, Tezuka gathered his themes and characters from all sources: Asian and European history, the world's fairy tales and myths, American science fiction films, and English detective stories. In the treasure trove of Tezuka's manga, one can find all possible genres with the idiosyncratic narrative patterns and the characters associated with them. Tezuka's manga are populated not only by samurai and ghosts, and robots and extraterrestrials, but also by actresses like Marilyn Monroe and comic book heroes like Dick Tracy. Through his manga, many motifs and characters from Western popular culture found their way to Japan.

At the beginning of his career, Tezuka was able to strike the right chord for the children who were his readers with his adventure and science fiction stories. In the 1950s, he dominated the manga industry, monopolizing it to a degree that would be impossible for any one artist to accomplish today. Like all who are involved in popular culture, he was sensitive to the dictates of his readers: works that did not appeal to their tastes were quickly abandoned for projects that would sell. However, he was also at the mercy of his readership's changing preferences. By the 1960s, Tezuka was no longer considered a trendsetter. His predominance was challenged when new kinds of stories gained popularity. Called *gekiga* (dramatic pictures), these comics were new in several respects. First, they came from a new generation of artists located in Osaka, not Tokyo, where the established artists lived. Second, they were new because they were realistically drawn and featured graphic scenes of violence. Tezuka found himself fending off journalists who declared that he was all washed up. Envious of gekiga's success, Tezuka fiercely attacked his new artist-competitors, but he also responded by adapting gekiga's stylistic innovations to his own work. Gekiga spurred Tezuka to abandon old formulas that he had favored for new themes, plots, and character concepts. Finally, after this phase of experimentation, Tezuka hit on a winning synthesis that used the gekiga format to embellish his dramatic manga epics about key moments in world history.

In terms of narrative style, we can distinguish three periods in Tezuka's career: (1) his early "classical" period from 1947 to the mid-sixties, (2) his horror-gothic period in the seventies, and (3) his historical-realistic period from approximately the mid-seventies to his death in 1989.

From 1947 to the Mid-Sixties: Tezuka's Classical Period

Tezuka's first manga, *Shin-takarajima* (New Treasure Island, 1947), is an adventure story combining elements of *Tarzan*, *Treasure Island*, and *Robinson Crusoe*. It became a best-seller with about 400,000 copies sold. *Shin-takarajima* marked a turning point in the history of manga: for the first time, children could read an exciting story not as a serialized newspaper column, but as a manga book of nearly 200 pages from beginning to end.

After the success of *Shin-takarajima*, Tezuka drew other manga that were published as "red-book manga" (*akahon manga*), so named because they were printed on cheap paper and bound in a red cover. They were sold by sweets merchants in the Matsuyamachi district of Osaka. His ideas came from a supply of approximately 3,000 pages that he had drawn and bound into books as a youngster during the war. Here, one can find a major reason for the great success of Tezuka's early publications; most of the adventure and science fiction stories of this early phase are revised versions of those that came from the pen of a boy who was not much older than his readership, rather than an adult who saw manga as a didactic tool to educate children.

In this early phase, Tezuka wrote three kinds of tales: adventure stories, science fiction stories, and period romances. In contrast to *Shin-takarajima*, these manga were not originally published as books but appeared in magazines running over many, many years, with a form and content that always responded to readers' changing tastes. For each type he drew manga from dozens to hundreds of pages long. In the early fifties, when he developed his cartoon stars, these stories became long-running bestsellers. All were hits, such as the adventure story *Janguru taitei* (*Kimba the White Lion*, 1950–1954, literally, "Ruler of the jungle"), the science fiction story *Tetsuwan Atomu* (*Astro Boy*, 1951–1968, literally, "Ironarm Atom"), and the period romance *Ribon no kishi* (*Princess Knight*, 1953–1956, literally, "Knight with Ribbons"). The publication of these three serialized manga marked the first triumph of Tezuka's career. They were so successful financially—all three even gained popularity abroad—that Tezuka was able to establish his own anime studio.

Stamp of Osamu Tezuka and his most famous characters—Astro Boy, Leo, Princess Sapphire, and Black Jack. (Copyright Tezuka Productions)

Adventure Stories

Adventure stories contain all the exotic locales and extraordinary situations that one can imagine: The heroes struggle to survive in a tropical jungle, either because they had to make an emergency landing or because they are on an unusual expedition to solve some mystery. En route, they find strange old towers, ruins of Inca towns, springs of immortality, and so on. The adventurers are attacked by eagles, crocodiles, black panthers, and gigantic poisonous spiders, as happens in *Sharigawa no himitsu kichi* (The Secret Base of Shari-River, 1948). The plot of these wilderness adventure stories is always structured upon the opposition between civilization and nature: "civilization," personified by the heroes, is characterized by advanced scientific thinking, whereas "nature," personified by the ignorant savages they encounter in the jungle, means silly superstition.

Science Fiction Stories

Tezuka's science fiction manga are radically different from his exotic adventure stories. Examples of this type include *Chiteikoku no kaijin* (The Mysterious Men Down in the Earth, 1948), *Metoroporisu* (*Metropolis*,1949), *Kitarubeki sekai* (*Next World,* 1951), *38 doseijō no kaibutsu* (The Monster on the 38th Parallel, 1953), *Taiheiyō x-pointo*

Ken'ichi—A character in Tezuka's early manga with whom fans could closely identify.
(Copyright Tezuka Productions)

(Point X in the South Pacific, 1953), and *Daikōzui jidai* (The Age of the Great Flood, 1955). Rather than being escapist fantasies, these manga directly reflect Japan's war experiences and the privations of the postwar period. The stark realities of the time are made clear in Tezuka's sharply detailed portrayals of life, down to the small details of its cruelties. The young Ken'ichi, for example, who appears in almost all of these early manga, is a character with whom many Japanese could closely identify. He has lost his parents in the war, and now his uncle, Hige Oyaji, has to take care of him.

In Tezuka's science fiction stories, the conflict that structures the narrative is based upon the opposition between democracy and dictatorship. While "democracy" stands for sincerity and responsibility, "dictatorship" stands for unscrupulousness and callow, self-serving egotism. Tezuka penned many stories about how the policies of an irresponsible government run by a dictator end in disaster. The characters who are part of the totalitarian regime ruthlessly oppress their subordinates and torture any dissenters. The people, lacking will and incapable of action, have no influence on the decisions of the selfish rulers. While the officers and governmental officials prosecute the war from a safe distance, the populace—a mob whipped into a frenzy—is exposed to a hail of bombs. Panicked, they try to flee, while others—buried alive and shouting for help—are abandoned to their miserable fate. Reading these manga, Tezuka's readers could not only reexperience the horrors of war, but also feel fear about the possibility of new ones. As such, these stories are a reaction to contemporary history, and, above all, to the outbreak of the Korean War.

Tezuka's story lines, therefore, are generally deeply pessimistic. The world has become a slaughterhouse; there is no corner left to withdraw to and be safe from violence. He repeatedly portrays the destruction of the world as a flood that buries everything under it, as in *Daikōzui jidai* (The Age of Great Flood,1955). He expresses his hope for a rescue using the biblical image of Noah's Ark. People try to escape on rafts or leave the earth in spaceships. If enough time remains, pairs of animals are entered on inventory lists to be taken along on board. These stories often have heroes, too—young adventurers who rescue Earth and humanity. Here the opposition, narratively, is between children and adults. The adults are selfish, uncompromising. and incapable of handling the awesome powers of new technologies responsibly. Great rulers end up being egotistical maniacs who cut ridiculous figures. By contrast, the young are reasonable, self-sacrificing, and fight valiantly against the corrupt evil adults to save the world.

As in all good science fiction stories, things do not occur by happenstance but can be explained (pseudo)scientifically. For example, the apocalyptic flood is caused by global warming after nuclear test explosions. Many stories end happily after the evil knowledge that has wreaked havoc has been destroyed, but it is also clear that scientific progress is unstoppable; the danger remains that some mad ruler will get his hands on this new technology once again and use it for nefarious purposes. Tezuka's ambivalence toward science is personified by different scientists who appear as characters. He repeatedly uses scenes of conferences and congresses where scientific experts gather from all over the world. Among them, there is always a mix of personalities. Invariably, along with the few modest and far-sighted researchers who warn of the consequences of new discoveries, there are also arrogant braggarts who announce smugly that "$1+1 = 2$," and greedy scientists hungry for money and ready to sell their inventions to the highest bidder, as in *Meturoporisu* (1949, 18–19).

Romantic Fantasies

In Tezuka's romantic fantasies one can see influences from three main sources: German fairy tales, from which he borrows plots; Disney characters, from which he takes stylistic features; and the Takarazuka women's revue, from which he takes scenes that he incorporates into his manga tableau.

Tezuka's stories are full of fairy-tale motifs. For example, *Akai yuki* (Red Snow, 1955) tells the story of an outcast orphan girl who later marries the son of the czar, a version of the Cinderella tale that, in this manga, is set in old Russia. Extremely implausible plot twists lead finally to a happy ending. The girl's key talent, which allows her to rise socially, is her singing. Thus, notes dance across the manga's pages with little birds, which flit around twittering the melody. Replete with romantic moments, Tezuka won over girls as manga readers with these pieces.

Animal figures, which play an important role in all early manga of Tezuka, appear

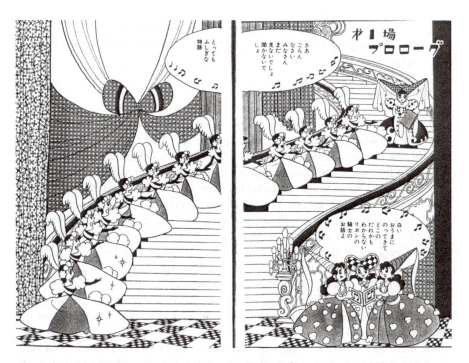

The opening scene of *Ribon no kishi* (*Princess Knight*, version drawn 1958–59) shows a giant staircase, like the illuminated one on the stage of Takarazuka, the trademark of the revue.
(Copyright Tezuka Productions)

in these stories in great numbers. Their resemblance to Disney deer, squirrels, bunnies, and so on is obvious, and one can even encounter famous Disney versions of characters from Western popular culture, such as Snow White or Peter Pan. Many of these manga are set in czarist Russia. In sharp contrast to the ultramodern skyscrapers and high-tech factories that form the backdrop of his science fiction stories, the scenes in Tezuka's romances are reminiscent of postcards of Russian Orthodox churches, filled with round onion turrets covered with snow.

Many also call to mind the Takarazuka all-women revue's costume plays, which still remain popular today with sold-out performances at their Osaka and Tokyo theaters (Robertson 1998). As a boy, Tezuka went to many of their performances with his mother, and he liberally imported themes, plots, scenery, scene sequences, and characters from the stage into his manga. Thus, these had enormous influence on Tezuka's girls' manga.

Tezuka's most famous costume drama is *Princess Knight*. It is the story of Princess Sapphire, a medieval European princess who has to disguise herself as a prince to succeed to the throne. The basic plot device in the story is that the princess must play a double role, constantly changing her dress, and thus her identity, to fool everyone. This gives Tezuka a wide latitude for thinking about gender roles and female identity.

As girls' manga (*shōjo manga*) developed, it is this exploration of what it means to be a girl, fathoming the inside world of the heroines, that became a central element of the genre.

Influences from Abroad

The adventure and science fiction manga of Tezuka's early phase reveal his thorough knowledge of American and European adventure tales like *Tarzan, Treasure Island*, or *Robinson Crusoe*, Hollywood, and the UFA (the former German film production industry) films. Over and over again, one finds famous film scenes reappearing in Tezuka's stories. For example, the being that is brought to life by scientists and slowly rises from the operating table in Tezuka's *Metoroporisu* (1949, 29) is inspired by Fritz Lang's robot woman in *Metropolis*, and the automatic food dispenser for factory workers in *Shinsekai Rurū* (literally, New World Lurue, 1951, 192) comes originally from Charles Chaplin's *Modern Times*. Tezuka altered the scenes for his young Japanese audience, gave them an entirely new context, and enriched them with the biological knowledge he had acquired while studying medicine.

Tezuka had mixed feelings about the United States, a love-hate relationship that alternated between rejecting and borrowing from American popular culture. On the one hand, the United States was Japan's former enemy. In one of Tezuka's science fiction stories, *Sekai o horobosu otoko* (The Destroyer of the World, 1954), for example, American generals discuss dropping another newly developed bomb on Japan. On the other hand, America positively symbolized adventure, progress, and the future. Tezuka's manga often featured idealized utopian American cityscapes depicting a way of life that was still foreign to Japanese children. Popular culture scholar Mitsutoshi Ishigami describes his ambiguous feelings as a boy toward Tezuka's manga by saying that he felt a sense of strangeness (*iwakan*) and curiosity when looking at Tezuka's cityscapes filled with their skyscrapers and foreign letters on the roadsigns because English was the language of the enemy. Japanese children did not learn English before 1945 (Ishigami 1977, 36). More and more American English crept into the titles of Tezuka's manga. At first, Tezuka ornamented his title pages with transcriptions in the Roman alphabet, which added an exotic flavor to them. Later, he added English subtitles that were more or less correct translations of the Japanese originals, and finally, he used English titles, as in *Metropolis* written in Latin script and in the Japanese katakana (Ishigami 1977, 28–37).

In addition, Tezuka added American cinematic features to his manga. In particular, he adapted the technique of cinematic montage by making sequences of panels to mimic movement or scene changes. For example, he might use a sequence of several panels that depicted a figure moving closer to the "camera" (viewer) of a scene.

A typical Tezuka narrative illustrates his special talent as an innovative borrower, an artist who could seamlessly fold Western plots into Japanese stories. Tezuka alternated his basic five-part plot structure in various manga, such as *Astro Boy, Mitsume ga tōru*, and *Dororo*. His five-part structure consisted of the following:

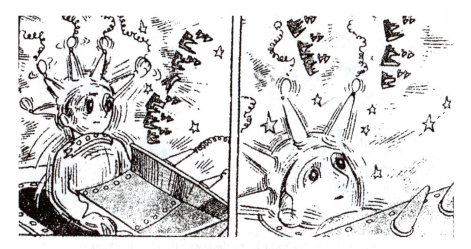

A trembling robot comes to life in *Metropolis*. (Copyright Tezuka Productions)

1. An imperfect child is born or created. In one version, the father promises the body of his child to demons to enlist their help so he can stay in power (Hyakkimaru in *Dororo*). In the other, more frequently used version, a mad or obsessed scientist creates a son, as in the case of Astro Boy; this son starts life as a child rather than a fully grown adult like the Western Frankenstein or the Terminator. In any case, the child has physical problems that were caused by his father. Angry about the child's imperfections, the bad father abandons him against the wishes of the weak mother.

2. The child is found by a man who lovingly takes care of him. Here, we see a central motif of Japanese fairy tales at work. This is the motif of the child sent by the gods *(mōshigo)*, as in the tale of the peach boy, Momotarō. Every Japanese child knows this story, which exists in countless variations.[2]

3. The stepfather, who is a brilliant scientist or doctor, provides the boy with special augmentations (e.g., Astro Boy's special equipment, radar, rocket drive, Hyakkimaru's artificial organs that allow him to live).

4. Through these special enhancements, the boy gains new powers, but also suffers a split in his personality. While living like an average schoolboy, an experience he shares with children his same age (and also the readers), he uses his unusual abilities for good. Because he is largely artificial, the boy wonders about his identity: Is he a human being or a robot?

5. The child rewards his stepfather by fighting criminals or ghosts. This plot becomes a kind of hero myth that also has the character of a detective story, like Batman in American comics. Tezuka's most famous crime fighter is Astro Boy.

Scenes from the western *Remon kiddo* (Lemon Kid) in which the villain (in black) burns the "wanted" poster of his face, and duels with the hero (in white).
(Copyright Tezuka Productions)

The Cast of Characters

Tezuka authored several instructional books on drawing manga that provide insights into his understanding of style, character development, and narrativity. In *Manga no kakikata* (How to Draw Comics, 1977), he compares manga to children's drawings. In his eyes, children draw innocently, not in the sense of a realistic portrait, like a photo, but expressively, directly putting down their impressions of their surroundings. Similarly, Tezuka argues that drawing good comics involves omission (*shōryaku*), exaggeration (*kochō*), and variation (*henkei*). Correct proportion for a realistic sketch is unnecessary. On the contrary, to express an emotion, abrupt alterations in figuration are appropriate. Thus, his characters may look like rubber dolls whose heads can reach the ground when submissively bowing and whose arms become elastic, unnaturally extending far out to grab a beer bottle they desire. During a fight, the head, arms, or legs can even fly away temporarily from the body. Strictly speaking, Tezuka's ideal is to make manga with a childlike innocence, but also in a way that takes its cue from early American animation, which is like a stack of images that simulate movement when flipped at high speed. The only component absent in Tezuka's manga is the musical background that accompanies the animated film.

It is in his treatment of his characters that Tezuka comes closest to the role of a modern film director or stage manager. The science fiction and adventure stories of Tezuka's early period are not serials. Content-wise they stand as independent works. Nevertheless, all his stories from 1947 to 1955 have the same characters in them. They may get a little older or have slightly different names, but they look the same and have the same personalities, jobs, and, therefore, the same social status. Like Hollywood studios with their stables of stars, Tezuka gradually built up a cast of dozens of char-

Lamp threatens Hige Oyaji. (Copyright Tezuka Productions)

acters that was like an actual theater troupe. Just like real actors who are typecast to
fit particular roles, these characters appear in different manga playing their assigned
bits. Tezuka called this his "star system."

For example, Hige Oyaji is the most pleasant, most engaging character in Tezuka's
oeuvre. He acts as the protective (step)father or uncle of the orphan boy Ken'ichi, a
figure for whom many Japanese children of the postwar period certainly yearned. A
dear old man with a moustache, Hige Oyaji is a traditionalist who is dependable and

intelligent, although sometimes a little bit clumsy and irritable. Having lived through the horrific defeat in the war, he is an ardent opponent of nuclear weapons and atomic bomb tests. In Tezuka's stories, like *Mahō yashiki* (Satan's House, 1948), *Metropolis* (1949), and *Janguru taitei* (Kimba, 1950–54), Hige Oyaji plays either a responsible doctor or a good-hearted detective.

In almost all of Tezuka's early manga, Ken'ichi plays the youthful hero with whom Tezuka's young readers could identify. Ken'ichi has a strongly developed sense of justice and responsibility, and does his utmost not only for his friends, but also for world peace. His uncompromising idealism is astonishing, because Ken'ichi repeatedly faces situations that show how naive he really is.

A third key character in Tezuka's star system is Acetylene Lamp, or "Lamp" for short, a character who is the embodiment of evil, the mirror opposite of Hige Oyaji. He plays various roles, such as the sadistic criminal and the unscrupulous saboteur. He murders people without showing the slightest touch of remorse. While Lamp is always meticulously dressed, he almost always is a fierce-looking man. His peculiar name comes from a candle's flame that flickers on Lamp's head when he is surprised or annoyed. Lamp had his debut as the mean newspaper journalist in *Rosuto wārudo* (Lost World, 1948) (Ishigami 1977, 111). Acetylene Lamp is one of the few of Tezuka's characters who also appears in his later manga as well. Even after Tezuka had abandoned the star system, he still cast Lamp in sadistic roles.

These and many other characters inhabit Tezuka's early manga, even if most of them never became the main characters in any of Tezuka serialized works.[3] Tezuka used this ensemble, giving his "actors" roles that would fit the specific genres in which they appeared (e.g., the gunslinger hero in the western, the brilliant scientist-inventor in the science fiction story, etc.).

An unpublished manuscript of Tezuka's, on exhibit at the Tezuka Memorial Museum (Tezuka Kinenkan) in Takarazuka, hints that he actually imagined his characters to be actors that he had hired (Tezuka Productions 1994). He had drawn a lineup of their faces, provided a short description of them, a curriculum vitae of their acting careers (who worked when for which studio), and a salary chart of the fees they should receive for appearing in a manga. Since his readers understand that Tezuka's manga are "cinematic," most Japanese critics rarely mention this idiosyncratic way in which Tezuka conceived his characters as real actors.

Having stock characters who are unambiguously either good or evil does not allow much flexibility in terms of a story's development. But it does allow for the possibility of humor. For example, Tezuka frequently drew himself, first as a doctor or manga artist, then as the head of his anime studio, Mushi Production. Sometimes, his characters quarrel with each other, intrigue against each other, or argue with Osamu Tezuka as the studio head about their "roles," "salary," and so on.

Tezuka also invented characters who have nothing to do with the plot per se, but appear in cameo roles for comedic effect. The most famous of these is a strange being called "Hyōtantsugi." It is shaped like a gourd bottle and covered with patches.

Hyōtantsugi. (Copyright Tezuka Productions)

Ordinary characters can suddenly mutate into Hyōtantsugi when they get angry, excited, or are ashamed, only to be restored to their original form in the next panel again. When Tezuka wants to stress strong emotions, the Hyōtantsugi bursts straight out of the panel. When something stupid happens in a story, it rains Hyōtantsugi.

Occasionally, the gags are more interesting than the events at the center of the story since they are inside jokes that only true Tezuka fans would comprehend. For example, characters often step out of the proper story (and even the actual panels) to remark upon the storyline and the cast of characters. They take on a life outside the stories as if they were famous film stars. In *Kitaru beki sekai* (Next World, 1951), a foreigner meeting Hige Oyaji remarks, "You say you are private detective Hige Oyaji! I am familiar with your name from several manga" (*Kitaru beki sekai,* quoted from a reprint of 1995, 87). Or, in another, when Hige Oyaji makes his first appearance in *Atomu taishi* (later, *Tetsuwan Atomu* or *Astro Boy*), he asks the other characters if they know him. They reply, "Of course, you are Hige Oyaji, the private detective in Tezuka's other manga." Hige Oyaji then tells them, "Yes, now I am teacher, but in former manga, as a private detective, I was an indispensible character of Tezuka's manga" (*Tetsuwan Atomu* 1995, vol. 1, 53). On this secondary comedic level, the close bond between Osamu Tezuka and his contemporary readers becomes clear.

Osamu Tezuka often drew caricatures of himself surrounded by his characters, which make him look like a theater or movie director with his actors. (Copyright Tezuka Productions)

The Hero—Astro Boy, Leo, and Princess Sapphire

The three serialized manga that made Tezuka's career all have good, strong heroes who fight against despicable villains. Indeed, the stories of these three heroes mark the zenith of popularity of Tezuka's adventure, science fiction, and romantic fantasies. The answer as to why Tezuka's work became so popular lies perhaps in the new ways he frames his heroes as characters. These stories are not a simple battle between good and evil—something that we see, for example, in the American *Superman* comics where the man of steel (aka Clark Kent) battles against the likes of Lex Luther and other unrecalcitrant criminals. Tezuka's heroes are also struggling against a corrupt society filled with prejudice of which they are a part.

For example, the small robot Astro Boy lives in the Tokyo of 2003, a world of skyscrapers and aircars that very much resembles today: the children are bored at school, the police provide law and order, and the Ministry of Science charts a course for society's technological future. On the one hand, these stories are conventional myths of the hero who protects society from evil outsiders. Like the American heroes in *Batman*, *Superman*, or *Spiderman* comics, Astro Boy works on society's behalf to hunt for dangerous criminals who threaten the public order. With the extraordinary powers that the boy received from his stepfather, he is often the only one able to fight the villains and save Tokyo, or even the whole of Japan, from their attacks or from environmental disasters.

On the other hand, these stories do not portray a simple "us versus them" in which society is good, and evil comes from outside dualism. In fact, the stories raise disturbing questions about modern society. Unlike today, robots live among humans. Thanks to scientific advances, in fact, the latest robot models are indistinguishable from humans. Thus, the underlying theme of *Astro Boy* is that tension arises when robots and humans live together. Using this fictional device, Tezuka is exploring real problems in contemporary Japanese society. Astro Boy repeatedly confronts the problems that minorities typically face today, particularly the evils of racism.

While Astro Boy faces down the evils of human prejudice, other manga heroes engage in different battles. In *Kimba the White Lion*, the white lion Leo desperately fights for the harmonious co-existence between humans and animals, and in *Princess Knight*, Princess Sapphire has to deal with gender discrimination by disguising herself as a young man, her only means of succeeding to her rightful place on the throne. By overcoming their difficulties, all three heroes become more than stick figures. They attain an unusual psychological depth because they are liminal figures. They stand between different groups and thus have difficulty finding their place in society. Astro Boy stands between humans and machines, the lion Leo stands between humans and animals, and Princess Sapphire stands between men and women. Their identity issues open up worlds that they would never have known if there were simply a machine, a wild animal, or a woman who fits conventional gender-role expectations. Their new insights make them long for another life and, at the same time, complicate any possibility of fitting into the status quo.

The Seventies: Tezuka's Horror-Gothic Period

In the sixties, artists like Sanpei Shirato, Shigeru Mizuki, and Yoshiharu Tsuge became famous for drawing stories that they called gekiga. In their new, more realistic drawing style, they created stories about the oppressed and outsiders with plots that were often disturbing. Their stories frequently featured ambiguous heroes, often social misfits or losers, in stories that were graphically violent—something that had been taboo in manga before this time. The stories, often set in Japan's past, were also explicitly marketed to teenagers and young adults, which soon made them popular with students. In 1964, the magazine *Garo* was founded to publish gekiga. In reply, Tezuka's company Mushi Pro set up its own magazine, *COM*, in January 1967. Most of the serials in *COM* came from Tezuka's pen but, at the same time, the magazine also served as a venue for lesser-known manga artists.

Graphically, as well as in terms of content, gekiga had a great influence on the further development of manga; new serials for children adapted its motifs, and, at the same time, more and more publishers tried to market not only to children, but also to teenagers as readers of manga magazines. For the first time in his career, Tezuka's sales figures dropped, and in 1968, after eighteen years, his most important serial, *Astro Boy*, ceased pubication. Again and again, publishers pleaded with him to change his drawing style to make it more like gekiga.

Tezuka had to do something, so he began to draw more realistically, in a style completely incompatible with his artistry until then, especially with regard to his preference for caricature and his whimsical incorporaton of sight gags into scenes to break up the narrative. Most of Tezuka's graphic jokes from this time reflect his own inner conflict as he uneasily searched for artistic compromises and changed stylistically over time. Many of his gags make clear that he was self-conscious about the clash of these two different styles, especially when portraying characters. He also tried to mute the exaggerated expressiveness present in his earlier work. Characters now had realistically drawn faces and longer legs and arms in proper porportions, and no longer did he include Disney-like figures.

Tezuka's darker gothic stories break stylistically with his earlier work. First, Tezuka made changes in plot and content. Like gekiga, his stories lost their dualistic worldview: right and wrong became blurred, reason and common sense vanished, and, often, the figures discovered evil in themselves as something endemic in their character that they could not shake off. Desire, jealousy, and hatred now took center stage. In his search for new heroes to appeal to the tastes of sixties readers, Tezuka also experimented with new genres as well, like ghost and horror stories that accented the fantastic and the grotesque.

Second, the action now unfolded in an alternate reality, typically in dreams, nightmares, or fantasies that blurred the distinction between what is real and what is not. Without warning, the plots might suddenly veer into the realm of the fantastic and the absurd, sometimes without providing any clear resolution at the end. A typical plot often starts with a normal, everyday situation that quickly goes wildly awry because a character suddenly acts unpredictably. This often happens because characters are driven by a dark side of their soul of which, until that moment, they are unaware. This dark side is a manifestation of absolute evil. It makes them devilishly deceitful, emotionally cold, and devoid of any moral scruples. Examples of this are found in *Barubora* (1974) or *I.L.* (1969–1970, reprint 1987). The former is a story about an artist who needs to live a decadent life consuming drugs in order to be creative. On the surface, the best-selling author Mikura seems to be a nice man, but he lives with Barubora, a lascivious and vulgar alcoholic. She gives him the fantasies he needs for writing. Although she is ruining his life, when she is absent he is unable to come up with ideas for new books. They have a bizarre and unhealthy relationship.

Third, Tezuka's character portraits include new stylistic features that signal their ambiguous nature. In his manuals on drawing manga, Tezuka explains how important it is to express the character's inner feelings graphically. His detailed descriptions of how to draw faces and bodies to evoke certain emotions like joy, grief, surprise, and/or fear are borne out by current research. For example, in their work on nonverbal communication, Paul Ekman and Wallace V. Friesen distinguish six basic emotions: surprise, fear, disgust, anger, happiness, and sadness. They see all other emotions as combinations of these basic emotions. These researchers systematically described, for the first time, how all emotions express themselves in the eyes, mouth, and forehead. On the basis of photos, films, and a computer program, they developed the so-called Facial Action Coding System (Ekman and Friesen 1975, 1978). In *Manga no kakikata,* Tezuka combines different schematically drawn mouths, eyes, and eyebrows into thirty-two facial types and demonstrates their different emotional effects, which correspond to a high degree to Ekman and Friesen's own typology.

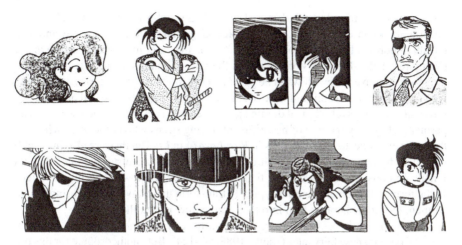

Some famous one-eyed evildoers in Tezuka's comics. (Copyright Tezuka Productions)

For Tezuka, the most important feature with which to reveal a character's inner feelings is the eyes. Tezuka creates an ocular lexicon for his fans that gives them immediate insight into the true nature of the characters who appear in his stories. For example, a one-eyed character always has a bad nature. Characters who are either blind in one eye or have one eye covered or injured are typically obscure, mysterious, and dangerous. They are usually perfidious cowards, betrayers, and even murderers.

One can find several examples of these odd-looking characters in Tezuka's work. As early as 1951, in his manga *Kitarubeki sekai* (*Next World*), Tezuka draws a young woman called Poponia whose one eye is covered by a hair lock. She turns out to be an opponent of the good characters (among them Hige Oyaji). An unwavering loyalist to a dictatorial regime, she fights her old friends. In *Dororo* (1967–1969), the brutal brother of Hyakkimaru always winks one eye, while an evil demoness, who tries to tempt the hero Dororo by altering her face to appear like a gentle lady, has one eye covered by her hair. In *Ayako* (1969–1973), Tenge Jirō seems to be nice at first, but it then becomes clear that he works for the American secret service and does not hesitate to kill people. Behind his eye patch, he hides politically important material, smuggled goods, or explosives. In *Burraku Jakku*, Black Jack's nasty opponent, Dr. Kiriko, always wears an eye patch. In *Shumari,* Hanamoto Danshaku has thick glasses that make it impossible to see his eyes. He shoots his wife Tae because of her supposed infidelity. In *Budda* (serialized in different magazines from 1972 to 1983), the one eye of Ahinsa always waters. He is one of the most dangerous opponents of Buddha. In *Hi no tori* (*The Phoenix*) in the "Book of the Cosmos" (*Uchū-hen*, which appeared first from March to July 1969 in the magazine *COM*), it turns out that the astronaut Makimura has brutally killed the bird people, alien inhabitants of another planet.

In his horror-gothic tales, metamorphosis is Tezuka's central theme. They are all about the shift that takes place when a character changes from his ordinary, apparently innocuous self to reveal that darker, evil side. Metamorphosis is the principal cause of uncertainty because the sudden, inexplicable change can come upon anybody and blurs the sharp borders between good and evil. This is the case, for example, in *Banpaiya* (Vampires, 1966–1969), a story in which the likeable main character is unwittingly transformed into a werewolf when he gazes at a full moon. In other stories, it is women who typically manifest this hidden evil side. It is their suddenly revealed preternatural physical but also psychological dominance that ends up destroying their weaker male partners. They play the role of beautiful entrancing sirens who attract men who need them, for example, to be creative, as in *Barubora* or in *I.L.* But they are also invariably menacing figures who constantly threaten men. In Tezuka's historical tales they are female demons, and in his science fiction stories they are powerful feminine aliens. In the former, the female demons typically transform themselves into alluring human women, luring the hapless men into their trap before eating them.

This motif of the shape-shifting woman who can become an animal or demon comes from Japanese fairy tales (Kawai 1988, 84–124). But another source for this plot comes from outside Japan. Ever the eclectic, Tezuka found many ideas in the works of Franz Kafka and Edgar Allen Poe, which he often alludes to in his manga. Indeed, Tezuka even gave a collection of seven stories published in 1974 and 1976–1977 the title "Metamorphosis," from Kafka's famous short story. All the stories are about transformation, either in a literal or metaphysical sense, and examine its effects—the physical or psychological entry into mystic worlds. Turning into an animal is regarded as a punishment. The more disgusting the animal, the worse the crime that resulted in this punishment. The process of metamorphosis is often painful, and by becoming the beast, the character loses his or her cultural and social abilities, above all the ability to communicate. By changing into a beast, the character also loses consciousness of the former human self. Tezuka's use of metamorphosis adds psychological complexity to his characters; the more ambiguous they are, the more terrifying they become. This makes them more interesting for Tezuka's more mature readers.

The Ambiguous New Hero Black Jack

Tezuka's most successful serialized manga of the seventies was *Burakku Jakku* (1973–1978). In many respects, this work successfully employs the character device of ambiguity discussed earlier. But in this case the comic features a powerful, ultimately good male hero who is self-assertive, decisive, and in control. Black Jack is a mysterious doctor who is officially unlicensed, but is famous as the most brilliant surgeon in the world. He is, however, an ambiguous figure, not only physically but also psychologically. While initially he seems unapproachable and emotionally cold, this is only a mistaken, surface impression. When he operates on a patient, he does whatever it takes to find a cure, showing his deep sense of responsibility, perhaps even compassion, for his patients.

Because of his fame, his patients (human beings, animals, and intelligent computer systems) come from all over. Before an operation, Black Jack sets his price, which often seems ridiculously high and unfair, given the severity of his patients' sicknesses. He does not make contracts or send bills for his services, but relies only on the good will of his patients. Most of the time, he uses the money he earns for good.

Initially, Tezuka wanted to make Black Jack an unscrupulous doctor. But his readers reacted so enthusiastically to him as the misunderstood but good loner who acted freely on the basis of his personal moral code that Tezuka left him as he was—not a greedy villain, but a dedicated doctor with a dark side who plumbs his limits as well as those of modern medicine.[4]

Mid-Seventies to 1989: Tezuka's Historical Realistic Period

Over the decades, Tezuka's manga had increasingly attracted teenage and adult readers. By the 1980s, he was an established artist whose works were published not only in manga magazines, but also in newspapers and periodicals. Sometimes they were even sold in the literature sections of bookstores.

In contrast to the imaginary worlds that formed the backdrop to his earlier works, Tezuka's later stories are set in clearly recognizable historical times and places. The specific political, social, and cultural context has an important place in the narration. These stories run for thousands of pages with numerous subplots and fascinating asides. No longer is the focus on single heroes whose force of character moves the drama. The historical context plays a key role because it puts its stamp on their character, motivating their actions. Adding historical details gives credibility to Tezuka's fictional tales. For dramatic effect, Tezuka also chooses revolutionary periods, times of momentous social upheaval that force his characters into perilous situations. This lends these stories a dynamic quality unlike the mood in his earlier stories. The stories underscore the fact that nothing lasts forever or is eternally true; in particular, they reveal that all political and social systems are ephemeral. For example, *Hidamari no ki* (Sunlit Tree, 1981–1986) is the story of the young doctor Ryōan Tezuka and the young samurai Manjirō Ibuya, which takes place during the turbulent final years of the Tokugawa era. It is a time when feudalism was crumbling in the face of internal political dissent and foreign pressures. In the story, the characters are witnesses to the political chaos that follows on the heels of the opening of Japan to the Western world, momentous events that culminate in the Meiji Restoration (1868), which marks the beginning of Japan's rapid technological, industrial, and political modernization. The two characters react differently to these changes. Manjirō Ibuya, who remains loyal to the old regime, cannot adapt and is ruined. Ryōan Tezuka, who embraces the new scientific techniques that make him a better physician, flourishes in the new Japan. The key plot twist in this and other tales of this period is that the two characters, once friends, find themselves confronting new political, social, and cultural changes that force them to choose different paths.

In this third period of his career, Tezuka also changes the way he draws. His characters become more angular and taller. He finally abandons his old star system, making way for a new cast of characters who represent an array of recognizable modern figures, like absentminded scientists, corrupt politicians, modest monks, successful businessmen, rebellious students, and so forth. Tezuka's new characters are not stars like Astro Boy, who appeared in a host of different works. In the course of a single story they age, sometimes change their personality, and cannot be simply typecast as either completely good or evil.

As we have seen in the example of *Hidamari no ki*, Tezuka usually builds his stories around at least *two* central characters who incarnate different worldviews and values. In the beginning of the story, the two know each other personally as close relatives or friends. However, as they grow older, their relationship inevitably changes. When they meet again as old friends, they now have different political or religious views that create complications; they come into conflict, and have to decide whether or not to fight each other. Later in these stories, Tezuka shows how the changing historical context forces the characters to change as well. They become uncertain because it is not clear what the best path is: should a sister hide her brother who has become the member of a resistance group, or does she betray him because he wants to overthrow the government she supports? Many scenes highlight these internal personal conflicts of characters who are caught in situations fraught with ambiguity and tormented because they are unsure about what they should do. Because Tezuka allows us to enter into the psyches of his characters, we are able to learn what motivates them. Thus, it often becomes difficult for readers to choose sides in these stories. A case in point is the story *Adorufu ni tsugu* (*Adolf*, 1983–1985). It is a story about two boys, Adolf Kaufmann and Adolf Kamil, who are best friends when they are children. As their lives become entangled in the political storm of Nazi Germany in the 1930s, they tragically end up becoming sworn enemies by the time they grow up. When they meet each other again during the war, they have mixed emotions. While they are happy to meet, they realize that they are now archenemies. Initially they embrace, but immediately feel uncomfortable and end up pulling apart, facing each other with unmistakable hostility.

Tezuka uses his new character types to tell stories about famous historical or literary personalities too. By doing so, he undermines the good public image they have enjoyed over the centuries. This is especially evident in *Hi no tori* (*The Phoenix*), a nearly 4,000-page classic story manga consisting of sixteen stories. The eleven that form the core of the work alternate between historical and science fiction stories. They unfold both in the distant past and in the far future. The stories cover a time span beginning with Japan's prehistory in the *Reimei-hen* (Book of Dawn, 1967), dealing with important events from ancient Japanese epochs (e.g., Kofun, Nara, Heian). Here we find that those whom history lauds as brilliant figures become, in Tezuka's retelling, moody, complaining egoists. In *The Phoenix*, Tezuka reveals that the wars fought throughout Japanese history are not simply for political power, nor are brothers assassinated solely to secure a tyrant's succession to the throne. All these evils are done to obtain the blood of the Phoenix so that people can become immortal.

A perfect example is *Dawn*, a story in Volume 1 about the empress-shamaness Pimiko, a half-legendary figure who is noted in the third-century Chinese *Wei Chih*. In this record she is described as a shamanic medium who ruled over the kingdom of Yamatai, the first actual ruler of Japan as verified in non-Japanese sources. In Tezuka's account, however, Pimiko is not a benign ruler. Quite to the contrary, she is an authoritarian megalomaniac who rules by fear. She grows insane with grief over the fact that she is growing old and losing her looks. *Dawn* is about her fruitless quest to find the Phoenix, whose blood can give her the eternal life that she craves (Phillipps 1996, 34–35; MacWilliams 1999, 78–79).

Very often, instead of the rulers and generals who are the major agents of history according to Japanese high school textbooks, Tezuka focuses on fictional characters in his stories. One such story, in Volume 4 of *The Phoenix*, is about the poor vagabond Gao, whose genius as a sculptor is juxtaposed with the famous priest Rōben's attempt to erect the huge Sun Buddha at Tōdaiji in Nara. The grandeur of Tōdaiji and the imperial history of the Nara period at the capital forms the backdrop of Gao's tragic life. He is arrested and tortured by governmental officials, who eventually perform an act of utmost cruelty, cutting off his arms. Yet, Gao does not despair. Living as a hermit far from the capital, he still carves his statues by holding a knife in his mouth. Gao's folk art is his only lasting testament to his triumph over the Japanese state's oppression. Other than this, all that remains of Gao's existence is one oblique reference in a government gazetteer (*fudoki*) (Phillipps 1996, 41–42; MacWilliams 1999, 98–99). In *The Phoenix*, Tezuka offers a revisionist history that is highly critical of the conventional, officially approved one.

In the *Mirai-hen* (Book of the Future, 1967–1968), Tezuka tells a science fiction story that takes place in the far future with interesting new characters. The story takes place during the destruction of the world in 3404 and the following long period of desolation when life becomes extinct. Before the disaster, the main character, Masato Yamanobe, fled to the earth's surface, making him the sole survivor of the subterranean nuclear war. To preserve humanity from extinction, the Phoenix makes him immortal and tells him to watch over Earth until new life can develop. Millions of years pass, but never again does human existence arise to lay waste to the planet. All the scientific experiments Yamanobe tries to produce new life fail pitifully. In the end, he realizes that he has to wait patiently until nature takes it course to create new life. At the end of the *Mirai-hen*, life finally evolves again, repeating the creation of the world that Tezuka describes at the beginning of *The Phoenix*. This suggests that the universe is an everlasting cosmic cycle of creation and destruction.

In this and other science fiction stories in *The Phoenix*, the hunt for the blood of the Phoenix becomes unimportant. Thanks to progress in the fields of medicine and technology, human life has been artificially extended and robot androids do all the hard labor. Now the stories turn to questions about the value of everlasting life, and what features distinguish humans from machines. Throughout, the magical phoenix is a unifying figure that links the individual stories. The collection of tales form a mosaic that allows glimpses into different cosmic eras of a boundless space and time. *The Phoenix* does not have any characters who have reached the cult status of Astro Boy. Rather, as is typical of Tezuka's late phase, individual heroes come and go, without falling into earlier stereotypes.

During his lifetime, Tezuka created a huge universe of characters featured in narratives that he had adapted from many sources. Over the decades, his Japanese readers

Tezuka as a taxidriver and a nineteenth-century medical doctor.
(Copyright Tezuka Productions)

became familiar with his repertoire of graphic conventions. By the end of the sixties, 90 percent of artists had grown up influenced by Tezuka's works, a fact that suggests Tezuka's critical role in the making of modern manga. His works were fundamental, often copied, occasionally ridiculed and satirized by other artists, but always there in the background exercising enormous influence. Moreover, Tezuka has become the face of Japanese manga outside of Japan as well.

On February 9, 1989, Tezuka died of stomach cancer. He had hidden his illness from the public. However, some of his late manga give hints to his state of health, as Tezuka had introduced elderly, physically ill male characters into his stories. For instance, the industrial tycoon Sakane in the story *Neo Fausuto* (Neo-Faust, 1988–1989, unfinished) dies of stomach cancer. In *Hidamari no ki* (Sunlit Tree, 1981–1986), Volume 9, Tezuka drew a poignant scene in which a physician called Tezuka, who is the father of the protagonist and looks just like Osamu Tezuka, dies (1981–1986, 70–80).

In 1997, Tezuka's complete works, comprising 400 volumes, were finally published, and even today Tezuka's manga are still published anew as paperbacks or as big color editions. A gigantic amount of secondary literature about his life and work has also recently become available. Osamu Tezuka has come to be recognized as one of the most important Japanese artists of the twentieth century.

Selected List of Tezuka's Manga

TOMZ = Tezuka Osamu Manga Zenshū

1.   The Classical Period from 1947 to the Mid-Sixties
     Chikyū no akuma. 1995. Tokyo: Kadokawa Shoten (including *Chikyū no akuma, Sekai o horobosu otoku, Kasei kara kita otoko*).
     Chiteikoku no kaijin. 1994. Tokyo: Kadokawa Shoten (including *Chiteikoku no kaijin, Mahō yashiki*).

Daikōzui jidai. 1995. Tokyo: Kadokawa Shoten (including *Daikōzui jidai, Ogon toshi, Taiheiyō x pointo, 38 dosenjō no kaibutsu*).

Fausuto. 1979 Tokyo: Kōdansha (including *Fausuto, Akai yuki*) (TOMZ 60).

Janguru taitei. (*Kimba the White Lion*) 1997. Two volumes. Tokyo: Shōgakukan.

Kitarubeki sekai (*Next World*). 1995. Tokyo: Kadokawa Shoten.

Metoroporisu (*Metropolis*). 1995. Tokyo: Kadokawa Shoten (including *Metoroporisu, Fushigi ryokōki*).

Ribon no kishi (*Princess Knight*). 1987. Two volumes. Tokyo: Kōdansha.

Rosuto wārudo (*Lost World*). 1982. Tokyo: Kōdansha (TOMZ 130).

Sharigawa no himitsu kichi. 1995. Tokyo: Kadokawa Shoten (including *Janguru makyō, Sharigawa no himitsu kichi, Yūbijin*).

Shinsekai Rurū. 1995. Tokyo: Kadokawa Shoten (including *Shinsekai Rurū, Taigā hakase, Gessekai shinshi*).

Shin-takarajima. 1984 Tokyo: Kōdansha (TOMZ 281).

Tetsuwan Atomu (*Astro Boy*). 1995 Fifteen volumes. Tokyo: Kōbunsha.

Tsumi to batsu. 1995. Tokyo: Kadokawa Shoten (including *Tsumi to batsu, Chin Arabian naito, Remon kiddo*).

2.   The Romantic-Fantasy Period of the Seventies

Ayako. 1996. Two volumes. Tokyo: Kadokawa Shoten.

Banpaiya. 1995. Three volumes. Tokyo: Akita Shoten.

Barubora. 1996. Two volumes. Tokyo: Kadokawa Shoten.

Burakku Jakku. 1993. Twelve volumes. Tokyo: Akita Shoten.

Dororo. 1994. Three volumes. Tokyo: Akita Shoten.

I.L. 1987. Tokyo: Daitosha.

Metamorufōze. 1977. Tokyo: Kōdansha (TOMZ 88).

Miraijin Kaosu. 1978–1979. Three volumes. Tokyo: Kōdansha, (TOMZ 131–133).

Mitsume ga tōru. 1998–1999. Eight volumes. Tokyo: Kōdansha.

Shumari. 1995. Three volumes. Tokyo: Kadokawa Shoten.

3.   Historical-Realistic Period from the Mid-Seventies to 1989

Adorufu ni tsugu (*Adolf*). 1985. Four volumes. Tokyo: Bungei Shunjū.

Budda (*Buddha*)1987–1988. Eight volumes. Tokyo: Ushio Shuppansha.

Guringo 1993. Three volumes. Tokyo: Kōdansha (TOMZ 304–306).

Hi no tori (*The Phoenix*). 1992. Thirteen volumes. Tokyo: Kadokawa Shoten (Kadokawa Bunko 8754–8766).

Hidamari no ki. 1983–1987. Eleven volumes. Tokyo: Shōgakukan.

Neo Fausuto. 1992. Tokyo: Asahi Shinbunsha.

Rūdouihi B. 1993. Two volumes. Tokyo: Shio Shuppansha.

Instructional Manuals by Tezuka

Manga no kakikata. Nigaoe kara chōhen made. 1996 (first edition, 1977). Tokyo:

Kōbunsha. (Republished as *Manga no kokoro. Hassō to tekunikku.* 1994. Tokyo: Kōbunsha.)
Manga senka shokyūhen. 1969. Tokyo: Mushi Puro.

Notes

1. A survey of Tezuka's manga is found in the exhibition catalog edited by the Tokyo Kokuritsu Kindai Bijutsukan/The National Museum of Modern Art (1990). On the life and work of Tezuka, see Ishigami (1977), Shimizu (1989, 1998), Takeuchi (1992), Natsume (1992, 1995), and Haruyuki Nakano (1993, 1994). For information about translations of Tezuka's works into other languages see "Tezuka in English" at http://tezukainenglish.com.

2. A boy is born from a peach that an old woman has fished from the river. The stepparents give the boy the name Momotarō (Peachboy) and raise him lovingly. The boy grows up astonishingly fast and one day explains that he wants to go to the devil's island to defeat the demons. With the help of a dog, a monkey, and a pheasant whom he wins as comrades, Momotarō defeats the demons and returns home with their big treasure.

3. For detailed catalogs of Tezuka's characters, see Oki (1996), and Tezuka Productions and Hiroaki Ikeda (1998).

4. In the 244 short episodes of *Burakku Jakku*, Tezuka had the opportunity to jump freely from each episode, telling new stories and introducing several new characters—some very witty and others scurrilous. All his former "star system" characters, even Astro Boy, appeared one more time for their swan song, as if to say good-bye to their loyal fans.

4

From *Metropolis* to *Metoroporisu*

The Changing Role of the Robot in Japanese and Western Cinema

LEE MAKELA

*My own beliefs say that we are machines, and from that I conclude that
there is no reason, in principle, that it is not possible to build a machine
from silicon and steel that has both genuine emotions and consciousness.*
—Rodney A. Brooks

Introduction

Early in the twenty-first century, robots are becoming ever more integrated into our
everyday world. The International Federation of Robots estimated that at the end
of 2006 approximately 875,000 multipurpose and dedicated industrial robots were
operational around the world, while another 638,000 service robots were also added
to the world's stock of mechanized helpmates.[1] In the world of home entertainment,
Sony introduced a second-generation "AIBO" robotic pet, the ERS-210, which it
claimed "has a greater ability to express emotion for more intimate communication
with people" (Sony 2000). Other robots mow the lawn, provide home security, carry
dishes, deliver mail, lead guests to conference rooms, and vacuum the carpet.[2] The
Japanese often describe their country as a *robotto ōkoku* (robot kingdom), "the result
of a collective infatuation with advanced technology" (Schodt 1988, 23).

The distance between human beings and robots appears to be growing ever narrower
as well. Some observers, philosophers Roger Penrose and David Chalmers, argue that
our unique human consciousness comes from some as-yet-uncovered "juice." Others, such as Rodney Brooks, director of the Artificial Intelligence Laboratory at the
Massachusetts Institute of Technology, foresee not only intelligent machines but also
the gradual merger of humans with the machines we strive to create (Brooks 2003,
180; Perkowitz 2004).

Science fiction in both Japan and the West has long been fascinated by the possibilities
inherent in the "humanization" of robot machines. Prime examples of films about this theme

Two movie posters; on left is for Rintaro and Ōtomo's Japanese version of *Metoroporisu,* **and on right is artist Heinz Schulz-Neudamm's famous 1929 poster for Fritz Lang's original film,** *Metropolis.* (Reproduced with permission from the Australian National Museum and Sony Pictures Entertainment)

include Ridley Scott's *Blade Runner,* the movie version of Masamune Shirō's award-winning *Ghost in the Shell,* Steven Spielberg's *A.I.: Artificial Intelligence,* Alex Proyas's *I, Robot,* which was inspired by Isaac Asimov's short story collection, and George Lucas's *Star Wars* series. Each of these futuristic science fiction films explores a different aspect of the several consequences emerging from the development of intelligent machines; each film also reflects the historical and cultural context in which it was created.

One early example of this interest in the interplay between robots and human beings (and the consequences of this interaction) lies at the heart of Fritz Lang's classic silent film *Metropolis,* which premiered in its original form in Germany in 1927.[3] The Japanese animated film version of this classic, *Metoroporisu,* appeared in Japan in 2001, directed by Rintaro (Shigeyuki Hayashi) in collaboration with Katsuhiro Ōtomo.

These similarly titled films, produced nearly seventy-five years apart in dramatically different historical and cultural contexts, provide an opportunity to inquire into how the question of the soul in the machine is dealt with over time. Both films focus on the interaction between robots and human beings and reflect perceptions of the place of the robot in their respective historical and cultural settings. How do Lang and Rintaro engage the assumed uniqueness of sentient beings and the consequences that might ensue if robots were to enter the realm of emotion and "immortality"?

Examining this question also gives us insight into the way the films are affected by the respective cultures within which they are produced. The robots we meet in the sundry versions of *Metropolis,* we will find, reflect prevailing views (both positive and negative) on what it means to be human. Moreover, our investigation will illustrate how the manufacturers of these mechanical beings, as well as their respective cultural and historical circumstances, are reflected in the robots' activities. The "toolmakers" find themselves and their times animated in the "tools" they have fabricated.

In this essay, we will move from the German *Metropolis* of 1927 to the Japanese *Metoroporisu* of 2001, examining the differences present in these two cinematic masterpieces and their literary antecedents. Their respective storylines' treatment of robots will establish some basic insights into differing Western and Japanese conceptions of "the soul in the machine," as well as the way those portrayals depend on different cultural contexts. These contexts, as we will see, result in disparate interpretations of the robot; Rintaro's view is more favorable and sympathetic overall, while Lang's view tends to be more frightening and threatening.

These general perceptions, however, vary as a result of specific cultural and historical influences, on both a local and a global scale. Thus, the temporal and cultural differences in the plots of the two versions of *Metropolis* offer us a better understanding of differing cinematic perceptions of the place of the robot in modern life and the cultural and historical reasons for these varying interpretations.

Fritz Lang's *Metropolis* (1927)

German film came into its own during the days of the Weimar Republic. At its peak in 1921, the German film industry was cranking out some 500 films annually, making it Hollywood's most serious competitor (Flippo 1997a). The Austrian-American director Fritz Lang (1890–1976) played a major role in that success. Wounded four times while serving in the Austrian army during World War I, Lang began writing screenplays during his year-long convalescence in a Viennese hospital. After the war, Lang, along with producer Erich Pommer (of the 1919 expressionistic horror classic *Das Cabinet des Dr. Caligari*), worked in Berlin as a script reader, writer, and director for the Decla Bioscop Company, later absorbed by Universum-Film-Aktiengesellschaft (UFA). In 1920 he married Thea von Harbou, a popular writer of the day who collaborated with him on his German screenplays and wrote the original novel on which *Metropolis* was based (Harbou 1975). After nearly bankrupting UFA, Lang formed his own film production company in 1927.[4] He fled Nazi Germany in 1933, immediately after being invited by Joseph Goebbels, Hitler's propaganda minister, to supervise Nazi film production. After a brief time in Paris, Lang immigrated to the United States where, as a naturalized citizen, he continued his directorial career for the next twenty years (Scheuer 1996).

Lang claimed that the inspiration for *Metropolis* came as a result of a visit he made to New York City in 1924. The city's imposing skyline particularly sparked his imagination, and his eventual cinematic recreation of the urban setting at the heart of the film itself.[5]

Looking out over the city from the deck of the SS *Deutschland,* Lang "saw a street lit as if in full daylight by neon lights, and topping them oversized luminous advertisements moving, turning, flashing on and off, spiraling . . . something which was completely new and nearly fairy-tale-like for a European in those days, and this impression gave [him] the first thought of an idea for a town of the future" (Harbou 1988, 1).

The film built on this urbanized vision of the future is still regarded as a visual feast, but critics consider the plot much less engrossing. A brief summary of the narrative seems in order at this point. The story takes place in 2026, a century after the movie was produced. We are immediately plunged into the cold, crowded, mechanical, industrial city of Metropolis. We quickly learn that vast numbers of the lower class live underground, where they run the machines that keep the above-ground world in working order. In contrast, the elite play and delight in sunlit, peaceful gardens and vast athletic stadiums.

Fritz Lang's futuristic world reflects fears rooted in the very present European world of the early twentieth century. Industrialization, mechanization, and urbanization were wreaking havoc on the work habits and lifestyles inherited from the mid-nineteenth century. To many early German viewers, the world portrayed in *Metropolis* represented the unhappy end product of unfettered industrial development run amok. While these changes had originally been viewed as socially beneficial, this evaluation had already begun to give way to a less optimistic assessment. The much-heralded industrialization process had also given rise to the exploitation of workers, the quickening pace of factory work under the machines' relentless demand, the growing concentration of wealth in the hands of a few, and the virtual enslavement of many industrial workers, with attendant poverty of mind and spirit. Given these problems, many citizens began to question whether this modernization was worth the price exacted from the majority. Lang's portrayal of this future world, especially in the opening scenes of the film, masterfully captures this unease in a parade of evocative imagery: relentlessly whirling gears; dispirited workers marching in lockstep to and from their job assignments; the horror of an industrial accident.

The film reflects not only this growing wariness at the prospect of a "modern" mechanized industrial future, but also an optimism that comes from early twentieth-century humanism. Lang believes that both parties to the transactions at the heart of this new society must recognize their mutual dependence. Without the labor of the worker, the elite would wither away; without the leadership and direction of the capitalist elite, the workers would lose their way in anarchy and directionless activity. The two are bound together for the mutual benefit of both parties.

Against this backdrop, Lang sets his plot in motion. While frolicking with a female temptress in the Eternal Gardens, Freder Fredersen (actor Gustav Froehlich) turns suddenly to see Maria (Brigitte Helm) burst into the tranquil garden space, surrounded by a swirling flock of children, to protest the economic disparity that characterizes Metropolis. Freder is immediately smitten by Maria and pursues her into the underground city. Here he is astonished by the horrific world he encounters; upon his return to the surface, he seeks out his father, Joh Fredersen (Alfred Abel), the Master of Metropolis, for an explanation of these appalling conditions.

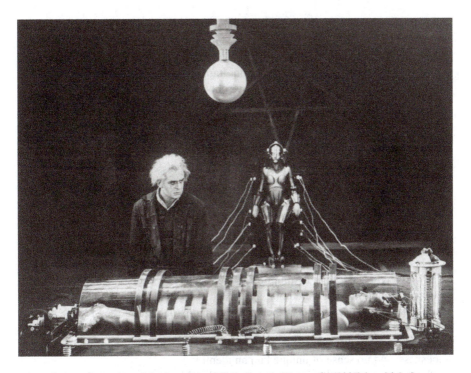

A scene from the original version of Fritz Lang's *Metropolis* (1927) in which the inventor and scientist C.A. Rotwang (Rudolf Klein-Rogge) watches over the body of Maria (Brigitte Helm) connected with electric wires to a female robot.
(Reproduced with permission from Hulton Archive, Getty Images)

The next portion of the film introduces Rotwang, an inventor and scientist consumed by the memory of an old flame named Hel. Hel, who had been involved in a love triangle between Rotwang and Joh Fredersen, married Joh and died giving birth to their son Freder. Joh arrives at Rotwang's laboratory seeking help deciphering coded plans for a workers' revolt. Rotwang instead presents Joh with his new invention, a strikingly beautiful robotic recreation of their shared love interest, Hel.

The gleaming metallic female-featured robot we first meet in Rotwang's workshop embodies the woman Hel literally as a "love object," an icon meant to be worshipped and adored by a bereft male admirer. The robot "objectifies" both feminine beauty and the emotional attachment felt by Rotwang, providing a comforting substitute presence for a love now lost to betrayal and death. Nothing seems to be expected from the robot except her acceptance of Rotwang's admiration and care, which the real Hel denied him. The expected relationship in this instance is conceived as a one-way street; the robot represents a controllable and dependent/dependable "love object." She is not meant to have a soul of her own, an independent emotional presence, a human consciousness, or a sense of her own unique identity as a substitute (human) being.

Meanwhile in the film, Freder also comes across plans for a workers' rebellion; soon thereafter a coworker confides that "Maria is having another meeting." Freder joins the workers as they file down into the catacombs to hear Maria speak. Joh and Rotwang likewise witness Maria's sermon. Impressed by her charisma, Joh suggests that Rotwang should make the laboratory robot he has constructed look like Maria. Fredersen believes that with a duplicate of Maria he can manipulate the workers, undermine the real Maria's authority, and avoid the planned revolt.

After the sermon ends, Rotwang captures and takes Maria to his laboratory. Here, she and the robot are hooked up to a myriad of machines and contraptions; amidst glowing rings and bolts of lightning, the robot's face dissolves into that of Maria's.

When robot Hel morphs into robot Maria, we are provided with yet another view of the place of the robot in the thinking of the times. Robot Maria (also played by actress Brigitte Helm) epitomizes evil and deceit. She misleads her worker devotees by suddenly arguing for the use of violence to redress the wrongs visited upon them by the Metropolis elite and their machines. She is not governed by any ingrained sense of right or wrong, by any remorse over the consequences of her call to destruction, or by any misgivings over her assumption of the real Maria's persona and charisma.

Robots, Lang intimates, are not to be trusted. They will lead human beings astray. The unintended consequence of the unbridled industrialization they represent must be resisted if human beings are to maintain their humanity and their unique emotional interpretation of reality. Robots have no soul, no emotional presence, no human consciousness, and no sense of unique human identity.

Plot twists bear out this interpretation as robot Maria urges her followers to take up violence and orders the masses to destroy the machines in the underground city. The workers fail to realize that destroying the machines will not only flood the entire area but also drown their children.

After the flooding has been forestalled, the workers set off to avenge themselves on Maria. They find her seemingly celebrating the fiasco she has created. The crowd captures and brutally incinerates her. Freder initially thinks the real Maria is being martyred but eventually sees the robot beneath the burned-away flesh. He then seeks out the real Maria and rescues her from the evil Rotwang.

The masses, meanwhile, march to the city's central cathedral square where they come to realize that Freder is the mediator they have been seeking. All come to realize there can be no understanding between the hands and the brain unless they are reconciled by the heart. At Freder's urging, the leader of the workers and Joh Fredersen clasp hands to seal their rapprochement. Order is restored to Metropolis, and all ends well.

The tenets of Christian Socialism are apparent throughout this optimistic prescriptive assessment, underlined by Lang's pervasive use of biblical symbolism—Maria as a Madonna, Freder as a Christ-like reconciler, the robot Maria as a devil temptress. Yet despite this inescapable theological context, the question of the robot's "soul" goes essentially unaddressed. In Lang's view, the robot is merely a plot device, fulfilling a variety of different roles in the tale being told.

The original novel by Thea von Harbou subordinates the robot even more to the overarching plotline and the emphasis is on the social turmoil created in Metropolis by the mechanization/industrialization process. The novel's plot centers much more on the human relationships, involving Freder and Maria on the one hand and Joh Fredersen and his son on the other. Secondary relationships among these and other characters are also much more developed in Harbou's prose version of the plot than in the film. Even minor characters get more attention in the novel than Rotwang's robotic creation does. The robotic Maria, because of her resemblance to Freder's love interest, causes the deception that is central to the plot, but Harbou does not emphasize her unique characteristics. The ornate, late-Victorian prose of the novel focuses much more directly on the disruption of human and social relationships brought about by the increasing dependence on machines than on any meaningful consideration of the role played by the robot in that society.

In many respects, this reflects an emerging German ambivalence regarding the role of mechanization and those technological advances that played such a major role in the development of Europe during the early decades of the twentieth century. The Great War had already thrown into doubt the assumption that industrialization itself represented an unalloyed improvement of the human condition. Moreover, in the era after the war, "German technological modernization did not bring with it the social progress for which most Germans had hoped" (Brio 1994, 97). Indeed, authoritarian interests, which had been eclipsed at the end of the 1920s, began to reassert themselves, embracing science and technology in support of their own brand of politics. In the eyes of those who had enthusiastically promoted modernization as the harbinger of democratic socialism and cultural purification, this was hardly a harbinger of social progress. Those favoring modernism found themselves in full retreat, their anticipated utopia subverted by the very forces they had unequivocally embraced.

This is the source of the negative role assigned to the robotic mechanical man in *Metropolis*. Both Rotwang's attempt to use robotics to recreate a lost love and Federsen's hope of subverting the charismatic voice of Maria (and her challenge to the control exercised by the Master of Metropolis) are frustrated in the film; indeed, technological advances are thwarted at every turn. Instead, the emotional "humanity" of human beings is reconfirmed in the end while robot alternatives are forthrightly rejected and vilified. They are seen as part of the problem rather than the solution their creators had hoped they would be, and the film denies the possibility that such an instrument might harbor a soul of its own.

All this mirrors a contemporary German cultural movement away from a surrealist synthesis championing the "liberation of the human subconscious" and toward a more pessimistic expressionism aware of the horror and violence of modern warfare and "the pervasive corruption of Weimar society" (Kleine-Ahlbrandt 1993, 323). The robot in Fritz Lang's *Metropolis* reflects this increasingly negative assessment of contemporary German realities and the dashed expectations for a technologically enabled utopian future.

Fritz Lang's *Metropolis:* The Edited Version

Interestingly, Fritz Lang's initial vision as analyzed in the preceding paragraphs was itself subverted in the reediting undertaken by UFA and the film's American distributors shortly after the film's initial release.

The full version of the film premiered at the Palast am Zoo cinema in Berlin in January 1927 and then played at the 600-seat UFA Pavillon am Nollendorf for four months. During that period, it was seen by approximately 15,000 people. The length of the film (showings were scheduled at three-hour intervals) undoubtedly contributed to the relatively poor attendance figures and UFA's resulting fiscal concerns. The film was withdrawn from circulation and rereleased in a considerably shorter version in August 1927.[6] UFA editors decided that Lang's version was overly complex as well as overly long, and they reshaped the plot in reediting, omitting key scenes and plot sequences. A similar reshaping was undertaken by American version's editors of the film, Adolph Zukor and Jesse L. Lasky, prior to its release in the United States in March of 1927.

In both these new retellings, Rotwang's desire to recreate his lost love Hel is entirely omitted. The explanation most often cited for this excision (initiated in the American version) lies in a key scene in which Fredersen unveils a bust of Rotwang's obsession emblazoned with her name: "Hel." Her name was considered so close to "Hell" that the American editor deleted all references to her, including scenes about her key relationship to Rotwang, Fredersen, and Freder (Rutsky 1993, 7). The result muddied the plot, but it avoided the inevitable snickers from the audience.

This deletion was further justified by Channing Pollock, the film's American editor. He commented that the very idea of a robotic love interest was ridiculous; he considered a metallic "second wife" nothing more than "an uncomfortable bedfellow on winter nights." Pollock's answer was to rearrange the existing scenes and reword the subtitles to reflect a mechanical monster theme, borrowed from *Frankenstein.* In this version, Rotwang's role was changed from Fredersen's rival in love to his faithful assistant, dedicated to the creation of a robotic worker (Lydon 2003b).

The consequences of this plot reconfiguration were little remarked upon until the full digital restoration of the film was undertaken by Kino International in 2002. However, these early changes removed the quest for a mechanical substitution for an absent emotional relationship from the film's narrative, significantly altering Lang's underlying purposes.

In fact, another interpretation of the robot presence in the film is introduced as a direct result of these alterations. Rotwang now initially presents the robot to Fredersen (renamed "John Masterman" in the American Paramount release) not as a recreation of their mutual lost love, but as a mechanical replacement for the city's human workers. The robot thus is presented as a direct threat to the workers' livelihood, transforming "men" into "machines." This is a far more explicit reflection of the suspicions increasingly attached to technological modernization than was conceived and presented in the original unaltered German version.

In this reworking of the original *Metropolis* plot, one can see the expansive growth in the German context of a European expressionist concern with the destructive potential of an out-of-control, unbridled technology threatening the very livelihood of the continent's industrial work force. The altered plot also fit remarkably well into the American context as well, removing some of the ambiguities present in the original to clarify the threat posed by robots as creatures of capitalism run amok in the ongoing battle over factory unionization and workers' rights in the United States. Rotwang, the inventor, and "Masterman," the industrialist, are seen in this version to be working in concert toward the creation of a mechanized factory system freed from the constraints of inefficiency and error. Such a system would be endlessly available for exploitation, freed from emotional attachment, and constrained only by greed.

In this new cinematic version, Fredersen's motivation for seeking the transformation of the robot into a Maria look-alike is altered as well. Fredersen/Masterman now appears to realize his son has become enthralled by Maria. His order to Rotwang to alter the robot's features now incorporates not only his hope to subvert Maria's control of the workers but also to regain his son's affection and loyalty (Brio 1994, 92).[7]

Another analytical perspective is also highlighted in this reworking of Lang's original film. If Hel has been excised as an emotional pivot point in the plot, the question immediately arises as to why Rotwang's robot is cast with feminine features, since it is meant to replace a largely male workforce. Here again, the reconstruction of the storyline serves to place emphasis on a heretofore less obvious correlation. If one assumes a "male gaze" as representative of the point of view being expressed in the film as a whole, both "robot" and "woman" become emblematic of "the Other," one a representation of out-of-control technology and the other of dangerous female sexuality. Robot Maria indeed transforms the mechanical man into a vamp, a seductress. She uses her feminine wiles to inflame the elite males who gather to watch her dance at the club Yoshiwara in exactly the way that she utilizes her erotic appeal to urge the workers to revolt against their masters. From a controlling masculine perspective, the feminized robot presents the most threatening prospect imaginable: an attempt to undermine male dominance and control over both women and the industrialized economy.[8]

These altered plot elements accentuate the negative interpretation of the machine man's perceived social and cultural role in the conflict between human beings and mechanized industrialization. While the earlier notion of the robot as a "love substitute" has been abandoned, the robot in these recut versions of *Metropolis* now threatens not only the relationship between capital and labor but also the very place of human labor in the industrial economy, the familial social ties connecting father to son, and the cultural and social control exercised by men over women. The robot, soulless and expressly dehumanized in this recasting, has become more threatening than ever!

For an American audience, the disappearance of the Hel subplot underscores another early twentieth-century conflict in the United States, that between urban and rural cultures and lifestyles. "[T]he opening shots of the film make clear that even for

**The actress Brigitte Helm plays the charismatic Maria in both her human and robotic forms
in the Fritz Lang film.** (Reproduced with permission from Hulton Archive, Getty Images)

the privileged of Metropolis that urban future is an urban nightmare" (Lydon 2003a).
Aside from the idyllic stadium playing fields and the Eternal Gardens of Pleasure, the
film's urban settings are depicted as shadowed and dark, a motif maintained by most
subsequent science fiction directors.

The troubled social and economic milieu portrayed in the film's narrative adds
to the discomfort level experienced by viewers. Most contemporary viewers were
increasingly ambivalent about the transformation taking place around them as urban
populations grew and the idealized "yeoman farmer" drifted further into obscurity.
Lang, who had grown up in Vienna—the heart of a heavily urbanized corner of Europe—was especially aware of this phenomenon, as were those Germans who were
drawn to Hitler during his rise to power. American audiences who viewed *Metropolis*
would find an iconic confirmation of their worst fears; this further confirms the impact of the contemporary culture and events on the film's depiction of a supposedly
far-off future world.

Michi, the central character in Tezuka's manga version of *Metropolis*, flying.
(Copyright Tezuka Productions)

Osamu Tezuka's *Metoroporisu*

A little over two decades after *Metropolis* was first released, a photograph of the robot from Lang's film inspired Osamu Tezuka (1928–1989), the originator of the modern Japanese manga, to incorporate "an artificial being" into the three-volume exploration of the future which he began in 1949. As the artist himself recalled: "This manmade person [the hero of the manga, a robot named Michi] was based on the image of the female robot in the famous pre-war German film *Metropolis*. That said, I hadn't seen the movie at the time and I didn't even know what it was about. During the war, in *Kinema junpō* or some other such magazine, there was a single still from the movie of the female robot's birth scene. I remembered it and it gave me a little hint. I also really liked the sound of the word *metropolis* so I used the same title, but other than that there was no real connection to the movie" (Tezuka 2003, 164). Tezuka drew inspiration from numerous other sources as well. Emmy, the violet seller, and her criminally inclined older sister, Gracy, are reflections of the Thenardiers in Victor Hugo's *Les Miserables*. The scenes of the robot Michi flying through the air, Tezuka thought, were "influenced by the American comic *Superman*, which had just entered Japan at that time, but I have no memory of having read *Superman* back then" (Tezuka 2003, 165).

A product of multiple sources, then, Tezuka's *Metoroporisu* differs significantly from the film that Fritz Lang had made some twenty years earlier. The latter obviously inspired the former, but his treatment presents a dramatically different vision. Like Lang's original, Tezuka's comic book raised such classic science fiction themes as the individual's search for identity in the modern world and man versus machine. But Tezuka gave them a Japanese twist, says Jonathan Clements, coauthor of *The Anime Encyclopedia:* "Tezuka, like many other people in Japan, was trying to work

MICHI IS NEITHER HUMAN NOR ANIMAL NOR PLANT NOR
MINERAL. MADE ENTIRELY OF SYNTHETIC CELLS, MICHI, TO
PUT IT SIMPLY, IS AN ARTIFICIAL BEING. DUE TO VARIOUS SECRET
APPARATII IMPLANTED IN THE BODY, MICHI EXHIBITS NUMEROUS TEN-
THOUSAND HORSEPOWER SUPERHUMAN ABILITIES, MAKING HIM WITHOUT
EQUAL ON EARTH. MICHI'S LUNGS EXHIBIT A HELIUM GAS ANALYSIS
REACTION SUCH THAT IF HE BREATHES IN AS DEEPLY AS POSSIBLE,
HE WILL FLOAT UP INTO THE AIR. THE EARS ACT LIKE FISH GILLS
AND ARE ABLE TO CONTINUE BREATHING FREELY EVEN UNDER WATER.
THERE IS A BUTTON IN THE THROAT, WHICH IF PUSHED WILL
CHANGE MICHI TO EITHER MALE OR FEMALE FORM...

At a critical juncture, Ken'ichi finds Michi's hidden journal and, reading it, discovers the true nature of his friend's unusual abilities. (Copyright Tezuka Productions)

out what this Cold War thing was and whose side should the Japanese be on. . . . If you look at *Metropolis,* you'll see it seems to be half American—every now and again you see American architecture, especially art-deco architecture—and half of it seems to be brutalist Soviet artwork going on in the background. Because at the time Tezuka was writing, he was confused about which side to be on" ("An Anime Metropolis" 2002).

One of the major distinctions between the two versions lies in Tezuka's determination that Michi, the robot, should be a biological, rather than a mechanical, "artificial being"; the robot is animated throughout the manga by the radiation emanating from mysterious black spots dotting the sun. Michi is given other superhuman characteristics as well; another character, Detective Mustachio's nephew Ken'ichi, discovers them in a hidden journal that reads: "Michi is neither human nor animal nor plant nor mineral. Made entirely of synthetic cells, Michi, to put it simply, is an artificial being. Due to the various secret apparatii [*sic*] implanted in the body, Michi exhibits numerous ten thousand horsepower superhuman abilities, making him without equal on earth. Michi's lungs exhibit a helium gas analysis reaction such that if he breathes in as deeply as possible, he will float up into the air. The ears act like fish gills and are able to continue breathing freely even under water. There is a button in the throat, which if pushed will change Michi to either male or female form" (Tezuka 2003, 84).

Each of these characteristics, of course, ends up playing a major role in the complex plot animating the 160 pages of Tezuka's manga. Other complications arise from the inclusion of a trio of detectives (Mustachio from Japan, Ganimarl from France, and none other than Sherlock Holmes from England); an environmental disaster taking the form of supersized creatures including giant bees and a phalanx of marauding "Mickey Mouse Walt Disney" rats; and the release of Toron Gas, a fearful weapon of mass destruction that turns those suffering its effects from human beings into animals.

Interestingly, the resulting narrative, despite its relatively newly minted manga form, exhibits characteristics inherited from earlier forms of Japanese literature. The storyline proceeds from episode to episode, introducing new characters willy-nilly along the way. It veers off time after time in unexpected directions and returns to weave forgotten threads back into the plot, seemingly without much regard for readers expectations of cohesion and continuity. As in more traditional forms of art and literature, *mitate* (metaphoric, often humorous, and satirical) allusions appear again and again—to Mickey Mouse, the British actor Charles Laughton, and Superman as well as to the atomic bombings of Hiroshima and Nagasaki, Heike crabs, and foreign interventionism in Japanese affairs.

The overall effect plays up the entertainment value of the manga. The story moves along at a furious rate, cinematic in its pacing, by skipping rapidly from scene to scene, while avoiding in-depth exploration of any specific plot twist. Humorous asides reflect the thoughts of those caught within the frame of crowd scenes; pratfalls abound. The reader is propelled along without regard for extended explanations or discursive consideration of the plot points raised in the narrative. This is lighthearted entertainment for the masses, Tezuka's rendition of the popular culture of postwar Japan.

What, then, of the search for "the soul in the machine"? Tezuka's "artificial being," Michi, is a surprisingly multifaceted creation. He/she (an ambiguity not so overtly present in the original since the Japanese language lacks gendered pronouns) displays characteristics seen as positive by human observers. Michi sticks up for the downtrodden, rescues the threatened, yearns for family connections, forms fast and loyal friendships, participates in sport activities, and values education. Michi is also naïve, seeking only kindnesses from others, single-mindedly intent upon finding its father/creator at all costs. Yet, in the end, when discovering its true identity, Michi flies into a rage and ruthlessly seeks revenge by leading a robot revolt with the goal of destroying the entire human race. There is no middle ground here; Michi exhibits two extremely contradictory personalities, perhaps reflective of the ambivalence with which Tezuka and many Japanese regarded their American occupiers between 1945 and 1952.

The radiation animating Michi is also the cause of the biological crisis threatening the citizens of this future world. Both "good" and "bad" emerge as a consequence. The Red Party (a group of "shadowy assassins" led by Duke Red) appears intent on

Michi as a female. Tripping a switch in the robot's throat allowed it to transform its gender.
(Copyright Tezuka Productions)

subverting technology for its own nefarious ends, yet key plot elements also rely on the advances promised by this same technology.

This appropriation of nuclear technology is reminiscent of Ishiro Honda's 1954 biologically based creature, called the "preeminent movie monster of the 1950's": Gojira, Americanized as Godzilla. In the original Japanese version of that film, this creature, too, carried a great deal of metaphorical gravitas as a deeply ambiguous postwar figure. Besides being, as *New York Times* film critic Terrance Rafferty stated, "an obvious—gigantic, unsubtle, grimly purposeful—metaphor for the atomic bomb," Gojira might just as easily have represented "Japan's former imperial ambitions, which finally unleashed the retaliatory fury that leveled its cities." Whatever the case, Rafferty—writing in 2004 on the fiftieth anniversary of the original film's release—finds the movie fundamentally to be about "a society's desire to claim its deepest tragedies for itself, to assimilate them as elements of its historical identity" (Rafferty 2004, 26). For both Tezuka and Honda, the world had been dramatically altered by the events of August 1945; their creative efforts both seem directed toward bringing into sharp relief resulting issues and concerns, some portraying Japan as victim, others as perpetrator.

In the midst of all this ambiguity, however, the human citizens of Tezuka's *Metoroporisu* seem willing to regard robots sympathetically and to grant them human attributes. In some cases, they are even moved by the dilemmas these mechanical beings face. Detective Mustachio, for example, encounters Fifi, a worker robot from

Duke Red's workshop, to whom he becomes both attached and beholden; Mustachio is distraught and angry when Fifi is crushed at a critical juncture in the plot. This sacrifice causes the detective to try to assure that Duke Red's underground army of "robot drudges" is later turned against its master in a revolt (led by Michi) that eventually threatens Metropolis itself.

At the very end of the narrative, an angry crowd, attributing the destructive events of the attempted revolt directly to Michi, marches off to confront the robot at the hospital where it has been confined. En route, however, they learn that the destruction visited on Metropolis was in large part due to the robot's frustration over being unable to locate its father. This seems to the now-mollified crowd a reasonable, very "human" response; they continue on to the hospital but now come to wish the patient a speedy recovery.

They are shocked when they arrive and are confronted with an immobilized figure doomed to disappear due to a lack of sustaining radiation from distant sunspots. Michi soon expires. He is not burned alive, like Lang's robot Maria, but is destroyed because of humanity's hubris in attempting to change the natural order to suit itself.

Likewise, later Gojira epics directed by Honda increasingly portrayed their monster heroes as (in Rafferty's phrase) "loveable entertainers" (2004, 26). Tezuka's manga and Honda's pop films place the blame squarely on those creating the artificial beings in the first place, not on the robots/monsters themselves. As Tezuka writes in his manga's afterward: "Michi's lifetime is over. He was science's greatest work of art. And yet the creation of animate existence only resulted in the wasteful destruction of human life. Perhaps, might the day not come when humans also become too advanced and, in actuality, as a result of their science, wipe themselves out?" (Tezuka 2003, 162).

This attribution of an essentially innocent guilelessness to the robotic creations of human beings reflects a distinct variation of the themes introduced in Fritz Lang's *Metropolis*. Machine men in Tezuka's world are not perceived of as capable of committing "evil deeds" intrinsically, but instead are seen as creations of aberrant, overly self-confident human beings who are indeed capable of such malevolence. This in turn clearly reflects a widely shared sentiment found everywhere in postwar Japan, the only nation on earth to directly experience the devastation of nuclear attack—yet another product of human ingenuity with destructive capabilities beyond initial imaginings.

Lang's human Maria is something of a Madonna; robot Maria, on the other hand, freely participates in the raucous nightlife of Metropolis, dancing provocatively at the Yoshiwara nightclub for the entertainment of the male patrons and later proving an accomplished agent provocateur. Her skillful rhetoric alone is capable of starting a riot. Even though nominally only a machine, robot Maria carries a kind of moral stain that causes her evil deeds. Michi, Tezuka's robotic creation, on the other hand, enters the human world an innocent who only assumes leadership of the robot revolt when s/he becomes frustrated over not finding his/her father. Such frustration seems natural even to the riot's victims. Compared to their human counterparts, then, Japanese robots seem untainted by any moral defilement since they are dependent on their human creators for life.

Another factor that links robots and humans together here derives from a Shinto

Detective Mustachio meets the robot Fifi, who saves his life but is destroyed later in the story.
(Copyright Tezuka Productions)

perspective that does not draw distinct lines between the animate and the inanimate. Shinto blurs boundaries between human beings and all other manifestations of our common shared experience. Shinto *kami* (deities) reflect not just spiritual entities but human beings (both historical and mythological), geological features (from mountains to waterfalls), unusual physical objects in the natural landscape (unusual rocks and ancient trees). Even dolls, in addition to being playthings in human form or items for display and admiration, "have since ancient times been created . . . as the embodiment of spirits to be worshipped, as objects endowed with magical powers" (Kitamura 1990, 4). If a human being, a rock, and a volcano can all be labeled *kami,* how difficult could it be to extend that category to include machines and robots (or legendary monsters)? And, if that be the case, can empathy and acceptance be far behind? If little divides human and robot, if we ultimately share a common origin and if transformation is possible, what is to keep a robot from "becoming" human?

Jane Marie Law, in discussing the use of puppetry in Japanese religious ritual performance, contends that "[w]hat actually happens in the rite is that a puppet is transformed from inert matter to a moving being" (Law 1995, 255). If, in Japanese thinking, "inert matter" can be "brought to life as the sacred possesses the puppet" (253), there exists a cultural and religious predilection to accept a positive assessment of robot transformation as nothing to fear. The animation of the inert becomes an indication of the intrusion of the divine into the everyday. It is evidence of the sacred at work "vitalizing the human world" (255) rather than threatening its very survival.

Moreover, in Japanese religious thought, we all inhabit the same cosmic setting, and we are separated only by a permeable membrane from both the surrounding natural world and the divine. Everything observable in our surroundings shares a common ontological origin. Shinto even allows for movement from one form to another; at death, a person might become a *kami,* for example.[9]

The unbridgeable divide between human beings and robots found in other cultural settings seems altogether absent in the Japanese context, as is apparent in Tezuka's *Metoroporisu.* The robots may not yet have souls, but each is given its due as a unique entity worthy of respect and freed from the Western assumption of "otherness."[10]

Katsuhiro Ōtomo and Rintaro's *Metoroporisu*

The anime version of Osamu Tezuka's manga took nearly fifty years to arrive, appearing in 2001. Critical reviews, however, instantly and emphatically placed it among the genre's best examples. As one reviewer enthused: "Osamu 'God of Manga' Tezuka wrote the *Metoroporisu* graphic novel from 1949 to 1951. Katsuhiro Ōtomo (*Akira, Domu*) retooled the manga into a screenplay, and veteran anime director Rintaro (*X, Galaxy Express 999*) fused the script, Tezuka's distinctive art style, computer animation, and a Dixieland soundtrack to make a high-tech movie with a delightful retro-futuristic feel" (Blackwell 2002). Again, however, significant alterations are made in the storyline from Fritz Lang's 1927 film and Tezuka's version of the narrative. According to Blackwell, "Rintaro hails the Lang film as a personal favorite, but made no conscious homage to it." His anime, like Tezuka's manga, does not follow Lang's original characters or plot and is more of an homage to Tezuka's *Metoroporisu,* in that Rintaro, an unabashed Tezuka fan, deliberately mimics Tezuka's characteristic drawing style (2002).

Nonetheless, visually speaking, both Japanese artists are heavily indebted to Lang's seminal work. Particularly, in their portrayal of futuristic cityscapes in which the stories take place they appear strikingly similar. The Metropolis of anime and manga, like Lang's, houses the rich humans in heavenly aeries and the poor humans in hellish caves, but Tezuka and Ōtomo (the scriptwriter) add a layer to Lang's simple have/have-not society: the robot slaves.

> Rintaro remarks that it would be difficult to make a retro-futuristic movie about robots and a big city without mirroring some aspect of the Lang's classic, but the plots and characters of the two *Metropolis* films stand on their own without reference to one another. Villainous Duke Red comes across as more of a megalomaniac than Lang's cold, but not irredeemable, Fredersen. Rintaro's robot girl existed in the manga not as a daughter, but as [an androgynous figure] named Michi, becoming Tima only in Ōtomo's screenplay. Unlike Lang's witchy and willing Pandora-like Maria, Rintaro's childlike Tima refuses to believe that she is a robot—and when Tima unleashes her powers, it's through anger, not calculation. Aside from stock mad scientists, none of the other characters bear any resemblance to one another (Blackwell 2002).

There are other important alterations in Ōtomo's script. In the anime, Duke Red has acquired a ward, a foundling named "Rock" who was taken in as an infant after "the last war" and now serves his benefactor as the reckless and violent head of a vigilante group known as the Marduks. In this version of the narrative, Duke Red's daughter is the one who has died. The film's "mad scientist," Professor Laughton, has been given carte blanche to create a robot substitute (Tima), who is to be installed atop the duke's newly constructed ziggurat skyscraper as its ruling authority and chief power source. What was a companionable friendship between Ken'ichi and the robot Michi in Tezuka's manga becomes a more emotionally involved relationship between the detective's nephew and the female-appearing Tima. The manga subplot, which centered on the mechanical robot Fifi and Detective Mustachio, has been recast to bring together Ken'ichi, Tima, and Fifi instead, although Fifi's self-sacrificing altruism is still firmly in place. In this newest film version, robots also assume an even more central role, while human beings are much less worthy of respect, admiration, or adulation.

This plot twist where robots are more enviable characters than the film's humans is made plausible in a number of ways. First, Ōtomo's script situates the story in the far future. Second, since it is an animated rather than live action film, it creates a fantasy world where the impossible seems not only possible, but plausible. Anything can happen, and there are no live actors getting in the way of the illusion of the real. At the same time, the film's Japanese audience can easily enter into the fanatasy world of *Metoroporisu* because, just like Tezuka's original manga, it has a Japanese detective and his nephew as characters with whom they can identify. Just like these two characters who are startled by what they see on their first visit to Metropolis, Japanese audiences are also shocked, also feeling like aliens (*gaijin*) within this foreign fantasy city.

As the Japanese detective and his nephew search out a fugitive wanted for human rights abuses, we too explore the city, come to know its culture and habits, meet its inhabitants, and experience its tensions. But, all along, we are "just visitors." The citizens of Metropolis are not "us" but rather "them"; their story has its lessons for us, but these insights are delivered at a remove, unlike the unsettling realities that marked Fritz Lang's much more direct and involving version of the plot.

Therefore, it becomes easier to accept the essentially negative interpretation of the human beings portrayed in the animated version of the plot. That Duke Red (modeled on Lang's Fredersen) refuses to acknowledge Rock as his son and heir might well strike a Japanese viewer as unusual, given the culture's ready acceptance of adoption to extend the survival of a household enterprise into the next generation. However, that same viewer is less likely to take the implied criticism of this behavior personally since Duke Red does not live in present-day Japan, but rather in an animated version of some distant future urban world.

Likewise, Rock's penchant for using violence to secure his "father's" dominant role in the city seems less an indictment of the viewer's personal acceptance of violence and more a negative assessment of the character himself as a human being. In fact, each of the major human characters in the anime is seriously flawed. Duke Red is obsessed by the desire to place a "super robot" constructed to resemble his dead daughter on the "throne" atop his newly constructed ziggurat to "rule the world." Rock perpetually seeks his "father's" acceptance through acts of violence to protect Duke Red's power. Laughton has nefarious plans to use Tima, the robot, for his own ends. The city's mayor plots his own power grab, and his military subordinate betrays him for selfish reasons—clearly no one in a position of elite authority is meant to seem worthy of respect.

As if to underline this "distanced" reading of the human anime characters, at the film's conclusion, Shunsaku Ban, the Japanese detective, departs for "home," leaving behind the world of Metropolis as he flies off into the distance aboard a huge airplane headed back to "the real world" of Japan.

The robots appearing in the movie, however, are treated quite differently. There are now many of them integrated into the storyline, not just the Hel/Maria of Lang's version. In fact, the variety of robots displayed in Rintaro's film equals that of the human players. At the very outset of the film—a celebration surrounding the opening of Duke Red's ziggurat—a debate about the place of robots in Metropolis is on everyone's lips. Below the city's glistening facade, the working-class humans who were the builders have lost their jobs to cheaper robot labor. However, many of the city's citizens also realize just how dependent the entire population has become on the jobs that they perform, often far beneath the earth's surface. As the extended celebration continues, gunplay breaks out as robots stray from their assigned roles and levels far below the city's surface grandeur. Despite evidence of thought and emotion, the robots are treated by most humans as machines, not thinking beings. The deviants among them are tracked down and violently disposed of by the Marduks, the vigilante political cadre secretly funded by Duke Red and commanded by his ward, Rock. Rock's chief aim, in fact, appears to be the eradication of the robots.

Yet the robot population is shown in a flattering light as well. When Shunsaku Ban arrives from Japan and needs the services of a local detective, he is assigned a specialized robot, Pero, a competent and astute guide to the inner workings and conflicts that rile the city. Later Ken'ichi, the Japanese detective's nephew, and Tima, Laughton's robotic creation, are rescued by Fifi, a garbage-gathering robot who works on the third underground level. Fifi's kindly maternal instincts and willingness to protect Ken'ichi and Tima at all costs help make this R2-D2 clone one of the most attractive characters in the entire production. Other robots appear as an effective firefighting brigade and as bit players in other scenes throughout the film, demonstrating their indispensability to the efficient operation of the community.

What, then, of that elusive "soul in the machine"? The robots emerge in a dominant position in the end of Rintaro and Ōtomo's *Metoroporisu;* the destruction wrought by Tima and the last desperate attempt by Rock to thwart her rise to power allow the robots to seize control of the city. Ken'ichi, whose love for Tima does not recognize a boundary between animate and inanimate, throws his lot in with the victors. Perhaps this is emblematic of just how far human beings have come since Fritz Lang first gave us a cinematic vision of a relationship between human beings and robots.

Robots are still robots and human beings are still human beings; however, in the Rintaro/Ōtomo *Metoroporisu* the robots have assumed control in the face of human inabilities to maintain their own authority, overcome as they have become by selfish concerns. As in each of the earlier versions of the narrative, the plot reflects the current state of affairs in its culture of origin, using the robots to drive home an ethical and moral stance. Unless we (re)learn empathy for our supposed inferiors (the robots, who could stand in for immigrants who perform essential tasks), unless leaders return to selfless devotion to national goals, and unless we acknowledge our social responsibilities to one another, human beings are doomed to be replaced by our own creations.

Another important distinction between this version of the Metropolis narrative and those preceding it emerges from a comparative examination of the place accorded women in the storylines. Terrence Rafferty, writing in the June 8, 2003, issue of the Sunday *New York Times* entertainment section, declares the following in his article about Asian ghost stories committed to film: "[a]n unusual number of their ghosts are women who left this world too soon, unsatisfied and uncelebrated, and, as you watch *Ugetsu* or *Kwaidan* (or read [Lafcadio] Hearn's evocative tales), you might begin to suspect that the function of the ghost narrative in Japanese culture is precisely to honor the suffering of generations of the country's women. When they return as spirits they have, at last, a bit of power; and their youth and their beauty remain, unchanging" (2003, 13).

Applying this observation to Rintaro and Ōtomo's *Metoroporisu,* one might say that Tima's destructive rampage upon finding she is a robot is at least partially attributable to her realization that she is being denied her humanity. Others might argue

Rintaro and Ōtomo's helpful robot, Pero, who escorts Detective Shunsaku Ban throughout his visit to Metropolis (pictured above). Fifi (pictured below) also reappears, but now assists Ken'ichi and Tima in their escape from Rock's vigilante forces, the Marduks.
(Reproduced with permission from Sony Pictures Entertainment)

that this reflects the status accorded women in contemporary Japan. In provoking this interpretation, Rintaro and Ōtomo's *Metropolis* infuses the narrative with references to a very contemporary set of social, political, and economic concerns, such as late marriage, workforce pay discrepancies, and job responsibility inequities. Robot Tima is no longer the symbolic representation of feminine passivity or destructive female evil and deceit; she has become instead emblematic of the Japanese woman's quest for true equality within the human frame.

Conclusion

In early twentieth-century Europe and the United States, those who viewed Fritz Lang's epic silent film masterpiece version of *Metropolis* could find an empathetic confirmation of their worst nightmares: an impersonal industrialized world in which robots embodied evil and deceit, threatening to replace their human counterparts in the workplace and depriving them of their livelihood and human dignity in the process. Robots were the unwanted end products of the emerging modernization process, which was centered in a crowded and darkly sinister urbanized environment, far removed from the bucolic world of the independent artisan and the yeoman farmer.

Twenty-two years later, Osamu Tezuka, in a similarly titled manga inspired by the original film, gave his robotic creations an essential innocence, to some extent reflective of long-standing empathetic Shinto beliefs, and a historically determined ambivalence derived from recent wartime experiences. The robots in Tezuka's time and place were not perceived as truly independent actors but instead as creations of aberrant, overly self-confident human beings. Human beings, not robots, had become the core of the problem.

In the 2001 animated version of Tezuka's *Metoroporisu,* Rintaro and Ōtomo give their viewers robots that were evolved enough to assume control of their own destinies and that of the world in the face of humans' inabilities to free themselves from self-serving goals and selfish concerns. As with the earlier versions of the narrative, the plot here embodies the time in which it appeared.

The nature of the ongoing relationship between robot and human being remains equivocal even today; however, the several views we have explored in this essay provide a variety of possibilities put forth by various artistic voices in the recent past within distinctly different cultural settings, each framed in a specific historical context. From these insights emerges a more nuanced consideration of the possibilities inherent in any search for the "soul in the machine" and its place in human affairs.

Notes

1. The International Federation of Robots maintains an Internet Web site at www.ifr.org.
2. See some of the latest examples at "Robotics," *21stCentury.co.uk, Your Portal to the Future,* at www.21stcentury.co.uk/robotics/index.asp.
3. The film, initially some seventeen reels long, was drastically reedited for its American release, losing some seven reels in the process until Giorgio Moroder's version, released in

1984, restored many of the cuts (see Rutsky 1993). A digitally restored version of the film from KINO International appeared in 2002, incorporating even more original material.

4. *Metropolis*, at 5.3 million marks the (equivalent of some 2 million U.S. dollars), was the most expensive film ever produced in Germany up until that time. Yet it failed to make a profit when initially released (Flippo 1997b).

5. Lang's futuristic architecture and overall urban vision likewise inspired numerous other visionary "cities of the future" in later films, including other classic science fiction films such as Jean-Luc Godard's *Alphaville* (1965), George Lucas's *THX1138* (1970), Richard Fleischer's *Soylent Green* (1973), and Terry Gilliam's *Brazil* (1985).

6. The original seventeen reels were reduced to ten; the 4,189-meter original length, to 3,241 meters (Lowry 2003).

7. This plot point is much more prominently featured in the Harbou novel than in the original Lang film version.

8. Elaine L. Graham (2002, 178–181) offers an extended analysis of Robot Maria and her human counterpart, concluding: "The female robot engenders only irrationality and chaos, hinting at the unreliability of women who, like machines, rob 'us' (coded as male, in a gendered unity that transcends the class division between labor and capital) of 'our' humanity (constituted as sexual control, reason, labour and freedom)" (181).

9. A nuanced discussion of Shinto animism can be found in Clammer 2000, especially pages 28–29 and 33–34.

10. In 1951, Tezuka, inspired by the rocket-propelled Michi character in *Metoroporisu,* also created a manga (and later, anime) series revolving around a robot called Astro Boy. In this series, the boy robot—seen by Tezuka, despite his multiple destructive powers, to be "first and foremost a boy with a good and open heart . . . [wherein] lies his true power"—struggles to become accepted as a thinking, feeling being after having been brought to consciousness by a grieving robotics expert to replace a deceased son. Many episodes in the ongoing narrative revolve around Astro Boy's quest for acceptance given his extraordinary powers. Astro Boy is often portrayed as the victim of the all-too-human foibles of his creators or the misapprehensions of the human beings surrounding him, misunderstood and ostracized by many humans with whom he attempts to interact as a conscious being.

5

Opening the Closed World of *Shōjo Manga*
MIZUKI TAKAHASHI

Introduction

In the past few decades, manga has become one of Japan's most important pop culture industries. Over ten thousand new titles are published every year, and many of these provide the inspiration for anime (Japanese animated films), TV shows, and even contemporary theater productions. As manga's influence on popular culture grows, Japanese universities are offering classes in manga studies, and government agencies now eagerly tout manga as an important Japanese cultural export (Nakano 2004). Manga genres have been divided along gender lines, however, and until recently comics for boys or young men have received far more critical attention than those for girls.[1] Although girls' comics *(shōjo manga)* can rightfully claim a large share of the medium's current success, they have been regarded as "second-class citizens" in the manga world (Schilling 1997, 206). It was only in the mid-1970s that male critics paid any attention to them at all, and even then, the critics dealt with masterpieces that were unrepresentative of the genre as a whole. As a result, the history and generic structure of girls' comics have not been studied as thoroughly as those for boys. Primarily aimed at girls from their teenage years to their early twenties, the genre of shōjo manga features distinctive decorative and expressive artwork, along with stories that emphasize the inner feelings of the characters; thus, it is best defined as a genre that combines poetry with illustrations (Ōtsuka 1994, 333).

Shōjo manga as a distinctive genre is intimately linked to the subculture of Japanese girls known as *shōjo bunka*. This subculture first emerged in the early twentieth century when literary magazines developed distinctive modes of storytelling and art styles that appealed to girl readers. In the postwar period, these magazines shifted from a text-based to a manga format, but the aesthetic style that marked them as "authentically" speaking to a girl audience remained. The contemporary genre of shōjo manga is inextricably linked to the subculture of the girls and young women who both produce and consume it. Although men have always been involved in the production of shōjo manga as creators and editors, female artists have gradually taken over the art form, starting in the 1960s. Back then, women, who grew up immersed in the shōjo subculture of prewar novels and magazines, formed a new generation of artists. They expressed their own inner emotions for contemporary female readers who were eager to enter this world by, for, and about girls.

In this chapter, I examine how Shōjo manga developed historically from prewar girls' magazines to its postwar generic form. These magazines addressed girl readers by representing idealized images of girlhood. These early-twentieth-century young women's magazines and novels typically focused on the inner feelings of their young girl heroines, who personified desirable feminine virtues and expressed those feelings in a flowery, emotional prose style. The illustrations that accompanied these stories in prewar magazines were portrayals of young girls who exhibited the same ideals. It is precisely this set of literary and visual conventions that was inherited by female comics artists when shōjo manga developed as a distinct genre after World War II. In addition to the tradition they could draw upon, artists deployed the pictorial side of their medium creatively to convey the psyche of their heroines; in other words, they used an aesthetic idiom that spoke particularly to girl readers by engaging their emotions. While many critics have disparaged shōjo manga for the lack of sophisticated action or plot, they have not understood that it is not so much the story, but the emotive power of the images that appeals to fans. As a reader who has been deeply influenced by shōjo manga, I will concentrate on explaining the pictorial features that made this genre distinct and powerful for me. In contrast, comparatively little attention will be paid to its "literary" particularities. Instead of introducing typical stories in detail, I will focus on the general characteristics that lead readers to embrace or reject shōjo manga.

The Invention of the Shōjo Gender

Before discussing shōjo manga, however, it is important first to understand what the word "shōjo" means. Usually glossed with the English word "girl," the term shōjo specifically indicates a young woman who is not allowed to express her sexuality (Treat 1996, 281–283). While a shōjo may be sexually mature physically, she is socially considered sexually immature and is therefore identifiable as neither male nor female. In fact, the term was not customary before the late nineteenth century; prior to that, the term "shōnen" (originally meaning "children," today meaning "boys") was widely used. Signifying both boys and girls, this term allowed for a distinction by age (children/adults) rather than by gender (Honda 1990, 49–51). However, as Japan modernized, the term "shōjo" came into common usage; referring specifically to girls, and differentiating young people on the basis of perceived gender differences. This category for teenage girls emerged with the new educational system, and was utilized to justify the emerging state-sanctioned patriarchal hierarchy that privileged boys over girls (Kume 1997, 195–221). Although gender bias obviously predates the Meiji period, it was only in the early twentieth century that the shōjo emerged as a distinct entity in need of state (and not merely parental or familial) definition and control. As John Treat writes, the shōjo is "a definitive feature of Japanese late-model consumer capitalism" (1996, 280); in other words, it is closely tied to Japan's modernization.

The term shōjo refers to a socially conservative gender role that owes its origin to the formative phase of the educational system in late nineteenth and early twentieth centuries. Masuko Honda has noted that the new educational law of 1887 was the major impetus in this regard. Known as the *chūtōgakkō rei* (the junior high school law), this law sacrificed girls' education in favor of boys'. Since girls were destined to be future housewives, they supposedly did not need an advanced education (Honda 1990, 178–205). In 1899, a second piece of legislation, the *kōtōgakkō rei* (the high school law) opened the way for girls' higher education. While this new law established some schools for girls, most had a limited curriculum, focused on the training of future *ryōsai kenbo* (wise mothers, good wives), and were only accessible to girls of the urban middle and upper classes. These schools did not teach young women how to function independently as adults, but rather inculcated what could be called the shōjo ideal—the dream of becoming happy future brides, isolated from the real-life public world outside the family. Ariko Kurosawa argues that these schools had the effect of isolating girls in order to enforce their purity as virgins, that is, as "unused sexual resources" (1998, 444–448). While in waiting, shōjo were forbidden from taking on any public or private role—either as part of the workforce or as wives. This use of the shōjo gender category became widespread during the Sino-Japanese War of 1894–1895, which forced the Japanese government to propagandize about young boys as the nation's strength and as the future soldiers who would defend the Japanese archipelago. In contrast, girls, particularly of the urban middle and upper classes, were not expected to contribute to civil society during their adolescence.

The shōjo gender role offered girls few resources to negotiate the adolescent process of identity formation. In keeping with their image as "unused sexual resources," representations of shōjo emphasized their elegant, nonlaboring, nonproductive bodies, or what Kunimitsu Kawamura calls a "bourgeois body" (1994, 32). Kawamura argues that the portrayal of the young female body as pale, frail, and fresh was enforced by a rejection of aging and labor. He deduces this from shōjo magazines, which, through the 1920s and 1930s, instructed girls to avoid any activities involving exposure to the sun. As Kawamura points out, shōjo magazines promoted an ideal of girlhood that was modeled on girls of the upper classes and the nobility, but marketed to and eagerly embraced by girls of the middle classes. The model shōjo was not only protected from sexual activity and any kind of social obligations in general, but from physical labor in particular. The illustrations of girls' magazines from the 1910s through the 1930s show this kind of shōjo—idle and daydreaming within her own imaginary world of novels, poetry, and painting.[2] Thus, the shōjo image that appeared in these magazines can be regarded not only as a modern invention in general, but one that was specifically aimed at the urban bourgeois girl.[3] The shōjo body was a privileged body.

Drawing the Shōjo Image

Images have been presented in shōjo magazines almost since the appellation of "shōjo" first appeared. Starting with *Shōjo kai* (The World of Girls), which was launched in 1902, the typical magazine in the 1910s and 1920s would begin with an editorial followed by articles and would also include readers' letters in order to encourage communication between writers and readers and to help enforce the ideal shōjo image in the readers' real lives, not merely on the magazine page. An example of this underlies the following excerpt from an article by Rippō Numata, editor of *Shōjo kai:*

> To pretend to read a book that you cannot understand, to pretend to know what you do not know, and to pretend to be an adult are all what you should not do. These behaviors are disliked and laughed at rather than liked and appreciated. . . . Thus, you, shōjo must be neither babies nor adults. You must be loved as shōjo for your gentleness, innocence, and wholesomeness. (Numata, quoted in Kume 1997, 217–218)[4]

Numata focuses on the proper comportment of a young girl but does not touch upon her physical appearance. It was the task of the illustrations in these magazines to visualize the inner qualities of sexual naiveté as something that must shine through, whereas the often serialized novels alongside with the poems promoted the innocence and sweetness of the shōjo by describing her verbally as a "fresh flower in the field." Mentioned in passing, the story lines of shōjo novels were highly formulaic and didactic, inculcating the cardinal virtues of girlhood while utilizing a lyrical style that favored elegant rhetorical flourishes over narrative progression. The main characters were always girls, and the plots always revolved around school or other sites of their daily life.

Illustrations were key to developing a recognizable and appealing image of the perfect shōjo. One of the most popular illustrators in this early period was Yumeji Takehisa (1884–1934), whose portraits of thin, frail-looking models with pale faces epitomized the shōjo ideal of the 1910s and 1920s. Not professionally trained as an artist, Takehisa first became famous as an illustrator of his own novels and poetry (Takumi 1978, 185–192). He also designed and marketed his own line of fashions, stationery, accessories, and home decorations, which in turn were regularly advertised in girls' magazines. Particularly popular among girls were letter sets and hair accessories with his signature. Thus, Takehisa offers a good example of how artists erased the border between the fictional and real worlds by providing young girls with the opportunity to literally buy into the shōjo look featured in the respective magazines.

Takehisa was the first and most important illustrator to create a coherent style that reflected the ideal shōjo image. His aesthetic approach persists in shōjo manga to this day. Initially a poet, Takehisa regarded his work as visual poem-scapes: "One day, I wrote a poem in the form of an illustration. Since it happened to be published in a magazine, my timid heart was delighted" (quoted in Takumi 1978, 192). His loose and sketchy pictorial style, which made the shōjo he drew look weak, soft, and dreamy,

Yumeji Takehisa's 1926 cover illustration of *Fujin gurafu* **(Illustrated Women's News).**
(Reproduced with permission from Minami Takehisa)

was soon given the name *jojō-ga,* which literally means lyrical painting/illustration (Kuwahara 1998, 1036–1037). Kaoru Sudō, a later jojō-ga artist, defines the genre in regard to its emphasis on feelings:

> The defining characteristic of jojō-ga is the visual representation of the artist's delicate sensibility in a way that combines the artist's imagination with realism. The difference between mere illustration and jojō-ga is that illustration simply depicts the narrative of the novel, while jojō-ga reflects the emotions of the artist, such as his view of nature or life. . . . I think that jojō-ga, like poetry, conveys the feeling of the artist and provokes an emotional response in its audience. (Sudō 1984, 30)

This kind of shōjo illustration contributed significantly to the aesthetic style that distinguished shōjo manga in the postwar period. Other influential jojō-ga artists of the 1920s include Kashō Takabatake (1888–1966) and Kōji Fukiya (1898–1979). Takabatake's shōjo are relatively sensual, while Fukiya's girls tend to have large, round eyes and maintain more of a childish innocence. But although each of them had their own individual style, they had one thing in common: to portray the shōjo as a girl staring vaguely into space as if she were daydreaming. This empty, wandering gaze became

Kashō Takabatake's 1928 cover illustration, "Asagao," for *Shōjo gahō* **(Girls' Journal).**
(Copyright Yayoi Bijutsukan)

typical of the shōjo image. It was spread, first and foremost, by illustrations created by Takehisa, Takabatake, and Fukiya for novels or poetry published in shōjo magazines.

This stereotypical image changed temporarily during World War II. When a magazine editor asked Fukiya to draw more realistic bodies, he represented his girls as soldiers protecting the nation (Hanamura 1989, 121–129). Due to the war effort, shōjo in magazines were no longer allowed to dream; instead, they had to face the real world at war. Or, to put it differently, for the first time, an active image emerged on magazine pages. After World War II, however, the demand for it decreased. In tune with that, Jun'ichi Nakahara (1913–1983) revived the jojō-ga of the prewar period. Having begun his career as an illustrator in the 1930s for the magazine *Shōjo no tomo* (The Girl's Friend), he was forced to quit during the war (Takahashi 1999, 150), but in 1946, he picked up his pen again, drawing for the magazines *Soreiyu* (Soleil) and *Himawari* (Sunflower). His illustrations of shōjo with willowy bodies, exaggerated eyes, and dreamy expressions soon became popular in a newly emerging genre, that is, manga for girls. Like Takehisa, Nakahara not only illustrated trends in fashions for young women, but drove such trends himself. With a background in both art and the fashion industry, he worked as a fashion designer, stylist, and editor, as well as an

Kōji Fukiya's cover illustration for *Reijo kai* (World of Ladies, 1926).
(Reproduced with permission from Tatsuo Fukiya)

illustrator. Although he updated the clothing and hairstyles of his shōjo, the illustrations that he created in the 1940s and 1950s were highly reminiscent of his prewar work, particularly in the exaggeration of the eyes.

The shōjo in Nakahara's illustrations have stick-like bodies without musculature, typical of jojō-ga. What distinguishes them from Takehisa's depictions are their extremely enlarged slanting eyes, thick black eyelids, and thick eyebrows. However, whereas before the war these girls had gazed contemplatively upward, unconscious of those viewing them, in the 1950s they began to address the viewer directly—as illustrated by means of the light shining in their clear black eyes. While his contemporary, Fukiya, had already invented this special effect, Nakahara's achievement was to use this light to animate the previously doll-like shōjo.[5]

Another important stylistic feature of jojō-ga that Nakahara developed after the war

**Jun'ichi Nakahara's cover illustration for the May issue of *Shōjo no tomo*
(Girls' Friend, 1940).** (Copyright Jun'ichi Nakahara/Himawariya Inc.)

**Jun'ichi Nakahara's 1958, cover illustration for the magazine *Junior Soreiyu*
(Junior Soleil, no. 24, 1958).** (Copyright Jun'ichi Nakahara/Himawariya Inc.)

are the backgrounds of shōjo portraits, now often decorated with flowers. Flowers not only lend a refined atmosphere to the figures, but also reflect their inner personality. For instance, adding roses to the background might indicate that a girl is cheerful, while balloon flowers suggest she is reserved. This language of flowers invites the viewer, who would otherwise just concentrate at the external features of the illustrated girl, into the character's inner world. Thus, a powerful affective link between audience and image can be formed.

Large eyes and symbolic flowers are the two stylistic features that later became the most important conventions in shōjo manga. An early example of this is found in the work of Makoto Takahashi (1934–). Like Takehisa and Nakahara before him, Takahashi not only illustrated manga, but also designed items, such as stationery, for purchase by his fans. In 1956, he collaborated with Sugako Hashida to produce a serialized manga for a magazine appropriately named *Shōjo* (Girls). Since Takahashi was an illustrator rather than a manga artist, it was Hashida who wrote the scenario while Takahashi was in charge of the artwork. Their stories look more like illustrated novels than comics, in that they contain many drawings of shōjo with large eyes and racy dresses in the jojō-ga style, and the narrative does not flow smoothly from one panel to the next. However, Takahashi's floral backgrounds and undulating waves of hair were to reappear in later shōjo manga. It was Takahashi's accomplishment to fully integrate the artistry of jojō-ga into the manga format by making decorative visuals his most basic convention.[6]

Interpreting Shōjo Manga Iconographic Conventions

The style of shōjo manga, which reached its maturity in the 1970s, is markedly different from shōnen manga. This difference was often misunderstood by Japanese manga critics. Around 1980, for example, Yoshihiro Yonezawa expressed the then-typical disparagement of shōjo manga when he dismissed shōjo figures as risible because of their absurd doll-like saucer eyes and their minimalist stick-like bodies. Moreover, he also found the complicated panel designs distracting and even aesthetically unpleasing (Yonezawa 1980, 10). In a similar vein, another critic, Hiroshi Aramata, complained that most shōjo manga were poorly drawn (Aramata 1994, 139). What these critics overlooked was that the main purpose of shōjo manga is to show the complex inner psychology of the characters, not to create a realistic or action-filled tale. The aesthetic features, such as enormous eyes with long eyelashes, full-body portraits, and complicated panel designs are crucial for fans to engage emotionally with the story. Rather than simply deriding the distinctive shōjo manga art style, it is more productive to analyze how these aesthetic traits invite readers to identify with the characters.

As mentioned above, large, shining eyes were first invented by Jun'ichi Nakahara in the 1930s, and further popularized by Makoto Takahashi around 1956. In the 1950s, artists often placed a star-shaped highlight next to the pupil. This became the key visual marker for identifying a comic as a shōjo manga (Schodt 1993, 91).

In regard to what these eyes signify, some have argued that starry eyes symbolize

A page from Makoto Takahashi's *Puchi la* (Petit la, 1961).
(Copyright Makoto Takahashi and Parco Co. Ltd)

A page from Yoko Nishitani's *Konnichiha Suzanu* (Hello Suzanne, 1971).
(Copyright Yoshiko Nishitani)

"the love and dreams" of the characters (Nakayama 1997, 7). In contrast, Inuhiko Yomota points out that they play at least two roles: they identify a story's main character, and they also serve as mirrors that reflect the character's emotions (Yomota 1994, 168). In other words, the eyes literally are the windows of the soul; by looking at the eyes, the readers can intuit the character's feelings, which remain unexpressed in dialogue. Using oversized eyes, therefore, is a key technique used by the shōjo artist to evoke empathy from readers. Such an artistic convention supports Jaqueline Berndt's observation that manga provoke strong emotional responses in their readers— intense feelings of happiness, sadness, and anger that make the story powerful for them (Berndt 1994, 143).

The importance of this convention is indicated by its staying power. Many new artists appeared in the shōjo world during the 1970s, when the number of shōjo manga magazines peaked (Yonezawa 1980, 176). While these artists experimented with new plots, expanding their repertoire into fantasy and sports stories, they preserved this visual feature—as can be deduced from the fact that the basic image of the young girl heroine remained unchanged: the head of the figure was disproportionately large in comparison to her body; the trunk, arms, and legs were elongated; and the eyes so large that they occupied half the face. What hints to the latter's significance is also the individual artist's attention to detail when drawing them. For a long time, the eyes were the only body part in this highly regulated genre where artists could exercise their freedom of expression. Their size and form, the number and shape of highlights in them, and the heaviness of the eyelashes differed according to the artist's idiosyncratic style and became their distinctive trademark.

Another convention often misunderstood by critics is the full-body portrait of the young heroine, the use of which was, in regard to Makoto Takahashi, for example, even called "unsophisticated" (Iwaya and Hagio 1995, 20–47). Such portraits were regarded as "clumsy" because they appeared suddenly in the middle of the story, interrupting the narrative. But to readers familiar with shōjo manga, full-length portraits are anything but an intrusion. A convention inherited from Nakahara's illustrations, part of their allure for women has always been that they were all about fashion—full-body images appear on the page like mannequins modeling the latest ensembles in store windows.

While most shōnen manga are action or adventure stories, the focus in shōjo manga tends to be on the psychological development of the characters. For this reason, most panels depict characters conversing, or revealing their inner thoughts to the reader, and generally showing only the upper part of body or the face. The face and body offer nonverbal cues to the main character's inner feelings, something that is much more important for fans than action scenes. Of course, not all the pages are composed this way, but their prominence shows that they serve a vital function; they create an emotional intimacy that communicates the emotions and interiority of the main characters. By contrast, when the whole body is displayed, the reader is put into the position of an observer. The implicit appeal not to identify too closely with the character is underpinned by the convention of drawing the full-length body unrealistically as a stick-like figure. Thus, faces and figures serve opposing functions: close-ups of the former draw the reader inside the emotional life of the character, while, simultaneously, more distanced views of the latter allow for a consideration of external aspects like physical appearance or clothing style.

Since the main focus of shōjo manga stories is the psychological development of the main character, panels and page layout are also designed to illustrate complicated inner feelings. In shōnen manga, the panel arrangement moves seamlessly, unfolding the plot in a predictable temporal sequence from beginning to end. As a genre that emphasizes physical action, its panels are typically arranged to be read from the right to the left and top to bottom, mirroring the traditional Japanese writing system (Natsume 1995a, 168–183). However, since the 1970s, shōjo manga have often discarded this temporal principle. As we have seen, full-body shōjo portraits are frequently inserted

**A page from Kimiko Uehara's *Yukidoke michi de . . .* (By the Slushy Road, 1974)
showing the convention of accenting the upper body and face of the characters.**
(Copyright Kōdansha Mai Daiyamondo and Kimiko Uehara)

into the story to break its narrative flow. This forces readers to stop to take stock of the emotional atmosphere of the moment, as the emotions of the characters are more important than what happens next.

In addition to the insertion of full-body portraits, the spatial arrangement of the panels in a collage-like way, which actually favors the page of the single frame, is crucial for the distinctive style of shōjo manga. It was Shōtarō Ishinomori (1938–1998) who invented this "spatialization," which has become a staple for shōjo manga since the 1970s (Ōsuka and Sasakibara 2001, 66–72). Ishinomori was an innovative manga artist who experimented with the space between the panels. He transformed this space into decorative grids that break up the temporal flow of the panels. Eliminating the space between the panels allowed for a layering and juxtaposing of various images. Thus, the panels no longer emphasized the passage of time. Instead of heading forward hastily to the next page, the reader became immersed in the character's feelings, dreams, and memories (Yomota 1994, 55). Now, there was also space for extended monologues that contributed further to the emphasis on the character's state of mind.

As the above example shows, the rectangular form of the panels makes it easy for the artist to arrange them sequentially for laying out the plot. Readers simply scan from right to left to follow the story. However, by manipulating the size, form, and location of these panels, the artist can express the emotions motivating the action. Altering the shape of individual panels reflects the emotional significance of the respective images—for example, bigger panels may highlight an important scene. Panel arrangements and page layouts play a significant role for involving readers in the story, not through intense action sequences, but through access to the inner feelings and thoughts of the character.

The artwork of shōjo manga is not limited to showing one action in each rectangular panel, like a window, canvas, or film frame. Since this genre has developed a highly sophisticated way of intertwining a so-to-speak "cinematic" sequentiality with the spatial simultaneity characteristic, it raises doubts about the definition of the comic as a "film strip laid out on a page." Shōjo manga's disparate panel sizes and forms, which occasionally break up the film-like continuity of narrative flow, can even be understood as a visual kind of internal monologue insofar as pictorial and narrative devices focus more on what the respective characters feel about a certain event rather than on the actual event itself (Yomota 1994, 55).

From this perspective, it does not seem appropriate to refer exclusively to Osamu Tezuka as the artist who created the genre of shōjo manga in the 1950s. As is well known, Tezuka pioneered the "story manga" format by applying a so-called "cinematic" method, that is, by incorporating cinematic conventions such as different camera angles, shots, and transitions. Although he mainly published manga for boys, he is also frequently credited with founding the genre of shōjo manga because he wrote *Ribon no kishi (Princess Knight)*, which was published in the magazine *Shōjo kurabu* (Girls' Club) from 1953 onward. Although his drawing style differed from jojō-ga and his influence on the most innovative female artists of the 1960s and 1970s was, in fact, secondary compared to that of artists such as Jun'ichi Nakahara and Makoto Takahashi, manga critics usually attribute to Tezuka the innovation of shōjo manga stylistic features such as large eyes, gender-bending plots, and romanticized foreign settings (Schodt 1996, 253; see also Murakami 1989a, 45).

It is certainly true that complex narratives such as *Ribon no kishi* did not exist in the pages of shōjo manga magazines before Tezuka successfully adapted his shōnen manga adventure stories for girl readers; he definitely raised the narrative bar by introducing his sequential manga style (Murakami 1989a, 45). However, the point critics usually miss is that crucial elements of shōjo manga existed long before Tezuka came on the scene. While Tezuka is rightfully celebrated for this narrative innovation, he contributed almost nothing to the distinctive visual style that was to define shōjo manga as a genre.

An example of full-body portraiture from Kyōko Fumizuki's *Nocturne* (1977).
(Copyright Kōdansha "Mai Daiyamondo" and Kyōko Fumizuki)

His *Ribon no kishi* appeared at a transitional period when jojō-ga was integrated into the story manga format, as exemplified by Makoto Takahashi.

A key sign that Tezuka is an exceptional rather than a key figure in the world of shōjo manga is his disinterest in the expression of the inner feelings of his heroines. In *Ribon no kishi,* a straightforward narrative without any temporal or spatial ambiguities, the interior monologues of the heroine Sapphire are expressed in thought balloons pointing to her head, rather than in free-floating text. By using such thought balloons, Tezuka ties the interior monologue to the passage of time in the frame, appropriate for an adventure story. Most shōjo manga, however, use free-floating text to indicate the main character's vague inner thoughts, approximating first-person narration.

Large eyes, full-body portraits, complex page designs, and free-floating text are the basic visual language of the genre, used to convey the inner feelings of the char-

A page from Osamu Tezuka's *Ribon no kishi* (*Princess Knight*, 1953–1956).
(Copyright Tezuka Productions)

acters and to invite the readers to identify with them. The specialized visual language of shōjo manga has often not been understood by male readers; one could say that shōjo manga functioned as a secret code that allowed girls to become absorbed in the intimate world of shōjo culture. Only those with the ability to decipher the code were welcomed into that private realm, to share girls' concerns with love, family, human relations, or their interest in fashion and trendiness. Thus, girls used the visual idiom of shōjo manga to quietly exclude those who did not understand the shōjo.

What Marginalized Shōjo Manga?

Shōjo manga began to fully develop as a genre in the early 1970s. This growth was led by a group of innovative young female artists known collectively as the *24 nen gumi,* which indicated the year of their birth, Shōwa 24 or 1949. They successfully combined the aesthetics of jojō-ga with stories that addressed the emotional lives of adolescent girls. However, as discussed above, the aesthetic idiom they created was (and in many ways still is) only accessible to informed, predominantly female readers. As a result, uninformed readers were not privy to the fascination shōjo manga has for girls, and their evaluation of the genre reflected this prejudice. The illegibility of the shōjo manga visual aesthetic to the reader outside of shōjo culture is one reason why the genre has been ghettoized. Moreover, the treatment of shōjo manga within Japanese discourse on the history of manga has only served to increase its isolation.

When shōjo manga received some early critical attention in the 1970s, critics focused on a few artists of the time rather than analyzing the genre as a whole (Kimura 1996, 61–69). 24 nen gumi artists Motō Hagio (1949–), Riyoko Ikeda (1947–), Toshie Kihara (1948–), Keiko Takemiya (1950–), Yumiko Ōshima (1947–), and Ryōko Yamagishi (1947–) are usually included in this group. While their artistic styles are distinct, they do share some commonalities. They are a generation who grew up reading Tezuka's manga. Hagio and Takemiya are explicit in their indebtedness to Tezuka, identifying him as a major influence behind their decision to become manga artists, and his cinematic style is apparent in their work. Their works, like Tezuka's, also explored bold new themes, such as science fiction, religion, sexual problems, and history, instead of the standard shōjo manga fare of school life or love stories. One female critic, Azusa Nakajima, describes this group of artists as follows:

> Not all artists now associated with 24 nen gumi were born in 1949. Clearly, it was because of their artistic style, not their age, that they were categorized as a group. Shōjo manga did not really exist as a genre until these artists created it. Some of the generic features they innovated include characters with shining eyes, stories of everyday life and first love, and emphasis on the delicate feelings of the shōjo. Although shōjo manga was popular and skillfully depicted the emotions of ordinary life, it was derided as cheap trash for women and children. Men dismissed shōjo manga not on literary grounds, but because of sexism, and a disregard for the world of women and children. . . . The challenge of the 24 nen gumi to sexism in society at that time was very striking; one could even call it a social phenomenon. (Nakajima 1991, 88–89)

Before the 24 nen gumi appeared, shōjo manga were dismissed as the lowest form of Japanese manga. The 24 nen gumi's work changed this. What did critics find so worthwhile in their artistry? Some argue that they were exceptional because they revivified the genre, incorporating new visual techniques, such as the montage-like panel arrangement, which ushered in "the golden age" of the genre (Okamoto 1998,

A page from Moto Hagio's *Pō no ichizoku* (The Poe Family, 1973).
(Copyright Moto Hagio and Shōgakukan 2006)

134). But critics evaluated only the story lines in shōjo manga and, thus, overlooked the most significant innovations these artists made, which were in the visual aesthetics. Critic Kunio Iwaya takes this narrow view in evaluating the work of 24 nen gumi member Moto Hagio, who is not only one of the most influential artists of the group, but who also introduced groundbreaking themes in her stories, including death and religion. It is because her stories are narratively complex that Iwaya singles her out for praise:

> I think that Hagio is one of the best manga artists in the postwar period, because her writing has depth. In fact, her work transcends the so-called shōjo manga, although it shares many of the genre's typical features. Indeed, she has a strong influence on today's shōjo manga artists, even though her works are more diverse than theirs. . . . Her works are stark and objective. . . . This distinguishes them from the majority of shōjo manga which is shamelessly subjective, emotional, and childish. (Iwaya 1980, 136–137)

This is a fairly typical critical assessment of these authors. Iwaya does not classify Hagio's work as shōjo manga because he thinks the genre is "childish." The value of her work for him lies in the fact that it is different from "the usual" shōjo manga. As further proof of her creative excellence, he claims that her works cannot only be enjoyed by girls but also by male readers (Iwaya and Hagio 1995, 20–47). Similarly, Yoshihiro Yonezawa argues that Hagio, like Tezuka, is an outsider to shōjo manga (Yonezawa 1980, 146). Although she began her career as a shōjo manga artist in 1969, and published in shōjo manga magazines, her work appears to be highly idiosyncratic. Most of her characters, for example, are boys, and they do not have shining stars in their eyes or long eyelashes. Of the 24 nen gumi, Hagio is often singled out for special critical acclaim, because critics see her as "transcending" a genre they regard as lacking in artistic value.

Another significant reason why critics tend to misread shōjo manga is that they do not understand the artistic tradition from which it evolved, namely jojō-ga and shōjo novels. Even more problematically, the artists themselves do not mention the influence of the jojō-ga and the shōjo novel tradition in their work; they seem complicit in a conspiracy of silence about that aspect of their work. Yet, as I have argued, the influences are apparent. The 24 nen gumi's fondness for Western countries as the backdrop for their stories, for example, can also be found in Jun'ichi Nakahara's and Makoto Takahashi's work. They improved upon the delicate drawing techniques of jojō-ga and fashion illustration so important in the world of shōjo art. Despite Tezuka's obvious narrative influence on them, the undercurrent of shōjo style runs strong in their visual aesthetics.

Critics ignore shōjo elements in the manga to which they give rave reviews because they tend to be unreflective of their own critical bias, which prizes shōnen over shōjo manga. When they deal with shōjo manga, they tend to favor artists who reinforce their aesthetic predispositions. This is why other members of the 24 nen gumi, such as Toshie Kihara and Riyoko Ikeda, are less well analyzed. Kihara's manga have been remade in other media, including as a stage play by the all-girl Takarazuka Revue theater troupe. Ikeda's seminal manga about the French Revolution, *Berusaiyu no bara* (*The Rose of Versailles*), has become one of the best-selling shōjo manga of all time, not only in Japan, but also in translation in Europe; it has been made into a Takarazuka play, an animated television series, and a live-action film. In spite of the cultural importance of Kihara's and Ikeda's works, they have received very little attention from male critics. One reason why they have been overlooked is that the jojō-ga influence is clearly apparent in their work.

Female critics have written about these manga, but they do not attempt to explain the appeal of shōjo manga to readers not already familiar with the genre. Interestingly, when they discuss shōjo manga, they do so by analyzing the works in light of their own lives. Yukari Fujimoto, Rika Yokomori, and Kazuko Nimiya are typical in this regard; they always move the discussion toward their own biographies, especially how much shōjo manga means to them. They regard shōjo manga characters as their alter egos whose fictional lives mirror their own real lives as modern women (Nimiya 1994; Yokomori 1996; Fujimoto 1998). For instance, in *Watashi no ibasho wa doko ni aru no?* (Where Do I Belong? 1998), Yukari Fujimoto analyzes shōjo manga from the 1970s through

A page from Toshie Kihara's *Utsukushiki iitsukushiteyo* (Express Your Beauty, 1978).
(Copyright Toshie Kihara)

the 1990s in terms of topics such as "love," "sex," "family," and "employment" in order to demonstrate how these works reflect women's changing values. Although this is one of the few scholarly works to treat shōjo manga in depth and from the point of view of an informed reader, Fujimoto begins by stating, "I have written this book not only as a history of shōjo manga (and for the sake of comparison, shōnen manga), but also as the history of my own personal struggle to find where I belong [in society]" (Fujimoto 1998, 4). By beginning her book in this way, Fujimoto makes it clear that she is not writing objectively but in a way that combines critical analysis with personal history. Another well-known and widely quoted female critic of shōjo manga, Rika Yokomori, suggests in the title of her book *Ren'ai wa shōjo manga de osowatta—ai ni ikite koso, onna!* (I Learned About Love from Shōjo Manga, I'm a Woman, Living in Love, 1996) that the purpose of her analysis is to examine how reading shōjo manga as a teenager influenced her ideas about love. In other words, although these critics explain in detail how shōjo manga powerfully affected their lives, their work is little more than a case study of the reception of these texts by girl readers. Symptomatically, they analyze the plots extensively but not the artwork. For that reason, it is very difficult for anyone who does not share their reading experience to follow their arguments.

To analyze the distinctive emotional power of the genre, we must be aware that manga are not only pictorial narratives but also an interactive medium. By forcing the reader to infer the action between the panels, manga draw the reader into the fictional world. In other words, the division of the images into panels and pages helps to absorb the reader in the world of the manga. While this is true of the comic book medium in general, shōjo manga in particular use this trick to draw the reader into the emotional world of the story. All elements in manga require the readers' active participation, integrating the words and pictures on the pages in order to understand the story. However, readers do not only use their eyes when enjoying the unfolding story. They can also control the speed of page turning.

This is exemplified in the work of Yumiko Ōshima, who is recognized as the most influential shōjo manga artist of the 24 nen gumi. Ōshima's important artistic contribution was developing the repertoire of visual techniques in panel design that enhanced the representation of emotions (Yonezawa 1991b, 82). One of her more important innovations was to free the characters' interior monologues from word balloons, allowing the text to float freely like flower petals scattered across the page. This free-floating text is equivalent to first-person narration in a novel. Another of Ōshima's innovations was to draw panels with delicate, thin borders, which are occasionally broken, making the page resemble a mosaic or a collage. The panels are not sequential, which forces readers to look at the whole page in order to understand the atmosphere of a scene rather than just read ahead in the story.

Ōshima often dwells on characteristic shōjo themes, particularly girls' anxieties revolving around adolescence. For instance, in Ōshima's *Kisuika akasuika* (Yellow Watermelon, Red Watermelon), one of the main characters shoplifts while suffering from PMS. This shows the character's difficulty in accepting her body as an adult body, capable of menstruating and reproducing, while at the same time denying the abandonment of youthful dreams and willingness to lead an ordinary life. That is, she represses her fear of becoming an adult, both physically and emotionally, even as her body matures on its own. As that gap between physical and psychological maturation widens, and the terror of becoming an adult consumes her, she dreams in one sequence that cracks appear on her face. In her dream, she sees a terrifying vision of herself as a reflection of her mother, breaking apart and scattering like sand. When she awakens from her nightmare, the light coming in from her window, broken by the trees outside, creates a sense of fragmentation.

Ōshima's manga thematize girls' adolescent insecurities as illustrated in the figure on page 135. Here, her style lends itself to the expression of intensely felt moments of angst in adolescent life. The nonlinear structure of shōjo manga allows the reader the freedom to pause and fully experience the emotions of the character. But to appreciate this effect,

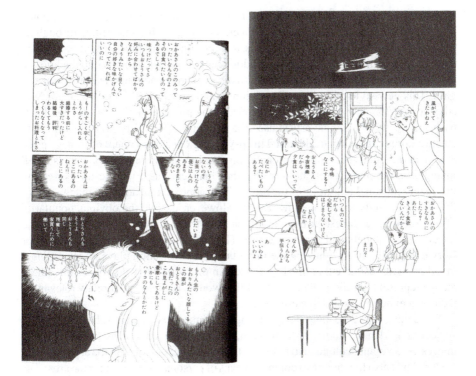

A dream sequence revealing a girl's anxieties, from Yumiko Ōshima's *Akasuika kisuika* (Red Watermelon, Yellow Watermelon, 1979).
(Reproduced with permission from Hakusensha General Editorial Department)

a reader must be open to these highly gendered experiences, something that is difficult to do if one has not experienced what the artists and the readers have. When critics analyze comics, they should discuss the visual elements as well as the plot. Although manga is made up of both text and pictures, the overwhelming majority of criticism only considers the text and ignores the visuals. Shōjo manga in particular utilizes many visual idioms, including the full body image, large sparkling eyes, and flower backgrounds, which serve to add depth to the plot and convey emotions that cannot be expressed in words, but critics have not undertaken to explicate this visual code. As a result, not only does the visual code of shōjo manga remain a secret known only to writers and readers, but the community of girls hidden within that code remains closed to outsiders.

Conclusion

I have referred to shōjo manga in this essay as a "closed world." This closed world has existed since the "shōjo" gender category was created in the modern period. The idea of the adolescent girl developed out of the ideology behind state educational policies of the late nineteenth century. Later, the category became reified through its representation in shōjo magazines, novels, and fashion illustrations, which established for the first time the visual image of the adolescent girl that developed into the jojō-ga. Inspired by poetry, jojō-ga emphasized artistic self-expression instilled in portraits of girls. This new style of fashion illustration, popularized by Jun'ichi Nakahara, was adapted into the new genre of shōjo manga in the postwar period by Makoto Takahashi. In the 1970s, female artists used the aesthetic idiom of prewar illustration to create complex stories that addressed the psychological development of teenage girls, and invited them to become emotionally involved in the narrative. The panels dwell lovingly on the portraits of shōjo so that they can serve as a vehicle for expressing the deeply personal emotions of the artists. This approach made shōjo manga attractive predominantly to teenage girl readers. However, despite the obvious popularity of these manga, Japanese critics unfamiliar with the traditions of jojō-ga and shōjo novels fail to understand the new genre. They criticize them as examples of poor storytelling without recognizing the important role illustration plays in generating a mood or an atmosphere that involves readers in the story. They do not see how these manga represent psychological problems that women readers find directly relevant to their own experiences in Japanese society.

Since the late 1990s, shōjo manga, along with other manga genres, has become the subject of academic inquiry. As a medium, manga tells a story using both letters and images. As a popular culture text, it reflects the social situation of both the artists and the readers, but it also functions as a complex means of personal expression for the artist. For that reason, when researchers and scholars discuss manga, their criticism must include multiple perspectives, not simply a discussion of the plot. If research is to progress, then the paradigm for studying shōjo manga must also change.

Notes

This essay is based on my M.A. dissertation for the University of London, the School of Oriental and African Studies, 1999.

1. This categorization is not always absolute. Sometimes it is reported that a large number of female readers purchase *shōnen* (boys') manga (Nakano 2004, 186–187). The reverse is not true: most boys do not read shōjo manga.

2. Of course, this does not address the full range of real girls' experiences in the early twentieth century. For instance, the idealized shōjo image purposely leaves out girls working on farms or in factories in order to promote a fantasy of wealth and privilege.

3. The formation of an idle class of young women devoted to literary pursuits can also be found in the Heian period. However, as a gulf of nearly one thousand years separates the culture of the Heian court from the bourgeoisie of the 1920s, it is deeply problematic to suggest a cultural continuity. Moreover, the magazines themselves do not reference this earlier culture.

4. All translations are my own unless otherwise noted.

5. Mieko Minagawa studied the chronological transition of the style of Nakahara's illustrations, noting the differences in his style before and after World War II in her *Himawari to Junia Soreiyu*. Shōichi Inoue also pointed out the unique style of Nakahara's depiction of the eyes.

6. Takahashi discusses this in detail in his illustrated book, *Shōjo Romance* (1999).

6

Situating the *Shōjo* in *Shōjo Manga*
Teenage Girls, Romance Comics, and Contemporary Japanese Culture
DEBORAH SHAMOON

Although *shōjo manga*, or comics for teenage girls, has been a popular and innovative genre since the 1970s, until recently it has been largely neglected by critics, especially those writing in English.[1] The study of shōjo manga as a distinct genre, however, can enhance our understanding of discourses of girlhood in Japan and also of the narrative and aesthetic capacities of comics as a medium. In the previous essay, Mizuki Takahashi draws connections between the private, closed world for girls depicted in prewar girls' magazines and shōjo manga's generic emphasis on the exploration of the inner psychology of teenage girls. She also demonstrates the aesthetic roots of shōjo manga art in girls' magazines of the 1920s and 1930s, particularly in illustrations by Jun'ichi Nakahara. This chapter will elaborate further on the connection between prewar girls' magazines and postwar shōjo manga. One of the features of prewar girls' magazines is the depiction of close friendships and even romance between girls as a substitute for depictions of heterosexual romance. As a result, the stories and illustrations in these magazines featured what I call an "aesthetic of sameness" in portraying same-gender romance. As the narrative and aesthetic heirs to girls' magazines, shōjo manga inherited a tendency to sameness in portraying romantic pairs. Even while relying on an aesthetic of sameness, artists beginning in the 1970s developed a visual idiom emphasizing sentiment and depth. While the classic shōjo manga of the 1970s were a powerful means for exploring the interiority of teenage girls, more recently, experimental artists have sought to move beyond the limitations of the genre. I will end with a look at how a more recent manga, Kiriko Nananan's *blue* (1997), recycles the sameness and flatness of the genre into a story that speaks to adult readers and redefines shōjo identity to accommodate contemporary social realities.

Of course, singling out the shōjo manga artists of the 1970s as a distinct group is historically and ideologically problematic, as Takahashi points out. Rather than considering shōjo manga of the 1970s as an isolated movement in time, it is more useful to think of those works as part of a continuing process of generic experimentation and innovation. The late 1960s and early 1970s were marked by experimentation in the arts, especially in youth culture; iconoclastic art forms such as New Wave film were reaching a wide audience, and manga as a whole was diversifying and finding a more mature audience with the publication of the experimental magazines *COM* and *Garo*. A group of young women who became known as the *24 nen gumi* (literally, the Showa 24 group, so-called because many of the women were born in or near Showa 24, or 1949) began to write shōjo manga that dealt openly with politics and sexuality. These manga also explored the psychological interiority of their girl protagonists, a change that Eiji Ōtsuka claims rivals the discovery of interiority in the early Meiji novel (Ōtsuka 1994, 65). Many of the artists categorized as 24 nen gumi, who created the classics in the 1970s, have continued to influence the genre, particularly Moto Hagiō and Yumiko Ōshima. With Takahashi's qualifications in mind, it is important to understand the larger context of shōjo manga—how it developed out of girls' magazines, how that early history had a limiting as well as a freeing influence, and how more recent authors have attempted to appeal to older audiences while referencing the teenage girl culture from which it arose.

Shōjo Culture and Girls' Magazines

Girls' magazines were instrumental in forming the aesthetic and literary qualities that appealed to teenage girls and that would later shape shōjo manga magazines. Magazines directed specifically at teenage girls began to appear at the beginning of the twentieth century, as school-aged children and teenagers began to be singled out as discrete marketing demographics and literary culture in general became more diversified. The late Meiji and Taishō period (1900–1926) saw a proliferation of magazines aimed at many different audiences, in addition to those aimed at teenage girls. Magazines with titles such as *Shōjo sekai* (Girls' World) and *Shin shōjo* (New Girl) began to appear around 1902 (Horie 2003, 114). One the most popular girls' magazines of the prewar period was *Shōjo no tomo* (The Girls' Friend, 1912–1955), which, along with other girls' magazines, was part of a larger girls' culture (*shōjo bunka*) that emerged in the 1910s and 1920s. In this period, girlhood was considered a time of sheltered innocence in which girls formed close relationships only with other girls. The prevalence of sex-segregated education and the popularity of the all-girl Takarazuka Revue theater troupe also contributed to the construction of girls' culture as a closed, homosocial space (Robertson 1998, 61–70). As an expression of that private world, girls' magazines presented a (supposedly) unmediated view of how the girls saw themselves. Of course, the content of these magazines was in fact mediated both by male editors and by increasingly strict government control. However, readers perceived these magazines as speaking directly to them, creating a private realm apart from the pressures of patriarchal society and impending marriage (Endō 2004, 30–34; Kawamura 1993, 43–49).

Girls' magazines, or more specifically, the *shōjo shōsetsu* (girls' novels) and accompanying illustrations serialized in them, developed a recognizable aesthetic and literary style that came be associated with the "authentic" representation of girls' culture. In the postwar period, girls' magazines shifted dramatically in content, from text-based stories with occasional illustrations to featuring manga almost exclusively (Horie 2003, 28–31; *Shōjo manga no sekai* 1991, 4–8). As Takahashi points out, nearly all the aesthetic features of shōjo manga derive from conventions created by illustrators working in prewar girls' magazines, most notably Yumeji Takehisa and Jun'ichi Nakahara. I would add that girls' magazines were also instrumental in the development of the narrative aesthetics of postwar shōjo manga; the novels serialized in girls' magazines by Nobuko Yoshiya and other authors were as influential in the creation of shōjo manga as the illustrations that accompanied them. These magazines were one expression of girls' culture, a discrete discourse premised on a private, closed world of girls that embraced not only close female friendships but also uniformity, sameness, and same-gender romance.

Same-Sex Desire and Sameness

One prominent feature of prewar girls' culture is the prevalence of female-female romantic relationships; however, it is important not to confuse these relationships with twenty-first-century Western constructions of homosexuality. While "homosexual" identity in Western culture has recently come to specify a distinct lifestyle, this identity is not absolute across time and cultures. As French philosopher Michel Foucault explains in *The History of Sexuality*, the category of "homosexual person" did not appear in the West until the end of the nineteenth century, when Freudian psychoanalysis, among other institutional forces, changed a loose set of behaviors into a single pathology. Foucault writes, "[T]he homosexual became a personage, a past, a case history and a childhood, in addition to being a type of life, a life form, and a morphology, with an indiscreet anatomy and possibly a mysterious physiology" (Foucault 1990, 43). In other words, while today homosexual acts are considered indicative of a specific social and political identity, this was not always the case. Same-sex desire should not be read uniformly as evidence of a more or less repressed lesbian or gay persona.

The process of deriving a homosexual personality from specific sex acts, moreover, did not occur in Japan until the introduction of Western sexology and psychology, and even then it developed slowly. Historian Gregory Pflugfelder argues that before Japanese society opened to the West in 1868, "the notion that each individual possesses a deeply rooted personal identity based on the biological sex of the preferred sexual object or objects . . . held no currency in Japan" (Pflugfelder 1999, 5–6). While Pflugfelder's study concentrates on the nineteenth century, he also argues that even in the 1920s and 1930s designations of "homosexual" or "heterosexual" were not absolute signifiers of social identity as they are today. Girls who engaged in same-sex relationships were not "lesbians" in the twenty-first-century sense of the word, nor were they necessarily rebelling against a society where heterosexuality is the norm. While Pfulgfelder's study concerns male-male relationships, primarily in the Edo period (1600–1868), many of his conclusions regarding the study of sexuality in twentieth-century Japan are relevant to the discussion of female-female relations as well. Pflugfelder explains that even after the introduction of Western psychology and sexology in the early twentieth century, older traditions, which considered some forms of homosexual activity normal or beneficial, still persisted.

> When in 1935 the sexologist Tokutarō Yasuda described same-sex crushes among contemporary schoolgirls, he similarly noted that it was at times difficult to distinguish "scientifically" between "normal" and "perverse" behavior. The possibility that some forms of "same-sex love" might be in fact "normal" found seeming confirmation not only in the nonpathologizing manner in which earlier native discourses had represented them, but also in more recent theories, such as those of Freud, that framed them as a necessary, or at least harmless, part of psychosexual development. (Pflugfelder 1999, 287)

Through the 1920s and 1930s, homosexual acts or desires did not necessarily preclude eventual heterosexual marriage. Sabine Frühstück similarly concludes that same-sex relationships between students at all-girls' schools were widely considered a normal part of female development. She quotes pioneering sexologist Senji Yama-moto as claiming that the affection girls displayed for each other was "harmless" (Frühstück 2003, 70). Whereas today, same-sex behaviors or desires among girls are often read as subverting or rebelling against a patriarchal order, in prewar Japan these relationships were an accepted means of delaying heterosexual experience until girls were old enough for marriage. The girl-girl romances of girls' magazines were nearly always within the context of girls' schools and did not imply rebellion against the patriarchy or a hidden feminist agenda. For this reason, rather than using misleading terms such as homosexual or lesbian, I will henceforth use the Japanese term *dōseiai* (same-sex love).

Japanese prewar society condoned same-sex relationships between girls, but only within the context of a larger homosocial group, usually an all-girls' school, and only as long as both girls maintained a feminine appearance. Jennifer Robertson explains that sexologists condemned and pathologized what she calls a "heterogender" rela-tionship, meaning that one of the female partners adopted masculine clothing, speech, or behavior (Robertson 1998, 68). The all-girl Takarazuka Revue theater troupe was particularly prone to such criticism because it featured cross-dressed female stars. In the 1920s and 1930s, the revue was frequently attacked in the mainstream media for provoking heterogender relationships, which were considered deviant.[2] Still, in her overview of sexology of the prewar period, Robertson acknowledges that dōseiai was not only accepted, but lauded. She writes, "Overall, it seems that much more print space was devoted to defending the typicality and relative 'normality' of dōseiai (homogen-der) relationships among shōjo and to insisting on their—ideally, at least—platonic character" (Robertson 1998, 69). Dōseiai relationships were premised on sameness (the *dō* of dōseiai). Another common term for this kind of bond between girls was *S kankei* (S relationships), in which the S stood for the English word "sister." It was a coupling not merely with someone of the same sex, but with one who exhibited the same modes of dress, speech, and behavior. The uniforms girl students wore, usually some variation on the sailor suit with a blue pleated skirt, contributed to this ideal of sameness in that they promoted a similar appearance among schoolgirls. The dōseiai relationship celebrated in girls' magazines was between two girls who were not only feminine, but who dressed exactly alike. The ideal of dōseiai encouraged sameness, loving the one who looks just like the self.[3]

The prominence of dōseiai in prewar girls' culture, then, should not be read uncritically in terms of twenty-first-century lesbian identity.[4] The significance of prewar girls' magazines was not their rebellious or subversive potential, but the creation of a private space for girls to support each other through adolescence. Although the magazines were edited and controlled primarily by men and subject to strict state censorship, the prominence of a few young women contributors lent the magazines an air of authenticity and gave the impression that in these magazines, at least, girls were representing themselves. This impression much later contributed to young women artists and writers' taking over production of shōjo manga in girls' magazines in the 1970s. The private world of girls' magazines was a powerful means of engaging girl readers from the 1920s through the 1960s. It was powerful because it constructed the narrative and aesthetic style that encouraged girls to recognize texts addressed to them.

Prewar girls' magazines were able to create a private world for girls by evading heterosexual romance, that is, through emphasizing dōseiai relationships. The illustrations that accompanied these stories also reinforced an aesthetic of sameness. The illustrator whose work would come to be most closely associated with girls' magazines and who would have a lasting impact on the look of postwar shōjo manga was Jun'ichi Nakahara (1913–1983).[5] Many of Nakahara's illustrations feature girls in pairs, fitting for the stories of dōseiai he was illustrating. Girls with similar facial features and wearing identical uniforms strike poses that reflect their close emotional bonds.

Even when Nakahara's figures appeared individually, the uniformity of the girls' faces indicates an aesthetic of sameness. Nakahara's other contribution to shōjo aesthetics was his style of drawing girls who had hugely exaggerated eyes, with many highlights and thick lashes. In the postwar period, the large eyes became associated in manga with the emphasis on sentiment and the exploration of interiority.

As shōjo manga entered a period of creativity in the 1970s, artists and writers continued to employ many of the aesthetic and narrative features developed in prewar girls' magazines: not just hugely exaggerated eyes and elongated limbs, but a tendency to make the people in romantic couples resemble each other. Girls' magazines left shōjo manga not only a private space for discourse about the experience of female adolescence, but also the generic conventions that could not easily accommodate heterosexual or heterogender desire and romance.

Although same-sex love among schoolgirls continued to appear, by the early 1970s girl-girl relationships were eclipsed in popularity by portrayals of boy-boy love, which also operated within an aesthetic of sameness. Dōseiai allowed writers to create nonthreatening love stories, and by making the characters boys rather than girls, writers could infuse the stories with far more sensuality and blatant eroticism than

Sameness, uniformity, and same-sex romance in an illustration by Jun'ichi Nakahara, *Shōjo no tomo*, **March 1938.** (Copyright Jun'ichi Nakahara, Himawariya, reprinted Endo 41)

previously seen in prewar magazines. Midori Matsui, in her essay "Little Girls Were Little Boys," argues that the stories of dōseiai among beautiful boys (*bishōnen*) stage the repressed desires of the female readers: "It was apparent that the boys were the girls' displaced selves; despite the feminine looks that belied their identity, however, the fictitious boys were endowed with reason, eloquence, and aggressive desire for the other, compensating for the lack of logos and sexuality in the conventional portraits of girls" (Matsui 1993, 178). As Matsui suggests, the boy characters in these manga invite the girl readers to identify with them because of their feminine appearance, marked with ectomorphic bodies, long flowing hair, and huge eyes. Even in shōjo manga stories that portray heterosexual love, the male or female characters, or both, often magically change sex or cross-dress. The appearance of male characters in shōjo manga in the 1970s did not reconcile girls' romantic fantasies with patriarchal society, but as in the Takarazuka Revue, domesticated the male body within the homogender world of shōjo culture.

Homogender romance in Riyoko Ikeda's *Berusaiyu no bara* (*The Rose of Versailles*, originally serialized in *Margaret*, 1972). In this scene, Oscar admits her love for Andre. Notice the similarity of facial features, hair, and clothing (2004, 4: 247). (Copyright Riyoko Ikeda Production)

In classic shōjo manga, the romantic couples, no matter what their biological sex, often share feminine features and have similar faces and bodies. An example of this is *Berusaiyu no bara* (*The Rose of Versailles*) by Riyoko Ikeda (serialized in *Margaret* 1972). Although the story was begun as a biography of Marie Antoinette, the title character was soon eclipsed by the fictional Oscar, a girl raised as a boy who becomes the captain of the queen's guard. Although Oscar gains power and prestige as a result of her masculine attire and bearing, she is tormented by her ambivalent gender when it comes to marriage. Indeed, she only allows herself to feel romantic and sexual desire for her longtime sidekick, Andre, after his physical appearance has been altered to more closely resemble her own.

When Oscar finally consents to marry Andre, she describes the two of them as the mythological twins Castor and Pollux, and he responds by referring to himself as her shadow (Ikeda 2004, 4: 292). In this case, the relationship is heterosexual but homogendered; the similarity of the characters enables them to enter into a romantic relationship as equals.

In stories of heterosexual but heterogender romance in classic shōjo manga, the female character inevitably loses her sexual and social agency. Yukari Fujimoto points out that at the heart of many classic shōjo manga stories is a girl who finds her identity and self-worth through a close emotional bond with a boy (Fujimoto 1998, 12). The shōjo manga heroine sees herself as awkward and ugly, but she always finds a boy who loves her anyway, in spite of her defects. Thanks to his love, she finds the courage to do anything because she is not doing it for herself, she is doing it for him. Having made passivity a virtue, the only way a girl can find true love is by sacrificing herself to her boy, saying, "His happiness is my happiness"; Fujimoto calls this the "love trap" (1998, 114). The girl protagonists that emerge are relentlessly passive; even characters who seem energetic or self-aware can never escape the love trap. Dōseiai stories, or stories of single-gender relationships, allowed writers to avoid the love trap and invest characters with agency. At the same time, dōseiai allowed girls to express their sexual desires safely, while maintaining the physical purity and innocence required of shōjo.

Narrating the Shōjo Self

Along with a tendency to depict single-gender relationships and an aesthetic preference for sameness, shōjo manga also inherited from prewar girls' magazines a narrative style that emphasized emotional interiority. As shōjo manga developed in the 1970s, this expression of emotion became an exploration of psychological interiority. This narrative emphasis on the deep self also found expression in the visual style, which used a layered panel arrangement to create the illusion of depth.

The author most closely associated with creating a recognizable prose style in girls' magazines is Nobuko Yoshiya (1896–1973), a prolific writer in the 1920s and 1930s whose stories of dōseiai and of female friendships had a direct impact on later shōjo manga. Her distinctive narrative style with its gentle tone of nostalgia, lyrical descriptions of beauty, and polite, feminine diction seemed to be an authentic expression of the innocence and purity of the shōjo identity. Her most popular and influential work is *Hana monogatari* (Flower Tales), a massive collection of vignettes, each named after a flower. These stories were originally published in girls' magazines between 1916 and 1924 and were subsequently compiled into a three-volume collection in 1934. Yoshiya's prose is filled with words such as "delicate," "slender," "lithe," and "exquisite," echoing the aesthetic of the ideal girl image seen in Jun'ichi Nakahara's artwork. For example, one story, "Sazanka" (Camellia), begins as follows:

> The tale I am now going to relate is about an outstanding poetess named Ruriko.
> "The flower of memory that blooms in my breast is the camellia."
> That modest flower possessed of a splendid simplicity. Oh, that thing whose every petal appeared to me like the whisper of a beautifully refined lyric poem—
> Many years ago, I had an elder sister with graceful eyebrows who tragically passed on while still quite young. (Yoshiya 2003a, 1: 32)

Words such as "refined" (*yukashii*), "lyrical" (*jojō*), "tragic" (*itamashii*), and "graceful" (*uruwashii*) appear with great frequency in Yoshiya's prose. Yoshiya also tends to repeat certain phrases and words two or three times to heighten the emotional impact. Her narration has a breathless, rushed tone, as if the narrator is so caught up in passion of the moment that she can barely express herself. Many of the sentences are fragments held together with ellipses or dashes or left dangling in successive rows, like poetry. In this example from *Yaneura no ni shōjo* (The Two Girls in the Attic),[6] the protagonist, Akiko, returns from visiting relatives in the country to the boarding house room where she has a dōseiai relationship with Akitsu.

> Akiko left behind the morning of the country town railway station and departed for the capital.
> Aah, her distant freedom!
> At once Akiko's chest swelled in anticipation.
> [. . .]
> —Ah! To the attic!
> —Oh! To the triangular blue room!
> —To the attic! To the attic!
> The locomotive ran along on Akiko's fevered imaginings and tears of longing.
> The locomotive came to rest at the station in the capital—the pain of separation lessened with every passing moment. (Yoshiya 2003b, 256)

This repetition of words and use of dangling phrases creates a style approaching poetry. Shōjo manga writers appropriated this prose style as a means of expressing the inner thoughts of the main character. The throbbing, palpitating excitement, readily flowing tears, and lushly blooming flowers of Yoshiya's fiction allowed the expression of the passions of teenage girlhood in ways that were not only acceptable to authority figures but also aesthetically pleasing to girls themselves. This narrative style became as recognizable a feature of shōjo manga as the large eyes and willowy limbs of Nakahara's illustrations.

In shōjo manga, the fragmented narration expressing the emotions of the main character became a means of exploring the character's interiority. Eiji Ōtsuka argues that extensive use of interior monologue is the fundamental difference between shōjo manga and shōnen (boys') manga, as well as other action-oriented genres in which the story progresses through dialogue (Ōtsuka 1994, 60). Furthermore, shōjo manga usually do not feature third-person narration. The interior monologue of the main character appears outside word or thought balloons; this approximates voice-over in film or first-person narration in the novel.[7] Ōtsuka states that, therefore, in shōjo manga, the feelings of the characters become as important as the dialogue, and the reader is drawn into the inner world of the characters (Ōtsuka 1994, 61). As in girls' magazines, the emotional lives of teenage girls are given weight and significance. Interior monologue remains one of the dominant modes of expression in comics by women artists, even when those artists have moved beyond the bounds of classic shōjo manga in other ways.

The exploration of interiority in shōjo manga also encourages the reader to identify with the main character. The inducement to identification is an inherent part of the comics medium, which shōjo manga exploits. In forms of visual narrative that rely on photographed images, such as film or video, the viewer's primary identification is with the camera; identification with the characters on screen is secondary. In comics, on the other hand, as Scott McCloud points out, the more generalized or iconic quality of the drawn face has the effect of drawing the reader in (McCloud 1993, 36). McCloud also points out that Japanese comics, which often juxtapose a simply drawn or "cartoony" figure against a more detailed background, emphasize this effect (1993, 37); shōjo manga often use this technique. According to McCloud, this contrast encourages the reader to identify with the characters. In this case, that identification by the reader complements shōjo manga's exploration of the subjectivity of teenage girls.

As part of the attempt to invest shōjo manga with emotional depth, the artists of 1970s shōjo manga created a three-dimensional effect on the page through layering. This can refer to layering panels on top of each other; laying dialog, narration, or sound effects over two or more panels; or laying the faces or full bodies on top of or beside other panels.

In addition, artists also made liberal use of white space and diagonal lines, with the result that the panels appear splintered or exploded, while characters and scenes appear to float in space. Because the stories emphasize emotion and are not action-oriented, the composition of the panels is intended to create a mood rather than to guide the reader's eye from one moment of action to the next. The effect is dreamy and nonlinear, which is appropriate to the tone of the stories, and illustrates the inner psychology of the shōjo characters. The use of layering to create depth is analogous to the narrative attempt to give the characters emotional and psychological depth.

Flat and Superflat

While the extensive use of layering and the lyrical, emotional prose style inherited from Nobuko Yoshiya both suggest a preoccupation with depth, the reliance on dōseiai generic conventions and an aesthetic of sameness has, in the long run, frustrated the attempt to bring depth to shōjo manga. One of the central generic tensions in shōjo manga is between flatness and depth; on the one side, there is the two-dimensionality of the manga medium and the uniformity of dōseiai and single-gender romance, while on the other side artists desire to depict depth of character and emotion, as well as to present heterosexual romance in a believable, satisfying way. As shōjo manga has continued to change, some artists, including Taku Tsumugi and Ai Yonezawa, have continued to experiment with depth and layering, but a significant number of artists, most notably Kiriko Nananan, have moved in the direction of visual flatness, while still favoring emotional depth. This perhaps signals a change in the meaning of flatness, both visual and psychological, in the context of contemporary Japanese popular culture.

Since the 1990s, shōjo manga, especially stories aimed at older readers, have shown a marked decline in the use of layering. Some new female artists, including Moyoko Anno, Kyuta Minami, Kiriko Nananan, and Erika Sakurazawa, have created a new visual style as part of their attempt to appeal to an older audience by using the shōjo manga genre to show contemporary heterosexual dating and sex realistically. Nozomi Masuda refers to this new style as "flat" because it does not use layering. She argues

**Classic shōjo manga composition showing the use of layering, open panels,
and an emotive flower motif, from Keiko Takemiya's *Kaze to ki no uta*
(The Poem of the Wind and the Tree, 1976) (1993, 1: 310).** (Copyright Keiko Takemiya)

that in writing manga aimed at readers in their twenties and thirties, these artists have tended to create stories that emphasize action over interior monologue. For this reason, they have not only used layering less, but they have tended to draw contiguous panels, eliminating the white space in between (Masuda 2002, 112). According to Masuda, whereas layering created an effect that was emotional, dreamy, and nonrational, the flat style is more orderly, action-oriented, and implies speed (2002, 115). Certainly, some shōjo manga artists have moved away from some elements of classic shōjo manga in favor of action manga styles. However, although these artists tend to favor square or rectangular panels over diagonals and a more linear approach over layering, they still make extensive use of interior monologue outside word balloons, indicating that they are still interested in the interiority of the main characters. In this regard, the term "flat" refers only to the visual style; if anything, the stories have greater psychological depth and realism than classic shōjo manga.

However, Masuda's use of the term "flat" in relation to contemporary shōjo manga is worth considering in regard to trends in Japanese popular culture generally. Some social critics of Japan have used the word "flat" in the sense of "meaningless" or "lacking content" to describe post-bubble Japan, implying an emotional emptiness or anomie. In her essay "Between the Technique of Living an Endless Routine and the Madness of Absolute Degree Zero," Yumiko Iida claims that Japan in the 1990s experienced a "representation crisis." She writes, "This crisis concerns the increasingly visible gap, an allegorical failure between . . . the form and its content, between the image and its substance" (Iida 2002, 455). This lack, she argues, is what allows for all kinds of antisocial behaviors, from *enjo kōsai* ("compensated dating," a euphemism for teenage prostitution) to the Aum Shinrikyō sarin gas attack. In this light, flatness can refer to the loss of meaning inherent to the postmodern condition.

The more prominent recent use of the term "flat," however, is in artist Takashi Murakami's "Superflat Manifesto," written in conjunction with the Superflat art exhibition he curated in 2000. Murakami begins his one-page manifesto with the lines, "Japan is perhaps the world's future. And Japan's present is superflat" (Murakami 2000, 4).[8] On the most literal level, superflat refers to the two-dimensional nature of certain types of Japanese art, most prominently nihonga and manga/anime. Murakami argues that this two-dimensionality is one of the defining characteristics of Japanese art and links classical and modern styles; for this reason he includes eighteenth-century screen paintings in this mostly avant-garde collection. Murakami argues even further that this different artistic tradition causes Japanese and American viewers to perceive realism in two-dimensional images differently. Taking video games as his example, he argues, "one [the American] finds realism in looking at the photograph of a living person, while the other [the Japanese] finds realism in the movements of a three-dimensional polygon figure that resembles a human" (2000, 123). Murakami points to the tendency of Japanese audiences to perceive two-dimensional manga, anime, and video game characters as extremely realistic and hints that the current popularity of anime in the United States is "training the American eye" to appreciate superflat realism (2000, 123).

In coining the term superflat, however, Murakami refers to a larger social phenomenon beyond the realm of high art. In his manifesto, Murakami elaborates, "One way to imagine superflatness is to think of the moment when, in creating a desktop graphic for your computer, you merge a number of distinct layers into one" (2000, 5). He goes on to explain that this flattening of accreted layers occurs not only in art, but also in postmodern pop culture in general, which is capable of homogenizing and domesticating any and all cultural objects or influences. Murakami ends his introduction by bringing the concept of superflatness to the real world: "No one has yet taken a serious look at the image resulting from the integration of layers of entertainment and art. But that integration is already occurring. Much integration is still under way. That integration is producing yet another 'superflat' image: us" (2000, 25). Thus, Murakami's description of Japan as "flat," like Iida's, derives from a basic idea of confusion between signifier and signified; rather than an empty gap, however, he sees the conflation of ideas, capable of forming new meanings.

In a commentary on Murakami's art, Hiroki Azuma draws connections between superflat and Western, particularly French, critical theory. Azuma sees in the superflat rejection of linear perspective an expression of Derrida's "spectre" or Baudrillard's "simulacrum" (Murakami 2000, 147). Taking Azuma's analysis further, if three-dimensional perspective in art is connected to Western philosophy and the idea of transcendence, then perhaps two-dimensionality is an expression of what Deleuze termed "immanence," in which there is nothing outside life and our experiences. Furthermore, Deleuze posits that the perceived differences between subject and object, inside and outside, and surface and depth, are false binaries; instead, he suggests the "fold" as an alternative topology that creates a network of relationships without resorting to dualist concepts (Deleuze 1993). In this light, then, superflat is an expression not of some gap or lack in meaning, as Iida suggests, but an expression of multiplicity within a single immanent plane of being. Experimental shōjo manga artists' embrace of flatness can be read as more than a simple attempt to escape the generic tendency toward fantasy and dreaminess. It becomes a means of reviving critical themes in a genre that has become formulaic.

Black Eyes and *blue*: Refiguring Shōjo Manga

blue by Kiriko Nananan is an example of an experimental work that plays with many of the generic markers of shōjo manga. The plot of *blue* concerns a dōseiai romance between two students, Kayako and Masami, at an all-girls' high school. Nananan illustrates this very conventional dōseiai narrative with an unusually flat, unornamented art style. By breaking the link between standard shōjo narratives and standard shōjo manga art style, she is able to give her story a remarkable freshness and a surprising level of emotional and psychological depth. In other words, Nananan breathes new life into a standard shōjo manga story by embracing the limitations of the genre, namely, sameness and flatness.

Nananan's artwork lacks many of the aesthetic traits of classic shōjo manga but still evokes the sentimental mood associated with the genre. She uses closed, rectangular

blue. **Another dramatic departure in aesthetic style from classic shōjo manga is the way Nananan deliberately hides the girls' faces, When Kayako and Masami kiss for the first time, their faces are obscured, but the left middle panel highlights their hands, which express their emotions (Nananan 1997, 68–69).** (Copyright Kiriko Nananan)

panels rather than splintered, opened, or layered ones. Rather than flowers, clouds, or abstract emotive lines, she exclusively uses stark backgrounds, punctuated only with solid black or gray screen tone. The overall impression is of a striking contrast between black and white and of an extremely flat picture plane, because of the lack of background or shading. Within the rectangular frames, however, Nananan makes extensive use of white space, which still imparts a dreamy, floating atmosphere, even without accompanying flower or cloud motifs. In spite of the flatness of the art style, the combination of the extensive use of empty space with the standard dōseiai story imparts a sense of longing and nostalgia.

Another dramatic departure in aesthetic style from classic shōjo manga is the way Nananan deliberately hides or obscures the girls' faces. The faces tend to be obscured most often during emotional high points in the story. For instance, when the girls kiss for the first time, their faces are completely obscured.

Nananan also frequently shows only the lower half of the face or the back of the head in a panel. The careful arrangement of the figures frustrates the reader's attempt to identify with the characters. More significantly, by obscuring the face, Nananan hides the characters' eyes. Even when the eyes are visible, they are quite small, black, and flat, without any of the highlights usually associated with shōjo manga.

The huge, starry eyes of both male and female characters are one of the most important generic traits of shōjo manga. The large eyes not only impel the reader to identify and empathize with the characters, but also signal a thematic interest in the characters' emotional lives. Both visually and narratively, the large eyes are another example of the attempt to add depth to shōjo manga.[9] Azuma points out that the stylized manga/anime eye has become more than a simple representation of a body part, but an "object of empathy" (Murakami 2000, 149). Because of their symbolic, overdetermined status, however, Azuma argues, the eyes of anime characters do not "look back" in the way that viewers might expect in more mimetic art styles. Azuma takes the proliferation of anime eyes in Murakami's art as another example of the Derridean "spectral"; he writes, "[W]e are unsure whether they are living or dead, watching or being watched" (Murakami 2000, 151). Because the manga/anime eye is so ubiquitous and symbolic, *blue* cannot exist outside the generic conventions that call for it; even the absence of the eye is overdetermined.

By obscuring the faces and making the eyes flat and unreflective, Nananan also forces the reader to look to other body parts, or to other images in the frame, for expression of emotion. Furthermore, by drawing a flat rather than a symbolic eye, she reorients the body of the shōjo manga character so that all body parts can be equally expressive. In particular, the girls' hands become one means of conveying emotion. For instance, on the double-page spread just after the girls kiss, the middle left frame shows their fingers slightly entwined. While classic shōjo manga would have shown the characters looking meaningfully into each others' eyes, here the entwined fingers speak to the girls' hesitant desire. Later, when Kayako sleeps over at Masami's house, there are several close-ups on the girls' hands with their fingers entwined, emphasizing their growing friendship (Nananan 1998, 90–91). When they argue, there is a close-up of Kayako pushing Masami's hand away (Nananan 1997, 145), then of her pulling her wrist out of Masami's grip. In obscuring the eyes, Nananan does not forsake sentiment; instead, she moves the emotional symbolism to the hands. The very simple line drawings of hands suggest an emotional response equal to any in shōjo manga, in spite of the very flat picture plane.

Although the art style is flat and the narrative is sparse, the extensive use of interior monologue, placed outside word balloons, highlights sentiment and connects *blue* to the shōjo manga genre. As in classic shōjo manga, the interior monologue outside word balloons approximates the first-person narration of Kayako in her relationship with Masami, and *blue* operates on a discourse of longing, nostalgia, and purity. The disconnect between the depth of the characters' emotion and the flatness of the drawings gives the manga a melancholy tone. The standard dōseiai theme paired with a non-shōjo manga art style also invites the reader to feel a sense of slightly jarring, displaced recognition. Indeed, this may be Nananan's purpose. *blue* originally appeared in the manga magazine *Comic Are!*, which is aimed at adult readers and not associated exclusively with the shōjo manga genre. Although *blue* is a story about teenage girls, it appeared in a magazine marketed to readers in their twenties and thirties. These readers might consider the conventional aesthetic style of shōjo manga trite or childish, but they embrace the sentiment of shōjo manga with nostalgia.

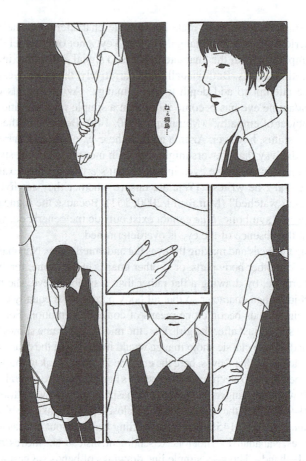

blue. **The central composition highlights the motion of Kayako's hand as she pulls it out of Masami's grip when they argue. The hands here stand in for the eyes, which are conspicuously concealed in the lower middle panel (1997, 154).** (Copyright Kiriko Nananan)

Nananan makes this standard shōjo story relevant to older readers both through her flat art style and by combining the rhetoric of shōjo sentiment with the harsh realities of contemporary high school life. Toward the end, in an interior monologue scattered in fragments over a completely empty page, Kayako's thoughts read: "I'm sure we are completely pure/That's all/And even if we have done dirty things/Are they really so bad?" (Nananan 1997, 172). As Kayako implies, the girls are far from "pure" in the strictest physical sense. Masami has had an affair with a much older, married man, become pregnant with his child, and had an abortion. Even Kayako, the more innocent of the two, casually loses her virginity to a boy she hardly knows. By the standards of shōjo culture, which emphasizes the purity and innocence of virginity above all else, the girls are certainly "dirty." But Kayako rejects this judgment, saying, "If you love someone, no matter who it is, you can't help yourself. You're not the only one. It's not your fault" (Nananan 1997, 168). Nananan inserts the uncomfortable reality of unhappy sexual relationships into the standard shōjo manga story, but by affirming the spiritual purity of the shōjo characters, she reassures her readers that even if they are not virgins, they are still shōjo. Moreover, by making the dōseiai relationship the center of the plot, she reaffirms the importance of love, even when heterosexual love proves disappointing.[10]

Contemporary shōjo manga and its many generic offshoots, including experimental manga based on shōjo conventions, are a key site of cultural production in Japan. They provide a space for women artists to explore the tensions and contradictions of shōjo identity. This medium would not have existed without prewar girls' magazines, which developed a narrative and aesthetic idiom for the private discourse on girlhood. But with this legacy, shōjo manga also inherited certain generic limitations from girls' magazines, in particular a reliance on sameness and certain difficulties in portraying realistic heterosexual romance narratives. In *blue*, Nananan responds to those limitations not by challenging or inverting them, but by expanding and magnifying them, using flatness and dōseiai to create a more sophisticated, socially relevant story that still speaks to female readers, even if they have outgrown the shōjo manga stories of their teen years.

Notes

1. The few critics writing on shōjo manga in English include Jennifer Robertson, Midori Matsui, and Mizuki Takahashi. One factor contributing to this critical neglect might include the tendency, both in Japan and in the United States, to disregard or disparage the culture of teenage girls. Another factor might be the cultural bias in the United States that has designated the comic book medium as an exclusively male domain, which has until recently limited the importation and translation of shōjo manga.

2. For example, see Robertson's description of the failed love suicide between Eriko Saijo and Yasumare Masuda (Robertson 1998, 194–196).

3. This affinity for sameness and the desire to erase or reject difference also relates to Japan's imperial expansion of the 1920s and 1930s. Robertson argues that masculinization of the cross-dressed Takarazuka star was similar to the way in which the colonial subject was supposed to become Japanese (91). Just as the Greater East Asia Co-Prosperity Sphere was based on ideas of the sameness of all Asians within the Japanese empire, so too was the assimilation of the threatening other carried out at home. Robertson writes, "This vision of co-prosperity was premised on a doctrine of assimilation (*dōka*, lit. "same-ization"), or Japanization (*Nipponka*), which, by the 1930s, was a central issue in Japanese colonial affairs" (Robertson 1998, 92). In other words, dōseiai and dōka, or assimilation of colonial subjects, are homologous and complementary systems. This is true not only in the Takarazuka Revue but in girls' magazines as well. While a thorough investigation of colonial ideology in relation to girls' magazines is beyond the scope of this chapter, I hypothesize that girls' magazines promoted an ideal of sameness not only of gender but of national identity as well, and that this ideology of sameness continues to haunt shōjo manga and girls' culture in general.

4. For an example of the equation of dōseiai with a subversive lesbian ideology, see Sarah Fredericks's discussion of Nobuko Yoshiya (Fredericks 2000).

5. Nakahara also married a Takarazuka star, another indication of the level of his participation in the world of shōjo culture.

6. According to Nobara Takemoto's notes on the reprinted edition of the novel, although the word shōjo in the title is written with kanji that now mean "virgin," at the time it was simply another word for girl, implying a general sense of innocence rather than specifically referring to sexual experience (Yoshiya 2003b, 327 n. 29). The English word "maiden" is perhaps a better translation.

7. Contrast this to the style of narration in American superhero comics by Stan Lee and Jack Kirby, in which the characters' thoughts are represented in cloud-like balloons pointing at their heads, and exposition of the plot appears in square boxes. This style is approximate to third-person omniscient narration.

8. "Nihon wa sekai no mirai ka mo shirenai. Soshite, Nihon no ima wa superflat." Murakami uses the English words in Roman letters. The English translation provided with the bilingual book *Superflat* written in conjunction with the exhibition compresses the original two sentences into one: "The world of the future might be like Japan is today—superflat" (Murakami 200, 5).

9. The appearance of large starry eyes not only in shōjo manga but also in some shōnen and seinen manga and anime is also an indicator of the relative importance of emotion versus action within a given story; boys' genres are frequently no less melodramatic than girls'.

10. The relationship between dōseiai and homosexuality has become complicated as Japan has taken on the Western concept of the homosexual person. I have heard anecdotally that some self-identified lesbians have embraced *blue* as a lesbian text. While some readers are perhaps unaware of the history of sexual relationships in prewar Japan, this history does not preclude a more subversive reading.

7

Intellectuals, Cartoons, and Nationalism During the Russo-Japanese War

YULIA MIKHAILOVA

Japanese studies scholars have recently highlighted how the formation of a cultural canon led to the creation of a distinctive national identity during the rise of Japanese nationalism in the Meiji /Taishō periods (1868–1926). Often the approach centers on high culture and the fine arts. For example, Christine Guth has shown how Takashi Masuda (1848–1938), the wealthy industrialist who headed the Mitsui financial combine and an avid art collector, helped define modern Japanese self-identity by collecting and identifying the key master artists and masterpieces of Japanese art. Masuda created what was, in effect, an authoritative canon of classical Japanese art that rivaled what he had seen in his travels to the museums and palaces of Europe. Guth argues that art collections like Masuda's played a vital role in creating a clearly defined sense of Japan's own unique culture, which was not only a source of pride, but also seen as constituting an inherently distinctive cultural identity—a visual and material archive that distinguished the Japanese national essence (*kokutai*) (Guth 1993; 1997, 35). Moreover, it remains powerful today, as evidenced in Japanese tourism advertising with its pictures of the tea ceremony, Zen gardens, famous Buddhist sculptures, and so on.

And yet, while art collecting and museum building were important for forging Japanese identity and, by extension, modern nationalism, other artistic practices also critical for defining Japanese national identity were at work. One new cultural form that Western scholarship has generally overlooked is the political cartoon. Political cartoons are often dismissed as "low" art, especially when compared to literature and painting. However, since they appealed not only to the intellect, but also to the emotions, political cartoons attracted a wide popular audience. As a means for whipping up fervent, often chauvinistic sentiments that quickly spread among the masses through newspapers and weekly magazines, they became a major force in shaping popular opinion.[1]

In this essay, I first examine how a new genre of political cartoons was born in Meiji Japan by combining comic pictures of the Edo period with the imported Western art form of the caricature. Second, I argue that political cartoons acquired a particularly significant political role during the Russo-Japanese War (1904–1905). Here, it is important to recognize that political cartoons benefited from the new power of the mass print media in which they occupied a prominent place. As James L. Huffman has argued, following Benedict Anderson, these new newspapers and magazines played a key role in creating modern Japan's "imagined community" (Huffman 1997). Widely published in popular magazines and newspapers of the time, they were instrumental in shaping Japanese nationalistic sentiment. Third, as other scholars have argued, defining "the other" is critical in stimulating the quest for national identity and a nationalistic spirit (Hijiya-Kirschnereit 2000, 81). In the Japanese case political cartoons were essential for defining "us" against "them" and constructing a sense of Japaneseness. They visually identified the foreign "other" against which the Japanese defined themselves, Japanese nationhood, and nationalism by the end of Meiji.

Many scholars have noted how vital Japan's victory in the Russo-Japanese War was for the building of the modern Japanese state (Wray and Conroy 1983, 150–157; Iriye, 1989, 777). Less clear is the psychological mechanism that lay behind it. Cartoons in comic magazines and newspapers reveal their artists' views about Japan's domestic and foreign policies that inexorably led to armed conflict with Russia. Cartoonists conveyed not only their own observations, but also simultaneously reflected and formed popular opinion, shaping the way their readers viewed the events.

Political cartoons were inspired by the unease caused by the period's tumultuous events. On the domestic front, such events included the cultural dislocation caused by the opening of the country to the West in the Meiji period and Japan's domestic political instability over establishing a parliamentary system. The humiliation of the unequal treaties, Japan's precarious position in an international arena where the law of the jungle prevailed, its domestic political instability over establishing a parliamentary system, its war with China, and, ultimately, its conflict with Russia, were the main themes in the political cartoons of Meiji Japan.

Like other contemporary forms of Japanese visual culture, political cartoons synthesized graphic conventions from two sources: indigenous art illustrations from the earlier Edo period and cartoons from the West. It is remarkable that the development of this new cartoon style coincided with Japan's political triumph at the end of Meiji when it became a new "power" on the international stage. The new political cartoons were especially effective in achieving the "great national goal." They were instrumental in two important ways. First, they incited passion among their readers, effectively antagonizing them against Russia. Second, they peddled a self-serving positive image of Japan, successfully instilling in Japanese a powerful sense of national pride as citizens (*kokumin*) of the new nation-state. Cartoons had a huge impact because they took advantage of the new print technologies that allowed for mass communication. How did this happen?

The Formative Years

In the Edo period, Japan had a rich visual culture including aristocratic paintings in *yamato-e* style, *ukiyo-e* pictures, which served the tastes of merchants and other town-dwellers, as well as various comic pictures (*warai-e*) that enjoyed great popularity among the people, but were considered second-rate. There was no one single word to name them, but they were known by such terms as *toba-e* (comic pictures first designed by the Buddhist priest Toba), *hyakki yagyū* (hundred demons walking in the night), *hyakumensō* (one hundred faces), *numazu-e* (pictures with catfish), *odoke-e* (funny pictures), and so on. Those pictures were used mainly for entertainment, rather than performing the role of political or social satire.

However, after the unsuccessful Tempō (1841–1843) reforms, Kuniyoshi Utagawa (1797–1861), together with his students, began to draw cartoons criticizing the policy of old Tokugawa period military government (*bakufu*). These pictures represented people who had starved to death as "hungry ghosts" while authorities were ridiculed as "spirits of the dead." Their monstrous figures were marked with the coats of arms of politically powerful figures, such as Tadakuni Mizuno, the principal force behind the Tempō reforms. These pictures quickly spread throughout the country so that authorities had to issue several laws regulating their content. To escape punishment, artists tried harder to draw pictures with ambiguous content that could be interpreted in multiple ways. As pictures critical of the government, they are the predecessors of modern political cartoons (Minami 1999, 2–3).

By the middle of the nineteenth century, European cartoonists already used the zinc letterpress or offset technologies to produce more and better pictures with a sharper contrast between light and shadow. But in Japan, illustrators continued to use traditional woodblock printing until the middle of the Meiji period (Shimizu 1991, 70). Despite this technological lag, as well as official controls over their circulation, woodblock cartoons were widely sold, suggesting that they were a part of mass culture.

It was during the closing stages of the Tokugawa era or *bakumatsu* period that the Japanese first learned about Western-style cartoons. One well-known example is the magazine *Japan Punch*, published by the Englishman Charles Wirgman (1832–1891), who arrived in Yokohama in 1857 as a correspondent for *Illustrated London News*. He married a Japanese woman and worked as a graphic artist for over thirty years. His satirical pictures poked fun at issues like diplomatic relations between the Japanese government and foreigners, and Japanese efforts to imitate exotically new Western manners and customs (Shimizu and Yumoto 1994, 12–13, 22–23, 30–31). Another Western cartoonist who worked in Japan for many years was the Frenchman George Bigot. An art teacher who came to Japan in 1882, Bigot became friends with Chōmin Nakae, one of the leaders of the Movement for Freedom and Popular Rights (1874–1889) who was deeply influenced by French liberal philosophy. Together, Bigot and Nakae founded the satirical magazine *Tobae*. Its satire of Japanese authorities was so biting that, to escape the censors, it had to be published secretly and circulated mainly among the French-speaking community of Tokyo and Yokohama (Shimizu 1991, 81–101). The influence of these foreign artists was multifaceted—they taught the Japanese how to use the new print technologies, such as lithograph and copperplate, how to publish illustrated magazines, and how to select picture topics of everyday life and political events.

The Japanese studied cartoons not only directly from the Western cartoonists mentioned above, but also through imported foreign books and magazines. One of these was the English satirical magazine *Punch*, which inspired Wirgman himself as well as many Japanese. Another example is Thomas James's (1809–1863) English translation of Aesop's fables. A copy of this book was owned by Tazumu Watanabe (1837–1898), a scholar in Dutch studies (*rangaku*) who also taught English. He was the major figure behind the publication of its Japanese translation, which appeared under the title *Tsuzoku isoppu monogatari* in 1873. Illustrations for this book were done by the talented and versatile artist Kyōsai Kawanabe (1831–1889) and showed the artist's unique ability to adapt freely, creating his own illustrations using Japanese stylistic conventions that did not exist in the original (Johnson 1994, 203).

In the early Meiji period, illustrated magazines with cartoons became one of the most popular genres. During 1870–1871 alone, over three hundred satirical magazines appeared, often going out of print after a short while (Ishiko 1979, 78). The cartoons were mostly about Japan's uneasy encounter with the West. Cartoonists brazenly ridiculed the government's pro-Western policy, which they saw as blindly imitating foreign customs. One of these pictures was a witty parody on the policy of *bunmei kaika* (civilization and enlightenment) by Kyōsai Kawanabe. It has the Buddhist deity Fudō together with his two youthful attendants, Kongara Dōji and Seitaka Dōji, dressed like English gentlemen. Fudō is traditionally considered to be the defender of Buddhist doctrine and the protector of the nation who can be called upon in times of crisis. In Kawanabe's cartoon, the Buddhist divinity sits absorbed reading the "*Shimbun zasshi*" (literally, "news magazine") while his two attendants are cooking a red meat dish. As a Buddhist being, Fudō would, of course, have avoided eating red meat, and, if he read anything, it would more likely be a sutra, rather than a modern newspaper. However, the cartoon implicitly questions the new Meiji law of 1872 that deregulated Tokugawa era laws of clerical deportment, including the prohibition on eating meat (Jaffe 2001, 4). As Jordan notes, Kawanabe is suggesting that the rage for occidental things has even reached the top of the hierarchy of the Buddhist pantheon (Jordan 1994, 94).

An important event that further stimulated the development of political cartoons was the Movement for Freedom and Popular Rights (1874–1888). It began when a group of former samurai from Tosa and Hizen domains submitted a petition for the establishment of a representative government, decrease of the land tax, and a revision of the unequal treaties. However, soon the supporters of "popular rights" included merchants and peasants from all over the country and the first political parties were established. In the middle of the 1880s, the movement's ideology instigated several peasant uprisings that were suppressed by the government. On the other hand, promulgation of the constitution in 1889 and establishment of the parliament in 1890 demonstrated that public opinion could really become an influential political force.

The Movement for Freedom and Popular Rights created a politically volatile situation that gave rise to many new illustrated magazines. Some of these switched to Western production technologies to increase their circulation. One of the most famous of these was Fumio Nomura's *Maru maru chimbun*. It was first published in 1877 and enjoyed a wide, loyal readership during its thirty-year run. Nomura was born into a samurai family from Aki province (now Hiroshima prefecture). In his youth, he often copied pictures from the English *Punch*, which, along with Wirgman's work, inspired him to create his own satirical magazine. Nomura was also a pioneer technologically, using a zinc printing press that allowed for the mass publication of five thousand copies of his first issue.

The extraordinary popularity of *Maruchin* (as this magazine was usually called) is partly explained by its feature of humorous or satirical verses and phrases sent in by its readers. Some show popular support for the government's policy of *bunmei kaika*, particularly, the emphasis on universal education, noting its advantages for Japan's modernization. One clever wordplay, published in 1893, averred, "It is the intellect that is the real property, not fields of rice." Another optimistically exclaimed, "Education relieves us from hardships and may even feed you." However, the very fact that these verses appeared in a comic magazine leaves room for speculation that they might be simply ironic, since not everyone admired the new policy of compulsory education. There were also other verses emphasizing the important role of the new mass media. "The power of newspapers moves the hearts of people," proclaimed one such verse published in 1903. On the eve of the war with Russia, an unknown author wrote what he thought of public opinion (*kokuron*): "Public opinion bursts into flames like wood thrown [in the fire]" (Shimizu and Yumoto 1989, 2, 228).

The artists who drew the most pictures for *Maruchin* were Kinkichiro Honda (1851–1921) and Kiyochika Kobayashi (1847–1915). Honda was Nomura's townsman and was sent by Hiroshima authorities to study land surveying at the Ministry of Industry. Simultaneously, he took lessons in Western painting at the school of Shinkurō Kunizawa and began to draw *koma manga* (sets of comic pictures) for the magazine *Kibi dango*. His compositional style imitated the comic strip format found in American newspapers. Unlike many other artists of his time, he had no experience in woodblock prints so he was not bound by the legacy of traditional painting.

Around 1881, Honda collaborated with Fumio Nomura on making cartoon illustrations in support of the Movement for Freedom and Popular Rights. His most famous picture, "Minken toboe" (Barking of the People Rights' Supporters, February 1880), was published when the movement was at its height (Shimizu 1976, 80). The pun in the title comes from the word *minken*, which originally means "people's rights," but is written here with the character for "dog" (*ken*). A huge dog with the word "people's rights" written in English on its tail (a hint at the Western origins of the movement's ideas) leads a crowd of people attacking hapless government officials. This obviously demonstrated the strength of the opposition. Reportedly, the cartoon had a huge impact on the public, urging even more people to join the ranks of "people's rights" supporters. It also shocked the authorities. Surprised by the power that cartoons had over popular opinion, the government promulgated a new law prohibiting antigovernment cartoons (Shimizu 1991, 60).

Kobayashi sympathized with the antigovernment movement and was always ready to criticize the authorities using his pencil and crayon. He even drew several cartoons expressing support to peasants' uprisings in Fukushima (1882) and Chichibu (1884). His political leanings may be partly explained by his background. Kobayashi came from a family of Tokugawa vassals who lost all their privileges and wealth with the rise of the new Meiji imperial government.

Like other cartoonists of the time, Kobayashi often traveled to Yokohama where he studied Western books, particularly those with cartoons, and learned lithographic and copperplate printmaking technology.[2] In 1882, after he began working for *Maruchin*, Kobayashi became acquainted with George Bigot, who also contributed several illustrations to this magazine in 1885. This was a fortuitous meeting that greatly aided Kobayashi's mastery of Western-style cartoon composition.

On March 23, 1889, *Maruchin* published his famous picture "Gokuraku otoshi" (A Trap They Are Enjoying), in which Taisuke Itagaki and Shōjiro Gotō, leaders of the Movement for Freedom and Popular Rights, are depicted caught inside a mousetrap eating food from the hands of officials—an allusion to their trip to Europe made at public expense (Shimizu 1976, 3). This picture was created using a lithograph and crayon technique that made it possible to mass-produce the magazine, thereby substantially increasing its readership. During its heyday, *Maru maru chimbun* was published every Saturday with a print run of 15,000 copies (Ishiko 1979, 80).

Kobayashi often faced legal prosecution for his pictures, and was even imprisoned several times while the magazine was closed under the Law Regulating the Newspapers (1869). Even after the demise of the movement, he continued his political activities by supporting the struggle of the Ashio miners, one of the first signs of a labor movement in Japan (1907). According to Isao Shimizu, Kobayashi was the only artist in Meiji Japan who persistently struggled against governmental oppression. (Shimizu 1982, 3). However, with the outbreak of the Russo-Japanese War, Kobayashi acquiesced in the face of the overwhelming nationalistic fervor of the time, drawing a series of pictures that glorified Japan's victory. Subsequently, he quit drawing political cartoons and focused completely on painting.

Another famous illustrated magazine of the time was *Kokkei shimbun* (Comic Newspaper), founded by Gaikotsu Miyatake (1867–1955), an outstanding journalist and noted historian of popular culture. As a young man, he was fascinated by cartoons after reading a collection of comic songs and verses from *Maruchin*. In 1887, he tried his luck as an artist by founding a small comic magazine in Kyoto called *Tonchi kyōkai zasshi* (The Wit Association Magazine). This quickly made him rich and famous. However, soon after the promulgation of Meiji Constitution in February 1889, his magazine published a cartoon drawn by Ginkō Adachi entitled "Dainihon tonchi kenpō happushiki" (The Promulgation of Laws on How to Polish Wits in Great Japan) (Shimizu 1991, 78). This cartoon openly mocked Emperor Meiji, who had promulgated the constitution. It represented him as a skeleton—*gaikotsu* in Japanese (the word also used as Miyatake's pen name)—standing on a dais and reading a document to members of the Wit Association Magazine. Gaikotsu was fined 100 yen and was imprisoned for three years for his impudence toward imperial authority (*Nihon no manga sanbyakunen* 1996, 61). On his release from jail, he moved to Tokyo and founded another satirical magazine, *Tonchi to kokkei* (Wits and Comics). It poked fun at various social mores. However, the authorities again banned Gaikotsu's magazine because they thought it "destabilized the public morals." The indefatigable Gaikotsu then moved to Osaka and, in 1901, published the *Kokkei shimbun* with a print run of 80,000 copies per issue. This magazine survived much longer that its predecessors, probably because it began at a time of heightened nationalistic fervor during which Japanese ire was directed mainly toward Russia. Although Gaikotsu, one of the most ardent political critics of his generation, tended toward socialism, he was still anti-Russian to the point that his magazine was among the first to publish cartoons calling for war. In this respect, he actively supported the government.

In general, satirical magazines published in the first half of the Meiji period created an image of Japan as a nation torn apart by social and political contradictions. However, as soon as the Japanese realized that the road to parity with the West went not through borrowing Western cultural patterns and political institutions, but rather through successful military conquests, the contents and tone of cartoons changed as well. From then on, artists concentrated their efforts on discussing Japan's place in the international arena. Due to its geographical proximity to Japan and its own growing political presence in the Far East, Russia was destined to play a special role in this discourse.

Nationalistic Fervor

Japan's anxiety over Russia arose with Russia's active alliance with France and Germany in the Triple Intervention (1895), an initiative that robbed Japan of the Liaotung Peninsula, which it had seized in the Sino-Japanese War. The Japanese were also alarmed by the construction of the Trans-Siberian Railway, which ran across Manchurian territory. In 1900, Russia sent troops into Manchuria to suppress the Boxer Rebellion and was in no hurry to withdraw them. In June 1903, seven Tokyo University professors submitted a petition to Prime Minister Tarō Katsura; it stirred additional nationalistic ardor by calling for war against Russia, characterizing this as a just punishment for its deceitful aggression. The *Asahi shimbun* immediately sensationalized this story as major news. In October 1903, when Russia did not abide by the terms of the agreement to withdraw its troops from Manchuria, the chauvinist mood in Japan grew stronger. Several so-called patriotic societies that were blatantly anti-Russian, such as Genyōsha (Dark Ocean Society) or Kokuryūkai (the Amur River Society), became very active. Given the rising tide of war hysteria, no one wanted to buy antiwar newspapers such as *Yorozu chōhō* anymore. With few exceptions, the spirit of the times transformed former pacifists into warmongers. James Huffman has argued that the mass media of the time editorialized "the need for Japan to stand strong on the international arena" by joining the West as an imperialist power (Huffman 1997, 273). Foreign newspapers also whipped up anti-Russian sentiment. This can be seen in the British tabloid *Japan Daily Mail*; it should be recalled that the British government was allied with Japan against Russia. The head of the Japanese Russian Orthodox Church, Archbishop Nikolay, noted of the *Japan Daily Mail* in his diary in the autumn of 1903 that "every issue of this newspaper contained attacks and swear words about Russia, most vile, nasty and malicious" (Nakamura 1994, 324).

The Japanese government also put controls on publicly disseminated information. On October 16, 1903, the Minister of Home Affairs, in accordance with the wishes of Army Headquarters, instructed the editors of the major Tokyo newspapers and magazines that they were prohibited from publishing anything about the present political crisis, particularly news of any troop movements. On January 5, 1904, the Army Ministry instructed newspaper editors that any information "on diplomatic relations or about army and navy activities had to be preliminarily approved" by authorities (Iguchi 1998, 146). Because of this policy, journalists could not give eyewitness accounts of the war. The instructions had the effect of sanitizing their war coverage, producing news reports that triumphantly announced a continuous chain of victories. The reality, however, was far different. Soldiers and sailors experienced grave hardships on the battlefield. The war took a high toll, with over 118,000 combat deaths and a high price tag that left Japan financially exhausted. Yet, the grim news did not appear in newspapers. Most papers took the easy route of selling the war, spinning it as a righteous struggle to protect the Japanese motherland from its belligerent northern neighbor. While rabidly attacking Russia at every opportunity, newspapers flatteringly portrayed Japan as a peace-loving country that was Russia's victim, and sang the praises of the glorious Japanese military. Japanese journalists relished spreading this propaganda.

Government censorship, coupled with the newspaper industry's penchant for ultra-nationalistic propagandizing, eventually caused great disillusionment. The paltry spoils of victory granted in the Portsmouth Treaty, which testified to Japan's military weakness, scandalized the Japanese public. Japan received no war compensation and only half of Sakhalin Island for its trouble. For a public convinced by the war propaganda of Japan's military prowess, this unimpressive outcome came as a great shock.

What was the role of political cartoons during the war? The Japanese were thirsty for news from the battlefield. Every report of a successful operation caused great excitement and enthusiastic celebrations. Although cable lines existed, they were not easily accessible to reporters, so detailed accounts of battles were dispatched by mail or by hand (Huffman 1997, 280). Moreover, since photography was still not widely available, pictures from the front seldom appeared in newspapers. This put newspapers in the awkward situation of being unable to satisfy the demands of a news-hungry public.

Illustrated magazines responded to the dearth of hard news by publishing war cartoons. These became so popular that magazines often had to publish additional issues. A cartoon by Shōkoku Yamamoto's *Gisen to gogai* (Sham War and Extra Editions), which appeared at the end of 1903 in the series *Kokumin no tekikaishin* (Anxieties of People), grasped the atmosphere of the time well. The image is of a crowd of Japanese holding national flags and running excitedly after the newspaper peddler (Sugiura 1978, 4). The cartoon suggests that the Japanese public wanted to hear only about the victories of its forces, regardless of whether the news corresponded to reality. To meet this demand for "good news," stories had to be invented. Here cartoons opened up enormous possibilities since the genre itself permitted unlimited possibilities for exaggeration and invention. So, while cartoons did not necessarily convey any real facts, they did express strong emotions about the war, something their authors knew would appeal to their readership.

Early on, when the situation at the front was unclear, only well-established magazines such as *Maru maru chimbun* or *Kokkei shimbun* dared to publish war-related cartoons. The cartoonists were cautious, waiting until the first obvious achievements in the war theater before they published anything. The cartoons that were published focused mainly on the violence of the enemy. It was not until the siege of Port Arthur began (July 1904), in which Japanese military superiority was incontrovertible, that artists began to pour ridicule on the enemy. They knew all too well that Western cartoons had often cruelly caricatured the Japanese as small, weak, and ape-like in appearance. The war victories gave the Japanese cartoonists a good opportunity to resort to similar slander against the Russians.

The war stimulated a new boom in illustrated magazines. One of the first to appear was *Nipponchi*, a temporary supplement to *Fuzoku gahō* (Pictures of Customs of the Time 1997) that was published from 1889 until 1916.[3] Its founder, Kensaburō Azuna, was familiar with polychrome lithographic printing technology, which, at that time, was not widespread in Japan. The longtime editor of this magazine was Shigetami Yamashita (1857–1941), who also worked at the Ministry of Finance. The main purpose of *Fuzoku gahō* was to familiarize the public with new places of interest in Tokyo and the customs of its inhabitants, which suggests that the editor and authors knew the public taste well. Apart from its regular run, special issues of *Fuzoku gahō* were occasionally published to cover important news, such as earthquakes, art exhibitions, or military campaigns. (Altogether, 487 regular issues were published with extra issues bringing the total to 517). Unfortunately, the spread of photography ultimately doomed this magazine since it relied on sketches for illustrations.

The title, *Nipponchi* (The Land of Japan), contains a clever pun. The middle syllable *pon*, written in *katakana*, can be combined with either the first or third syllable making it *Nippon* or *ponchi* respectively. *Ponchi* was a term for Meiji-period cartoons, but the word also evokes the English word "punch," as in *Japan Punch*. *Chi*, signifying "land" in the wartime magazine's title, also signifies more than the Japanese homeland—since Japan was trying to expand its territory militarily in Korea, Manchuria, and even Russia. This same sort of wordplay is found throughout the entire magazine (Mikhailova 2001, 69).

Nipponchi was a wartime magazine. Its first issue appeared on September 7, 1904, at a time when the Japanese had already trapped the Russian army in Port Arthur and the battle for Liaoang had begun. The publication ceased in spring 1905, leaving an impression that its artists and writers exhausted their creativity in poking fun at the Russians.

The magazine was rather straightforwardly pro-war by employing the typical tabloid approach of constructing a negative stereotype of the Russians as the evil other. Before the war, Japan feared Russia as a menacing foreign power, but during the war, this fear turned into scorn in the unsophisticated pictures of *Nipponchi*. Its artists gave the Japanese public sweet revenge with a biting satire that worked cathartically to ease the strain of war. It usually mocked the Russians as a people of low morals and bad warriors.

Kinshō Otei (1868–1954) was the inspiration behind the comics in *Nipponchi*. He was a newspaper writer specializing in the *rakugo, gidaiyū, kōta, chaban, kyōgen*, and *kyōka* styles, all of which were short, often vulgar popular comic songs and stories. Shōkoku Yamamoto (1870–1965) was the leading artist of the magazine, and Shunkō Nakashima usually drew the artwork. Yamamoto, originally trained as a Nihonga artist of the Kanō school, was hired at *Fuzoku gahō* in 1894. Later he became famous and was awarded several prizes for his artistry (*Nihon jinmei daijiten*, 2001, 412; *Bijutsu techō* 1956, 109–118). For *Nipponchi* he mainly drew color frontispieces (*kuchi-e*). Nakashima was probably hired on a daily basis to do the artwork.

Nipponchi, while rightly criticized for its overly simplistic style and vulgar drawings, is still important. For its cartoons, the magazine drew on familiar art forms, particularly standard Edo-period humorous pictures, historical anecdotes, and story lines (Inagaki 1988, 8–9). Nowadays, much of this traditional humor has long been forgotten, but it is important to see how it still underlies comedy in modern Japan.

The Meiji period also introduced a completely new style of cartooning with the work of Yasushi Kitazawa, more widely known as Rakuten (1876–1955). He was the son of a samurai family who had been vassals of the Tokugawa. After graduating from elementary school, he studied *ukiyo-e* painting, but also delved into Western painting for two years at the Taikokan painting school at Nagatachō, Kojimachi, under the tutelage of Yukihiko Ono, and then at the Kanritsu Bijutsu Gakkō. Rakuten's first job was at the *Box of Curiosities*, a weekly newspaper published in Yokohama by the American E.B. Thorne. At this time Rakuten met an Australian cartoonist, Frank A. Nankivell, who taught him the Western cartooning technique of caricature portraits. He also translated English picture captions that were published in the *Box of Curiosities*. Rakuten's artistic experience at the *Box of Curiosities* laid the foundation for his future work as a cartoonist. Moreover, the cosmopolitan atmosphere of the port city of Yokohama, where he had daily contact with foreigners, gave him a keen awareness of modern Japan's foreign relations.

In 1900, Rakuten was noticed by Yukichi Fukuzawa, who invited him to work as a cartoonist at his famous newspaper, *Jiji Shimpō*. Every Sunday, Rakuten, together with another artist, Ippyō Imaizumi, published *Jiji manga*, comics that were primarily about the increasing political tensions between Russia and Japan after the Triple Intervention and the Boxer Rebellion or dealt with other social problems of the time. This period also marks one notable innovation—using the word *manga* for comic and satirical pictures instead of *ponchi-e* or other terms.[4] Rakuten was the first who consciously called himself a manga artist and began to publish both manga of one-page size and serialized manga, something previously unknown in Japan. Rakuten borrowed this idea from American "yellow papers." By choosing the word manga, he was attempting to raise the low cultural status of cartoons as a type of low-brow humor (*Kindai manga-no so* 1991, 12). The word manga, after all, had a certain cachet given its association with Katsushika Hokusai's famous work, *Hokusai manga*. The war with Russia inspired Rakuten to publish his own cartoon magazine, which he named *Tokyo Puck* after the American magazine *New York Puck*. This name choice also reveals Rakuten's strong desire to distance himself from the traditional *ponchi-e*. It is reported that he refused to name the magazine *Tanuki* (Racoon dog), the name suggested by its sponsor, Yajirō Nakamura (Suyama 1968, 56). The sound *pon-pon*, which is supposed to be the sound that a *tanuki* makes, reminded him of *ponchi*. Rakuten's first issue appeared in April 1905, soon after the battle at Mukden. *Tokyo Puck* was initially printed two and then three times a month, with a circulation that soon reached 100,000 copies (Ishiko 1979, 84). It was also the first magazine to publish all its cartoons in color in large paper size, a format that was very appealing to the public.

Fighting the Enemy

As Ryūichi Narita has observed, "writing on the war is the most rapid construction of the sense of community of us," and thus, it creates a worldview that clearly delineates between an "us" and a "them" (Narita 2000, 147). The same is true about war cartooning. Cartoons praised the heroism of Japanese soldiers while disparaging the cowardice of the Russians. They portrayed Japan as a united nation while offering an unflattering portrait of a Russia driven by internal dissent, and they created a sense of Japanese nationhood, fostering great pride in Japan's national spirit, or "*yamato damashii.*" Needless to say, this feat was achieved at the cost of sacrificing the truth.

The Russo-Japanese War began with Japan's attack on the Russian navy in Chemulpo and Port Arthur. As in the Sino-Japanese War ten years earlier, this was a preemptive, surprise attack carried out before Japan's declaration of war was received by the Russian government, a strategy designed to bridge the gap between Japan's large political ambitions and its limited military power. The Japanese mass media colluded with the government by instigating a campaign of disinformation. For example, although Japan had launched the first attack on February 8, 1904, cartoonists blamed Russia for initiating hostilities. They relentlessly caricatured their enemy as the "devilish man-eater," who gobbled up the territories of its weaker neighbors. One of the cartoons that illustrates this appeared in *Kokkei shimbun* on February 25, 1904. The devil in this cartoon has the face of the Russian emperor Nicholas II, whose sinister demeanor and rapacious grin leave no doubt about his greed and cruelty. The artist also depicts people of different nationalities being digested in Nicholas's stomach.[5] In the age of imperialism, when state power was measured in terms of territorial expansion, Japan perceived Russia as its rival and envied the Russian Empire's holdings in the Far East. However, in this cartoon, the unknown artist imagines Japan not as an imperial rival of Russia, but as the liberator of the Asian people (Yoshino 1993, 117).

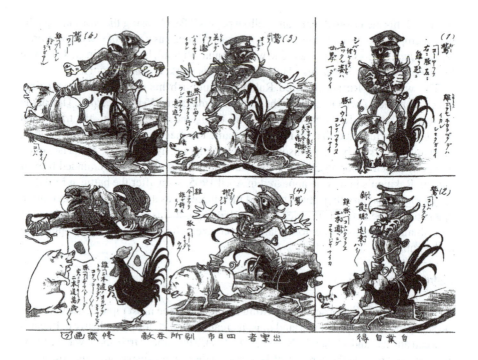

Shunkō Nakashima's "Jigyō jitoku" (Benefits of Enterprise), *Nipponchi,* **October 20, 1904.**
Fuzoku gahō **CD-ROM edition.** (Reproduced with permission from Yumani shobō)

Cartoons about Russia's military aggression were a regular feature in illustrated magazines of the time. For example, a six-picture set called "Jigyō jitoku" (Benefits of Enterprise) poked fun at Russian expansionism in Korea and China. In the cartoon, an eagle symbolizing Russia is perched with its talons dug into the backs of a pig (China) and a rooster (Korea). Both animals seem to be enjoying being its beasts of burden for a while, because the bird of prey is not heavy. However, when the road forks, the pig runs right, while the rooster runs left. The final picture has both animals happily holding a Japanese flag, the Hi-no maru, signifying that they rejoice in being the new livestock of Japan. The Russian eagle, however, lies torn apart and crying in despair. The comic effect comes from several puns. The word *nippon* means both "Japan" and "two roads"; China is a pig because the usual Chinese hairstyle of the time was *bempatsu* (the pigtail), and pork was considered Chinese food since the Japanese ate it infrequently. Korea is a rooster because the Koreans like cockfighting, but also because Korea itself became a fighting ground between Japan and Russia. It is interesting to note that, although *Nipponchi* usually employed traditional Japanese visual cues, these symbols for Manchuria and Korea are international, also appearing in European cartoons of the period (*Kikeriki* 1904, 1).

These cartoons, which exaggerated Russian and ignored Japanese imperialism, actually indicated how unsure the Japanese were about the war's outcome. The Russians were not always the losers. For example, the Japanese attempt to blockade the entrance to Port Arthur's harbor in spring of 1904 ended in failure when the five vessels used in the operation were either blown up or ran aground. Russia's Vladivostok squadron was also quite successful attacking even the Japanese archipelago. It took Vice-Admiral Kamimura three months, from April to June 1904, to track them down. Unfortunately, because of fog he mistook his own vessels for the Russians and sank them by mistake. Kamimura's blunder looked like betrayal, and a cartoon, "Kamimura jo-no hanake-o nuku" (Lady Kamimura Pulling the Hair Out of Her Nose), appeared in the magazine *Bijutsu gahō*. It lampooned the vice admiral, drawing him as a geisha primping herself before Russian military men and carelessly throwing out the trumps as if trying to find out the location of the enemy. The cartoon reflects the popular irritation at Kamimura's ineptitude and also the suspicions that he was a Russian spy (Haga and Shimizu 1985, 25).

At the end of August 1904, the Japanese and Russians engaged in their first serious battle near Liao-yan. At this time, when the war obviously began to turn in Japan's favor, cartoons celebrating the great victory appeared more frequently, although they did underscore how difficult the victory was.

Many cartoons ridiculed the commanders of the Russian army, such as the viceroy of the Maritime Province Alekseev and Generals Kuropatkin and Stoessel. A good example is "Roshia Shichifukujin" (Russian Seven Gods of Luck and Virtue), which poked fun at General Kuropatkin. These seven gods—Daikokuten, Ebisu, Bishamonten, Benzaiten, Fukurokuju, Jurōjin, and Hotei—are well-known divinities in Japanese popular religion. For comic effect, the artist Shunkō Nakashima used the so-called *chikuchi-e* art form that was popular during the Edo period. This type of art involved wordplays using rhyme. The original words are substituted with those that have a similar pronunciation. Since the new words use different *kanji* characters, they change the meaning in humorous ways. For example, Daikokuten is a guardian god or a god of war who is usually portrayed with a hood on his head, a sack in his left hand, and a mallet of good luck in the right. However, in this picture, the central character, *koku* (black), is replaced by the similar sounding *goku* (prison). We see a Russian tied to a tree with his good luck mallet cast aside. Next comes Ebisu, also a popular god known to bring prosperity in trade and sea voyages. Usually, he is portrayed with a happy smiling face holding a mackerel. Here, the character *imi* (mourning) is added to his name, and the mackerels are biting him; he is their dinner rather than the other way around. We also see a triangle on his head, which in Japan is typically festooned on the heads of the dead. This signifies the Russian general Kuropatkin's bad luck—his failure as a commander that brought death to thousands of Russian soldiers under his command and, indeed, to Russian fame as a military superpower of the time.

With the exception of the tsar, Russians never have identifiable features in those cartoons. They are usually depicted with *washibana* (beaks) or as demons, which were de rigueur portrayals of "foreign barbarians" in pre-Meiji Japan. The *washi* (eagle) also alludes to the double-headed eagle on the coat of arms of the Russian Empire. In

Shunkō Nakashima's "Roshia Shichifukujin: (Russian Seven Gods of Luck and Virtue),
Nipponchi, **November 25, 1904.** *Fuzoku gahō* **CD-ROM edition.**
(Reproduced with permission from Yumani shobō)

Shunkō Nakashima's "Senji Yanagidaru" (Yanagidaru on [the topic of] War),
Nipponchi, **September 27, 1904.** *Fuzoku gahō* **CD-ROM edition.**
(Reproduced with permission from Yumani shobō)

some pictures, Russians resemble the goblins drawn by Kyōsai Kawanabe (Kawanabe 1994, 114–115), or the famous *Hyakki yagyō* (Hundreds of Demons Walking in the Night) of Mitsunobu Tosa (Komatsu 1993, 78).

Ordinary Russian soldiers were also the butt of jokes, though in reality Japanese and Russians often cooperated with one another (Kowner 2000, 134–151). A "gallery" of portraits of Russian prisoners of war gives a good illustration of how the mass media demeaned the Russians as gluttons, loafers, deserters, warmongers, pickpockets, bribe-takers, Neanderthals, and so on. While Russian cartoons always emphasized their soldiers' raw physical strength, Japanese cartoons accented the low morale and moral caliber of their adversary. Popular games, such as *irohagaruta* and *rokujū musha*, a kind of game like Japanese chess (*shōgi*), were also used to entertain the public and raise its military spirit by depicting Japanese victories over the Russians.

Every issue of *Nipponchi* published a cartoon called "Senji Yanagidaru" (Yanagidaru on [the topic of] War), usually drawn by Shunkō Nakashima. It was designed as a large-cell matrix within which smaller images were placed. Each image includes a *senryū*—a comical seventeen-syllable poem mocking the foibles of ordinary people in everyday situations.[6]

In the example on page 169, the small picture in the top left corner makes fun of Alekseev, the vice-regent of the Russian Far East, a man whose primary job qualification was that he was close to the imperial family. At first, he was appointed as the commander-in-chief of the Russian army, but he was dismissed in October 1904 because of his incessant military blunders as well as his quarrels with other generals. He is portrayed here with a Red Cross flag and embracing a woman, which suggests that Alekseev preferred having a good time over fulfilling his duties at the front. The accompanying *senryū* poem adds, "Alekseev vice-regent says, 'After me the deluge,'" obviously hinting at his lack of interest in Russian military fate.

In the bottom right corner, there is a picture-poem mocking Vice-Admiral Hikonojo Kamimura, whose servant is seen here boasting about his master's success destroying the Russian squadron. In reality, we know that this victory was achieved with great difficulty; Kamimura won only after he received secret intelligence from a Russian spy. Although many cartoons depict Japanese rejoicing over their victories, some occasionally do offer the Russians sympathy. One example is a cartoon that shows an injured Russian soldier begging a Japanese nurse for help. In any case, this traditional genre was useful for producing relatively unsophisticated cartoons with comical verse on various topics of the day.

As they increasingly gained self-confidence during the war, officials thought that people should know more about Japan's wartime achievements. No cartoonist was better suited for this task than Rakuten Kitazawa, a man knowledgeable about international politics as well as foreign cultures. Rakuten wrote captions to his cartoons not only in Japanese, but also in English and occasionally Chinese, indicating that he was trying to address an international audience. Rakuten's art demonstrates how Japan hungered for a new international stature as a great power.

Rakuten's main target for satire was the Russian emperor in the "company" of the European powers. Thus, the front cover of the first issue of *Tokyo Puck* contained a masterfully drawn cartoon entitled "Repentance of the Russian Tsar." It has a twisted figure of the Russian tsar trying in vain to bite his own navel (i.e., trying to achieve the impossible). This conveys the desperate situation the Russian government found itself in, crushed between defeat at the front and revolution at home, and is intended to underscore how wrong the Russians were in their prewar scornful attitude to Japan. By emphasizing the enormous size of the country, the cartoon reminds readers about the incredible strength of Japan's adversary. Drawing upon Western caricature, this cartoon stands in sharp contrast graphically with the primitive pictures of *Nipponchi*.

Many of Rakuten's cartoons reveal his familiarity with Western news and gossip. For example, in "Surgery of His Tongue," created in August 1905 at time of the Portsmouth negotiations, he portrays Kaiser Wilhelm being punished for labeling Japan the "yellow peril." It was widely known in the West that after the Sino-Japanese War, Wilhelm drew a picture of the "yellow peril" and sent it as a warning to his relative, the Russian tsar. Rakuten also penned a cartoon like this in August 1905, calling it "The Czar at His Wit's End—Holding Up the 'Yellow Peril' Bogey." It pictures a

Rakuten Kitazawa's "One Strike Is Enough," *Tokyo Puck*, **vol. 2, no. 3, 1905.**
(Reproduced with permission from Kokusho kankōkai)

yellow specter with Asian features looming above the kaiser, who stands beside the globe with an easel and brush.

Another cartoon by Rakuten, "Changes at the Front," shows a tall figure of a Japanese general mounted on horseback above a ruined Russian church, while soldiers are running around in disarray. The Orthodox Church is a symbol of the Russian monarchy, and the cartoon's depiction of a road marker for Harbin, a city in Manchuria, means it was supposed to become Japan's next conquest in the war. In reality this goal was not reached, but the picture demonstrates how the pride in military achievements was gaining force in Japan.

The principal Japanese victory was the Battle of Tsushima, which took place on May 27, 1905. Rakuten commemorated it with his cartoon "Ichigeki mijin" ("One Strike Is Enough"). In the center of the picture is a Russian ship, commanded by Admiral Rozhdestvensky, that is sinking to the bottom of the sea. The tall, portly figure of Admiral Tōgō is standing proudly on the right and the other Great Powers are found in the top left corner, symbolized, as in Western cartoons, by John Bull and Uncle Sam. These two are applauding Japan, while Germany and France, the friends of Russia, look shocked. A Chinese and other Asians joyfully dance to celebrate Japan's triumph. Clothes serve here as the main markers of nationality—a typical device of Western cartoonists. Waves, fish, and water plants are drawn in the traditional Japanese manner, but as a whole, the picture resembles Western-style political cartoons with its sparse lines for the figures and emphasis on caricature.

The front cover of the same issue of the magazine pictures Japan as a huge sumo wrestler with a face like General Iwao Ōyama, Head of General Staff, who is staring scornfully at the tiny Russian tsar, Nikolas II. The caption has the tsar exclaiming, "What a monstrous fellow! He is no match for me. I now surrender." As usual in Rakuten's cartoons, the Great Powers, consisting of Uncle Sam, John Bull, a Frenchman, and a German, are watching admiringly from a distance. Nevertheless, the historical fact is that Japan was not such a threatening bully, but was exhausted by the war, and had even asked the U.S. president to be an intermediary in the peace negotiations by this point.

Although adept at Western artistry, Rakuten had far more success drawing caricatures of Westerners. His caricatures of Japanese politicians seem bland by comparison, without the artist's characteristic sting (Ishiko 1979, 84). For example, in the cartoon "Peaceful Warriors," Rakuten wanted to point an accusing finger at Japanese politicians who had concluded a disgraceful (from the Japanese viewpoint) treaty with Russia. Yet, the cartoon is ineffective because all the faces have the same expression.

Another element in Japan's political cartooning is its critical view of the Russian Revolution. In number 4 of *Tokyo Puck*, Rakuten published a cartoon entitled "The Long Snake of Revolution." The cartoon shows "Bloody Sunday," which happened in Russia on January 9, 1905. This is by no means satirical even though it was published in a comic magazine. The large demonstration is drawn to look like a snake choking a church (the symbol of Russian monarchy) and the furious faces of the crowd are quite terrifying. The word *bakudan* (explosion), emblazoned on the snake's huge eyes, make it clear that the Russian state is in danger. Another cartoon in the same issue has a Russian *mouzhik* (peasant fellow), again with a furious face, tearing the crown from the tsar's head. Still another cartoon shows a sailor from the battleship *Potemkin* in a life-and-death struggle with an officer. The caption states, "The Navy and Army defending the country prove to be dangerous for Russia. It had better keep none of them." Similar cartoons appeared in other illustrated magazines of the time as well.

These cartoons created an unflattering image of Russia as a place of disorder and discontent. By contrast, Japanese propaganda of the time presented Japan as a country where the emperor and people coexisted in unity and harmony, so these images of revolutionary Russia were jarring in two ways. Compared with Japan, Russia showed a terrifying lack of social and political harmony, and it was dangerous because its revolutionary virus could infect Japan. After the war, this image of Japan's menacing northern neighbor was replaced with the image of Russia as a threatening, possibly contagious, example of domestic instability. Japanese officials' worst fears were realized when some Japanese citizens rioted over the terms of the Portsmouth Treaty. These domestic troubles were blamed, at least indirectly, on Russia's bad influence.

Most of these cartoons, whether in traditional or Western formats, emphasized unalloyed Japanese jingoism while offering contempt for the Russians. The mass media's brainwashing campaign is epitomized in the hapless Russian fellow—Roske—a

Rakuten Kitazawa's "No Match to Me," *Tokyo Puck*, **vol. 1, no. 3, 1905.**
(Reproduced with permission from Ryūkei shosha)

Rakuten Kitazawa's "Long Snake of Revolution," *Tokyo Puck*, **vol. 1, no. 4, 1905.**
(Reproduced with permission from Kokusho kankōkai)

popular cruel stereotype roughly equivalent to the racist "Jap" caricatures in American publications during World War II. Japan's victory at the front made this image more persuasive.

This does not mean, however, that Japan's mass media portrayed the war in a uniform way. Scholars are well aware of the antiwar ideas of socialists like Shūsui Kōtoku and Toshihiko Sakai, who published a newspaper entitled *Nichikan heimin shimbun*. They called for peace, as did the poet Akiko Yosano, whose famous poem begging her soldier brother not to die touched the hearts of many Japanese.

Antiwar cartoons were rare, but not completely absent. One example by the artist Hyakuho Heifuku, whose pen name literally means "one hundred seeds of peace and happiness," appeared in the first issue of the paper in 1907. The cartoon has a figure of a woman holding a placard with the word "socialism" written on it. This cartoon is often reproduced in school textbooks. Another example, "Heimin no chi" (Blood of Common People), also seen in modern textbooks, pointedly argued that the war was waged in the interest of each country's capitalists, rather than for the people. Still another artist, Misei Kosugi, who also worked as a war correspondent, drew Russian graves with crosses next to Japanese graves with wooden tablets. In another work, Kosugi conveys the tragedy of war by drawing a field of corpses with a wild dog eating the bodies (Suyama 1972, 113). Takashiro (Futō) Kanokogi, a leftist artist, drew

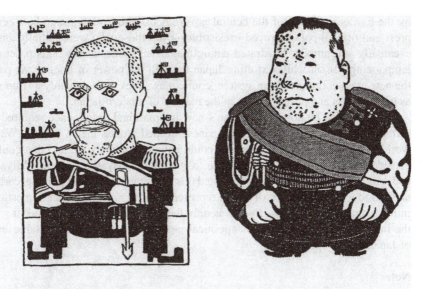

Takashiro (Futō) Kanokogi's "Heihachirō Tōgō Shōgun. Isao Ōyama."
Taishō hibijutsu gahō. **Banchō shobō.**

comical pictures of Tōgō, Ōyama, and other commanders who were to be idolized after the war. In his cartoons, they appear ugly and disgusting, without any manly features. These protests, however, were lost in the mass media's sea of boisterous nationalistic propaganda.

It is well known that after the war, the Japanese intelligentsia became fascinated with Russian culture and with Marxism. But for mainstream Japanese society, Russia (and subsequently the Soviet Union) continued to have negative connotations. The Russo-Japanese War was a significant cause of this. As we have seen, it was decisive in the formation of Japan's positive definition of its national identity. The mass media defined Japanese nationalism against Japan's negative "other" and antipode. Political cartoons were particularly useful for the state because they disseminated its ideology throughout Japan in the national press.

Conclusion

Yōichi Komori and Ryūichi Narita, in their recent book on the Russo-Japanese War, have acknowledged that the transformation of Japan into a nation-state (*kokuminka*) was stimulated by mobilizing the people psychologically, and that the war provided an "important chance" for this development. Nevertheless, these scholars are often highly critical of the hypernationalism of the mass media (Komori and Narita 2004, 11). Newspapers were a vehicle for communicating news that was deemed important by the hawks in charge of the central government. This collaboration between the press and official policy proved irresistible—even those who were initially antiwar eventually succumbed. Illustrated comic magazines contributed to this process by lampooning Russia while extolling Japan through the power of images. As part of the new mass communication system, comic magazines were arguably as important as the railroads and postal system in the making of modern Japan.

It should also be noted that Japan's new international prominence required new forms of political expression. The Japanese needed a mass media that the Western world as well as the Japanese people could equally comprehend, and that could be considered a feature of a modern state. Kiyochika Kobayashi, Gaikotsu Miyatake, and, especially, Rakuten Kitazawa created this new graphic idiom of political cartoons and introduced the practice of visual representation in mass media of domestic and international politics. *Tokyo Puck* was only the first magazine of this kind. It was in the Taisho period (1912–1926) that political cartoons became an indispensable feature of Japanese newspapers.

Notes

I would like to express my sincere gratitude to Ms. Keiko Morisaki, the librarian at Hiroshima City University Library, and to the staff of Hiroshima Manga Library, particularly its former director Mr. Hirō Kurui, Ms. Naomi Okumoto, and Ms. Yumi Takeyama. They assisted me in collecting materials for this article and generously shared their knowledge, helping me to understand the contents of cartoons.

1. There are numerous works in Japanese devoted to the history of cartoons in Meiji Japan, but they do not take the perspective I have taken in this chapter; that is, how cartoons contributed to the sense of the nation-state. Isao Shimizu is the most important authority on Japanese cartoons and manga, so his works are a major source for this essay.

2. His first famous work was a series of Tokyo landscapes called *Kosenga (Pictures in Light's Rays)* drawn between 1876 and 1877.

3. According to Keiichi Suyama, ten issues of *Nipponchi* were published twice a month until the spring of 1905. See *Nihon manga hyakunen*, 57 (1968). However, the CD-ROM edition includes only seven issues.

4. Contemporary researchers diverge in their opinions as to who was the main figure in choosing the word manga—Rakuten or Ippyō Imaizumi—because both worked at this newspaper.

5. For a full description of the cartoon titled "Hitokui rokoku," see Mikhailova 2000, 156.

6. *Senryū* are different from *haiku* in that they do not have seasonal topics and *kireji* (the cutting syllable). The first collection of senryū, the *Haifu yanagidaru* was authored by Senryu Kairai and appeared in 1765. New editions were published several times in the Tokugawa period with additional poems from Kairai's successors. The characters used for the original word, *yanagidaru* (willow, many, stop) were substituted in later editions with others, meaning "willow, barrel, sake." One rationale for this is that *senryū* are full of humor, and like drinking sake (kept in willow barrels), they make people laugh. So these pictures themselves were conceived as a sort of "barrel" with many comical pictures and poems inside.

8

Framing Manga

On Narratives of the Second World War in Japanese Manga, 1957–1977

ELDAD NAKAR

Introduction

Remembering is as much a collective as a personal act. Society has the power to frame people's individual memories by providing the means to classify and condense particular historical situations, actions, events, and experiences into organized and meaningful wholes (Snow and Benford 1992, 137). This chapter explores how society frames individuals' memories in a Japanese context. I examine how Japanese remember World War II, an epochal event in modern Japanese history that divides what came before and after it. Of course, one possible means of exploration is looking at various portrayals of the war in places such as school textbooks, monuments, and memorials. For example, Yasukuni Shrine offers one highly controversial particular perspective—an ultra-nationalist one—as a shrine for spirits of Japanese soldiers lost in battle. Yasukuni's sacred precincts and rituals, along with its war museum's jingoistic exhibits, which attempt to highlight Japan's "glorious" and controversial militaristic past, offer what Christian Smith has called a "living narrative" to visitors, providing them a particular story deemed collectively important about "what is real and significant, to know who [they] are, where [they] are, what [they] are doing and why" (Smith 2003, 67).

However, there are other equally powerful ways to access the Japanese people's recollections of World War II. One key means, which scholars have generally overlooked, is popular manga. In the postwar period, Japanese publishing houses produced many manga that explicitly dealt with the war. Japanese manga about World War II, which I am defining here as tales that take place during the war, first appeared in the late 1950s. Such works were first published and distributed through the *kashihonya* (pay-libraries), and later in the weekly boys' magazines that were created as early as 1959. In both places, works were classified by the Japanese term *senki mono* (records of war), giving the illusion the works were handing down real war stories. In fact, most merely combined fictitious details with real historical places, characters, dates, and figures. They were a regular feature in manga magazines over the next twenty-five years and still appear today.

In the pages that follow, I will explore the content of these early stories, showing that over time they developed two different types of "living narratives" that reflected the social, economic, and generational changes of the postwar period.

The Late 1950s to Late 1960s

Heroic Warfare—The Hegemonic Narrative

Early manga about World War II display two key characteristics. First, their stories ignore the home front while concentrating on the battlefield. Second, they are predominantly adventure stories about the air war, featuring brave pilots heroically flying to victory. This is illustrated in Table 8.1, which compiles a selection of several titles from the late 1950s to the early 1960s. Of the twenty-eight World War II manga that I found, twenty-four are about air battles, three are about naval warfare (items 6, 14, 17), and just one (item 23) features the ground war.

Some of these tales were very popular at the time and have become classics. Two well-known stories are Hiroshi Kaizuka's *Zero-sen reddo* (The Red Zeros) and Naoki Tsuji's *Zero-sen Taro* (Taro the Zero Pilot), both serialized in a *shōnen* magazine in 1961. In 1963, another noteworthy work by Naoki Tsuji called *Zero-sen Hayato* (Hayato the Zero Pilot) also appeared. This manga was first serialized in a *shōnen* magazine and was adapted into a television anime in 1964. Another popular example is Tetsuya Chiba's *Shidenkai no taka* (The Hawk in the Violet Lightning Fighter), which was serialized in *Shōnen Magazine* from 1963 until 1965. All of these early manga classics are adventure stories featuring aerial combat. Typical of their time, their cover artwork offers dramatic battle scenes embedded with pictures of courageous pilots and shiny warplanes in desperate dogfights. The fighter planes in realistic combat action, and the pilots with determined looks, were typical covers for these stories.

Also striking is the fact that many stories use the name of the Japanese navy fighter plane—the famous Zero (which was the nickname for the famous Mitsubishi A6M fighter plane)—as part of their titles. Ten such stories are listed in Table 8.1 alone. Moreover, stories usually offer a simplistic image of the war. The heroes are often drawn as "cute" (*kawaii*) childlike figures. This is especially true in the case of boys' magazines, though less prominent in manga published by the pay-libraries, which employed a *gekiga* (dramatic) style that had more mature characters. In both cases, however, the stories and images do not engage the starker realities of war, especially the omnipresence of death and suffering. If death occurs, it is briefly noted without any distastefully graphic illustrations. In other words, death is left to the reader's imagination.

While the main characters appear childlike, the stories strive for historical real-

Table 8.1

Major Japanese War Comics, 1957–1967

Year	Work	Author / Illustrator	Publisher
1. 1957	*Tokkō-ki ōzora ni chiru* (Kamikaze Are Scattered in the Sky), part of *Senjō Shirītzu* (The Battlefield Series)	Tarō Himoto	Akebono Shuppan
2. 1958	*Senjō no chikai* (The Battlefield Vow)	Shigeru Mizuki	Togetsu Shobō
3. 1958	*Akatsuki no totsunyū* (The Dawn Attack)	Shigeru Mizuki	Togetsu Shobō
4. 1958	*Kurogane no Zero-sen* (The Iron Zero)	Tarō Itai	Akebono Shuppan
5. 1959	*Shōnen Zero sentai* (The Boys' Zero Squadron)	Shinji Nagashima	Bōken Ō
6. 1959	*Senkan Yamato no saiki* (The Last Days of Battleship Yamato)	Kunio Hase	Akebono Shuppan
7. 1960	*Shōnen senki* (War Records for Boys)	Shigeru Mizuki, ed.	Togetsu Shobō
8. 1961	*Shōnen spīdo ō* (Boy Speed King)	Ippei Kuri	Shōnen
9. 1961	*Zero-sen reddo* (The Red Zeros)	Hiroshi Kaizuka	Bōken Ō
10. 1961	*Gekitsui* (Shot Down)	Shigeru Mizuki	Rikukaiku
11. 1962	*Zero-sen chanpion* (The Champion Zero)	Tatsuo Yoshida	Bokura
12. 1962	*Ōzora no chikai* (Vow in the Skies)	Ippei Kuri	Shōnen Sunday
13. 1962	*Zero-sen sōkōgeki* (All Zeros Attack)	Shigeru Mizuki	Akebono Shuppan
14. 1962	*Musashi* (Battleship Musashi)	Mikiya Mochizuki	Shōnen Gahō
15. 1963	*Zero-sen Hayato* (Hayato the Zero Pilot)	Naoki Tsuji	Shōnen King
16. 1963–5	*Shidenkai no taka* (The Hawk in the Violet Lightning Fighter)	Tetsuya Chiba	Shōnen Magazine
17. 1963	*Maboroshi no Yamato* (The Phantom of Battleship Yamato)	Seryū Mitsu, Takeshi Furushiro	Shōnen Magazine
18. 1963	*Zero-sen nanbā wan* (The No. 1 Zero)	Daiji Kazumine	Manga Ō
19. 1963	*Sora no san unsō* (Three Aerial Express Men)	Sanpei Wachi	Shōnen
20. 1963	*Moeru minami jūjisei* (The Burning Southern Cross)	Akira Matsumoto (Leiji Matsumoto)	Hinomaru
21. 1964	*Arawashi shōnen-tai* (Boy Air Ace Squadron)	Mikiya Mochizuki	Shōnen Gahō
22. 1964	*Nihon kessaku sentōki shirītzu* (Brilliant Japanese Fighter Planes)	Mikiya Mochizuki	Shōnen Book
23. 1964	*Shiroi hata* (The White Flag)	Shigeru Mizuki	Aa Taiheiyo
24. 1964	*Tokkōki dayo! Kantarō* (Kamikaze Kantarō)	Fujio Akatsuka	Shōnen Book
25. 1967	*Zero-sen shinkyoku* (March of the Zeros)	Hiroshi Kaizuka	Shōnen Champion
26. 1967	*Akatsuki sentōtai* (Dawn Combat Unit)	Shunsuke Sagara, Mitsuyoshi Sonoda	Shōnen Sunday
27. 1967	*Fuhai no Zero-sen ō* (Unbeatable King Zero)	Akira Ogawa	Shōnen Magazine
28. 1967	*Zero-sen Iga* (Iga the Zero Pilot)	Satoru Ozawa	Manga Ō

Shigeru Mizuki's cover artwork for *Senjō no chikai* **(The Battlefield Vow, 1958).**
(Copyright Mizuki Productions)

ism. This leads to an interesting visual ambiguity in these manga. On the one hand, by featuring cute kids as heroes, the tales tend toward fantasy. On the other hand, the enemy and senior Japanese commanders are always depicted as adults, which lends realism to the stories. This is augmented by the illustrations of the war machinery that are meticulously and accurately drawn. References to real battlegrounds and famous historical figures also anchor these manga historically. And as if to further empha-size their historicity, these manga typically include advertisements for actual plane or ship models that can be purchased separately (Natsume 1997, 61–62; Yonezawa 1996, 30).

The plots of early World War II manga are invariably consistent. They always emphasize that Japanese soldiers at the front are heroes, bravely fighting against an implacable foe. They are always volunteers, patriots who are willing to risk their lives in defense of the homeland. At the center of these stories is the battleground (more precisely the aerial battlefield), where the courage, persistence, and military expertise of the Japanese soldiers are vividly displayed. Very little attention is given to the soldiers' lives, either before or after their victories in battle. The same is true for the enemy soldiers, who are lumped together as the faceless and anonymous evil "other." Interestingly, they are always Americans or British soldiers who come off as halfhearted, cowardly, and unworthy opponents. The stories usually take place over the Pacific, often near the end of the war when Japan was on the verge of defeat.

What makes these stories distinctive is that they tend to exaggerate brief moments of aerial combat. The dogfights occupy the center of the narratives, and by adding extra cels the authors extend the action sequences over several pages. This has the effect of highlighting scenes showing Japanese pilots' courage under fire. Furthermore, the stories typically end with the war still dragging on, and we see the pilots valiantly flying off on their final missions to their inevitable deaths. In other words, these manga are heroic tragedies that emphasize the remarkable dedication of Japanese pilots doomed to defeat, something that the reader is left to ponder at the end (see Nakar 2003). This archetype, the tragic hero who loses a hopeless battle against an overwhelming foe, exemplifies what scholar Ivan Morris called "the nobility of failure." Morris identified this archetype as one of the most omnipresent tropes in Japanese literature (Morris 1975). This type of protagonist, the young and morally pure warrior, is also found in classic and modern literature. Examples include the famous samurai Yoshitsune Minamoto whose valor is glamorized in the *Heike monogatari* (Morris 1975, 67–105), and the doomed radical nationalist Isao in Yukio Mishima's novel *Runaway Horses*, who commits *seppuku* after failing in an assassination plot against the government in the 1930s.

Therefore, a clear cut, uniform, and familiar predominant narration of the war emerges from these early tales. It is a story of success, an account of dedication with no limit and of a heroic action taken by the weak party, despite its eventual loss. The actual winners of the war are set aside. To create this story, the artists situate the tales at the end of the war, putting the Japanese fighters in a defensive posture, and adopt a "bird's eye view." The war becomes what happens up in the sky, in a world far removed from the harsh realities on the ground. The enemy and death are rarely seen, and thus killing is less keenly felt, allowing the reader to concentrate on the defenders' heroism rather than on the war's tragic outcome. The superb flying abilities of the Japanese fighter planes can also take a leading role, allowing the readers to feel great pride in Japanese technological achievements. The overall effect is to avoid dwelling on the devastating defeat and destruction that resulted from the war. Given the number of stories of this type that were published, we can also conclude that heroic war tales were the hegemonic narrative type of this early postwar period.

The Rejected Narrative About the Tragedy of War

While heroic war tales were dominant, they were not the only war manga available to young postwar readers. There were other stories about the ground war that emphasized its pain and tragedy. One such story is Shinji Nagashima's *Shiroi kumo wa yonde iru* (The White Cloud Is Calling), which was first published in 1956. It details the hard lives of children who had been left orphaned by the war. Another important example is Sampei Shirato's 1958 work, *Kieyuku shōjo* (The Vanishing Girl), about a life-and-death struggle of a young girl exposed to radiation from the atom bomb attack on Hiroshima. Other examples of this story type are those by the famous manga artist Shigeru Mizuki. He depicted the war mainly from the infantry's perspective with tales conveying its sorrow, pain, and stupidity.[1] One particularly famous work of his (item 23 in Table 8.1) is *Shiroi hata* (The White Flag, 1964). It recounts the brutal realities of the "no surrender" policy for infantry soldiers. Raising a white flag to surrender was almost unheard of in the war. Mizuki's story tells of a commander who decides to surrender in order to give his wounded soldiers a chance to retreat. It raises questions about what exactly counts as true bravery—fighting to the death or retreating to live.

Another poignant example is the short work by Sampei Shirato, *Sensō sono kyōfu no kiroku* (The War Records of Terror, 1963), dealing with starvation and cannibalism on the front line.[2] It tells of a tormented Japanese army veteran who struggles to explain to his children why since the war he has refrained from eating rare fish meat, and it directly addresses one of the horrors that many front-line Japanese soldiers experienced. Even some of the heroic air combat manga discussed earlier had their critical side. Tetsuya Chiba's *Shidenkai no taka*, for instance, is not just another adventure tale, but also challenged the justification of going to what amounted to a foolish war. Although they were written early in the postwar period, antiwar narratives of this type were rarely published at that time (Natsume 1997, 56). Shigeru Mizuki himself has testified that he had great difficulty getting these kinds of stories published because the magazine editors were rarely interested in them (Hirabayashi 2000, 72–73). These stories, deemed unacceptable by the publishing world, became the rejected narratives of that time.

The Late 1960s to Late 1970s

However, by the end of the 1960s, a new kind of manga tale dominated the marketplace. These stories were as transparently critical of the war as those that had been rejected in the previous decade. However, they drew attention to their polemic with sharp-edged stories about the ground war and plots that focused not only on the front but also on civilians adversely affected by the war. New topics were introduced that explored the war's moral and political ambiguities. Some of these included the atomic bomb, the air raids on civilian targets, the Japanese army's atrocities in Asia, the American struggle against a totalitarian Nazism in Europe, the participation of second-generation Japanese Americans (*nisei*) on the American side, and also the Japanese army's mistreatment of prisoners of war. The fate of Jews in the Nazi concentration camps, the retreat of Japanese civilians from China, the fate of women and children, and even the fate of animals in war zones were addressed.[3]

There were several well-known artists of that time. Keiji Nakazawa, for example, drew several important works. One was *Kuroi ame ni utarete* (Black Rain Fell Over Me, 1968), a tale set against the atomic bombardment of Hiroshima. It is about a hired killer who has some "things to take care of" on that day but ends up badly wounded. Yet before he dies, he offers his eyes to a blind young girl named Heiwa (Peace), whom he had known before the attack. The story is replete with scenes of the destruction, misery and tragedy wrought upon the city. Nakazawa's other works in the same vein are *Aru hi totsuzen ni* (Suddenly, One Day, 1970), and *Ore wa mita* (I Saw It, 1972). Both are based on his experience in the bomb blast and were published in *Shōnen Jump*. However, his most famous work by far is *Hadashi no Gen* (*Barefoot Gen*, 1973–1975).[4] This long running work, based on the experiences of Nakazawa's family in Hiroshima, starts a few months before the blast and then focuses on the immediate aftermath, detailing the ordeals of those daring to speak up against the war, the scarcity of food, and the daily struggle to survive. His description is completely unvarnished, bluntly showing how people were vaporized, crushed, and mutilated by the explosion and documenting how the survivors were so extensively burned that their skin had melted away. Another artist who wrote about the atomic havoc is Koji Asahioka, whose *Aru wakusei no higeki* (A Tragedy of a Planet, 1969) is based on the diary of the storywriter Tatsuo Kusakawa.[5]

Yet another famous artist of this period is again Shigeru Mizuki. His *Haisōki* (The Flight, 1970) was part of a project called "manga writers writing themselves" that included works by famous manga writers like Osamu Tezuka and Jōji Akiyama. Mizuki chose for that project to recount his war experience of being wounded, losing his left arm, and being evacuated while the rest of his unit fought to the death. *Danbiru kaikyō* (The Strait of Danbiru, 1970) is another story of his, this time about the soldiers who were the bearers of the rising sun flag. It tells the story of one such soldier who struggles to defend this "piece of cloth" but instead loses his life. *Sōin gyokusai seyo* (The Banzai Charge, 1973), by far his famous work from that time, is about a unit that miraculously survives a suicide mission. Yet, since their "glorious death" has already been reported to headquarters, they are sent back to the front with orders not to return alive. Brutal stories like these showed the arrogant and callous way Japanese officers treated their soldiers. All of Mizuki's works reveal the tragedy of infantry units based upon the author's own bitter personal experiences.

Another notable author of the time was Junpei Gomikawa. His story *Ningen no jōken* (The Human Condition) was first published as a literary work in 1956 and was adapted as a manga in 1971. Drawn by Kenji Abe, it chronicles the cruelty of the Japanese army toward the Chinese.

The writers Joya Kagemaru and Shinebu Hashimoto are not as famous as the manga writers mentioned above. Nonetheless, they belong here. They are responsible for the manga form of the story *Watashi wa kai ni naritai* (I Wish I Could Become a Shellfish), published in 1969. The story was based on a television drama broadcast in 1958. It tells of an ordinary Japanese draftee who is ordered by his superiors to kill prisoners of war and is subsequently accused of committing war crimes.

Table 8.2 lists the titles of a selection of World War II manga from this period. Of the twenty-six examples found, twenty dwell on the tragic ground war, while only four focus on the air war (numbers 7, 22, 25, 26) and two (numbers 3 and 23) blend both into one plot. Looking at them iconographically, it is clear that manga of the late 1960s and the 1970s, unlike their predecessors, did not hesitate to picture the grotesqueries of war.

In Keiji Nakazawa's comic about the atom bomb attacks on Japan, *Ore wa mita* (I Saw It) for example, the horrific effect of the war on the human body is no longer hidden. In gruesome scenes (see page 186), readers see victims suffering from the deadly radiation burns. The pages are unsparingly graphic about the myriad grisly ways in which people and soldiers could die in war. This obsession with suffering and death appears on the covers in riveting portraits of the dead and dying, in stark contrast to the cute-hero fighters typical of earlier manga. This can be seen, for example, in the difference between earlier and later examples of Shigeru Mizuki's cover artwork. His earlier cover, done in 1958 (see page 180), has fighter planes in the skies with determined-looking pilots surveying the scene; in Mizuki's later cover (see page 187) for *Sōin gyokusai seyo* (The Banzai Charge, 1973), the pilots and planes are removed; what was left flying are the body parts blown up by the explosions.

The stories are usually about fighters who are led to war by tragic circumstances. In air war stories, too, tragic social circumstances that engulf the characters become the main focus of the narrative. The works of Reiji Matsumoto, Keiji Nakazawa, Machiko Satonaka, and other artists showed that even within the ranks of the "heroic" Zero pilots, there were those who joined reluctantly and because of social pressure. In many of these stories, the main characters become kamikaze pilots only because the Japanese society expected them to do so. A good example is Hiroshi Kaizuka's *Aa, Zero-sen tonbo* (The Dragonfly Zero Fighter, 1972).

It is the story of a boy who became a Zero fighter pilot despite his real desire to keep studying biology, specializing in what he loved most—insects. The war forces him to abandon his dream, and he eventually dies in the war, leaving his father, a teacher, tormented over his loss. Hiroshi Kaizuka is a manga author who wrote many stories about the air war that emphasized the bravery of the pilots. In this story, however, he casts an unsparing glimpse into the horror and misery of the war, with his main character clearly revealing how much he despises it.

Also prominent is the absence of heroes. The stories, of course, do have various protagonists, but these are no longer the type of heroes found in the earlier World War II tales. Rather than symbolizing unstinting self-sacrifice and honor in the service of the emperor, soldiers in these stories are ordinary people who epitomize the human will to survive. Shigeru Mizuki, for instance, depicts soldiers enduring the everyday indignities of army life at the front. His characters show the unheroic ways soldiers typically suffered and died, such as from disease, poor medical care, and starvation.

As noted above, many tales were based upon personal testimonies. Some authors who had drawn the earlier manga showing fictionalized heroic air battles now stepped forward to tell their real personal experiences. A good example is Tetsuya Chiba. From 1963 to 1965, he wrote the famous *Shidenkai no taka* (The Hawk in the Violet Lightning

Table 8.2

Major Japanese War Comics, 1968–1977

Year	Work	Author / Illustrator	Publisher
1. 1968	*Kuroi ame ni utarete* (Black Rain Fell over Me)	Keiji Nakazawa	Manga Punch
2. 1968	*Kono ai senka o koete* (Let's Move Beyond the Fire of War)	Masako Watanabe	Margaret
3. 1968	*Futari no Ōzora* (A Sky for Two)	Machiko Satonaka	Shōjo Friend
4. 1969	*Aru wakusei no higeki* (A Tragedy of a Planet)	Koji Asahioka	Shōnen Magazine
5. 1969	*Watashi wa kai ni naritai* (I Wish I Could Become a Shellfish)	Shinobu Hashimoto Joya Kagemaru	Shōnen King
6. 1969	*Cho wa koko ni sumenai* (A Butterfly Cannot Live Here)	Masako Watanabe	Margaret
7. 1970	*Aru hi totsuzen ni* (Suddenly, One Day)	Keiji Nakazawa	Shōnen Jump
8. 1970	*Haisōki* (The Flight)	Shigeru Mizuki	Shōnen Magazine
9. 1970	*Danbiru kaikyō* (The Strait of Danbiru)	Shigeru Mizuki	Bunshū Manga Yomihon
10. 1970	*Jigoku shima* (An Island of Hell)	Koji Asahioka	Shōnen Gahō
11. 1970	*Mata au hi made* (Goodbye Until We Meet Again)	Kenichiro Suzuhara	Margaret
12. 1970	*Mariko* (Mariko)	Riyoko Ikeda	Margaret
13. 1971	*Ningen no jōken* (The Human Condition)	Junpei Gomikawa Kenji Abe	Shōnen Jump
14. 1972	*Ore wa mita* (I Saw It)	Keiji Nakazawa	Shōnen Jump
15. 1972	*Akai rikku sakku* (The Red Rucksack)	Tomoe Satō	Ribon
16. 1972	*Ashita kagayaku* (It Will Shine Tomorrow)	Machiko Satonaka	Shōjo Friend
17. 1972	*Aa, Zero-sen tombo* (The Dragonfly Zero Fighter)	Hiroshi Kaizuka	Shōnen Magazine
18. 1973-5	*Hadashi no Gen* (Barefoot Gen)	Keiji Nakazawa	Shōnen Jump
19. 1973	*Sōin gyokusai seyo* (The Banzai Charge)	Shigeru Mizuki	Kōdansha
20. 1973	*Sokaiko kazoe uta* (The Song of an Evacuated Child)	Tomoe Satō	Ribon
21. 1973	*Yane ura no ehonkaki* (The Illustrations at the Attic)	Tetsuya Chiba	Shōnen Jump
22. 1973	*Reppū* (A Strong Wind)	Hiroshi Kaizuka	Shōnen Champion
23. 1973–5	*Senjō manga shirîzu* (Manga Battlefield Series)	Reiji Matsumoto	Shōnen Sunday
24. 1974	*Kami no toride* (The Paper Fortress)	Osamu Tezuka	Shōnen King
25. 1975	*Zero no shiro taka* (The White Hawk Zero Fighter)	Hiroshi Motomiya	Shōnen Jump
26. 1977	*Senki roman* (Nostalgic War Records)	Kaoru Shintani	Monthly Shōnen Champion

A scene from the English translation of the story *Ore wa mita* **(I Saw It, 1972) by Keiji Nakazawa.** (Reproduced with permission from Harupu Publishing)

Shigeru Mizuki's cover artwork for *Sōin gyokusai seyo* (The Banzai Charge, 1973).

Fighter), a heroic story about pilots and planes. In 1973, however, he wrote *Yane ura no ehonkaki* (The Illustrations in the Attic), which recalled the humiliating Japanese retreat from China as he had experienced it at the age of six. In the scene on page 189, a soldier consoles a dying woman. Those too weak to travel were left to die along the way.

A scene from *Aa, Zero-sen tonbo* (The Dragonfly Zero Fighter, 1972), by Hiroshi Kaizuka.
(Reproduced with permission from Harupu Publishing)

A scene from *Yane ura no ehonkaki* (The Illustrations in the Attic) depicting the hardships on the way back to Japan. (Copyright Tetsuya Chiba)

Other artists tackled the issue of the war for the first time by writing about their personal war experiences. Most famous among these was a newcomer to this genre, the "god of manga," Osamu Tezuka. In his *Kami no toride* (The Paper Fortress, 1974), Tezuka described the air raids in Osaka by drawing attention to the plight of the children, who were forced to give up school and any semblance of a happy childhood for "the sake of the country." Jun Ishiko notes that in the 1970s two other manga writers, Reiji Matsumoto and Hosei Hasegawa, also drew their personal war recollections, each detailing the horrors of the air raids (1983, 214).

Another interesting development in this decade is the increase of World War II manga in girls' magazines. For quite some time after the surrender, this genre was found exclusively in boys' magazines. However, starting in the late 1960s, this began to change. In girls' magazines, these stories were usually centered on heroines who were struggling through the war, and they tended toward the emotional, often revolving around the tragedy of lost love due to death or forced separation. Most were not directly concerned with Japan but described events in Europe, such as the resistance movement and the concentration camps (Ishiko 1983, 214). Two examples of these are Masako Watanabe's *Kono ai senka o koete* (Let's Move Beyond the Fire of War, 1968) and her *Cho wa koko ni sumenai* (A Butterfly Cannot Live Here, 1969). The former is an account of the Allied Forces' D-Day Normandy landing that also tells how Nazi soldiers, despite everything, were still merciful; the latter is a Holocaust story about the Jews who suffered horribly in Nazi concentration camps.

Manga in girls' magazines also shed light on the wartime fate of Japanese women and children. Some dramatized the forced retreat of Japanese civilians from China or Japanese women's struggles after the death of their loved ones. Good examples of the former are Tomoe Satō, *Akai rakku sakku* (The Red Rucksack, 1972) and Machiko Satonaka's *Ashita kagayaku* (It Will Shine Tomorrow, 1972). A classic example of the latter is Kenichiro Suzuhara's *Mata au hi made* (Goodbye Until We Meet Again, 1970), a story about two lovers who are forced apart, their longing and devotion to each other, and their final tragic deaths. There were also stories about the travails of children caught up in the forced evacuations (*sokai*), such as Tomoe Satō's *Sokai ko kazoe uta* (The Song of an Evacuated Child, 1973). This story gives a gripping account of a child who has become separated from his parents and must survive hunger and bullying from other displaced children; again, the story is based upon the author's own wartime experiences as a child.

Girls' magazines also published stories about the *hibakusha,* those who suffered from the devastating atomic bombings of Hiroshima and Nagasaki. Riyoko Ikeda's *Mariko* (1970) is a noteworthy example of this plot type. Set in the 1970s, the story follows a second-year high school girl who must cope when some of her closest friends die from diseases caused by the residual effects of radiation. She becomes curious about the war, asking her mother about her own experiences. The story ties the manga-reading youth of the 1970s directly to their parents' pasts by revealing how much pain and suffering inflicted by the war still lingered.

What I have tried to show thus far is that a narrative shift has occurred in manga war stories since the late 1960s. Heroic war stories are no longer the dominant discourse, since stories about the absurdity and tragedy of war have replaced them. These new stories do not look back nostalgically to the Japanese empire, nor glorify the ideals of duty, honor, and country, nor revel in Japan's war machines. Rather, they are complex and ambiguous. They examine the tragic flaws, from simple hubris to banal fumbling, that led to the human misery of the war years. These later stories no longer allow the reader to dwell above the fray, flying with heroic Japanese ace pilots. They have descended from the earlier romantic fantasy to Earth, and more specifically to the harsh realities of the muddy hell where Japanese soldiers and civilians suffered and died. In short, the story that had been marginalized a decade earlier was now the mainstream.

The new hegemonic narrative did not feature the tragic hero archetype. Rather, manga of the late 1960s and 1970s featured ordinary foot soldiers facing the ever-present realities of death, fear, hunger, and despair. These characters are older and wiser than those of the immediate postwar period. Worn out by the war, they have lost their innocence and wear rags instead of dashing uniforms. These soldiers are not the war's heroes, but its victims.

But beyond this, the later manga also addressed some new and troubling issues. Of particular interest is their treatment of Japan's role as aggressor. This is found in several cases. *Ningen no jōken* (The Human Condition, 1971) is an unsparing indictment of Japanese soldiers' cruelty toward the Chinese. Keiji Nakazawa also touches upon the victimization of Chinese and Koreans during the war. Osamu Tezuka's *Nagai ana* (The Long Hole, 1970) is another tale about the sad fate of Koreans, both during hostilities and later as displaced second-class Japanese citizens.

And yet, while this new narrative was gaining a growing readership in the late 1960s and 1970s, the previous hegemonic narrative of the early 1960s did not disappear. Some artists, like Hiroshi Kaizuka, kept drawing heroic air war tales even into the 1970s, like his *Reppū* (A Strong Wind, 1973). The same is true of writers like Hiroshi Motomiya (*Zero no shiro taka* [The White Hawk Zero Fighter, 1975]), Kaoru Shintani (*Senki roman* [Nostalgic War Records, 1977 on]), and Reiji Matsumoto (*Senjō manga shiirizu* [Manga Battlefield Series, 1973–1975]). This type of manga story was still present, although these manga had decreased dramatically in number by the 1970s as the new battlefield manga gained ground (Natsume 1997, 71; Yoshida 1995, 114–115; Yonezawa 1996, 146).

War Manga as Mirrors: Collective Representations of the Historical Moment

Now that we have identified the two types of war manga, it is necessary to explore the changing historical and social conditions that led to their creation and popularity. What was it that made the air war hero stories appeal to Japanese readers in the 1950s and early 1960s, but less so in the subsequent decade? Why did the historically realistic and anti-militaristic stories of the ground war become the reigning narrative in the late 1960s and 1970s? In both cases, the content of war manga shifted with the changing historical and social realities of Japanese society. As a pop cultural medium, manga served as collective representations of how most Japanese perceived World War II in the postwar periods.

1945–1954: Getting Distance from the War Experience

Generally speaking, Japanese in the immediate postwar years, from 1945 to 1954, were silent about the war. War stories began to appear mainly after the 1952 ratification of the Peace Treaty between the Allied Powers and Japan. Popularly known as the Treaty of San Francisco, this agreement officially terminated formal hostilities. By signing the treaty on behalf of Japan, Prime Minister Shigeru Yoshida legally forfeited all territorial conquests since 1895 and agreed to cede Okinawa temporarily to U.S. rule. A short while after signing the peace treaty, Japan and the United States signed a separate agreement, known as the Japan–U.S. Security Pact. In it, Japan agreed to the stationing of American troops on its soil for the sake of protecting Japan from outside aggression and assisting the Japanese government in suppressing internal riots. Both the peace treaty and the security pact entered into force on April 28, 1952, ending the postwar military occupation of Japan.

At this point, a vast narration of the war in media other than manga appeared (Yoshida 1995, 84–85; Hicks 1998, 24; Dower 1996, 129). The end of the U.S. military occupation, Igarashi argues, allowed the memories of the war to resurface in the popular consciousness (2000, 15), particularly through stories and reports circulating in the mass media of radio, television, and films. Yoshida, for instance, notes that as soon as the peace treaty was signed in 1952, a wave of *senki mono* (accounts of the war) written by former Japanese officers occurred (1995, 84). And, in 1956, when the government, in its annual economic White Paper, declared that "Japan is no longer in the postwar period," a record number of over sixty works was published (Natsume 1997, 32; Morton 1994, 210; Yoshida 1995, 106–107).

The new Occupation policies were doubtless behind this trend. Immediately after the war, the Occupation authorities had censored everything that discussed the recent military conflict (Natsume 1997, 25; Schodt 1983, 79; Braw 1997, 157; Richie 1996, 28; 1990, 41). But the postwar devastation also had something to do with it. Put simply, "Japan was too busy in digging itself out of the ruins to bother about those already dead, to worry about assigning guilt" (Richie 1996, 21). There was really no time to reminisce about the past. Treat (1995), who has studied Japanese A-bomb literature, has also noted the unprecedented difficulties that faced the first postwar generation of writers. These authors, he argues, faced "the problem of imagination." They faced the limits of language in relation to the overwhelming event. They needed time in order to digest their experiences and to make sense of them morally, politically, and spiritually, rather than simply dismissing them as inscrutable acts of god (Richie 1996, 20–54).

Manga were influenced by the same factors. They, too, initially faced the problem of censorship, and neglected the past during the Occupation years. Yonezawa maintains that the first manga about World War II was Taro Himoto's *Senjō shiirizu* (The Battlefield Series), published as late as autumn 1957 (1996, 42). This work, he points out, was actually a series written during the Occupation period, but, because it depicted World War II soldiers as heroes and showed no regret over the war, it was censored. What still needs to be addressed is why the manga world remained silent about the war until the late 1950s, when other forms of mass media had already begun to tackle the subject.

The first important reason is the fact that the manga of the 1950s were basically targeted at children. Such young readers would most likely find the subject of war unappealing. It was a time of acute poverty and of devastation in the bombed-out cities, and young Japanese were drawn to stories that gave hope for a better future or that provided escapist fantasies (Schodt 1983, 69; Tsurumi 1987, 32–34). Since war stories would evoke sad memories of the unpleasant recent past, they did not appear in the first decade after the end of the war.

But it is also tempting to regard this prolonged silence as indicative of the unwillingness of the Japanese to confront their past. By consciously excising the war from children's manga, Japanese adults revealed their own inability to come to terms with the war years. This absence is revealing since during the war, manga "reporting" on Japan's past and present battlefield glories had been popular fodder in children's magazines (see Akiyama 1998).

The initial lack of consensus about World War II left manga authors in a difficult position. It was easier to pick safer subjects that would not create any disputes. Manga writers and publishers at that time indeed chose to ignore history in favor of science fiction stories that provided uplifting dreams of a better time in an imaginary future (Schodt 1983, 61).[6] Focusing the reader's gaze forward with fun stories about the virtues of science and technological progress was, after all, a winning formula to attract a mass audience.

People's curiosity about science was particularly high in those days. First, in creating the atom bomb, science had proved its supremacy over the samurai spirit and the sincerity (*makoto* or *shisei*) of the kamikaze fighters in the waning days of the war. Second, the Cold War was beginning, ushering in the space race and the arms race. Finally, the new Ministry of Education placed an "emphasis on basic science" at the center of the postwar school system (Dower 1996, 119–121). All this stirred up interest in matters of technology, and writers, artists, and filmmakers filled the demand for technology-related stories.

Late 1950s to Late 1960s: The Emerging Positive Image of Japan's Military Past

By the late 1950s, most Japanese lived in small but functional apartments, and a growing number could enjoy the convenience of the so-called *sanshu no jingi*—the "three imperial regalia" (a refrigerator, a washing machine, and a TV set). The rapidly improving quality of life and the time distance from the events allowed people to reflect upon the war. What emerged was a new and interesting perspective.

First, it was readily becoming apparent that Japan's technological prowess, both before and during the war, had not gone to waste. People were aware, for instance, that through developing high-speed fighter planes, Japanese aeronautical engineers had acquired knowledge of great value in peaceful postwar Japan. When these engineers joined the civilian manufacturing industry, they contributed to the rise of a powerful automobile industry and later to the creation of Japan's high-speed rail network (Igarashi 2000, 148). Thus the reputation of Japan's technology once again reigned supreme, making Japanese feel great national pride. Likewise, their successful bid to host the eighteenth Olympic Games in 1964 symbolized Japan's reemergence as a player on the international stage, further boosting Japanese national pride. Indeed, social, economic, and political developments like these inspired a fair amount of national self-confidence.

At the same time, the late 1950s were also a time of acute internal conflict, centering on the Japan–U.S. Security Pact. In 1951, the signing of the security pact after the peace treaty had been an unwritten condition for ending the occupation of Japan. In October 1958, however, the Japanese government announced its intention to renegotiate the pact with the United States, rather than demanding its abolition. The announcement generated strident opposition within Japan. By now, the remarkable economic recovery of Japan made such security arrangements with the United States seem completely unnecessary. Many also viewed the treaty as one-sided: Japan had to provide military bases exclusively for the United States without having any control over them. Opposition intensified in late 1959, when the Soviet Union declared a right to retaliate against these bases, from which American spy planes freely operated. The apex of the political crisis occurred in 1960, when a surge of violent demonstrations (*ampo tōsō*) brought down the government of Nobusuke Kishi, who had himself been accused of war crimes but was released untried by the Occupation authorities.

The anti–Security Pact movement created a strange reality, in which the United States reemerged as an "enemy" that once again threatened Japan. It was a political crisis in which the Right and Left were ready to join hands. Both right-wing voters protesting the government's capitulation to American pressure and left-wing voters who feared a resurgence of Japanese militarism strongly believed that they were defending national pride. In this politically charged atmosphere, people could again enjoy manga that lionized a patriotic spirit. Put another way, many Japanese no longer felt uncomfortable about stories telling of the kamikaze pilot's unswerving devotion to the nation. In sum, the 1960s political conflict with the United States, Japan's rapid economic recovery, the anticipated Olympic glory, and Japan's postwar emergence as a high-tech powerhouse created fertile ground in which positive links between Japan's past and its present could grow. The passing of the years brought a more detached perspective and the circumstances of the present helped recast war memories in a rosier light. They helped to erase past failures and to transform wartime suffering into a positive and beneficial experience.

These changing political, social, and economic realities were reflected in the mass media. The literary magazine *Maru*, for instance, which early on began to specialize in accounts of naval and air war, added the following note to one of its first issues, dating from 1956: "Since the war we have tended to feel a sense of inferiority internationally. But the history of the war we fought against the world's greatest powers was, at some level, not necessarily a story of defeat. There was in some cases no lack of individual successes that can only lighten our hearts. We should never forget these facts" (Yoshida 1995, 85–86). Individuals were encouraged to remember the successes and not to dwell on Japan's ignominious defeat. Similar entreaties also came from the government. In a speech on the first War Dead Commemoration Day, held a full eighteen years after the war ended, on August 15, 1963, Prime Minister Hayato Ikeda observed that behind Japan's remarkable postwar recovery were the hopes and dreams of the many who had died for the country (Yoshida 1995, 110). A succession of prime ministers have echoed this view, ascribing Japan's postwar prosperity to the sacrifices made by the wartime generation. In their view, Japan's defeat had been a necessary precondition for the postwar Japanese "miracle" of peace and prosperity. In this revisionist view of Japanese recent history, World War II was no longer better left unspoken and forgotten. Japan's present and future success story was inextricably linked to the past through a continuous historical narrative of progress.

This logic was seductive. Many Japanese who had directly experienced the misery of the war were given an answer to the daunting question that haunted their postwar lives: Were the deaths of so many of their compatriots during the war utterly pointless? Here was a plausible answer: Their deaths had meaning because they had laid the foundation for Japan's current prosperity. And indeed, Yoshida points to the popularity of Fusao Hayashi as an instance of how such rationalizations of the war played out in the 1960s (1995, 127–128). In some widely read articles published in *Chūō kōron* (1963–1965), Hayashi justified the war by maintaining that Japan's military expansion had been designed to liberate the people of Asia from Western domination. Like the manga war stories of this era, Hayashi's argument neglects the awkward fact that Japan's imperial army frequently fought and killed fellow Asians.

This tendency to put a positive spin on the war is typical of literary works dating from the early to late 1950s. Most of the writers of these works were ex-navy and even former army soldiers turned authors, and therefore tended to write accounts that glorified the air war (Hicks 1998, 24–25). Stories emphasized courage, devotion to duty, and the technological marvels of the Japanese war machine. For the most part, they avoided moral or political questions about war.

It is not at all surprising, then, that manga from the same period share these narratives. Popular media, as well as literary media, generally reflected the spirit of the age. The resurgence of interest in Japanese war technology and Japanese war heroes reflected the renewal of Japanese nationalism from under the penumbra of the Occupation.[7] Under such circumstances it was easy for World War II stories to become permissible for children. Put another way, the war was tamed, miniaturized, and thereby rendered fascinating rather than terrifying, simply because the adults themselves were indulging in such memories and sugarcoating the wartime legacy. Manga merely replicated the larger hegemonic discourse about World War II that had taken hold of the Japanese public.

Of course, many manga authors were also falling back on their own personal recollections and on the war propaganda they had been exposed to as children. They had doubtless devoured stories about Japan's superiority in military technology, which had been highlighted in magazines like *Kodomo no kagaku* (Children's Science), or stories about the heroism of Japanese soldiers, which had been found everywhere in wartime children's magazines like *Rikugun no tomo* (A Friend of the Army) or *Kaiyō shōnen* (A Boy of the Ocean). Using these tried and true stories from their own childhoods helped manga authors to produce heroic pilot and plane stories under deadline. Shigeru Mizuki, the only manga writer of that time who saw active service, was made then to recall a different war, resulting in his stories of a much grimmer, darker tone. Yet Japanese society was not ready for Mizuki's version at that particular time and his stories were initially suppressed.

The Late 1960s to the 1970s: Revisioning World War II as a Dreadful Past

By the end of the 1960s, new circumstances emerged that transformed Japan's vision of its past. Renewed diplomatic ties with Korea and China, the oil crisis of the 1970s, and the Vietnam War, which lingered on for almost a decade (1965–1974) were the critical events of this time.

The Vietnam War saturated the media with images that resonated with Japan's wartime past. As early as 1965, images of casual American brutality were broadcast in the Japanese media. Reports of American atrocities and "body counts" became daily fare (Asada 1997, 175–176). The U.S. air raids on Hanoi and the scenes of Vietnamese peasants enduring American bombing evoked disturbing memories among Japanese TV viewers. Moreover, diplomatic ties were resumed with (South) Korea in 1965 and with China in 1972. This placed these two countries, which had been the focus of Japanese imperialistic ambitions, at the front and center of the Japanese public consciousness. The Japanese could no longer ignore their Asian neighbors' accusations of wartime atrocities. And if this were not enough, there was also the oil crisis that occurred during the 1973 Arab-Israeli war. Oil-producing Arab countries cut supplies to those countries they deemed hostile to the Arab cause. The shortages that followed in Japan brought back unpleasant memories of the prewar shortages of raw materials that had threatened the Japanese economy. Indeed, Japan's view that the West had cut off its access to vital raw materials had been a major impetus to its entry into the war.

It is not surprising, then, that the late 1960s and the 1970s produced a surge of reminiscences about the tragedy of the war—including the horrors of the Japanese invasion and occupation of China and Korea, Japan's war atrocities, and the devastation Japan inflicted upon others during the war (Yoshida 1995, 129; Dower 1996, 141). Famous among these was a series of reports by the Japanese journalist Katsuichi Honda, who wrote on the violence and atrocities committed by Japanese military forces in China. Honda's *Chūgoku no tabi* (The Journey to China) was published in the daily *Asahi* newspaper in 1971. It offered the first extensive coverage on how the Chinese remembered the war, generating a heated debate on the Nanjing Massacre of 1937 that still continues today. Another key work of that period to recall the horrors of the war was Katsumoto Saotome's book *Tokyo daikūshū* (The Great Tokyo Air Raids, 1971), which recounted for the first time the terrors of living under constant bombardment (Yoshida 1995, 154). Likewise, beginning in 1974, members of *Sōka Gakkai,* a new religious movement that was ardently antiwar, compiled their own wartime reminiscences, published under the title *Sensō o shiranai sedai e* (To the Generation

Who Does Not Know the War). It was released in two series. One consisted of fifty-six volumes published from 1974 to 1979, and the other was a twenty-four-volume set that appeared from 1981 to 1985. It offers graphic testimonies of Japanese acts of aggression, especially on the Chinese front (Yoshida 1995, 157; Hicks 1998, 42).

It was civilians rather than former soldiers who often wrote war reminiscences at that time, concentrating their attention on the devastating air raids (Yoshida 1995, 154–155). Another interesting feature is that many were women's memoirs (Hicks 1998, 41). In addition, reminiscences were often written by the many Japanese who had responded to the imperial call to settle in the "new world," particularly Manchuria in the 1930s, and who had been forcibly repatriated after the war (Gluck 1993, 77).

The mass media also participated in this project of providing an unvarnished picture of the brutality of the war, and turned from soldiers' recollections to civilian memoirs. The daily newspaper *Asahi shimbun* heralded this new tendency when, in 1965, it collected war stories of average Japanese into a work entitled *Chichi no senki* (Father's Record of War). The effort opened the way for war stories that broke down the customary division between front line and home front. As the title of the series indicates, it was a male-only memoir. Ten years later, however, women's memoirs finally appeared in the *Yomiuri shimbun* too, in a series called *Senshō* (The War) that ran from 1975 to 1984 and offered a forum for common people's stories.

The trend of publishing personal memoirs also occurred at the local level. Of particular interest in this regard was the island of Okinawa. The U.S. air bases in Okinawa were the staging area for bombing sorties to Vietnam at that time, which must have added a special impetus to produce wartime memoirs about the Pacific war. These accounts were characterized by the rejection of heroic interpretations of the Okinawan battle, which had killed over one-third of the civilian population (Yoshida 1995: 154–155).

By the 1970s, the now-famous husband and wife painters Toshi Maruki and Iri Maruki had also made their mark with murals depicting new perspectives on the war. The two were antiwar activists who had struggled against the Japanese imperial army's occupation of Manchuria in 1931 and Japan's entry into World War II. In August 1945, after the atomic bombing, they had rushed to Hiroshima, where they had relatives. The experience changed their art radically, according to Toshi Maruki: "Though we tried to paint with peace and optimism, our paintings were filled with anguish. A darkness emerged on the canvas, even when we didn't intend it. We realized we would have to confront that darkness" (quoted in *Hellfire: A Journey from Hiroshima* 1986). The two artists began to illustrate the "hell" that they had witnessed with their Hiroshima murals. Their works were allowed to be publicly exhibited in 1950. Drawing all along on the horrors of Hiroshima, it was only in 1971–1972 that they included images of the enraged survivors in Hiroshima, who tortured and murdered Caucasian prisoners of war and Korean nationals in the aftermath of the attack (Dower 1997, 44–45).

Generally speaking, by the 1970s Japan was comprised of the "same people, inhabiting the same self, status and daily life, except that the frame of social meaning had been suddenly changed" (Gluck 1993, 76). Japanese now soberly faced the truth of the war, including its melancholy stories of meaningless suffering and hopeless tragedy. A survey conducted in 1975, for instance, found that the number of people who discussed the atrocities committed by the Japanese army had increased significantly from previous surveys and that the number of those discussing the heroism of the Japanese soldiers had sharply declined (Yoshida 1995, 197–198). Evidence of this sudden change is found also in the war manga of the late 1960s and the 1970s. Manga, as a popular medium of social expression, simply added a visual form that helped disseminate the new narratives and perspectives to a mass audience.

The Social Frames of Manga Tales

In this study, I have focused on the representations of World War II in manga that were intended to edify and entertain young people in the first twenty-five years after the war. This genre consists of fictional works that neither the artists nor the editors pretended to present as an objective vision of history. However, as this chapter has shown, these stories are closely related to larger historical views and concerns prevalent in Japanese society over that period. Manga stories about World War II clearly reflect the different times in which they were produced, faithfully conforming to contemporary dictates of the collective moods and perceptions of the war. Manga, which were mainly sold to youth, gave this collective frame of memory a "childish" color and form, altering its representations as the predominant way of remembering the war changed over time.

The manga artist Go Nagai has noted that when he sits down to compose a manga, he always feels that some mysterious power joins him. "Saying such a thing," he adds, "is not to suggest that I am being possessed by some mysterious ghost or some other strange things, but rather to point out the existence of a so-called 'collective desire'; to suggest that in fact stories are written by the period. Many people, he explained, who share a certain experience together or just live in the same era, eventually develop a collective desire as for what they would like to read. I always then find myself trying to adjust to that collective desire and to represent it in my manga." (quoted in Tanigawa 1995, 174–175).

In the same vein, Vinitzky-Seroussi has noted that "[Mnemonic] narratives are never mere lists-assemblages of dates or facts—put together without logic or motivation. Rather, they are selective accounts with beginnings and endings, constructed to create meanings, interpret reality, organize events in time, establish coherency and continuity, construct identities, enable social action, and to construct the world and its moral and social order for its audience" (Vinitzky-Seroussi 2002, 34–35). Manga war stories are like any other narrative in this respect. They might be entertainment for a young audience, but they are nevertheless intimately connected with other discourses about the past, creating a vast symbolic system that gives meaning and an ethos for Japanese society in the early decades after the war.

Notes

1. Initially, however, Mizuki also depicted the war solely in terms of the air war. Examples are his story collections *Senjō no chikai* (The Battlefield Vow), *Zerogō sakusen* (Operation no. Zero), and *Akatsuki no totsunyū* (The Dawn Attack), all published in 1958.

2. To be exact, this work is comprised of three different stories. The first two deal with the European theater, and the third concerns Japan's wartime memories. The first two are about a young girl's struggle to survive during the Holocaust, the London bombing campaign, and the horrors of Nazi forced labor camps.

3. I know of two works dedicated wholly to animals. One was published in 1971 in *Shōnen Jump* and was called "Tonky monogatari" (The Story of Tonky), and the other, published in 1974, is a story from the famous *Doraemon* series called "Zō to ojisan" (The Elephant and the Uncle, by the publisher Shōgakukan). Both recall the fate of animals in Tokyo's Ueno zoo during the war, describing how they had to be put to death because of the lack of food. In his *Hadashi no Gen* (*Barefoot Gen*), a manga about the fate of Hiroshima's civilians before, during, and after the nuclear bombardment, Keiji Nakazawa also briefly touches on the fate of horses and other animals.

4. *Hadashi no Gen* was first serialized in *Shōnen Jump*, and was turned into a film in 1976, translated into English in 1978, published as a children's book in 1980, and became an animated television series in 1983.

5. Published in *Shōnen Magazine*, it was actually the first manga story about the atomic bomb. First published in a weekly boys' magazine, it was later turned into a literary work (Ishiko 1983, 236).

6. There were of course also some stories that dealt with the past. With the lifting of the Occupation rule in 1952, a spate of manga appeared that were set in Japan's past. Nonetheless, until the end of the 1950s, such manga works did not deal with the recent past, but with the more remote samurai period. These are the *chanbara* (sword fight) genre stories (Natsume 1997, 26).

7. Around 1960, more than thirty regional papers are recorded to call for former soldiers' memoirs (Takahashi 1988, 55), reflecting the renewed public interest in war veterans.

9

Aum Shinrikyō and a Panic About Manga and Anime

RICHARD A. GARDNER

During the postwar years, various aspects of Japan—including traditional arts such as the tea ceremony, the classics of modern Japanese film, and the phenomenal growth of the Japanese economy—have attracted foreign interest in Japan and even come to stand as emblems of Japan. For the past twenty years or so, manga and anime have also come to serve as emblems attracting people throughout the world to things Japanese. The recent success abroad of Hayao Miyazaki's *Spirited Away* has introduced this aspect of Japan's visual culture to an even wider audience and led some to predict a new "golden age" for Japanese film (Napier 2003, 22). In the midst of the accolades, it is important to recall that there have been moments in recent history when manga and anime have been regarded as potentially dangerous or as emblems of what is wrong with Japan.

Such was the case in the months following the release of sarin gas in several Tokyo subway lines by members of the religious group Aum Shinrikyō on the morning of March 20, 1995. As the extent of the Aum's crimes gradually became clear, Japanese journalists, scholars, intellectuals, and commentators of every sort attempted to explain the origin and rise of Aum, the reasons for the group's turn to violence, and what the appearance of such a group might mean about Japan. In the various theories and explanations presented, nearly every aspect of Japanese society, culture, and religion has been held to be at least partially accountable for the rise of Aum and the turn to violence by some of its members (see Gardner 1999, 221–222; 2002a, 36–42). In the efforts to explain Aum, considerable attention was given to the roles that manga and anime might have played. This resulted in what might be described as a panic about their possible negative influence on Japanese culture and society.

Rather than attempting to explain precisely how manga and anime might have contributed to the rise of Aum and its vision of "Harumagedon," or Armageddon, this chapter will simply present an overview of the ways in which both members of Aum and commentators on Aum understood the role of manga and anime in relation to Aum. Attention will be given, in particular, to how these perceptions were linked with broader concerns about the possible negative influence of various forms of media, technology, and "virtual reality."

Harumagedon in Popular Culture and Aum

While my aim is not to analyze in any detail the apocalyptic, cataclysmic scenarios and themes in 1970s and 1980s Japanese popular culture or in Aum's vision of Harumagedon, some background concerning these topics is needed. This should help explain why, following the Tokyo sarin attack, many drew parallels between Aum's teachings and the apocalyptic story lines of some manga and anime.

Growing out of a yoga group led by Shōkō Asahara (original name Chizuo Matsumoto), Aum emerged in the mid-1980s as one of the New New Religions (see Reader 1988, 235–261). From the beginning, Aum was preoccupied with the development of supernatural powers through the use of yogic practices and meditation. While presenting itself as a form of esoteric Buddhism and indeed drawing many of its teachings from Buddhist sources, Aum was eclectic. Though it claimed its origin was in ancient traditions, the link was usually mediated through very contemporary sources: the teachings and publications of other new religions, popular writings on Nostradamus, the writings of Buddhist scholars, and a variety of popular publications treating a range of religious, occult, and New Age topics. Though cast in a language and idiom that seemed bizarre to many in Japan, most of Aum's practices and concepts can nevertheless be traced to those found in many Japanese religious traditions (Shimazono 2001, 19–52; Reader 1996).

While Aum had an apocalyptic orientation from early on, its vision of the future became increasingly dark as its confrontations with society grew. Some have suggested a link, for instance, between Aum's increasingly pessimistic vision of a coming war and cataclysm and the suspicions surrounding the group after the disappearance of lawyer and anti-Aum activist Tsutsumi Sakamoto and his family in November 1989 (Aum members later confessed to the killing of the Sakamotos). Other possible sources of this shift in vision include the defeat of Aum candidates in the 1990 Diet elections, the arrest of Aum members for land fraud in 1990, a growingly vocal anti-Aum movement, and the group's increasing financial difficulties as its expansion slowed (Reader 2000, 126–161).

While Asahara's prophecies concerning Harumagedon were relatively optimistic throughout the 1980s, they became increasingly pessimistic in the 1990s. Because Aum's teachings were being ignored, Asahara pronounced that the world was inevitably moving toward a cataclysmic war that only a small fraction of the world population would survive. Pressure increased on Aum members to renounce the world, contribute their worldly goods to the group, and devote themselves to ascetic practices at Aum communities. A sense of Asahara's vision in the 1990s is gleaned from a quick overview of some of Aum's public statements concerning Harumagedon (Reader 2000, 162–195).

In *Risō shakai Shambala* (The Ideal Society Shambala), Asahara is presented as the blind messiah prophesied by Nostradamus and attributed powers of prophecy likened to those of Jesus and the Buddha (Asahara 1992b). Harumagedon will take place in 1999. Japan's shift to the right and militarism is taken as a sign of the approaching disaster. Hope lies, however, in members of Aum being able to develop supernatural powers similar to those of Asahara. While there is no longer hope of preventing Harumagedon, Aum adepts will be able to survive to establish a new one-thousand-year kingdom on Earth. This is the same one-thousand-year kingdom foreseen by St. John in Revelations, by Nostradamus, and by Adolf Hitler, whom Asahara considers another great seer. In *Asahara Shōkō, senritsu no yōgen* (The Shocking Prophecies of Asahara Shōkō), the date for Harumagedon is moved up to 1997. Freemasons and Jews are identified as agents involved in a conspiracy leading the world to disaster. Those who develop supernatural powers in time will be able to survive (Asahara 1993). In *Hi izuru kuni, saiwai chikashi* (The Land of the Sinking Sun, Disaster Is Near), published in manga form early in 1995, the date of Harumagedon is moved up to the fall of 1995 (Asahara 1995).

Even before nationwide attention focused on Aum, Japanese scholars of religion had been attempting to account for the rise of what they called "New New Religions" in Japan from the 1970s onward (Shimazono 1992, 1–8). To explain these somewhat distinctive new religions, considerable attention was given to relating them to a range of phenomena in Japanese culture: apocalyptic manga and anime, a science fiction subculture, a Nostradamus boom, an interest in the occult and supernatural powers, the growth of consumerism, the emergence of an information society, the influence of New Age spiritualities, and so forth (Haga and Kisala 1995, 236–241). There was, in other words, prior precedent for appealing to manga and anime to explain New New Religions such as Aum.

The apocalyptic or cataclysmic themes in manga and anime throughout the 1970s and 1980s must be understood, of course, within a larger context. Apocalyptic, millennial, or cataclysmic themes are not unknown in modern Japanese religious traditions and are particularly notable in many of the movements labeled as New New Religions (Shimazono 1986, 55–86; 1992, 46–50). Related themes have also been dealt with extensively in modern Japanese literature as well as film (Napier 1996, 181–219; 1993, 327–351). Also relevant are phenomena such as the "Nostradamus boom" in Japan, sparked by the publication of *The Great Prophecies of Nostradamus* in 1973 (Goshima 1973). There is not yet any compelling, definitive account of how all these apocalyptic or cataclysmic scenarios are related either to each other or to changes in Japanese culture and society. We must thus content ourselves with some preliminary, exploratory observations.

Among the manga and anime frequently mentioned in connection with Aum are Reiji Matsumoto's *Uchū senkan Yamato* (The Space Battleship Yamato, known in the United States as *Star Blazers*), which first appeared as an animated television series in 1973; Hayao Miyazaki's *Mirai shōnen Konan* (Conan, The Boy of the Future), an animated television series broadcast by NHK beginning in 1978; Miyazaki's *Kaze no*

Aum's apocalyptic representation of Harumagedon from its publication *Vajrāyana Sacca* **no. 5,
AUM Press, pp. 6–7.** (Reproduced with permission from Aleph Public Relations Department)

tani no Naushika (*Nausicaä of the Valley of the Wind*) which appeared in manga form
from 1982 to 1994 and as a feature film in 1984; Kazumasa Hirai and Shōtarō Ishimori's
Harumagedon: Genma taisen (The Great Battle with Genma), which appeared as a
feature-length anime in 1983 and did much to popularize the term "Harumagedon";
and Katsuhiro Ōtomo's *Akira*, which appeared in manga form beginning in 1984 and
then as an animated film in 1989.

Despite their many differences, these works share a few general features. All present
a situation in which an existing civilization has undergone a traumatic transformation (*Conan, Nausicaä*, and *Akira*) or is confronting imminent destruction (*Yamato*
and *Genma*). The destruction originates from either human evil or stupidity (*Conan,
Nausicaä*, and *Akira*) or an external evil civilization or force (*Yamato* and *Genma*). In
all cases, a small band of heroes must save themselves as well as whatever part of the
world they are still capable of saving. In all but *Yamato*, the heroes are set aside from
most people by virtue of the supernatural powers they have developed or mysteriously
acquired. In the cases of *Genma* and *Akira*, salvation seems possible only for those
who have developed extraordinary powers.

This brief account of apocalyptic scenarios in Aum's teachings and in manga and
anime should make clear that there are some intriguing parallels between the two.

Aum presented the world (and itself in particular) as threatened by various evil forces. While at times envisioning that disaster might be averted, as in *Yamato*, Aum eventually concluded that the coming cataclysm was inevitable and concentrated on surviving into the post-cataclysmic age. As in the case of many manga and anime, developing supernatural powers was considered key for survival. While most people might die, Aum members would live to carry on civilization in some form.

Aum's View of the Mass Media

While Aum at times successfully made use of the mass media to publicize itself, beginning in 1989 the group was involved in a series of confrontations with the Japanese mass media (Gardner 2005, 159–161). These confrontations, as well as the defeat of all Aum candidates in the 1990 Diet elections, seem to have alienated Aum members further from Japanese society. The perceived rejection of Aum's teachings was closely linked with Asahara's increasingly pessimistic view of the possibilities of avoiding Harumagedon. Given these confrontations, it is thus not surprising that the mass media came to play a prominent role in Aum's vision of the evil forces threatening the world. Aum developed a theory that mass media was an instrument of mind control that was being manipulated by evil forces conspiring to control the world.

Equally important is Aum's development and use of various forms of media. Publications of books by its founder, Shōkō Asahara, and other Aum leaders began in 1986. The monthly magazine *Mahayana* began appearing in 1987. In addition, Aum soon began producing manga, anime, promotional videos, music recordings, and tapes of Asahara's preaching. Some of the audio and videotapes were meant not only for proselytizing but also for use in Aum's religious practices. In the early 1990s, Aum began weekly radio broadcasts from Russia and also established its own homepage on the Internet. Developing its own forms of media, such as manga and anime, became a way of avoiding and counteracting the evil influence of mainstream media.[1]

Aum's understanding of the mass media is conveniently summed up in the February 1995 issue of the group's monthly journal *Vajrayāna Sacca*. Contained here is a special section of over one hundred pages entitled "The Devil's Mind Control: Exposing the Plot to Brainwash Humanity" (Aum Editorial Board 1995, 6–112; see also Aoyama 1991, 82–88). The opening essay, "Subliminal Seduction," details how subliminal images are being used to influence people: "Foolish Japanese Pigs! Devote Yourselves to Sex! First Public Report in Japan! Subliminal Japan up until the present, the Japanese mass media has kept silent and refused to discuss the use of subliminal techniques in Japanese advertising. That is because they have been using such techniques themselves. *Vajrayāna Sacca* will expose for the first time in history the use of subliminal techniques in Japan!" (1995, 8–9).

A number of images from advertisements are also presented here in "computer-enhanced" form to reveal that messages, such as the word "sex," are often included not only in ads but even on the potato chips we eat. If all of this seems implausible (which it is), it should be noted that some Aum members, with whom I spoke in an

お馴染みのポテトチップスにも、これだけのサブリミナルが……。最近、ジャンクフードの食べ過ぎで肥満に悩む子供が増えているが、その大きな原因の一つがここにある。

これは教えてもらえば誰にでもわかる類の象徴的サブリミナル。①は今まさに性交しようとしている男性性器と女性性器。②は性交中の図で、③は放出された精液。④の模様はすべて女性性器。⑤はそのまま、性交中の男女。⑥のトマトの水滴は、発情を連想させる。⑦のフレーズも、性的欲望に引っかけている。

①と②は、男女がセックスしている図。実はこれ以外にも同様の絵がたくさん隠れているので、自分で確認していただきたい。スナックが穴を貫いているのも、セックスの象徴である。

さあ、あなたは買いたくなる、買いたくなる、買いたくなる……

11　特集　悪魔のマインド・コントロール

Computer-enhanced image of potato chips revealing how they, like many common products, are marked with subliminal images and words such as "sex" from *Vajrāyana Sacca* no. 7, AUM Press, p. 11. (Reproduced with permission from Aleph Public Relations Department)

Aum bookstore in the spring of 1995, thought this was all a joke.[2] It should also be added, however, that one Japanese television station did make use of subliminal images in its coverage of Aum and had to issue extensive apologies once this came to light (Gardner 1999, 223).

The next essay in the magazine, "Do You Believe the Mass Media?" explores the various strategies mass media use to manipulate people. Included here are extensive quotations from *The Protocol of the Elders of Zion* (the well-known anti-Semitic text accusing the Jews of a conspiracy to control the world) that are used to argue that Jews and Freemasons are manipulating the media throughout the world. Returning to more local matters, "Don't Be Mind Controlled by School" then explains how Japanese schools use mind control on students.

"Dr. Sacca's Course on the Psychology of Mind Control" next offers a detailed overview of various brainwashing methods. Included here is a model of how people's lives are shaped emotionally and conceptually by their external environment. The words "information" (*jōhō*) and "data" (*detta*) appear frequently; people are compared to computers that are controlled by the data inputted into them. This is particularly important because Asahara frequently explained Aum's religious approach as a way of deleting "bad data" and inputting "good data." Though this is not explicitly stated here, Asahara in a sense justified "mind control" techniques as a necessary way of undoing "bad mind control."

The visual dimension of the media is deemed particularly dangerous and deceptive. Mass media, it is argued, are filled with visual images that lull us into forgetting there is a gap between them and the realities they ostensibly represent. There is a danger, for instance, that consumers will end up preferring the visual representation to the real thing (as in preferring to watch baseball on television rather than going to the ballpark). This section culminates with a warning concerning virtual reality: "In other words, there is the danger of misapprehending something as being the real thing even though it is not the real thing. Speaking of which, recently something called virtual reality has started appearing. It has become possible to produce a fake experience that is exactly like the real thing. This is another way in which we are going to go on being controlled by information" (1995, 65).

The next essay, "The Secret Order to Mind Control Japan," details how institutions like the Rockefeller Foundation, the CIA, the U.S. Embassy in Japan, the University of Pennsylvania, and Dōshisha University are involved in an elaborate plot to brainwash Japanese. The following essay, "The Start of a Strategy to Use Machines for Mind Control," reveals how new forms of technology, such as cell phones, are a part of this larger plot. The final essay, "Wrenching Off the Chains of Information," provides hope. The teachings and practices of Aum are offered as the way to escape mind control.

Aum's View of Manga and Anime

Aum's view of, as well as use of, manga and anime must be understood in the larger context of its understanding of the mass media. Though producing their own manga and anime, Aum publications occasionally portrayed these forms of media in general in a negative light. In *Jinsei o kiru*, published in 1989, an Aum member responds to letters from two high school students and suggests that some of their problems are a result of the influence of manga and anime. After outlining the relation of the phenomenal, astral, and causal worlds, the Aum member dubbed with the "holy name" of Milarepa offers a diagnosis of their difficulties.

> In the cases of A and S [the two high school students], their ability to concentrate and memorize is deteriorating. We can thus conclude that their mirrors [minds or spirits] have become soiled or dirtied. Considering what they say about scenes and images from anime and manga suddenly appearing to them, it is obvious that the cause of this deterioration is manga and anime. Looking at their letters more carefully, we can see that these images appear to them when they become separated from the everyday or superficial level of consciousness. . . . In other words, the information they have taken in from anime and manga has been recorded in the causal world as data and this data has fallen in turn into the astral world of images. (Aum Editorial Board 1989, 77; see also Aoyama 1991, 87, 1992, 239)

The dangers of manga and anime are explained by linking the ideas of information and data to Aum's notions of an astral world (a realm of data) and causal world (a realm of images), both of which greatly influence the phenomenal world and the beings residing in it. Thus, images from the mass media, including manga and anime, not only influence people on first exposure but continue to exert influence through their presence in the astral and causal worlds. Particular emphasis, it might be noted, is placed on the powers of visual images.

Despite this critical evaluation, later Aum publications portray manga and anime more positively. They do so by noting the parallels between Aum's vision of Harumagedon and depictions of the cataclysmic or apocalyptic scenarios found in many manga and anime. For example, *Vajrāyana Sacca* no. 5, which appeared in the spring of 1992, contains a five-part approximately 100-page "special report" devoted to the theme of "Terrifying Prophecies of the End of the World." Its first section, entitled "Images of Harumagedon: The World Is Awaiting Ruin," shows pictures, accompanied by brief explanations, from manga, anime, and films dealing with the theme of worldwide cataclysm and destruction (Aum Editorial Board 1992, 8–14).

On the first page of this section, the creators of such works are described as prophets: "We cannot make light of novelists, scriptwriters, and manga and anime artists. No one shows more interest in the future nor does more to express in vivid form images of the future. As a matter of fact, much of what they have envisioned in recent decades is becoming a reality in the 1990s. They are, in other words, contemporary prophets, and their works are the books of prophecy nearest to us in the modern age. So let us begin by taking a look at how the fate of people in the near future is portrayed in these modern prophecies" (1992, 8). Manga and anime here are seen not as symptoms of the evil mind control being carried out by the mass media but as potentially valuable prophetic works.

Scene from the Aum manga *My Guru*, that recounts the discovery that Asahara's body, unlike that of normal people, has no electrical resistance. From *Vajrāyana Sacca* no. 8, AUM PRESS, p. 138. (Reproduced with permission from Aleph Public Relations Department)

While it is difficult to determine whether the views expressed in Aum publications reflected those of Aum members in general, there is evidence that at least some saw a connection between apocalyptic manga and anime and Asahara's vision of a coming crisis. Hidetoshi Takahashi, a member of Aum's science team who managed somehow to correctly predict the Kobe earthquake of January 17, 1995, and subsequently left the group following its sarin attack on the Tokyo subway system, wrote the following in an account of his time in Aum: "Though there may be some who do not believe in Harumagedon, it is not a matter of belief in the usual sense. The notion of the 'end' was inputted into our generation as a general sense of things. . . . Our favorite anime such as *The Space Battleship Yamato*, *Nausicaä of the Valley of the Wind*, and *Akira* all dealt with the theme of the state of the world after cataclysmic destruction" (Takahashi 1996, 160). Making use of the metaphor "input," Takahashi sees apocalyptic manga and anime of the 1970s and 1980s as having created an atmosphere of expectation among those coming of age in those decades that helped render Asahara's vision of Harumagedon plausible and compelling.

There is also evidence that *The Space Battleship Yamato* may have held some significance for Aum members. A former member who once served as Asahara's chauffeur, for example, noted in an interview that "[w]hen we were traveling by car once, I sang the theme song of *The Space Battleship Yamato* with the Master. The Master said, 'Yamato was a ship carrying the last hope for the earth. It's just like us, isn't it?'" (Kiridōshi 1995a, 51). This connection is also made in an Aum-produced anime in which Asahara is depicted as captain of the "Spaceship Mahayana" in a way that clearly refers to *The Space Battleship Yamato* (*Oumu Shinrikyō no sekai*, n.d.). Moreover, by the time of the sarin attack in March 1995, at least some Aum facilities were equipped with Cosmos Cleaners, air purification systems named after the "cosmos cleaner" that the Yamato brought back to save the earth.

Aum, Manga, and Anime in the Mass Media

In the weeks and months following the Tokyo sarin attack, commentators saw nearly every aspect of contemporary Japanese society as a possible cause for Aum's violent behavior. More than a few identified manga and anime as a major factor behind Aum members' "bizarre" beliefs and actions (Ōizumi 1995, 42–43).[3] In addition, they often described Aum members as unable to distinguish between reality and the fictional worlds of manga or anime. Such a characterization, of course, implied that Aum members were mad because they could not distinguish fantasy from reality, visual representation from reality, and so on. What follows are some examples of the writings of journalists and social commentators as well as those who saw themselves somehow implicated in the *otaku* or fan subculture of manga and anime.

To understand the impulse to link Aum with manga and anime, it is first necessary to take note of earlier concerns in Japan about their possible negative influence on society. The early 1980s saw the appearance of otaku, who were at the time charac-terized as young people out of touch with mainstream social life but bound together by their "obsessive" interest in manga and anime (Schodt 1996, 43–49; see also Ishii 1989). Always regarded as odd from the mainstream perspective, otaku came under greater suspicion, at least temporarily, when Tsutomu Miyazaki was arrested in 1989 for kidnapping and killing three preschool girls. Miyazaki seemed to fit the profile of an otaku perfectly (Schodt 1996, 45–46; Hoffman 2005).

Public concern about manga and anime was also coupled with growing concern about "virtual reality" as witnessed in the burgeoning interest of youth in computer games and their possible link with the rising incidence of youth violence. For example, an article appearing as part of a series on violence in Japan in *Asahi shimbun*, a major national newspaper, in January 1995 noted that some of the fourteen junior high school students involved in a school bullying incident confessed that they had wanted to try out techniques they had seen in a computer game. The article went on to quote an expert, Akira Sakamoto of Ochanomizu Women's University, who concluded that computer games were dangerous because youth seemed to lose their ability to distinguish reality from illusion, fantasy, or simulation. Though not explicitly mentioned in the text of the article, a term for virtual reality (*kyozō riaru*) appears in a caption beneath a picture of a child playing a computer game. The dangers of virtual reality remained a recurrent theme in newspapers throughout 1995 and 1996. One series of articles entitled "The Creator God Virtual Reality," which appeared in *Nihon keizai shimbun*, the Japanese equivalent of the *Wall Street Journal*, from January 22 until January 26, 1996, even seemed to attribute divine creative power to virtual reality.

The term "virtual reality" was used early on to describe Aum after the sarin attack. For example, Sadao Asami, who, as a professor at Tōhoku Gakuin University and an anticult activist, was a major commentator on Aum, used this terminology in his description of the group: "As a result of isolation from society, it is easy for persecution complexes and antisocial behavior to develop. If a cult is composed mostly of young people, such behavior can intensify and cult paranoia becomes 'virtual reality'" (Asami 1995). In this and other cases, "virtual reality" seems to have lost any connection with its original meaning and simply becomes a way of saying that Aum members have lost touch with reality.

One of the first articles to link Aum directly with manga and anime, Keiko Ihara's "Their Shared Language Is SF Anime," appeared in the weekly magazine *AERA*. The article opens with a description of an imaginary village that draws on features of Aum's commune near Kamikuishiki and themes from *The Space Battleship Yamato*. Japanese readers are expected to grasp the connections immediately. Reports of Aum's use of Cosmos Cleaners had already alerted the public that Aum saw a parallel between their own situation and that faced by Earth in *Yamato*.

> In a village someplace on earth in the 1990s, there are repeated mysterious poison gas attacks. The villagers' health is deteriorating and the village is on the verge of destruction. But another country offers to help by providing both weapons and a cosmos cleaner, a device to clean the air of poison gas.
> The villagers attempt to make their way to the other country but they are obstructed

by a mysterious power until finally the final battle of Harumagedon breaks out with laser weapons, plasma weapons, and an earthquake machine being deployed. Attacked with new-style weapons by a mysterious power, the villagers respond with cutting edge science and supernatural powers. A heroic life-and-death struggle ensues. (Ihara 1995, 19).

Just as the earth in *Yamato* found itself under attack by an unknown alien power, Aum claimed that their commune was being attacked with poison gas by an unknown assailant (although Aum suggested at various times that it was the Japanese state, the U.S. military, or the Japanese new religion Soka Gakkai who were responsible for the attacks). Ihara adds that many Aum women, including high officials, had long straight hair resembling that of Stasha, the queen of the planet offering to help Earth in *Yamato*. Ihara suggests that Aum members, many of whom grew up in the 1970s and 1980s, were greatly influenced by popular manga and anime like *Yamato* that had plots about evil forces threatening the world with cataclysms and catastrophes. She also notes that Asahara, older than most Aum members, had grown up when robot anime were popular and was influenced by them, as indicated in his wish that he desired "to create a robot empire someday" (Ihara 1995, 20).

One of the most prominent journalistic critics of Aum, Yoshifu Arita, also gave considerable weight to the importance of manga and anime in explaining Aum by echoing many of the points made by Ihara. Interviewed in a popular weekly magazine, Arita claimed that "[w]ithout a doubt, a number of science fiction anime lay at the base of this Harumagedon Asahara talks about—*The Space Battleship Yamato,* for example. Aum named the air purifier it developed to protect against poison gas attacks 'Cosmos Cleaner' after the machine used in *Yamato* to purify the earth of radiation. In short, if Asahara borrowed much of his doctrine from other religions, the notion of Harumagedon is probably nothing more than a parroting of the occult and science fiction anime that he had seen" (*Shūkan taishū* 1995, 32). Like many others, Arita argued that Aum members could not distinguish the world of manga and anime from reality:

> It may be that the believers did away with the line between animated stories and reality to the extent that they could, without hesitation, even spread sarin gas and take part in kidnapping and forcibly confining people. . . . Of course, many Aum members were brainwashed by using drugs. They didn't necessarily cross over the boundary between anime and reality simply because they were fervent anime fans. However, it is true that Japan has been shaken by a childish fraud of a man who could not free himself from the illusory world of anime. (*Shūkan taishū* 1995, 32)

Though hesitating to unequivocally cite manga and anime as a cause of Aum, Arita clearly indicates that Aum's madness stems from an inability to distinguish between fiction and reality. Asahara himself, however, is clearly described as being unable to distinguish between anime and reality.

Some producers of manga and anime, such as Yoshiyuki Tomino, even accepted some responsibility for the appearance of Aum.[4] Best known for the animated television

An example of the use of images from Aum anime in articles in the popular press
exploring the influence of anime and manga on Aum. This is from Suzuki Takuma,
ed., *Oumu jiken manyuaru.* Special edition of *FLASH,* May 5, p. 44.
(Reproduced with permission from Aleph Public Relations Department)

series *Kidō senshi Gandamu* (Mobile Suit Gundam), which aired from 1979 through
2002, Tomino was involved in the production of a number of robot anime in the 1970s.
He acknowledges a connection between the content of these anime and Aum's vision
of Harumagedon. In *Kidō senshi Gandamu,* for instance, Earth is fighting a desperate
battle against an evil empire in which even teenagers are pressed into service and,

in the course of their training, gradually develop what might be termed supernatural powers. Members of Aum, he argues, took as real the fictional evil empire that was originally envisioned simply to create a scenario in which anime heroes could emerge (Tomino 1995b, 52; see also Kiridōshi 1995b, 58–61). Tomino notes here that the works of two other well-known makers of anime have been cited in relation to Aum, Hayao Miyazaki and Reiji Matsumoto, but they have avoided discussing the issue of whether they and their works bear some responsibility for Aum.

Tomino sees the 1970s as a crucial turning point in the history of anime. Before this time, teenagers and adults rarely viewed television anime. Such anime were intended for children. They were also roughly made as they were produced on a tight schedule and it was never thought, in the age before videotape, that they would be seen more than once. Most children abandoned anime in favor of reading books once they graduated from elementary school. Beginning in the 1970s, however, partly in response to the number of anime Tomino had helped produce, fan clubs began to form, indicating a rising interest among teenagers and adults. Tomino sees the anime of the 1970s as responsible for the loss of "aesthetic sensibility" among a whole generation (Tomino 1995b, 53). He suggests, in other words, a regrettable move from the visual experience of reading written words to watching manga and anime.

It is only possible to provide here a sampling of the various ways in which Aum was linked with manga and anime by journalists, cultural critics, and creators of manga and anime.[5] A final example worthy of note, because it sums up much of the earlier commentary in the mass media and had wide circulation, is an article that appeared in the Japanese-language edition of *Newsweek* entitled "An Age of Believing the Unbelievable: Virtual Reality Has Caused Japanese Youth to Enter Aum and Americans to Be Entranced by Paranormal Phenomena" (Ruisu and Ugajin 1995, 50–53). The article cites a number of experts to build the case that technological developments like the Internet, computer games, and advances in animation techniques have led to "an age of virtual reality" in which many have lost the ability to distinguish between reality and virtual worlds of various sorts. Here, too, use of the term "virtual reality" is less than precise yet serves to explain the power of manga and anime.

Scholarly Analysis of Aum, Manga, and Anime

A number of scholars have also written on the relation of Aum with anime and manga. While attempting to complicate "popular" discussions, they also echoed much of what was being said in such discussions. The sociologist and expert on subcultures Shinji Miyadai, for instance, did not deny the influence of anime and manga on Aum members but sought to deepen the discussion by pointing to the dynamic changes in anime, manga, and subcultures over the last thirty years.[6] While many seemed to lump together the popular anime of the 1970s such as *Space Battleship Yamato* and those of the 1980s such as *Akira*, Miyadai argues that they reflect important differences among generations and subcultures (Miyadai and Kayama 1995, 122–138).[7]

In particular, Miyadai points to two visions of "the end" found in subcultures of the 1980s. One he associates primarily with young women and describes as a sense of *owaranai nichijō* (the unending everyday), which might be described as a sense of ennui, a sense that nothing will ever change, coupled with an inability to generate any concern or motivation about the future. The other he associates with young men and characterizes as *kakusengo no kyōdōsei* (a sense of community after a nuclear war). Miyadai describes *Akira* as perfectly characterizing this latter view of the postapocalyptic that was greatly influential for some Aum members (Miyadai and Kayama 1995, 123; Miyadai 1995a, 166–167). Miyadai did not make use, however, of the term "virtual reality," and questioned (as early as 1994) efforts to understand otaku as having lost the ability to distinguish between reality and media representations thereof (Miyadai 1995b, 89).

Among religion scholars in Japan, it is Nobutaka Inoue, a leading authority on new religions, who has given the most attention to the issue of manga, anime, virtual reality, and new technologies. In one of the earliest books to appear on Aum.[8] The authors introduce the topic of manga and anime by presenting a summation of thought on the topic appearing in popular publications that they then respond to:

> Youth seem to feel that everything is like a computer game. Asahara seemed to have said in his childhood that "I want to create a robot kingdom someday." While we may think it ludicrous that they did such things as import a military helicopter from Russia and store up immense supplies of drugs and chemicals in order to survive Harumagedon, it might be that they tried to make real their fantasies derived from manga and anime. Envisioning a new state to replace the Japanese state, they structured their religious group in terms of government agencies and tried to create the world of *Space Battleship Yamato*. While it is just a hypothesis, the idea that they were developing the vision of *Yamato* seems persuasive. (Inoue 1995d, 29)

While not denying the validity of these views, the authors attempt to complicate the discussion by suggesting that the influence of computer simulation games, which allow the player to become "god-like," is of more importance in explaining Aum (Inoue 1995d, 165).[8] At later points in the book, however, manga and anime are presented as being sources for Aum's ideas and actions (Inoue 1995d, 32–34, 78–79, 106).[9]

Writing in the May 1995 issue of the monthly journal *Ronza*, Inoue presented a related analysis of Aum in terms of the dangers of the information age. According to Inoue, the information age, which began in the 1970s, is marked by the appearance of new forms of media and technology such as videotape, computer games, satellite broadcasts, and improved animation techniques. In addition, many religious groups made increasing use of some of these forms of media in proselytizing. These developments also coincided with a growing interest in the occult and apocalyptic scenarios in Japanese popular culture (Inoue 1995d, 48–57).

Inoue argues that these technological developments and the omnipresence of visual images have transformed Japanese youth. Instead of getting most of their information from parents and teachers, they now get it mainly from the new forms of media prevalent in the information age. This has resulted in Japanese youth developing a new way of grasping reality. Inoue, by way of explanation, links this claim with a reference to the "virtual reality" of computer games (1995d, 48–57). What Inoue, here and elsewhere, seems to be suggesting is that something called "virtual reality" marks much of the media of the information age and may be changing our sense of reality (and particularly that of youth) without our full awareness (Inoue 1995b and 1995c).

Inoue also links manga, anime, television, computer games, and virtual reality. Here, he suggests that such forms of media and technology distort our sense of reality to the point that the line between visual images and real life becomes ambiguous. Youth are particularly susceptible. "When we come to think about why the minds of our youth are taken with these forms of media, it is clear that one of the themes we must consider is the allure of virtual reality" (Inoue 1995c). The danger of virtual reality is that it has the ability to lead us to be unable to distinguish the difference between reality on the one hand and media representations and simulations on the other.

Inoue's views have had at least some impact on scholars of religion in Japan. On June 10–11, 1995, the Association for the Study of Religion and Society took as its theme, "Will the Information Age Change Religion?" with Inoue providing opening remarks raising the themes and issues to be discussed. The papers as well as the discussions were later published in a volume edited by Yoshimasa Ikegami and Hirochika Nakamaki (1996). Tetsuya Yumiyama began, early in his presentation, with the following observation: "Some have suggested that the Aum Affair is an 'information war.' We can also accurately describe it as a realization of the virtual reality of the science fiction–like virtual reality found in TV games, family computer role-playing games, and theme parks" (Ikegami and Nakamaki 1996, 25). While such theoretical discussions appear now and again in the proceedings of the symposium, they are usually, if not always, quickly abandoned in favor of the presentation of "information" concerning the relation of religion and the "information age." While the notion of virtual reality was evoked by some, with little if anything in the way of definition, it seems to have gone virtually nowhere.

Concluding Reflections

The discussions in Japan concerning the question of whether manga and anime somehow contributed to the rise of Aum and its turn to violence are inconclusive. There are, to be sure, a number of parallels between Aum's vision of Harumagedon and the themes and scenarios to be found in many manga and anime. In addition, there is evidence that at least some Aum members were conscious of these parallels. At the least, it might be concluded that manga and anime did provide some of the images that Aum members drew on both in creating and understanding their vision of Harumagedon. Beyond this, however, it is difficult to draw any conclusions about the role of manga and anime in relation to Aum. None of the discussions of the topic provides anything close to approaching a compelling argument concerning how manga and anime, in relation to other factors, "caused" Aum either to develop the view of the world it did or to resort to violence.[10] Perhaps the most percipient observation on the whole question has been provided by Frederik L. Schodt, a translator and writer who has done much to introduce manga and anime to English-language readers: "Ultimately, any attempt to directly link manga, anime, otaku, religion, and crimes against humanity requires a considerable stretch of logic" (Schodt 1996, 48).

Discussions of the topic, however, do tell us much about the reaction to Aum in Japan and efforts to understand it. Perhaps the most common understanding of Aum members was that they were mad or crazy; they believed the unbelievable and were incapable of distinguishing between reality and fantasy. Though some introduced the notions of cult and mind control to explain this madness, such efforts tended to simply rename rather than explain the phenomenon of "madness" (Gardner 1999, 220–221). Efforts to link Aum with the influence of manga and anime showed a similar pattern. Discussions of the topic moved from exploring how the content of manga and anime might have influenced Aum members to simply arguing, usually implicitly, that the similarities between Aum's views and some manga and anime showed that the group's members were incapable of distinguishing reality from manga and anime. As recently as February 2004, when Asahara was sentenced to death, describing Aum members as "manga-like" (*manga-teki*) or "anime-like" (*anime-teki*) became an alternative way of saying they were crazy.

A similar mode of argumentation can be found in the efforts to explain the power of manga and anime by linking them to the influence of the information age, computer games, and especially virtual reality. Robert Markley has argued that many popular accounts of virtual reality merely "demonstrate that Virtual Reality remains a semiotic fiction" (Markley 1996, 2). Markley thus remains "skeptical of a cyber-spatial metaphysics that assumes, rather than questions, the revolutionary nature of virtual worlds and electronically mediated experience" (1996, 2).

Critics would do well to bring Markley's skepticism to the discussions of virtual reality in relation to Aum. Though the term "virtual reality" was vaguely if at all defined, it became the key to explaining how manga, anime, and computer games could harm people's abilities to distinguish between reality and fantasy or reality and representations thereof. The term was even widely expanded to include media such as manga and anime, which would not be counted as instances of virtual reality in any precise definition of the term. In addition, there seems to be little evidence that manga and anime can cause people to be unable to distinguish between reality and what they read and view.

It is ironic that journalists, social commentators, scholars, and Aum members had basically the same thing to say about virtual reality. Indeed, Aum's account of virtual reality is about as coherent as the explanations found in any of the writings of those seeking to explain Aum. Leaving its more labored conspiracy theories aside, what Aum had to say about the dangers of the mass media also roughly paralleled discussions by others. In short, both Aum's writings on the information age and virtual reality and the writings of those attempting to explain Aum seem to recycle, without much reflection, discussions of the information age and virtual reality found in the mass media itself. While scholars attempted to complicate popular understandings of Aum by questioning notions such as cult and mind control, there was little in the way of critical examination of virtual reality.

These discussions of manga, anime, and virtual reality thus might be taken as an example of the ways in which people imagine problematic others. Such others are often, of course, simply perceived as being mad or crazy, or as being unable to make distinctions. At other times, seemingly more sophisticated terms such as cult, mind control, or virtual reality are used to either rename or explain this madness. Such perceptions of the other, it might be noted, parallel nineteenth- and early-twentieth-century theories of primitive mentality that viewed "primitives" as unable to make distinctions between things such as word and object or symbol and reality (Smith 1978, 296–297).

Such theories of "primitive mentality" were discredited more than a few decades ago by anthropologists and scholars of religion as empirically and theoretically unintelligible. It is thus ironic that at the end of the twentieth century, many, particularly scholars of religion, sought to explain Aum by reference to the concept of "virtual reality." The notion of "virtual reality," I would suggest, is a replay of the notion of "primitive reality." Both concepts imagine the other as being unable to discern the difference between symbol and reality, word and thing, "virtual reality" and reality, and so forth. In a sense, then, the writings on Aum reviewed here might be characterized as leading to an unexpected discovery of "primitives," not far away, but in our midst.

Notes

1. For a discussion of manga and anime produced by Aum, see Schodt 1996, 47, 228–232.
2. For documentation that Aum members did not always believe the unbelievable (and also had a sense of humor), see the film *A* by Tatsuya Mori (Gardner 1999).
3. For an early overview of writings on Aum in popular publications treating the theme of manga and anime, see Yoshimi 1995, 56–57.
4. At least one other writer of science fiction works, Shin'ichi Ichikawa, also expressed a sense of responsibility concerning the influence of such works on Aum members. Shin'ichi Ichikawa, "Seigi no kamen o tsuketa wakamonotachi," *Asahi shimbun* (July 19, 1995).
5. Not treated here is an important and influential essay by Eiji Ōtsuka, a cultural critic who sees himself as somewhat of an otaku, that appeared in May 1995 in the monthly journal *Shokun!* and links Aum with manga, anime, otaku subcultures, and Japan's inability to come to terms with its wartime legacy. Two collections of essays published on the Aum affair (Kitagawa 1995 and PLANK 1995) also contain a number of essays, listed separately in the bibliography, relating Aum to the influence of manga and anime.
6. In November of 1994, Miyadai published a book entitled *Seifuku shōjo-tachi no sentaku* (The Choices of Young Girls in School Uniforms), which explored questions such as why young girls were selling used panties and school uniforms to sex shops to resell to men interested in such objects. The book attracted media attention such that Miyadai, who often discusses "consumer society," became himself a bit of a commodity, appearing frequently on television and in popular magazines. As an expert on contemporary Japanese "youth subcultures," Miyadai was in demand when the Aum tragedy occurred.

7. Miyadai does, however, identify "subcultures" as the root of Aum. See here also, Miyadai (1995c, 35).

8. In a brief column appearing in the weekly magazine *AERA*, Inoue clearly identifies manga and anime as a major influence on, if not a cause of, Aum (Inoue 1995a, 3).

9. A further discussion of computer games and virtual reality can be found on page 165.

10. For a related discussion of efforts to explain Aum in English-language studies of Aum, see Gardner (2001a and b).

10

Medieval Genealogies of Manga and Anime Horror

RAJYASHREE PANDEY

Jigoku gokuraku wa kono yo ni ari [Heavens and hells are of this world].
—Japanese Buddhist Proverb

We are all familiar with what by now has become a common reading of Japan as the site of the postmodern. In one version of this reading, Japan has always displayed characteristics of the postmodern. The decentering and dispersal of modern subjectivity, the absence of logocentrism, and Japan's image as the empire of signs all point to a Japan that is postmodern before the fact (Barthes 1983).[1]

In another version, Japan's postmodernism becomes a cultural correlate of late capitalism, and Japan satisfies many of the conditions that are symptomatic of the postmodern world. These conditions include the complete commodification of culture, the effacement of the distinction between high and low culture, the proliferation of hybrid forms that lack depth, historicity, specificity or narrative closure, and the fragmentation and decentering of the subject. In this reading there is nothing specifically Japanese about postmodernism in Japan; indeed, part of postmodernism is the disappearance of national specificity and myths of national origin and uniqueness. In other words, the reason Tokyo, Hong Kong, and New York can all be postmodern cities is because they have ceased to be in any significant ways Japanese, Chinese, or American.

By contrast, those who see Japan as postmodern before the fact claim that postmodernity comes from something specific and unique in Japanese culture. They turn to Japan's deconstructivist tradition, which, they argue, is born out of a Buddhist—and more specifically Zen—philosophical framework. According to this line of thinking, Buddhist thought practiced a form of radical deconstruction for centuries before its appearance in the West. Indeed, the eminent literary critic Kōjin Karatani argues that there is no deconstruction in Japan, simply because Japan has never had a logocentric structure and there is therefore nothing to deconstruct (Ivy 1989, 40).

Robert Magliola argues that the Buddhist notion of *sunyata*, as expressed in Madhyamika philosophy, constitutes a Middle Way between the eternalist "it is" and the nihilist "it is not." He further argues that Nagarjuna's *sunyata* [devoidness] is Derrida's *différence*, as both represent a critical deconstruction of the principle of self-identity (Magliola 1984, 88–89). Barthes, in his *Empire of Signs*, turns to Zen to arrive at his reading of Japan as an open-ended text, free of a fixed center. Of haiku he writes, "the haiku ... articulated around a metaphysics without subject and without god, corresponds to the Buddhist *mu*, to the Zen *satori*, which is not at all the illuminative descent of God, but 'awakening to the fact,' apprehension of the thing as event and not as substance" (Barthes 1983, 78).

While these two readings of Japan's postmodernism pull in different directions, both have played an important part in establishing Japan as the site of the postmodern. As Marilyn Ivy puts it, "Perhaps 'Japan' describes the uncanny convergence of a cultural predilection for language dispersal with a postmodern capitalism whose powers of de-territorialization and differentiation seem to effect the same kind of dispersal" (Ivy 1989, 39).

It is not surprising that Japan's most popular cultural forms, such as manga and anime, contain some of the elements most emblematic of postmodernism.[2] Writing about the anime *Akira*, for example, Isolde Standish argues that the Tokyo of the film bears no resemblance to the historical place we call Tokyo. All specificity of time or culture has been effaced, and Tokyo could easily be New York, London, or any other city (Standish 1998, 66). In her view, *Akira* displays some of the characteristics of the postmodern as outlined by Fredric Jameson, namely, "an effacement of boundaries, for instance between previously defined stylistic norms (Eastern and Western) and between past and present, resulting in pastiche and parody; and a schizophrenic treatment of time as 'perpetual present'" (Standish 1998, 62). Likewise, Susan Napier points to *Akira*'s "almost total lack of a moral center," the celebration of disaster "for the fun of it," its "thoroughgoing denial or even erasure of the past and of the established order of the collectivity," and its "postmodern refusal of traditional narrative closure" (Napier 1993, 346, 347, 350).

Akira appears to fit well with the reading of postmodern texts as ones in which the past functions as pastiche, appearing as a mosaic of different cultural styles from different historical periods that have been emptied of all historicity. The references to the past are part of a playful intertextual game, one in which "the history of aesthetic styles replaces 'real' history" (Jameson 1996, 20). But there are also other ways of reading this text; for example, the cult of *Akira* and its leadership have strong resonances with Japan's "new religions" and many of the members of the Akira cult use quasi-Buddhist jargon. So too, the music at the moment when Tetsuo escapes from the torments of this world is "decidedly religious in nature" (Freiberg 1996, 102). I argue here that Japanese manga and anime can indeed be read as postmodern texts. Such a reading, however, comes in part from Japan's religious tradition, and therefore an understanding of the religious beliefs underlying Japanese culture is critical to our appreciation of Japanese articulations of postmodernism.

As Barthes's reading of "Japan" demonstrates, Zen Buddhism is often made to bear the weight of the entire Japanese Buddhist tradition. Removed from the framework of Mahayana philosophy within which it is located, Zen Buddhism too often emerges as an unchanging and essentialist aesthetic; indeed, the false distinction Western thought often makes between aesthetics and ethics tends to reinforce the view of Zen as preeminently aesthetic. Here I would like to restore both the ethical and aesthetic dimensions of Buddhism in my readings of Japanese manga.

The philosophical and ethical bases that underpin these works are evident from the way in which they treat areas such as human life and death, the relationship between human and nonhuman, and the notion of the self and the body. They are very different from the beliefs that arise out of a Judeo-Christian tradition, and they continue to animate contemporary popular texts in the most unexpected places and in the most unexpected ways. The point of view that appears in these texts, which dovetails with the contemporary postmodern moment, is also a legacy of Japan's particular history. In other words, it is Japan's past that enables the reading of popular texts as postmodern; history resurfaces in these works in ways deeper than mere pastiche would allow.

I begin by looking at some manga in the horror genre, written by Hideshi Hino over the last two decades. Depictions of the disintegration of the body or grotesque caricatures are not new to the world of Japanese visual arts. Medieval picture scrolls dwell on the decaying and putrefying corpse, while seventeenth- and eighteenth-century woodblock prints revel in the blood, gore, and spilling intestines that mark the samurai's performance of ritual suicide through disembowelment (*seppuku*). The horror manga that I consider draw freely on formalistic elements from traditional Japanese art. Beyond that, I hope to demonstrate that they employ traditional ways of making sense of the threatening and destructive—in other words, that which constitutes horror.

In drawing this lineage, I do not wish to ignore the fact that horror manga is very much a product of a "modern" sensibility or that it has close affinities with Western horror films. The very notion of a genre that calls itself "horror" and that ostensibly exists to entertain is a modern one. In the medieval world, horrifying images served a clear didactic purpose and were closely tied to religious themes and ideas. The medieval hell scroll paintings (*jigoku zōshi*) illustrated the horrific tortures awaiting those who fell—depending on the nature of their crimes—into one of 128 hells. *Kyōkan jigoku* (Hell of Screams), for example, was peopled by those who, among other things, had committed the crime of mixing water with sake and selling it for profit! The illustrations graphically highlight the torments of men and women as they are eaten by worms and insects that crawl out of their bodies. The written text tells us that the cries of suffering are unbearable in the extreme. In these works, the horrors of hell served to illuminate the futility of worldly attachment; they functioned as expedient means (*hōben*) that would help lead the way to enlightenment.

Horror in manga narratives is modern. Like Western horror novels and cinema, manga creates horror by using such themes as demonic possession, the transmutation of humans into animals, and destructive monsters created by technology gone awry. However, the normative discourse that brings horror to a closure in Western horror rests upon very different religious and cultural assumptions than those found in Japanese

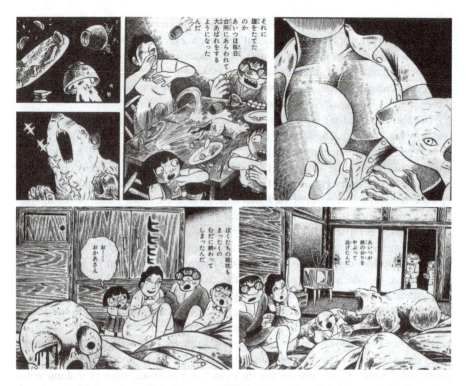

A sequence of frames from *Hatsuka nezumi* (White Mouse) in which Mouse wreaks havoc on nuclear family, suckling at mother's breast and attacking and killing the baby.
(Copyright Hideshi Hino)

manga. In this chapter, I will explore the techniques of incorporation, transformation, and fluidity in horror manga, as well as the very different modes of defining the self, which are a striking feature of these works.

Hatsuka nezumi (White Mouse) by Hideshi Hino is a very popular horror manga that was published in the 1980s for teenage girls and boys (Hino 1995a). It is the story of a mouse kept as a pet by a young boy. The mouse gradually becomes a monster, which lives off animals fed to it by the boy and his sister. It destabilizes the nuclear family and begins to compete for attention with the newborn baby, suckling with the baby at the mother's breast. After being cruelly treated by the family, the monster-mouse destroys the baby and acquires exclusive access to the mother's breast. The mother (now unhinged) treats the mouse as her own child and beckons it every day to her bosom. The other children resume their ordinary lives and everything returns to "normal."

In the last two pages, however, the story begins again exactly as it had at the beginning—with the boy arriving at the pet shop for the first time and discovering that it is like no ordinary pet shop . . .

The mother welcomes mouse to her breast, and everything returns to normal.
(Copyright Hideshi Hino)

This manga lends itself admirably to a psychosocial reading. It falls within a familiar trope, that of the horror that is introduced from the outside into the home. The home is the hard-won purchase of an overworked taxi driver who has at last realized his dream of *mai hoomu* (homeownership). The surroundings are idyllic, with fresh air and verdant forests, a far cry from Japan's urban sprawl. The monster takes over the lives of the family members and turns their surroundings into a nightmare landscape.

The mouse is the ultimate spoiled male child who presumes his mother's boundless love, even when his behavior is transgressive and antisocial. The destruction of the baby can be read as carrying out the fantasy of dealing with sibling rivalry by literally removing the rival. Much has been written about the concept of *amae* (self-indulgent dependence), which is seen by some as central to social relationships and particularly to close mother-son relationship in Japan (Doi 1973). *Amae* allows the child to rely upon the unquestioned love of his mother even when he is badly behaved. This is often offered as an explanation for why Japanese men are able to get drunk with impunity, secure in the knowledge that society at large, and women in particular, will look upon their excesses with indulgence.

My interest here is not so much in the psychodynamics of the tale, but rather in the modes whereby the animal is rehabilitated within the narrative. The monstrous mouse is the object of horror, but it is also allowed to be simply a creature that yearns for warmth of maternal love—a profoundly human desire. What does this tell us about the relationship between humans and animals?

Here I would like to suggest that the Japanese context, unlike that of the Christian West, offers a much greater fluidity between man and beast, which mitigates against the monstrous animal's merely being demonized as "the other." This fluidity owes much to a Buddhist understanding of the world and our place in it. It is to this paradigm that I now turn in order to read the mouse in the closing scenes of the manga.

All schools of Buddhism understand the universe in terms of a taxonomy called *rokudō* (six realms). These six realms, in hierarchical order, are the world of the gods, the world of humans, the world of *asuras*, the world of animals, the world of the hungry ghosts, and the world of the creatures of hell. In Buddhist doctrine, a human will be reborn in one of these six realms until he or she achieves enlightenment. Through karmic reward for deeds performed, a human can be pushed up and down this ladder. While this taxonomy is not totally different from the one accepted in medieval Europe, one major difference is that there is greater fluidity, a constant movement, "the possibility of either progress or slippage to another location in the taxonomy" (LaFleur 1986, 29). These worlds themselves are not inescapable; there is always the possibility of escaping from the cycles of births and deaths and breaking out of the confines of the six realms.

Animals in this order are part of a continuum, interchangeable with humans along the wheel of births and deaths. In the Pali text, the *Jataka,* for example, the Buddha explains his past births and identifies the particular animal that he was born as in a previous life. The *Jataka* stories are intended to teach human beings a moral lesson. In this context they are not unlike the didactic tales found in the *Bestiary*, or book of beasts, as it evolved in medieval Europe. The *Bestiary* is written with the assumption that the creator made animals in order to edify and instruct sinful humans. Each creature is therefore a moral entity, but not in its own right. It is simply the bearer of a message for the human reader, serving as an example for humans to redeem themselves. In the Buddhist world, on the other hand, there is no clear separation between animal and human worlds. Not only do they occupy the same space, but at times they are each other, as the stories of the Buddha's past lives testify.

In the manga about the mouse, nowhere is the human privileged over the animal. When the family has a chance to destroy the creature that they have rendered unconscious with sake, they choose, instead, to inflict the cruelest punishments on it. We have scenes in which the girl spears his eye, the boy cuts off his tail, and the mother exults over having snipped off his ear. The mouse cannot be the site of the monstrous "other"; the humans in the narrative incorporate many of the monstrous features that are to be found in the beast.

In a similar vein, another horror manga by Hideshi Hino, entitled *Kyōfu jigoku shōjo* (Hell Baby) blurs the boundaries between humans and the nonhuman other (Hino 1995b). Twin sisters are born on a dark and stormy night. One is beautiful while the other is a demon child with a grotesque appearance and a taste for blood. Abandoned in a garbage dump, the "hell baby" reemerges and keeps herself alive by feeding on live animals. There is nothing in her to suggest that she is human. However,

The family torturing the mouse. (Copyright Hideshi Hino)

an encounter with a discarded mannequin arouses in her inexplicable and only dimly understood feelings of desire and longing. An unaccountable instinct drives her to scour the streets of Tokyo in search of her family. When she succeeds in finding it, her quest seems complete, but the story does not end there. She is shot by the police and dies alone. Her death, however, takes on a redemptive quality; she crawls into a dark, warm hole—clearly an image of the mother's womb—where she is able to die, secure, and content.

Both the mouse and the monstrous child constitute horror in Hino's manga. However, what unites the mouse and the child is not only the violence and destruction that

Hell baby feeding on live animals. (Copyright Hideshi Hino)

Hell baby crawling into a hole and dying. (Copyright Hideshi Hino)

they wreak, but also that which ultimately salvages them—their craving for maternal love and recognition.

These horror manga draw on narratives from Japan's past, which envisage the world of nonhumans as being not radically different from our own. Of particular interest in this regard are the twelfth-century picture scrolls of hungry ghosts (*gaki zōshi*) (Komatsu 1994). Human beings who were filled with insatiable greed and lust in former lives are reborn in the realm of the hungry ghosts, where they are doomed to experience intolerable hunger and thirst that can never be satisfied. *Gaki* are depicted as grotesque, skeletal figures with enormous bellies and needle-thin throats. They are driven to eating excrement and carrion and are tortured by demons and vultures. At one level, they are the very embodiment of grotesque horror. They arouse fear in the viewer and serve as a moral lesson against avarice and greed.

At the same time, the way in which they infiltrate our world, quietly consuming excrement while people are defecating, begging food from monks, and so on, prevents them from being rendered as pure otherness. Their presence within our world is normalized; indeed, they are not dissimilar to the starving beggars who once populated medieval towns and cities—at once pariahs as well as part of the community (Ruch 1992, 124–127). The ultimate redemption of *gaki* in these scrolls is assured with the appearance of the compassionate Buddha, who has vowed to save all creatures.

It is no surprise, then, that one of the stories that has captured the imagination of Buddhists for centuries is about a disciple of the Buddha, Maudgalyayana, who journeys to the realm of the hungry ghosts to save his mother, who has fallen into this world.

The fluidity in the hierarchy of the six realms preempts any notion of being condemned forever to a particular realm. Indeed, the Tendai school of Buddhism espouses a doctrine of radical nonduality, arguing that each world includes the others within it. As William R. LaFleur has stated, "this means not only that there are Buddhas in hell but also there is something of hell in the Buddha" (LaFleur 1986, 53). Nondualism is fundamental to Mahayana dialectics and offers a radical challenge to a world seen in terms of binary oppositons. Human and beast, good and evil, *samsara* (this deluded world) and *nirvana* (the world of enlightenment), and life and death are mutually dependent and inextricably intertwined.

Yamai no sōshi (Handscroll of Illnesses), a collection of Japanese hand-scroll paintings of the late twelfth century, captures the sufferings of those who live in the realm of human beings (*ningendō*). Being born in the realm of the gods or the realm of humans is better than birth into the world of the hungry ghosts or the many hells; however, our world is akin to—and indeed, not distinct from—the other five. Hino plays with this concept of the interpenetration of the various realms and with the notion that hell is to be found in our world and within us. In one of his most famous manga, *Jigoku-hen* (*Panorama of Hell*), he creates a chilling vision of hell on Earth. "This world is a living hell, utter chaos terrifying to behold . . . the wheel of karma spins round spreading misfortune killing my brothers and sisters—that is my sin" (Hino 1989, 133).

In many contemporary texts, the topos of the nuclear bomb dropped on Hiroshima and Nagasaki serves as the trope for imagining a postnuclear hell. In *Panorama of Hell*, the diabolical artist, who destroys everything in order to be inspired to paint, is conceived at the precise moment of the nuclear explosion. He is corrupted even before he emerges from his mother's womb, and he becomes a devotee of his own painting of the mushroom cloud, which he refers to as the "Emperor of Hell." Where Keiji Nakazawa's antiwar manga, *Hadashi no Gen* (*Barefoot Gen*, 1987), gives a realistic account of the horrors of the nuclear bomb, Hino offers up an anarchic celebration

Gaki (hungry ghosts) receiving the Buddha's mercy in the *Gaki zōshi.*
(Reproduced with permission from Kyoto Kokuritsu Hakubutsukan)

Hell on Earth as depicted in Hideshi Hino's *Panorama of Hell*. (Copyright Hideshi Hino)

of destruction and an exploration of the various hells on earth. In the end, the painter in *Panorama of Hell* creates the perfect vision of hell by exploding a nuclear device that brings himself and the world to an end.

Death here is not seen as an unhappy experience. In fact, the moment of total annihilation is exhilarating in that it foreshadows the possibility of escape from our corrupted world and the various hells it contains.

In the modern horror genre in the West, horror often stems from the fear of the psychic descent of the rational and unified self, which ultimately leads to its virtual dissolution. In the *Nightmare on Elm Street* film series, for example, the child molester and murderer Freddy Krueger returns from the dead and disrupts the boundaries between the imaginary and the real. He wreaks vengeance on teenage children, entering their dreams and subsuming their very identities. In *Nightmare on Elm Street 2*, Jesse is possessed by Freddy, who gradually takes over his body. In one scene, when he kisses his girlfriend, he sprouts a huge Freddy tongue. When the teenagers become unable to distinguish between dream and reality, Freddy emerges whole out of Jesse's stomach, while Jesse falls to the ground, a hollow shell devoid of all substance. In *Nightmare 1*, Nancy is able to resist Freddy only when she regains control of herself and reasserts her own identity by recognizing that he is only an illusion.[3] These films lend themselves admirably to a psychoanalytic reading, and Freud's comments on the uncanny are particularly incisive in this context.

Freud argues that the uncanny (*unheimlich*) "invariably . . . can be traced back every time to something that was once familiar and then repressed" (Freud 2003, 154). For Freud, the uncanny is experienced when repressed infantile complexes, which arouse dread and fear, return to our consciousness. Horror is that "other" which is rooted in our own psyche and constitutes our deepest fears and obsessions. Julia Kristeva defines horror in terms of abjection and elaborates on Freud's insights, arguing that the abject is "something rejected from which one cannot part," and that it is at once an "imaginary uncanniness and real threat" (Kristeva 1982, 4). What is of particular interest here is Kristeva's suggestion that in the Judeo-Christian tradition, the corpse represents a fundamental pollution, "a body without soul, a non-body, disquieting matter" that is "to be excluded from God's territory." If the corpse is waste, she argues, then it is the opposite of spiritual and is fundamentally "accursed of God" (Kristeva 1982, 109).[4] It is the potential fragmentation and loss of self or ego that produces the ultimate horror: "the corpse, the most sickening of wastes, is a border that has encroached upon everything. It is no longer I who expel. 'I' is expelled" (Kristeva 1982, 3–4).

The dissolution of categories is essentially threatening to the social order. As Mary Douglas has argued, society strictly polices the boundaries of the individual body, which serves as a metaphor for the social body (Douglas 1967). In Hideshi Hino's manga, as in Western horror films, the sense of terror comes precisely from this border crossing—the grotesque transformation of a boy into a killer bug, the appropriation of the mother's breast by a foul rat, the birth of a monstrous child to a normal mother, and so on. And yet, as I have argued, the worldview that allows for containment and closure in Hino's manga deviates significantly from that which informs horror narratives in the West.

Hino's attitude toward death is strongly inflected by a Buddhist understanding of the essentially impermanent and insubstantial nature of all phenomena (*mujō*). In the Buddhist view, there is no self or ego that can claim a lasting identity. Indeed, in Buddhism, the body itself is used to illustrate the doctrine of impermanence. Indian Buddhist texts, like the *Visuddhimagga* by Buddhaghosa, spell out at great length the various categories of the foul body—swollen, discolored, festering, fissured, mangled, dismembered, bloody, worm-eaten, and so on (*Path of Purity* 1971, 205; see also Komatsu 1994, 110–119).[5] Buddhist monks were trained to meditate in the charnel fields and to observe in minute detail the putrefaction of the human body. The purpose of this training was to recognize the true nature of the body and the self and to experience the horror of attachment to a body whose essential nature is foul.

For Buddhism, the disintegration of the body does not produce anxiety about the dissolution of the self. Indeed, if the self itself is problematized, then the disintegration of the body takes on a radically different meaning and becomes the means for the attainment of enlightenment and liberation. It is the a priori assumption of a self and its valorization that is radically called into question in Buddhism. Let me illustrate this point more concretely by looking at the metamorphosis of a human being into a

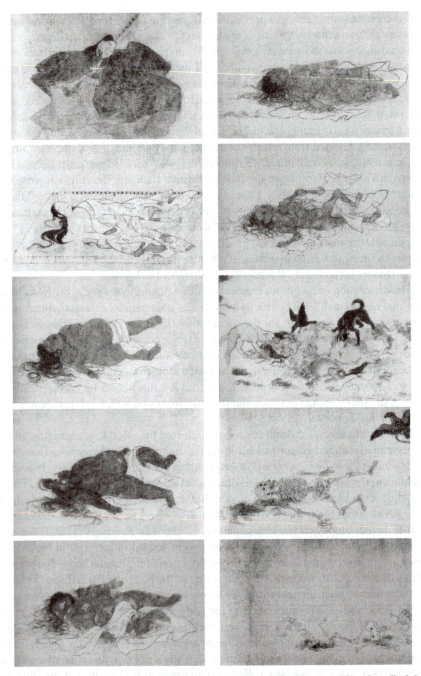

Images of the process of decomposition from the *Kusoshi emaki* (**Illustrated Handscroll of the Ten Stages of a Decaying Corpse**) (*Nihon no emaki* 7, 110–119). (Copyright Chūō Kōronshinsha)

fly in David Cronenberg's remake of *The Fly* and contrasting it with the transformation of a young boy into a poisonous bug in Hideshi Hino's *Dokumushi kozō* (*The Bug Boy*, 1975).

In *The Fly*, the brilliant scientist Seth Brundle is the victim of his own inventive genius. Through accident and his own inventions, he is turned into a fly. In the end, Brundle's redemption lies in the assertion of his humanity in the face of his terrifying metamorphosis. He urges his girlfriend Veronica to kill him; groaning in anguish, he pulls the trigger of the gun that she holds to his head, preferring to die rather than live as an insect. His conscious decision to die affirms the human will; in other words, even when he is being rapidly subsumed into a monster insect, he acts as a human being.

Hino's *The Bug Boy* is the story of a young boy, Sanpei Hinomoto. Sanpei is a sickly child, hopeless at schoolwork and at sports, and obsessively attached to bugs, snakes, and other creepy crawlies—an ideal candidate for being bullied at school and reprimanded at home. One day he is bitten by a bug, and soon his body undergoes a horrifying transformation, from young child to a rotting mass of jelly, and, finally, to a healthy and strong monster bug. Sanpei initially enjoys exploring rivers, oceans, and mountains as a free spirit. Gradually, he discovers his poisonous potential and becomes a vengeful killer who enjoys the destruction he wreaks. One day he finds himself close to his own home and remembers his former life with a wave of nostalgia and longing. When he makes his way into his home, his father shoots him with a gun and he escapes, mortally wounded. Throughout this narrative, the bug is accorded the consciousness and the accompanying emotional complexities that we associate with human beings.

One could say that the bug is a highly anthropomorphized figure and that we can relate to it because the human still inhabits the bug. This is no different from Seth Brundle's transformation into a fly. However, the conclusion of this manga deserves consideration. After being shot, the bug escapes from his home and finds his way into a sewer. This takes him to a river and then to the ocean, and it is here that he finally begins to sink in the waters. What he experiences is a profound sense of liberation and calm in the face of death: "I can feel myself drifting away . . . I can feel almost nothing . . . My wounds no longer hurt . . . Ahhh . . . what a wonderful feeling . . . Nothing. . . . There is . . . nothing more," and with these thoughts the creature vanishes into the setting sun (Hino 2004, 201–204). Here death is not a heroic choice, but a release from the suffering that comes from being trapped in this world. In the end, the bug understands the profound meaning of nothingness (*mu*), which promises a liberation from the endless cycle of being, and the conclusion suggests that our distinctions between the human and animal realm are meaningless, since both cause equal measures of suffering and misery. This state of quietude is a far cry from the celebration of the agency of the humanist subject in *The Fly*.

In many Western horror films, narrative closure is possible only when the horror, which is "other," is excised from the home and the world, and the stability and security of the "self" is reinstated. (When on occasion the monstrous survives, it is often for commercial considerations, to keep open the possibility of sequels.) In most instances, the "good" human lives and is able to overcome the "evil" force that attacks him or her. Even when the hero dies, his death, like Brundle's, has a certain tragic grandeur. In the world of Hino's manga, neither animals nor human beings are particularly laudable or celebratory. Both are suffering victims, even when they inflict cruelty on others. Both are trapped in a hell from which there appears to be no escape. Liberation usually comes in the form of death and the dissolution of the self.

I conclude by looking briefly at the 1997 animated film by Hayao Miyazaki entitled *Mononoke-hime* (*Princess Mononoke*), which was an extraordinary success with Japanese and Western audiences alike. A young Emishi boy, Ashitaka, kills one of the boar gods of the forest who has been shot by humans and therefore becomes a *tatarigami*, a malevolent and violent spirit. Ashitaka saves his village but now bears the curse of the boar in the form of a scar on his arm. He is obliged to leave the village and discover the secret of the boar's transformation into a *tatarigami*. He discovers a little community headed by an ex-prostitute named Eboshi who, together with a colony of outcasts, mines for iron ore. This has polluted the surrounding forest and angered the animals who live there.

Princess Mononoke, herself a human who is brought up by wolves and lives in the forest, is determined to save the forest and the creatures who live in it. In the end there is a huge battle between the beast gods and the men who work for Eboshi. An unscrupulous monk double-crosses Eboshi and makes her shoot Shishigami, the god of the forest, so that he can present the head to the emperor. The angered god walks the forest, looking for his severed head and destroying everything in his wake. Finally the head is restored to Shishigami, the villagers decide to mend their ways, and the forest slowly renews itself.

This story draws upon both Japanese and Western folklore. The idea of a child brought up by wolves and living with other beasts is reminiscent of the tales of Romulus and Remus as well as Beauty and the Beast. Miyazaki himself mentions folklore as a vital source for his work (McCarthy 1999, 183). Although *Princess Mononoke* is ostensibly set in the Muromachi period (1392–1573), Miyazaki moves freely across different historical periods. The young boy Ashitaka is an Emishi, while Mononoke-hime, according to Miyazaki, is like an ancient Jōmon pottery figure. This period of Japan's prehistory is one in which women had more freedom and society was less differentiated and more fluid (McCarthy 1999, 187).

Despite its medieval setting, the story speaks directly to contemporary issues—our relationship to nature and a world in which the land and oceans have become increasingly polluted. Finishing work on the film, Miyazaki explained that he could no longer make a movie "without addressing the problem of humanity as part of the ecosystem" (McCarthy 1999, 185).

The humanist message of this film is, however, undermined by its refusal to create a straightforward opposition between humans on the one side and nature, nonhumans, and science on the other. Eboshi does not simply represent the evil forces of industrialization, bent on exploiting nature and acquiring wealth. She works for the well-being of the community she has created—she has rescued *hinin*, or outcasts such as prostitutes and lepers, and provided them with a secure livelihood. The narrative of science and progress cannot be dismissed out of hand if human beings are at the center of our concerns. Equally, nature cannot be seen simply as bountiful and benign. When angered or wronged, the spirits that inhabit nature can turn into malevolent beings that destroy everything. Miyazaki refuses to let us identify completely with the story or any particular set of characters.

Ultimately, the anime resists a humanist reading because it refuses to privilege human life. Some of the minor characters seem to recognize the ephemerality of human existence (*mujō*) and to understand that true enlightenment goes beyond the struggles between human beings and nature and between science and ecology. Ultimately, these battles belong to the phenomenal world, and it is our attachment to this world that constitutes the real problem.

Thus, the leper who helps Eboshi make guns laments the fact that he (and by implication, all human beings) is foolish enough to be attached to worldly things and to hold grudges and curse others even when he is on his deathbed. The she-wolf Moro, who raises Mononoke-hime, refuses to ask the god of the forest to cure her wounds and save her life. She feels that she has lived long enough and is happy to accept her fate.

Wisdom lies in struggling but at the same time in recognizing our insignificance in the larger scheme of things. Ultimately, the film leaves us with a sense that the answers to questions about our relationship to the environment and the possibility of learning to live in harmony with nature have only a kind of contingent value. In the final scheme of things, humans are transient beings; human endeavor and passion are a form of attachment and a hindrance to the grasping of the ultimate truth. To the extent that our commitment to the ecological struggle helps us to grasp the ultimate truth, it is a battle worth fighting. This is all we *can* do as human beings.

I am suggesting, then, that the postmodernism that has been detected in Japan's popular cultural forms is enabled by certain—to be deliberately provocative—premodern sensibilities. In Hideshi Hino's manga about the mouse, the more diffuse sense of the separation between humans and animals is what allows the mouse to be brought into the family. Indeed, at the end of the manga, even this particular reading is called into question. We are no longer sure whether the whole story happened or whether it was a figment of the boy's imagination. In this deluded world, it is not possible to tell the difference between dream and reality. The monstrous child who dies in the closing sections of *Hell Baby* and the poisonous superbug of *The Bug Boy* find solace in death, which provides welcome relief from the tortures of this world. In *Panorama of Hell*, the vision of a nuclear apocalypse allows the monstrous painter to celebrate his own death, as well as the death of the world. As with Tetsuo in *Akira*, death is not the end. Both the hells and the higher realms remain open as possible futures for the shifting self.

The indeterminacy of the self, the universe that is not centered around humans, the view of life and death as a series of metamorphoses, and the narratives that resist closure are all informed by a Buddhist sensibility. They are also emblematic of postmodern culture. Japanese popular texts can be read as particularly sophisticated articulations of the postmodern position precisely because they are embedded in a history shaped by Buddhist values and ideas.

Notes

This chapter is a revised and expanded version of "The Pre in the Postmodern: The Horror Manga of Hino Hideshi," which appeared in *Japanese Studies*, December 2001. I would like to thank the journal for permission to use previously published material.

1. The issue of whether or not Japan had a native deconstructive tradition before the fact became the subject of debate between Akira Asada, Kōjin Karatani, and Jacques Derrida. See *Asahi jānaru*, May 25, 1984, pp. 6–14. It is noteworthy that it is precisely at a time when the West saw itself as undergoing a crisis of modernity that Japan came to epitomize the postmodern. Once again, Japan came to be constructed as radically "other," the antithesis of the West. However, this time it was no longer backward and premodern.

2. My argument here is not that *all* manga and anime produced in Japan lend themselves to a reading that is postmodern. There is a bewildering variety of manga genres catering to different age groups and interests. The enduringly popular domestic comedy *Sazae-san*, for example, can be viewed as a mirror of Japan's modernity in the postwar era, reflecting the changing roles of women and the family in this period.

3. For an analysis of the seductive power of Freddy for teenagers and its links with consumerism, see Conrich (2000).

4. Although Kristeva does gesture toward other ways of understanding the abject—for example, in the case of food remainders she recognizes in Brahmanism "a challenge to our mono-theistic and mono-logical universes" (76)—there is a sense in which the Western model is implicitly accepted as the universal and all other systems of thought become mere footnotes to the dominant narrative.

5. There are many verses in both the *Therigātha* as well as *Theragātha*, the poems of Buddhist nuns and monks respectively, that counsel the necessity of understanding the true nature of the human body. They recommend meditation on decomposing corpses in cemeteries as a means of achieving this end. See, for example, *Psalms of the Early Buddhists* (1980, 211–212). As the figure from *Kusō zukan emaki* demonstrates, in Japan, the female body often became the object of meditation and functioned as a pedagogical tool for the enlightenment of the male monk.

11

The Utopian "Power to Live"

The Significance of the Miyazaki Phenomenon

HIROSHI YAMANAKA

Introduction

It has been estimated that 23.5 million people in Japan have seen *Sen to Chihiro no kamikakushi* (*Spirited Away*, 2001), approximately one out of five Japanese people. The box office profits were said to be around 30.4 billion yen, which makes it the highest-grossing film ever released in Japan. The film also aired on television in January 2003, garnering a surprising audience rating of 46.9 percent. Even abroad, Miyazaki's animation has been well received, as his numerous international awards, including the Academy Award in 2001 for Best Animated Feature, attest. The astonishing popularity of his work, both in Japan and internationally, can be described as the "Miyazaki phenomenon." Even in Japan, anime has traditionally been regarded as an entertainment for children and young people, so the deluge of stories and articles concerning the film, which appeared in mainstream newspapers and magazines aimed at an adult readership, raises some interesting questions. Is there something behind Miyazaki's anime's phenomenal success other than its sheer entertainment value? Does the popularity of his anime among adults as well as children indicate important changes in Japanese attitudes toward anime as a form of cultural production? Beyond anime's current vogue as an enjoyable mass medium for young people, do Miyazaki's films and, especially, *Spirited Away*'s box office appeal reveal a deeper significance that his works have, not only for children, but also, increasingly, the adult audiences who watch them?

This chapter will examine some of the reasons why Miyazaki's anime are so popular in contemporary Japan, particularly focusing on what the unprecedented success of *Spirited Away* reveals about important socio-economic and religious changes that have recently taken place in Japan. I will argue that Miyazaki's animation can have a deep significance for contemporary Japanese, touching on spiritual issues of identity and the quest for a meaningful life. Miyazaki offers a new form of pop cultural spirituality, one that is based upon his own revision of the Japanese folk-religious tradition. At a time when formal institutionalized religious and cultic practices seem to be increasingly marginalized in today's secularized culture, Miyazaki's *Spirited Away* provides a powerful means of psychological healing for his Japanese audience.

Needless to say, there are many reasons behind the blockbuster status of *Spirited Away*. The first part of this chapter will delve briefly into the specific artistic qualities and special marketing campaign that have helped it to attract a large audience. Then we will analyze the power of the narrative itself. *Spirited Away* is about the hero Chihiro's quest to free herself, her friend Haku, and her parents who are caught in a bizarre magical fantasy world. What makes Chihiro's story so compelling is that it is a story of growing up. As her tale unfolds, she changes from a frightened, self-centered little girl into a young woman who learns to live independently, work for her own living, and find the wisdom to save her hapless parents. Intriguingly, Chihiro achieves her new emotional and psychological maturity not through a tumultuous struggle as a rebellious and alienated child who has escaped a troubled home life in order to find herself, but as a dutiful and hardworking employee who takes a job at a bathhouse for gods and goblins after being marooned in the spirit's fantasy world. Her quest is not a lonely individual journey or a solitary vision quest, but marks her transition, her move from a this-worldly life in the bosom of her family to an otherworldly life as an apprentice working at the quaint and magical bathhouse. Chihiro eventually solicits the help she needs from the network of strange friends she makes on the job.

In the third part of this chapter, I will explain how Chihiro's quest mirrors Miyazaki's own search for his personal identity as a modern Japanese. I will argue that Chihiro's success in recovering her true name and thus her true identity is a metaphor for the possibility that her audience can do the same in a time of economic, cultural, and spiritual malaise when what it means to be Japanese has become an open question. One of the film's attractions is its evocation of nostalgia for an idyllic past when people felt at home both in their communities and in the world itself. What is fascinating is that Miyazaki's appeal to "nostalgia" for a usable past is couched within his own imaginary fantasy world. This fantasy past has nothing to do with ultra-nationalistic forms of nostalgia with their culturally chauvinistic claims of a unique quality of Japaneseness. Rather, *Spirited Away* offers a new secularized spiritual vision of a world where Japanese can find salvation.

Miyazaki's Popularity and the Underlying Ideas Behind His Work

A number of factors have contributed to Miyazaki's popularity. The most obvious is that fact that large numbers of people find pleasure in his work. Since my approach puts more emphasis on the underlying ideas in Miyazaki's films, I should therefore clarify that I believe Miyazaki's popularity comes more from the entertainment value of his films than from the serious ideas that he presents in them. Needless to say, Miyazaki and his staff at Studio Ghibli are some of the most skillful professional animators in the industry today, and they know very well how to produce a commercially successful product.

The first important factor behind *Spirited Away*'s commercial success is the high quality of its animation. Miyazaki's anime are famous for their original character designs, beautiful coloration, attractive music, and skillful sound effects. These and his other remarkable achievements as a director have secured his reputation as a great master of anime, making him a household name in Japan, especially after the success of *Mononoke-hime* (*Princess Mononoke*) in 1997. Moreover, his works also enjoy favor among Japanese parents who are acutely aware of the barrage of tasteless television programs and magazines that their children encounter daily. Miyazaki's-anime—which are largely free of violence and sexually explicit scenes—have their tacit seal of approval. Even though his earlier hit, *Tonari no totoro* (*My Neighbor Totoro*, 1988), has been broadcast several times, the audience rating is always high, suggesting that Miyazaki has attained the enviable status as a creator of wholesome family entertainment, a kind of Japanese Walt Disney despite his disapproval of such a title. Miyazaki's impeccable credentials as a child-friendly animator doubtless contributed to the tremendous popularity of *Spirited Away*.

A second key to the film's success was the unique marketing strategy devised by Toshio Suzuki, who produced the film. Suzuki did not push the marketing of Miyazaki's films until a distributor threatened to stop carrying them because of declining box office profits from *Kaze no tani no Naushika* (*Nausicaä of the Valley of the Wind*, 1984) to *My Neighbor Totoro*. As a consequence, Suzuki began to extensively promote Miyazaki's animation. The promotion of *Spirited Away* was handled by four prominent companies: Dentsu Inc., Japan's largest advertising agency; Nippon Television Network Corporation, a leading broadcasting company; Nestle Japan, an international beverage company; and Lawson, an influential chain of convenience stores (Sawada 2003, 1–2). For instance, Nippon Television aired its promotional video repeatedly and aired a special program on the film before its release. Nestle Japan attached free gifts relating to the characters of this film to some popular products, and advance tickets were available at Lawson (Katagiri 2003, 51–56). In addition, Tōhō, the distributor, ran various advertisements in leading newspapers almost every week for more than six months (Studio Ghibli 2002, 96). It would not be an exaggeration to say that *Spirited Away* was foisted on Japanese people's minds after a well-orchestrated and relentless advertising barrage.

Given these factors behind *Spirited Away*'s commercial success, any attempt to interpret the film on a deeper level should be undertaken with great care. However, just because Miyazaki's anime are fun to watch does not mean that they are simply children's fare like Walt Disney's *Snow White* or Mickey Mouse cartoons. While Miyazaki himself has sometimes averred that his works are solely for children, he has also passionately argued that they convey a serious message.

Good evidence of this is Miyazaki's comments concerning *Princess Mononoke*, an anime set in Muromachi period (1392-1573). The tale is about a war that the gods and beasts of the forest led by Princess Mononoke are waging against the humans from an iron mining town who are thoughtlessly destroying their world. Miyazaki points to the contemporary relevance of his tale:

People lived, loved, hated, worked, and died without the ambiguity we find everywhere today. Here lies, I believe, the meaning of making such a film as we enter the chaotic times of the twenty-first century. We are not trying to solve global problems with this film. There can be no happy ending to the war between the rampaging forest gods and humanity. But even in the midst of hatred and slaughter, there is still much to live for. Wonderful encounters and beautiful things still exist. We depict hatred in this film, but only to show there are more important things. We depict a curse, but only to show the joy of deliverance. (Miyazaki 2000, 64)

As his comments show, Miyazaki takes great pains to explain the deeper meaning of his works, rather than leaving their interpretation to his audience or critics. Although his primary job is to produce entertaining stories, he believes that they have important things to say. This gives us reason enough to take Miyazaki's anime more seriously and to explore what he says about them.

Chihiro's Heroic Journey

At this point, a brief synopsis of the film's plot is in order. The hero of the story is a ten-year-old girl named Chihiro Ogino. *Spirited Away* starts with her sitting in the rear seat of an Audi 4WD, with a bunch of flowers and a card from one of her classmates. The card says "Take care and see you again, Chihiro. From Risa." Her family is moving to a new house in the middle-class suburbs and she is not only melancholy, but also scared about the new life ahead of her. As her father tries to take a shortcut, they end up traveling down a lonely old dirt road that grows increasingly creepy as they pass by bizarre-looking statues of folk-religious deities called *dōsojin* or *sai no kami*, which are typically found at village boundaries, mountain passes, or country roads. The dirt road takes them, not to their new home, but to a mysterious tunnel that leads to the front of a dilapidated gate. On the other side is a stream, and beyond that is a town that looks like a derelict theme park. The town appears deserted, but there are several eating establishments with dishes of food lined up on the counter. The parents walk into one of the restaurants and begin to help themselves, ignoring Chihiro's plea to stop.

As her parents gorge themselves on free food, Chihiro investigates a large building with huge chimneys at the end of the street. As she approaches the bridge that leads to the entrance of the building, a boy whom we later learn is named Haku appears and warns her not to cross the bridge. Chihiro runs back to her parents, only to find them turned into pigs. She is shocked to realize that she and her family are caught in a strange other world because of her parents' ignorance and greed.

Chihiro runs desperately to the stream, which is now a river too wide to cross. When she notices that her body is beginning to fade away and panics, Haku comes to her rescue. He warns her that in this bizarre world, those who do not work either vanish or turn into animals. Haku magically returns her body to normal and takes her to a bathhouse for the gods where he works so she can find a job to save her from that fate. There, she meets Yubāba, a witch who runs a huge old-style bathhouse named Aburaya that caters to traditional Japanese local gods and lesser deities (*kami*) who come to the baths to get clean. Chihiro ends up making a deal with Yubāba in order to get a job and stay in this strange, alternate world; the price is that the witch deprives her of her name, changing it to Sen. When this happens, Chihiro magically forgets her original name.

On her first day as an attendant, Chihiro comes across a shadowy masked figure, Kaonashi (literally, No Face). Seeing him standing in the rain, she leaves a window open. Later that night, after the bathhouse is closed, Kaonashi shows up again. He tempts workers with pieces of gold and then devours them. Meanwhile, Chihiro sees a wounded dragon fly into Yubāba's room. She instinctively feels that the dragon is Haku. Chihiro runs to Yubāba's office, where she sees her son Bō, the dragon, and Yubāba's sister Zeniiba. Zeniiba turns Bō into a rat and complains that the dragon has stolen a magic seal.

Chihiro leaves the bathhouse and gets on a train, with Kaonashi, the rat, and a bird. After the sun sets, the party finally gets to Zeniiba's house. She serves them tea and they talk; then, the dragon/Haku flies into the forecourt of the house. Chihiro, the rat, and the bird get on Haku's back. Just before they fly away, Chihiro remembers her true name and Zeniiba gives her a hair band, which Zeniiba calls an amulet. On the way back to Aburaya, when Chihiro tells Haku about her earlier experience of nearly drowning in a river called Kohakugawa, Haku suddenly remembers his true name, Nigihayamikohakunushi.

When they return to the bathhouse, Yubāba is waiting with a herd of pigs. She tells Chihiro to pick out her parents from the pigs: if she finds them, she may leave. Chihiro says that her parents are not among the pigs. She is correct and can leave. Chihiro reunites with her parents and they go through the tunnel, conversing exactly as they did when they walked through the first time. Coming out of the tunnel, the family finds their car completely covered with leaves. As the parents remove the leaves, Chihiro looks back at the tunnel. She still wears the hair band Zeniiba gave her but seems to have forgotten about her amazing journey to the other world. She gets in the car, and the family drives away to their new house. Chihiro has not only saved her parents and escaped Aburaya, but has learned to fend for herself.

In sum, *Spirited Away* can be described as an otherworldly journey. Chihiro travels to a mysterious otherworld of the gods. The several obstacles that test her mettle in her liminal fantasy world ultimately transform her from a callow child into a mature young lady. This kind of hero's adventure story is not particularly Japanese. As Joseph Campbell noted as early as 1949 in his book *Hero with a Thousand Faces,* variants of this story can be found throughout world literature.

According to intellectual historian Eric Leed, the ancients viewed travel as suffering rather than pleasurable, an ordeal or test as indicated by the original English word for it, *travail* (1991, 6). Leed observes that in the earliest stories of heroic travel, like the *Epic of Gilgamesh* or the *Odyssey,* the hero on his journey must face ordeals that test and ultimately transform him when he overcomes them. On the surface, the sacrifices and hardships seem like a loss, but, in actuality, they give something that the hero did not have before—wisdom and self-understanding. Most importantly, by losing one's old life by leaving home, the hero gradually sloughs off his old identity. The obstacles he faces on the road strip away his old persona, forcing the hero to discover a deeper level of the self that lies buried beneath. Gilgamesh, the impetuous king of Uruk, for example, crosses the waters of death to reach the island of Dilmun in a quest for immortality. Although he surmounts many obstacles put on his path by the gods, who are immortal themselves but have determined that humans must be mortal, he fails in his quest, returning to Uruk an older but now wiser king. Here the loss is that Gilgamesh, although a victor of many battles, fails to achieve immortality, the futility of which wears away his old bravura as the all-conquering hero. The gain is that Gilgamesh now realizes his all-too-human limitations and returns a changed man. No longer an impetuous and capricious warrior of his youth who was a danger to the gods as well as his people, the wiser king can now sagely rule his kingdom.

This idea that "the purity of the road" causes a loss, or a scouring away of the old self that leads, ultimately, to the hero's finding his or her true identity, is central to understanding the plot of *Spirited Away*. The key symbol of heroic loss and gain at the heart of *Spirited Away* is the magical loss and rediscovery of one's true name. Miyazaki pays considerable attention to the symbolic meaning of words and names, something people often take for granted. According to him, stealing people's names is a way of controlling them because they lose a sense of self that gives them meaning and purpose in life. Thus, Haku, like Sen after him, loses his name and ends up a faithful apprentice to Yubāba, forgetting his true identity as a powerful river spirit named Nigihayamikohakunushi. The point made here, symbolically, is that it is not enough for us to keep our own names; what matters most is keeping our own deeper individuality, which our names denote.

Miyazaki symbolizes this in terms of the power of words, an idea that has a long history in Japan, often associated with the power of sacred words (*kotodama*) in Shinto prayers (*norito*). For instance, Chihiro announces her willingness to work in the bathhouse by making a formal pledge to Yubāba that then automatically seals her fate. As Miyazaki has noted, "A word is one's will, oneself, and one's power" (2001, 1). Therefore, the individual must accept all responsibility for the consequences of his or her words.

By contrast, there are other denizens in Chihiro's fantasy world who cannot speak, and have at best a marginal sense of their own individuality. The key example is the character Kaonashi. Kaonashi, who plays a prominent role throughout the story, cannot or will not say anything; instead, he simply stands like a shadow near a bridge and utters inarticulate noises in a strange voice. If "a word is one's will," Kaonashi has no independent will; he is a caricature of a person with only a mask for a face and who exists as a shadowy figure whose key attribute is an insatiable, indeed monstrous, lust for consumption. Kaonashi finds money to be the most powerful way to win the workers' favor at Aburaya, the spirits' bathhouse run by Yubāba. Money talks for him and he orders them to serve him heaps of delicious food, paying for it with

Kaonashi facing a banquet at the bathhouse in *Spirited Away.*
(Reproduced with permission from Studio Ghibli)

magically counterfeited money. They all flatter him with compliments and entertain him with lavish dishes, which Kaonashi voraciously gobbles down until he turns into a gigantic bloated monster who terrorizes the bathouse by devouring its staff. It seems fairly clear that Kaonashi's story is meant to illustrate the tragi-comedy of living a superficial life driven by a lust for unlimited but ultimately meaningless consumption—a self-centered life that leads only to a horrible isolation and loneliness. This certainly is not Chihiro's final fate, however. Her heroic foray into this fantasy world of gods and goblins enables her to discover a hidden world within herself and, as a consequence, magically gain self-reliance. Her initial loss of her identity as a sheltered and somewhat timid middle-class child leads to a gain by the end of the story: she finds the power within to not only free her parents, but to free herself from her childhood dependency so that she can return to her own world ready to begin a new life.

Chiro and Modern Individualism

To understand how *Spirited Away* has a deeper significance for a Japanese audience, we need to see how different its story is from a comparable Western tale. Stories about heroic otherworldly journeys are replete in Western literature, but a useful example for our purposes is Daniel Defoe's 1719 novel, *Robinson Crusoe*, about a man who, rebelling against his father's desires for him, goes to sea and through happenstance or God's will is shipwrecked as the lone survivor on a deserted island.

Literary critic Ian Watt sees Robinson Crusoe's heroic story of survival as key example of what he calls "the modern myth of individualism." By "myth," Watt means a story that symbolizes a "larger and more permanent meaning" than the narrative action literally denotes (1996 xii). *Robinson Crusoe,* like *Spirited Away,* became popular not only because it is entertaining, but because its underlying ideas appeal to its readers. What Watt sees as central to the novel's mythic power is its secularized "religious individualism."

Watt argues that *Robinson Crusoe* does not mimic the typical Puritan works of the time that loudly sang praises of God's saving grace for sinners. At best "Defoe's pious intentions are no doubt sincere, but they are rather occasional, and in that sense . . . there is an element of 'Sunday religion' in the novel" (1996, 162). So what is Defoe's story about then? In order to survive, Crusoe demonstrates his heroism not as a devout Christian but as a rugged individualist, who spends his time on the island working hard to put everything under his dominion. While he enjoys the fruits of his labors, he embodies an ascetical ethic that values hard work. He fashions his homes, builds his walled defenses, learns by himself hunting, fishing, animal husbandry, and agriculture "by labor, application, and contrivance" until, he tells us "I found at last that I wanted nothing but could have made it, and especially if I had the tools" (quoted in Watt 1996,152).

Underlying Crusoe's story here is the Calvinist idea that individual responsibility, which includes working tirelessly in one's calling and "untiring stewardship of the gifts of God," is a spiritual-ethical obligation (Watt 196, 154). However, what makes Defoe's novel a modern myth is that Crusoe, while embodying the "Protestant ethic," is motivated primarily by a "secular spirit." Crusoe's is not a religious, but rather an economically driven man—his ultimate goal is to improve the material side of life, and to take joy in his accomplishments as he efficiently and methodically builds his solitary island empire (157). Everything Crusoe does, finally, is for his own profit, and, by the end of the story, he is a very wealthy gentleman (Watt 1996, 152).

What this myth symbolically points to as fundamental to human life, therefore, is an ethic of utilitarian individualism. It is the secular faith that the enterprising rational person can pull himself up by his bootstraps, that is, achieve independence and salvation solely through individual self-effort, what Robert Bellah has called "lonely individualism" (1985, 145). This accurately characterizes Robinson Crusoe, whose only companion on the island is his obedient slave named Friday. In a contemporary American movie that takes its cue from Defoe's novel, *Cast Away* (2000), this same ideal of the lonely individual is highlighted. The hero, Chris Noland (played by Tom Hanks), finds himself the lone survivor of a plane crash. His best friend on his desert island is not even a person, but a cast-off basketball that he names, appropriately enough, Wilson. While his time on the island is a constant struggle against loneliness, Noland is able to find his personal salvation only through his own wits and heroic will to survive.

By contrast, Miyazaki's hero Chihiro in *Spirited Away* is anything but a lonely individualist. Her story exemplifies a very different kind of heroism than what we have seen in *Robinson Crusoe.* Chihiro saves herself not through her own solitary efforts, but through the help offered by her friends. If Haku, Kamajii (the old boiler keeper), and Rin (a female worker of Aburaya) had not given her useful advice, Chihiro would have lost her will to survive. Despite being initially an outsider, Chihiro soon makes friends in her new job at the bathhouse. It is by joining rather than resisting her boss, Yubāba, and working diligently at Aburaya that magically transforms her, giving her the power to free Kaonashi, the old river spirit, Haku, and her own parents. Moreover, it is through her web of personal relationships that Chihiro finds a cure for her loneliness and achieves maturity. In *Spirited Away*, Chihiro is no alienated loner, but rather a joiner who quickly becomes socially integrated in her new workplace, gaining admiration and respect from her colleagues precisely because she works so well in the group.

A similar hero-type can also be seen in Miyazaki's *Majo no takkyūbin* (*Kiki's Delivery Service*, 1989). Based on Eiko Kadono's work, the story is about a little witch named Kiki, just thirteen years old, whose magical talent is the ability to fly. She leaves her loving home to become a full-fledged witch. This film deals more directly with Kiki's independence than *Spirited Away* does with Chihiro's story of growing up. Where Chihiro just happens to stray off into another world, Kiki initially appears to be satisfied with going to another town to improve her magical talent, even though she has little choice because there is a witch's rule that she has to leave her home at the age of thirteen in order to become a full-fledged adult witch. The way in which Miyazaki portrays Kiki's growing autonomy highlights her internal psychological struggle. Her initial motivation is obeying tradition—young witches need to move away from home, and, initially, she faces no obstacles or opponents that attempt to repress or interfere with her ability to realize her goal of developing her magical powers. Indeed, she finds herself in a deepening intimate relationship with her new boyfriend Tombo, whom she meets in the beautiful seaside city of Koriko.

Miyazaki's films understand individuality in a different way from the Western Robinson Crusoe type of rugged individualism. Crusoe as a hero stands alone. His wits, his abilities, and his will are all he has to fight against the seemingly implacable, forces that threaten his destruction. Bellah argues that in the United States, a young person's coming of age , which he calls "finding oneself," has much the same quality. It "sometimes appears to be a pitched battle only the heroic or rebellious wage against a coercive parental order . . . " (1985, 57). Neither *Spirited Away* or *Kiki's Delivery Service*, however, follow the Western model of finding oneself. Neither Chihiro or Kiki are loners or rebellious children struggling to reject parental authority that they perceive as infringing upon their personal freedom. Kiki, for example, leaves home not against her parents' wishes but because of them. Her personal crisis comes from a loss of self-confidence when her powers mysteriously disappear, rather than from any struggle against authority or personal conflicts. And like Chihiro in *Spirited Away*, she is able to become increasingly independent because of the care and kindness shown to her by those around her, including her parents.

In *Spirited Away*, Chihiro and Haku are also not in a pitched battle with the parental figure of the witch to get their names back. Instead, it is the love and trust between them that finally allows them to remember. Yubāba herself, although a frightening-looking witch, is not absolutely evil, and her twin sister, Zeniiba, is more like an affectionate mother who encourages Chihiro to remember her original name. Neither witch, beyond the superficial resemblance, is anything like the typical Western witch figures, such as those in Grimms' fairy tales or C.S. Lewis's *The Lion, the Witch, and the Wardrobe*, who often represent a seemingly all-powerful negative feminine authority figure with the power to snuff out the child's individual existence.

In both Miyazaki films, then, what I call an "invisible affectionate support network" is the underlying reason for the hero successfully achieving independence and a stable, more mature identity. Moreover, the path from Chihiro's and Kiki's independence to their final destinations does not lead to a rejection but a reaffirmation that they belong to their families and communities. In Miyazaki's world, the heroes never lose their old social ties in the process of achieving their independence. Rather, to survive in the new and sometimes frightening outside world they find in their journeys, they form new friendships, which, in turn, allow them to reestablish old family ties, albeit in a new way based on their new sense of themselves. By the end of their stories, Chihiro and Kiki remain close to their families, but they are no longer children.

Miyazaki's Utopian Faith

Another key difference between Miyazaki's heroic journeys and Western ones is that their focus is not on their struggle with external obstacles in the way of their freedom. Miyazaki's anime focus on their heroes' ways of internally awakening an invisible power within themselves. "Renewal" is typically connected with "the bottom" in Miyazaki's world, so his recurring motif of "discovery through a descent to the bottom" implies that something in the depths of our minds allows us to discover a new self and rekindle a sense of inner confidence.

Examples of this are found in other Miyazaki films. In *Nausicaä of the Valley of the Wind*, Nausicaä finds the power behind the renewal of nature at the bottom of Fukai (the sea of pollution). In *My Neighbor Totoro*, Mei, a young girl who has moved to the country with her father and sister while her mother is recuperating from a serious illness in the hospital, finds solace when she creeps down inside the big bole of a sacred Camphor tree in the forest and falls asleep on the bosom of Totoro, the mysterious being who lives there.

Miyazaki's motif of self-renewal is based on his reverence of life as the powerful force at work within nature and human existence. Miyazaki's anime affirm life. He pays attention to life exclusively—death does not intrude in his fairytale fantasies. However, one can think of many other stories that are powerful because of their focus on death. In these stories, life's significance—which we often forget while busy doing our everyday routines—comes to the fore when we are confronted by death, which can suddenly break through our normal lives as a catastrophic event.

A famous Japanese film centered on this theme is Akira Kurosawa's *Ikiru* (*To Live*, 1952). In Kurosawa's film, a civil servant who has been working for thirty years without

Mei asleep on Totoro's breast in *My Neighbor Totoro.*
(Reproduced with permission from Studio Ghibli)

any sense of purpose or satisfaction becomes aware of the richness of life only after he learns that he has terminal cancer. In facing his fear of death, he rediscovers the significance and dignity of life, and in order to spend the remainder of his life more meaningfully, he dedicates himself to helping people. By focusing on death, Kurosawa effectively questions the meaning of life.

In contrast with Kurosawa, Miyazaki takes a different path. He tries to express the richness of life without dealing with death, and rarely addresses the reality of death head-on in his works. Certainly, this is partly because his protagonists are almost always boys and girls who are presumably far from death's door. However, it also seems likely that he has consciously decided not to deal with death (or sexuality) in his works for a deeper reason (see Murase 1997, 53–66).

What drives Miyazaki to take such an approach? It would be incorrect to say that it is because of his optimistic view of human nature; he is quite sensitive to wickedness and stupidity, which seem ineluctably part of human nature. This is well illustrated, for example, in his comic book version of *Nausicaä of the Valley of the Wind*. There, Miyazaki sheds light on the dark side of human life, depicting the nihilism and disappointment Nausicaä feels as she faces the fierce power struggle of the princes in Tolmekia. Nevertheless, in his 1984 anime version of this tale Miyazaki deliberately altered the script. In the film, when the Tolmekian army invades the Valley of the Winds, the villagers obediently accept unconditional surrender after being persuaded to do so by Nausicaä.

One of Miyazaki's critics found this new simplified plot of good versus evil unsatisfactory. In an interview, the anonymous critic suggested to Miyazaki that it would have been more interesting to have a character like Dais, who was featured in Miyazaki's TV series *Mirai shōnen Konan* (*Conan, Boy of the Future*, 1978–79), among the villagers. In *Conan, Boy of the Future*, Dais is a captain of a ship of the evil military kingdom of Industria, which is trying to revive the use of dangerous energy sources. At first, he is depicted as a villain who tries to arrest Lana, the hero who was a refugee from Industria. But in later episodes, when he decides to heroically lend his help to Lana, his character becomes more ambiguous. Adding such a morally complex character like Dais to the cast of characters in *Nausicaä of the Valley of the Wind* might have made the plot more exciting and unpredictable. However, in response, Miyazaki firmly rejected he interviewer's proposal.

> Well, when the Tolmekian army invaded, we could imagine various responses among the villagers: some villagers might think that what Kushana [a princess of Tolmekia] told them was right, others might become a traitors, or some might ask for surrender or some might get angry with Nausicaä, saying "What an opportunist!" . . . Nevertheless, I doubt if these characterizations are meaningful. No! I'm fed up with exposing the differences between people. That's what human nature is all about. Rather, it seems more important to think about how we can live together. With the twentieth century coming to an end, and various problems piling up before us, don't you think there is no use dwelling on such things? (Miyazaki 2002, 473–474)

When the critic followed this up by asking what he thought was the solution, Miyazaki retorted, "My answer would simply be that power to live can solve any problem."

It is obvious that the "vitality" or the power to live mentioned here is also central to the plot of *Spirited Away*. The priority that Miyazaki accords to life is clearly linked to his firm belief that we must say "yes" to life without hesitation—like Nietzsche's idea of "life affirmation"—deliberately denying that dark side that haunts actual life and can drain vitality away. It is easy to see that this idea penetrates all of his works, which are based upon this faith. Indeed, it is this belief that underlies the powerful personal relationships that help Chihiro and Kiki to live freely and fully. If Chihiro's self-awakening to life through her intimate network of otherworldly friends is her salvation, then we can conclude that Miyazaki is making a more general theological statement: the web of life that naturally, socially, and cosmically links human beings with a mysterious other world beyond ourselves permits every being to find a place in which it is totally accepted and can thrive. Therefore, this powerful web of life, biologically, psychologically, ecologically interlinked through a web of personal interrelationships in his films, is the key symbol of Miyazaki's utopian ideal.

A scene in *My Neighbor Totoro* (1988) expresses this symbolism very clearly. The three leading characters—Satsuki, Mei, and their father—bow deeply to a big old tree near their new house, thanking it for its protection and asking it to take care of them. The tree symbolizes the source of life through which every creature is united

Satsuki, Mei, and their father bow before the *kami* tree in *My Neighbor Totoro*.
(Reproduced with permission from Studio Ghibli)

and supports each other. If we are linked with this source to some degree, it is natural for us to have a sense of sympathy for others, like Miyazaki's characters. In the story, Mei's family weathers their family crisis through the assistance not only of Totoro and other local spirits, but also the local villagers who take them under their care as members of their own group.

Miyazaki and the Japanese World

Individuality in *Spirited Away* is established through the help of an interpersonal network of friends, rather than through the lonely struggle represented in the modern Western mythic type. It is natural to assume that a Japanese way of thinking has influenced this understanding of individualism, and Miyazaki himself appears to believe this. In *Spirited Away*, he avoids a mythical world for the real one with an actual Japanese person as his hero; Chihiro lives in a specific place and time—1980s Japan. In discussing the setting of the film and its very Japanese locale, Miyazaki notes that

Japanese must "recognize again that [they] are inhabitants of this island country. In an era of no borders, people who do not have a place to stand will not be treated seriously. A place is the past and history. A person with no history, a people who have forgotten their past, will vanish like the mist" (Miyazaki 2001, p. 2).

Obviously, Miyazaki believes not only that people should be conscious of being Japanese, but also that Japanese identity should be based on a traditional culture. Interestingly, he had tried to avoid very Japanese settings in his work up to this point; his favorite settings lacked national identification and were, if anything, rather Western (e.g., *Tenkū no shiro rapyuta* [Laputa: *The Castle in the Sky*, 1986], *Kurenai no buta* [*Porco Rosso*, 1992]). He has said that once he did not like Japan. Due to his guilty conscience over the barbaric behavior and crimes committed by the Japanese army in China, Korea, and Southeast Asia during the Second World War, he denied his Japanese identity and hated Japan, her people, and her history. This led him to long for Western countries and places such as Russia and Eastern Europe. Thus, he said, "I worked as an animator later, and I preferred stories set in foreign countries. I didn't get interested in Japanese folk tales, legends, and myths, although I ought to have chosen Japanese settings" (Miyazaki 2002, 266). It is fairly safe to say that his tendency toward neutral or Western settings comes from his ambivalent feelings toward Japanese history and culture.

However, when Miyazaki actually went to Europe, which he had wanted to do for a long time, he realized that it was impossible for him not to be Japanese. He said, "In a village in Switzerland which I had longed for, I became acutely conscious of being an Asian, short-legged Japanese. In a Western town I identified the ugly figure in the mirror as myself" (Miyazaki 2002, 266).

This serious ambivalence—his strongly negative feelings toward Japan and his inescapable Japaneseness—bothered him. Miyazaki was able to recover from his identity crisis by reading the book *The Cultivation of Plants and the Origin of Agriculture*, written by Sasuke Nakao, a prominent botanist. According to Nakao, Japanese culture is not isolated or unique; it has much in common with other cultures in forests of evergreens with thick, dark green, and shiny leaves. Nakao calls this common culture "the shiny-leaf culture" and locates it in the northern part of Southeast Asia: Sikkim to the west, Myanmar and northern Vietnam to the south, and the southern Chinese coast to the east.

When Miyazaki imagined himself as part of the shiny-leaf culture, suddenly he felt relieved of his depression and guilt (Miyazaki 2002, 267). At that moment he realized the importance of not limiting his Japanese identity to Japan's national borders. Therefore, his shift from the West to Japan does not mean that he began to lean toward a nativist political nationalism; rather, he turned his eyes to the trees and the forests of Japan, a country located at the eastern end of the shiny-leaf culture. In other words, he awakened to the beauty and richness of the Japanese natural environment.

This natural world is at the center of many of Miyazaki's films. That being said, Miyazaki represents it not only as a physical environment, but as something living by its own will. Miyazaki's animistic view of nature is symbolized, for example, by

The river god, Kawa no kami, cleansed from pollution by Chihiro in the bathhouse in
Spirited Away. (Reproduced with permission from Studio Ghibli,)

the Shishigami, an awesome deity who controls the lives of every creature at the very
center of the dark forest in his anime *Princess Mononoke*, and, as we have seen, by the
tree-dwelling spirit of the forest, Totoro, in *My Neighbor Totoro*. It is no surprise that
his view of nature is heavily influenced by Japanese folk Shinto, in which everything
in the universe, like rivers and trees, is believed to have its own spirit. Such a view
is in sharp contrast to the Judeo-Christian tradition, in which nature is an impersonal
object created by a transcendent God and given to humanity to be conquered and
controlled. According to Miyazaki, "Gods live in the dark. . . . It must be a sense of
awe that inspires the Japanese people to venerate something like a forest; that is to say,
a sense of awe has something to do with the darkness in our mind. If we lost such a
feeling, it would result in the disappearance of that mental darkness and consequently
we would become shallow" (Miyazaki 2002, 493–494).

But even though Miyazaki sympathizes with the animism underlying many Japanese folk beliefs, the gap between his view and traditional folk Shinto should not be
overlooked. Most spirits and gods appearing in Miyazaki's works are harmless and
loveable. The Japanese *kami* depicted in *Spirited Away* are not awe-inspiring, but
are easygoing, often friendly deities. The same is true in *My Neighbor Totoro*. The
Totoro, a sort of incarnation of the forest, is not a fearsome pre-modern spirit of the
kind that Shigeru Mizuki, a famous popular cartoonist specializing in folkloristic
deities, depicts in his manga. Rather, Totoro is more contemporary, a product of
the modern Japanese culture industry that markets cute (*kawaii*) lovable teddy bear
creatures as collectibles to Miyazaki's anime fans. As such, Totoro, as well as other
anime *kami* appearing in Miyazaki's works, express a secular shift in response to

the three "izations"—Westernization, industrialization, and modernization. On the one hand, Totoro reflects perhaps a general anxiety his Japanese audience feels after having increasingly moved away from the deities and spirits that are evocative of nature's awe-inspiring power. Modern Japanese people are more comfortable with the more domesticated variety like the harmless Totoro, who personifies the power of mass culture over nature instead of a natural "other" world beyond the human one (Hirashima 1997, 164–169).

Princess Mononoke helps in understanding this shift from pre-modern to contemporary views of the *kami*. Shishigami, a god who appears in the film, is not a harmless spirit like Totoro, who lives quietly on the fringes of modern civilization. Instead, he is a god of the Muromachi period's pre-modern folk religion, a powerful and dreadful deity who is believed to control the source of life of the Japanese forest. No one can approach it without serious difficulties.

In the film, however, Miyazaki has Jiko Bō (a strange monk) and others cut off Shishigami's head. If the god is a center of the universe (an *axis mundi*) from which every creature derives its energy, Miyazaki seems to be telling us that we have lost the center by killing Shishigami. Assuming that the god is an incarnation of nature, the killing of the god appears to symbolize the modern person's struggle with the gods and spirits. Thus, after the death of Shishigami, the spirits living in Japanese nature must necessarily become like the harmless Totoro.

This pacification as well as the secularization of the *kami* is thoroughly accomplished in *Spirited Away.* For example, several traditional folk religious Japanese gods are turned into characters, like Oshirasama or Kasugasama. At best, they serve as a handy device to pull the audience into Miyazaki's world of fantasy. He portrays them from the point of view of a modern Japanese people who have lost the feeling of awe and fear in the presence of gods. As anime characters, they signify the decline of traditional folk animism rather than its contemporary revitalization. Their manifestation in films using advanced technology like computer graphics, displaces folk deities even further from their traditional cultic context. In *Spirited Away,* Oshirasama or Kasugasama are no longer awe-inspiring cultic figures worshiped in a specific locality and tied to a set of ritual practices and symbol systems, but have devolved into secularized, humorous characters consumed for mass entertainment. Oshirasama, for example, a deity of the home (*ie no kami*) found throughout the Tōhoku region in Northeastern Japan associated with silkworm production and blind shamanesses (*itako*), is now only a colorful figure on the screen. Here Adorno's observation about the culture industry seems particularly apt. It is "defined by the fact that it does not strictly counterpose another principle to that of aura but rather by the fact that it conserves the decaying aura as a foggy mist" (1991, 102). In the film, these deities' mysterious aura has faded away.

Miyazaki and Salvation

If *Spirited Away* offers a secularized vision of traditional Japanese folk Shinto, then is there still a spiritual dimension to his work? It is a mistake to think that Miyazaki's animation is simply co-opting religious imagery in order to add an air of mystery to his amusing stories. Miyazaki takes his films seriously and argues that his artistic vision carries with it a deeply spiritual message of self-renewal.

Chihiro's return to this world can be regarded as a story about the awakening of her power to live. This awakening is a discovery of a new self within that she has never realized before. Thus, Miyazaki's emphasis on Chihiro's powers to know herself shows his confidence in the mythic power of self-renewal and his rejection of nihilistic self-denial, both of which come from his utopianism.

Interestingly enough, this message is communicated throughout the film by the symbolism of hot water. As Susan Napier has pointed out, in *Spirited Away* Miyazaki emphasizes the purifying and renewing powers of water (Napier 2002, 458–460). The film is essentially about the need for spiritual cleansing. It is a story of a symbolic death and rebirth through ritual acts of purification that restore not only Sen to her true self as Chihiro, but the natural world as she cleans nature deities of the dirt and filth from the industrial waste that covers them, obscuring their pristine natural beauty.

This is illustrated in the episode involving a mysterious spirit named Okusaresama (Mr. Stinky), who visits Aburaya Spa unexpectedly. All of the workers are terrified of him because he is so filthy, and so Chihiro is ordered to wash him with hot water and herbs. Finally, after scrubbing hard, a large amount of dirt and garbage bursts from his body, and the face of the rejuvenated spirit flies up into the air to thank the startled Chihiro, gratefully, "Well done." It is hardly surprising that Miyazaki's utopian message of salvation through self-renewal is tied to hot water, which is the traditionally Japanese means of purification (as anyone who has stepped into a Japanese bath (*furo*) would know). Such symbolism evokes a spiritual understanding in Miyazaki's audience.

It is important to draw attention here to the fact that Miyazaki's optimistic message of renewal closely parallels folk and shrine Shintoism, which focus on nurturing the life-giving powers in this world. Miyazaki finds salvation based upon the immanent spiritual powers that infuse both human beings and the world, powers that work collaboratively, by uniting with each other, so that all can be saved. In this vision, all we have to do is to awaken that life-affirming spirit within ourselves, and to reach out to connect with those who have that same life-affirming spirit. As Thomas Kasulis has recently noted, this emphasis has much in common with a folk Shinto spirituality that "may be understood as an emphasis on connectedness—on the feeling of being at home in the world" (2004, 166).

The notion of salvation in Japanese folk Shinto emphasizes the importance of the power of the community as a whole to create the conditions of fertility, creativity, and life renewal (*musubi*). Miyazaki's work is filled with examples of how the life-affirming power of the community gives his characters what they need to live fully. For example, the workers at Aburaya cheer Chihiro enthusiastically when she sees through the witch's trick and saves her parents, and, at the end, the film reveals that while Aburaya is a business, it is not all about profits, maximizing efficiencies, and submission to the unquestioned authority of Yubāba. It reveals something entirely different; it is a community that displays what Victor Turner calls *communitas,* characterized by an egalitarian bonding among its members. It is Chihiro's intimate web of friends and colleagues who function collectively to guide her toward self-renewal. This contrasts greatly with the Calvanist form of Christianity that informs works like *Robinson Crusoe*. Such a Christian faith is rooted in the concept of individual salvation. The solitary soul standing before God is marked by original sin, a pessimistic view of a human nature, and is redeemable only in the next life by a transcendent God who bestows salvation if the sinner is predestined or justified by his or her own faith.

Miyazaki's fantasy vision of his utopian community is also filled with a sense of nostalgia. In fact, Aburaya and the quaint town around it are evocative of Japan's past. Its architecture is reminiscent of famous historic hot spring bathhouses, and the atmosphere of the streets and shops is like that of old Japanese downtown areas. Miyazaki got the idea for Aburaya from an actual local religious festival in which spirits from many regions are invited to bathe (Katagiri, 2003, 52–53). In other words, *Spirited Away* conveys a nostalgic feeling for the "good old days" in Japan, which it shares with Miyazaki's earlier works like *My Neighbor Totoro*. It is interesting that Miyazaki looks backward not forward for his vision of utopia; it lies there in the dusty memories of the old bathhouses or long forgotten farming villages that have disappeared with the progress of Japan's high-tech, increasingly globalized society. This nostalgia is at the heart of Miyazaki's modern myth—that such Japanese communities based on mutual caring and trust once existed in times now past, or at the very least persist today in the virtual fantasy reality of his anime.

Conclusion

It is no coincidence that the unprecedented success of *Spirited Away* coincided with dramatic changes in Japanese society after the collapse of the bubble economy. According to Chie Nakane, a noted social anthropologist, Japanese people enjoy a "web of comradeship" that they find within the limits of the circle or place of work, which have traditionally defined the narrow but nonetheless intimate confines of their social world around which they construct their personal identity (Nakane 1989, 26–67).

It is true that the old rural village communities have gradually disappeared in the face of modernization, but part of their function seems to have survived in Japanese companies. These companies—Toyota, Sony, Canon, and the like— became pseudo-communities where employees found refuge against the fierce competition of modernization through corporate policies like the lifetime employment system. Belonging to a company meant having a fixed identity as anyone who has seen a Japanese salaryman proudly wearing his company's lapel pin knows.

However, it is becoming increasingly apparent that the seniority system and the lifetime employment system, which were hallmarks of the postwar Japanese management system and the symbols of Japanese economic success, have disappeared with the collapse of the bubble economy of the 1990s. Big blue chip companies like the Yamaichi stock brokerage firm have disappeared overnight, falling into bankruptcy. The unemployment rate hit a record high and is still higher than before the collapse. Under such circumstances, Japanese people in the post-bubble economy are experiencing a serious identity crisis. Feelings of uncertainty and anxiety about the future prevail. I think this is one of the reasons why Miyazaki's *Spirited Away* appeals to Japanese people in various age groups. They likely empathize with his film, which is filled with nostalgia for a holistic rather than fragmented community, one that values cooperation over competition, and promises renewal through the mobilization of familiar and thus comforting Japanese cultural resources.

Nonetheless, it would clearly be a mistake to interpret Miyazaki's animation simply as a nostalgia trip that attempts to resuscitate Japanese traditional culture for modern audiences. We should not overlook the fact that he also incorporates many different cultural elements into this film. The twin witches' faces are certainly Western, and the elder sister's home is like a traditional thatched English country house. This suggests that Miyazaki did not want to be misinterpreted as promoting a form of Japanese ultra-nationalism. Miyazaki is also not a dreamer, but a realist who is conscious of the inevitability of modernization. This realism is at the heart of *Princess Mononoke*, which, after all, is a story of a war between the deities of the forest and humans living in a mining town that are destroying it. After all, the animation industry itself is a product of modern technology.

According to Mircea Eliade, in archaic ontology the renewal of the world is believed to take place through the imitation and repetition of an archetype (Eliade 1971, 34). If we accept this premise, Miyazaki's nostalgia for traditional Japan should be interpreted not as a call to return to a nativist past, but as the director's hope for the renewal of the Japanese people cursed by the collapse of the bubble economy. In this sense, Miyazaki's body of work might be considered to be an attempt to convey a modern "secular religious" myth that provides psychological healing to those Japanese people suffering from an ongoing identity crisis.

12

Heart of Japaneseness

History and Nostalgia in Hayao Miyazaki's *Spirited Away*

SHIRO YOSHIOKA

In 2001, *Spirited Away* (*Sen to Chihiro no kamikakushi*) established Hayao Miyazaki as the undisputed leader in a national obsession with anime. The film, however, was not unequivocally praised as a masterpiece. Many Internet commentators complain that *Spirited Away* was less enjoyable than Miyazaki's earlier films, especially those produced before *Princess Mononoke*. *Spirited Away* seemed somehow empty. Such was my own reaction; it was not as entertaining as *Laputa: Castle in the Sky* or *Kiki's Delivery Service*. It was not as didactic as *Princess Mononoke*. It seemed that the film wanted to say something, but I was unsure of its message.

The key to understanding *Spirited Away* is Miyazaki's attitude toward Japanese history and tradition, especially his idea of "Japaneseness." *Spirited Away* is an attempt to use fantasy to establish a link between contemporary and traditional Japanese culture. Seen in this light, it is clear that *Spirited Away* shares common ground with his other films set in Japan. All attempt to show a connection between traditional and contemporary Japanese culture, although they vary in their approach to and treatment of the relationship.

As a child, Miyazaki had a basic dislike of Japanese culture. He was born in 1941. His father was an executive member of Miyazaki Aircraft, a company owned by Miyazaki's uncle. During the war, the business was successful, and the family was well-off. His father was conscripted, but not sent to the front. From what he told Miyazaki, just before his squad left for mainland China, his superior asked if there was anyone who did not want to go. Miyazaki's father put his hand up and said, "I cannot go because my wife and children are here." As a result, he stayed home, working to produce parts for military aircraft. Miyazaki described his father as "a man who was unconcerned about his own self-contradictions" (Miyazaki 1996, 249–250). His father's association with war-related industries and the family's relatively high standard of living during the war affected the young Miyazaki, leaving him with feelings of guilt toward the victims of Japan's aggression in Asia.

During the rapid transition from militarism to democracy in the years immediately after the war, Miyazaki lost confidence in his own country. He recalled when "adults around me sarcastically described Japan as a 'fourth-rate country whose standard of culture and living is helplessly low with too many people, too few natural resources, and that all it can be proud of is its natural beauty and seasonal changes'" (Miyazaki 1996, 265). For Miyazaki, "Japanese history was the story of oppression and exploitation of the common people, and rural villages were representations of poverty, ignorance, and rejection of basic human rights" (265). However, by the 1970s, he began to reconsider his Japaneseness. It was then that he read Sasuke Nakao's book *Saibai shokubutsu to nōkō no kigen* (Domesticated Plants and Origin of Agriculture).

This book enabled Miyazaki to regard Japan as part of Asia in terms of both history and culture. His sense of Japanese culture as a part of Asia made his view different from conventional approaches to Japaneseness, which tended to focus on the uniqueness of Japanese tradition. Miyazaki was interested in the diversity of Japanese culture. For him, even Western things became part of Japanese culture.

The representation of the Taishō period (1912–1926) in *Spirited Away* is an important focal point, which I will discuss later in this chapter. The period is a favorite setting among many manga, anime, and computer game artists. This is also the case in *Spirited Away*. Miyazaki chose this setting because it allowed him to highlight the diversity inherent in Japaneseness. That, however, is not the only reason; his personal affection and longing toward the Taishō and early Showa eras also had a strong influence. Such personal affection might appear to reduce the setting to mere nostalgia. The reality, however, is the opposite. While the works of other artists treat the interwar years with affection, theirs is nothing but a wistful longing for a romanticized past. Miyazaki's affection, on the other hand, is based on personal experience, springing from childhood memories and from a more recent encounter with the Edo-Tokyo Open Air Architectural Museum. Miyazaki is gifted with the ability to merge personal experience into a larger sense of past.

Miyazaki's belief that all Japanese share a certain sense of past is another important focal point. The subtle blending of personal experience into historical "fact" formulates a sense of past that looks and feels familiar to the audience, even though they have never experienced it.

All Miyazaki films set in Japan relate to Japanese history. *Princess Mononoke* concerns a "historical" past and pan-Asianism. *My Neighbor Totoro* has aspects of both pan-Asianism and personal experience. *Spirited Away* also includes these aspects, but Miyazaki approaches the issue of Japanese tradition differently.

Generally speaking, Miyazaki's fantasy is not a mere tool to criticize society but a powerful weapon used to merge the past and present. A critical difference between *Spirited Away* and Miyazaki's other Japan films is the way in which past and present merge and fantasy and reality coexist. The films before *Spirited Away* are set in the past, and fantastic events take place within the "real" world of the film. Those films do not directly depict contemporary Japan; *Spirited Away* is the first to do so. Still, Miyazaki's fantastic world shows the strong influence of both Japan's "historical" past and of Miyazaki's own personal past as extensions of the contemporary "real" Japan that belongs to the audience. Thus, Miyazaki succeeds in establishing a seamless link between Japanese past/tradition and the present. *Spirited Away* can be called a folktale for the twenty-first century, which teaches that contemporary culture is an extension of, or even a part of, a much larger context of Japanese tradition.

Spirited Away can be read as a critique of contemporary society. As some scholars point out, Japanese fantasy has been "a kind of mirror image of modern Japanese history" (Napier 1990, 12), and "a mode of social critique" attached to a socially constructed reality "while at the same time putting the foundation of what constitutes the real into question" (Figal 1999, 156). *Spirited Away* is no exception. Social critic Takashi Tachibana sees *Spirited Away* in this way.

> In his previous works, Miyazaki never depicted negative aspects of Japanese society seen from a child's point of view. That's what he did in *Spirited Away*, and that's what makes it different from his other works. . . . In the relationship between Yubāba and Bō, you can find another, weird relationship between parents and children in contemporary society. That distorted maternity is a striking representation of the sort of relationship that corrupts our society.
>
> Kaonashi's rapaciousness is also shocking. That, I think, is nothing but representation of Japan during the era of bubble economy. . . . It is those spirits, guests of that bathhouse, and the workers attending them, who built up contemporary Japanese society. Although this is not explicit in the film, it definitely is a very striking representation of a specific historical period. (Tachibana 2001, 34)

Tachibana is agreeing with Napier and Figal's belief that anime fantasies are a social critique of contemporary Japan. *Spirited Away* criticizes, for example, the unhealthy relationship between mother and children. In Japan, the rapidly declining birthrate is a long-standing social issue. The average number of children per household has also declined, and as a result, parents end up spending more time and money on their children (or, quite often, their only child).

Tachibana also suggests that the movie is also a critique of the social devastation that was the result of Japan's bubble economy, which started in the late 1980s. After the Plaza Agreement in 1985, the strong yen and easy-money policy fueled a craze for speculation, especially in real estate and stocks. As a result, stock prices hit a record high of 38,000 yen, and land prices (especially in Tokyo) skyrocketed well beyond their actual value. The myth that land prices would keep on rising further fueled the craze. Banks loaned, holding mortgages on properties increasing in value. Tachibana regards Kaonashi's greed as a symbol of Japan during this time of "irrational exuberance."

Tachibana is right that the film can be interpreted as a social critique as seen from a child's perspective. However, Chihiro's parents are better personifications of Japan during this period. According to the official movie description found in *Roman arubamu* (Romantic Album), Chihiro's father is thirty-eight and her mother thirty-five years old (Saito et al. 2001, 56). This means that they were in their late teens to twenties during the bubble economy. It is also ironic that the father assumes the strange town to be the remains of an old theme park closed down after the collapse of the bubble economy. Chihiro's parents are typical members of Japan's newly affluent middle class. At the beginning of the film, they are driving a shining new Audi to a new house in the suburbs. The father is especially smug as a self-satisfied bourgeois who is thrilled when he speeds down a narrow path leading to what he thinks is the gate to his pricey dream home. When Chihiro asks him, "Daddy, are we lost?" he replies, "We're fine. We've got a four-wheel drive."[1] Nothing will get in his way. He takes a shortcut over an old country road, relishing the opportunity to ride roughshod over nature. None of the signs that foreshadow their approach to a different world, such as a deserted-looking *torii* gate next to many small shrines, and a weird-looking statue standing next to the path, catch his attention. After they wander into an empty street lined with old-fashioned shops, the family goes into a place to eat. The parents start to help themselves to the food that is set out. When Chihiro tries to stop them, the father says, "Don't worry, you've got Daddy here. I've got credit cards and cash."

Nevertheless, Miyazaki's comments on the film reveal that *Spirited Away* is more than a critique of contemporary Japanese materialism and consumerism. The anime is also about the loss of any sense of history or identity: "In contemporary society where borders are disappearing rapidly, those who have no place to return [to] are the most insignificant sort of people. A place is past, and history. Those who have no history, people who have forgotten their history, I reckon, cannot but simply vanish like ephemeral mayflies, or be turned into chickens and keep on laying eggs, until they are finally processed for food" (Miyazaki 2001a, 19). Noting this passage, Susan Napier points out that "[i]n *Spirited Away*, loss of history in every possible aspect, which produces the most dramatic suspense in the film, describes fear for loss, or corruption of cultural identity," and the most distinctive of all fears "is loss of memory/identity, or loss of power of words" (Napier 2001, 461). Later in his essay, Miyazaki emphasizes this same point:

> I designed the world where Yubāba dwells as a pseudo-Western person. One reason for that is to give the world an appearance that is somehow recognizable, but at the same time hard to know whether it is a dream or reality. The other reason, however, is that Japanese traditional art is a treasury full of myriad images. . . . [Traditional folktales such as] *Kachi-kachi yama* [Ticktock Mountain] and *Momotarō* [Peach Boy] have certainly lost their appeal. But to cram everything traditional into the tiny world of folklore is, I must say, extremely senseless. Our children, surrounded by high-tech machines and shallow industrial products, are rapidly losing their roots. We must show them what rich traditions we actually have.
>
> By integrating traditional motifs into a story that is connected to the present, and also by placing such a tradition into the present as a piece of a colorful mosaic, the world in the film gains its own persuasiveness, I believe. That also makes us realize once again that we are residents of this island called Japan. (Miyazaki 2001a, 19)

The abundant images of the bubble years in the movie represent a society without tradition and history. This loss may be the result of globalization, particularly America's creeping yet unstoppable cultural domination of Japan. Although such anxiety imbues Miyazaki's lament over the loss of Japanese tradition, it is not the only issue at stake, for Miyazaki sees Western culture as now a part of Japanese culture. What, then, does Miyazaki regard as traditional Japanese culture?

By "pseudo-Western," Miyazaki means a style that mixes Western and traditional Japanese features. The most ubiquitous example in *Spirited Away* is the shops facing the street leading to the bathhouse and the bathhouse itself, which look Western, but are covered with traditional Japanese tiled and gabled roofs. Miyazaki calls these pseudo-Western.[2]

One of the reasons Miyazaki gives for adopting this style is to emphasize the rich diversity that makes up traditional Japanese culture. For Miyazaki, Japanese art is not "purely" Japanese; it does not represent an unchanging ancient heritage, unsullied by foreign cultures. It is rather an ever-changing hybrid, combining ideas and styles from various cultures at various historical periods. Miyazaki sees the Japanese pseudo-Western style as itself "traditional" since it is a bricolage of the newest bits and pieces added to a dynamically evolving Japanese culture.

Such a view is not unique to Miyazaki. In the 1930s, the famous Japanese philosopher and cultural historian Tetsurō Watsuji argued that Japanese culture consists of multiple cultural layers that the Japanese people have assimilated. When a new layer is added, it sits on top of older layers. In his essay "Nihonjin no seishin" (The Spirit of the Japanese) from his *Zoku Nihon seishinshi kenkyū*. (A Further Study on Japanese Spirit, 1935), Watsuji cites everyday examples. Like Miyazaki, he sees Japanese houses as eclectic combinations of different styles (Watsuji 1989, 315–316). However, Miyazaki differs from Watsuji in his view of Japanese culture's hybridity. According to Miyazaki, Japanese culture does not consist of distinctive layers; it fuses diverse cultural elements into something new. The bathhouse and other buildings in the spirit world are neither imported Western architecture nor quaint traditional Japanese wooden townhouses (*machiya*). They are something new. Miyazaki doubts the existence of anything that could be called uniquely Japanese. He is highly critical of those who typically point to "unique" icons of the samurai, classic aristocratic literature, or Zen temple architecture as something "uniquely" and "essentially" Japanese.

There is a more important reason that Miyazaki uses pseudo-Western buildings in *Spirited Away*. After the heady years of the 1960s, many Japanese forgot about poverty. Miyazaki seems to regard Japan's experience in the Meiji (1868–1912) and Taishō periods as crucially significant in this respect. He explains:

The town, in which the bathhouse frequented by the deities is situated, is modeled after buildings in the Edo Tokyo Open Air Architectural Museum in Koganei Park, Tokyo. It is a museum in which houses and shops from the Meiji and Taishō periods have been moved in from elsewhere or reconstructed. I like the pseudo-Western style buildings from that period. They are interesting pieces of architecture. I often go there for a walk when I have some free time. There, I somehow feel really nostalgic [*yatara to natsukashii kimochi*]. . . .

The shops in the old amusement park leading to the bathhouse in *Spirited Away*.
(Reproduced with permission from Studio Ghibli)

We, I think, have all forgotten the sort of buildings and the landscape and lifestyle of this slightly distant past [*chotto mae no*]. . . . In this case, what we need to do now is to remember that lifestyle that dominated Japan just a little while ago, and cheer ourselves up [*genki ni naru*]. That's what I wanted to do with that town in the film. (Miyazaki 2001b, 52)

The Taishō period is very popular among anime, manga, and video game artists. In most cases, they consider the period as an imaginary past, replete with nostalgia. It has little, if anything, to do with the present. The significant difference between Miyazaki and these other artists is his attitude toward the past. For Miyazaki, fantasy is not a mere tool of nostalgia. The past for Miyazaki is a part of the present, and fantasy describes the relationship between past and present by virtually resurrecting the past. This role of fantasy can be observed in all of Miyazaki's Japan films.

Miyazaki's attempt to look back on Japan's past through fantasy is similar to Kunio Yanagita's project in his *Tōno monogatari* (The Legends of Tōno), compiled in 1910. Yanagita believed that these fantastic folktales preserved a *pure* Japaneseness, untouched by modernity. Yanagita's search for an essential Japaneseness later led him to the notion of the common folk (*jōmin*). Similarly, Miyazaki is anxious over the fate of Japanese traditional culture, whose enemies are globalization and postmodernity. However, Miyazaki's vision of Japaneseness in the film is not Yanagita's static and unchanging notion of tradition; it is diverse and dynamic. This is obvious from the pseudo-Western buildings and the characters who inhabit them—as reminiscent of Lewis Carroll's *Alice in Wonderland* as of premodern Japanese folktales.

The diversity of Japanese tradition is a major theme of *Spirited Away*; however, it is evident in all of Miyazaki's films. To understand this theme better, it is important to comprehend Miyazaki's peculiar vision of Japan's past.

This vision can be understood in two senses: the "historical" past and the personal past. By historical past, I mean a distant past that those living in the present cannot access directly. They can know it through records but have no firsthand experience of it. Such a "historical" view is usually a macroscopic national history. A personal past, by contrast, is a past that is experienced either firsthand or secondhand, perhaps through an artifact from the past. It is based upon an individual's concrete and unique experiences. *Spirited Away* is distinctive artistically because it merges these pasts into a cinematic whole. But Miyazaki always sets his artistic vision of Japan's past into some larger context.

Miyazaki's Historical Past

What view of the historical past is at the core of Miyazaki's films? Miyazaki's belief that Japan is not isolated from world history comes from Sasuke Nakao, a botanist who sees Japan as part of a wider pan-Asian culture. In his book, *Saibai shokubutsu to nōkō no kigen*, Nakao argues that the origin of Japanese culture is best understood in terms of the archipelago's ecology. Toward the end of the Jōmon period, an evergreen forest culture originally from Southeast Asia came to Japan and replaced the earlier hunter-gatherer culture. Forests were converted into arable land through slash-and-burn agriculture and the growing of cereals. Nakao argues that this early culture was very different from the later rice-growing culture, which became the mainstay of Japanese agriculture. In the evergreen forest culture, people depended on the forest and were anxious to coexist with it rather than destroying it. But since growing rice requires flat land for paddies, people had to dominate nature by developing it (Komatsu 1997, 49).

Nakao says nothing about the legends, myths, or rituals of evergreen forest culture. However, what Miyazaki does is to create his own *mythos* reflecting this "forest cosmology" (Komatsu 1997, 50). *My Neighbor Totoro* evokes this mythic forest world with the Totoros's den in an enormous tree of a Shinto shrine. In *Princess Mononoke*, Shishigami's forest, with the mysterious pond at its center, is an *axis mundi* that connects the spiritual world to this world. In both movies, the forest is a source of life power with which human life must harmonize spiritually. In discussing *My Neighbor Totoro*, Miyazaki argues:

> There are few people who like soft and sticky rice in the world. Japan, Yunnan, Nepal, that's almost all the places where you can find them. . . . The Japanese people were actually part of a culture that adores soft rice much earlier than the establishment of Japan as a state, or even before the formation of the nation of the Japanese race [*Nihon minzoku*]. So, you can find food that is very similar to *okowa* [rice boiled with red beans] in Yunnan even now, and if you go to Bhutan, the faces of people there look exactly like Japanese. Then, finding out that this country, Japan, has been

connected to the whole world beyond nation or race, I felt really refreshed. Because until then, I always thought that Japanese history was nothing but a lot of rubbish like the *Tale of Genji* or Hideyoshi Toyotomi. This unity of Asian culture is what "the culture of the evergreen forest" means. . . .

I came to be able to regard Japanese history, or our way of life, including all those stupid things during the war, more liberally than before, as a part of a much larger history. . . . Until then, I felt I was almost suffocated. But once I saw the Japanese again, from this new point of view, and reflected on myself, I began to wonder—what do such characteristics of mine—my fondness of sticky foods, for example—mean? Or, what about the shape of my nose? Isn't it just like that of a man from the Jōmon period? These are the questions that haunted me the most during my youth [laughter]. (Miyazaki 1996, 492)[3]

Because of his guilt over Japan's wartime atrocities in Asia, Miyazaki was initially attracted to Western culture; he often chose the West (mainly Europe or its look-alike) as the setting for his anime. But Miyazaki soon realized that he could not reject Japan; this interview discloses his liberating vision of merging Japanese with a broader Asian sense of identity.

Miyazaki's view of Japanese identity is significantly different from that of Watsuji. Both see Japanese culture as part of a larger Asian culture, are concerned about how Westernization affects Japanese identity, and agree that the historical past influences the present. But Watsuji discusses Asian culture to illustrate Japanese uniqueness and supremacy, while Miyazaki identifies Japanese culture as an instance of a larger Asian culture.

In *Fūdo* (1929; translated, *A Climate,* 1969), Watsuji asserts that after a thousand years of assimilation, Chinese culture in Japan has been transformed into something completely different. Nonetheless, he also claims that Japan preserves China's lost heritage if the Chinese wanted to "restore the power and grandeur of their noble culture of the past, lost from the China of today" (Watsuji 1961, 133). Watsuji suggests that Japan's adaptation of Chinese culture is superior to the original. This is precisely what Miyazaki considers a "suffocating" if conventional isolationist view of Japanese exceptionalism.

By contrast, Miyazaki views Japanese culture as linked to Asia. Indeed, he eliminates the very periods of Japanese history that Watsuji lauds as exemplary of Japan's genius. Miyazaki does not like the Heian period, which boasts the refined aesthetic of aristocratic Japanese culture (such as *The Tale of Genji)* or the Age of Civil Wars, which is famous as the time of the samurai (such as the great shogun Hideyoshi Toyotomi, who invaded Korea). Both periods are "rubbish," says Miyazaki, despite the fact that they are iconic of a Japanese "golden age" for many.

Miyazaki's Personal Past

Another reason why Miyazaki ignores the time between the Jōmon and the Taishō and early Shōwa eras of the early twentieth century is that they have no connection to his personal history. A past that is too distant to be part of his personal past does not mean much to him:

Japan has modernized. But it somehow still cannot finish this process so completely. Totoro is a spirit of that era of transition.

I felt this very strongly when I made the film [*My Neighbor Totoro*]. So I don't have the slightest intention to go back all the way to the spirits that Shigeru Mizuki[4] draws, and I don't feel any sympathy towards them at all. . . . So, when I try to think of a story set in the Meiji period, like *Oshin*,[5] it is almost like thinking of a story set in a foreign country. For me, an old roadside inn (*magome no yado*) contains nothing nostalgic. Buildings from early Shōwa period [1926-1989], or those which survived the war, are much more appealing. When you think about Japan, you could think in terms of shamans [*itako*] in Osorezan Mountain,[6] or a world full of haunting emotions, like the ones seen in *ōtsu-e* pictures.[7] That means nothing to me. In that sense, unfortunately, I myself am a modern man. (Miyazaki 1996, 489–490)

When Miyazaki made *My Neighbor Totoro* in 1988, he created a fantasy world of rural Japan in the 1950s, drawing on his own memories of the countryside in Saitama prefecture. Talking about *Totoro* and *Panda ko-panda* (1972, *Panda! Go Panda!* 2005), a short film he made in 1972, Miyazaki credits personal experience as his inspiration:

When I made *Panda! Go Panda!*, I realized how nice it is to make a film based on the scenery I really remember seeing—not somewhere in Europe or some fictitious town. In *Panda! Go Panda!*, I drew a street known as Sakura-jōsui as I remember it in the past. . . . Remembering such a street, I was really happy [laughter]. . . . While I was making *My Neighbor Totoro*, it was just the same. It was such an enjoyable thing to make something like that, and *I also really thought that everyone has got his own stock of such memories, just like mine* [italics added]. (Miyazaki 2002, 301)

The setting of *My Neighbor Totoro*, according to Miyazaki, is a mosaic of his personal memories: the area around the Kanda River in Tokyo, where he used to live in his childhood; Tokorozawa in Saitama prefecture, where he lived while the movie was in production; and an area in west Tokyo near Seiseki Sakuragakoka, close to Nihon Animation, where he formerly worked (Miyazaki 1996, 485). The road where Satsuki and Mei wait for the bus in the rain, for example, is modeled after a road in Tokorozawa. Miyazaki had an area around Nihon Animation in mind when he designed the home of Kanta, Satsuki's classmate (Miyazaki 2002, 200).

Miyazaki's anime, while based on his own memories, also resonate for his audience. Yūichiro Oguro, an editor of an anime magazine, and Risaku Kiritōshi, a popular culture critic, both identify with the children in *Totoro*. They find the quixotic Mei appealing—she quickly shifts her attention from watching tadpoles to investigating a bottomless bucket to searching for acorns and then to playing with the little Totoro—

The bucolic landscape that is the setting of *My Neighbor Totoro*. (Reproduced with permission from Studio Ghibli)

The mysterious wild forest in *Princess Mononoke*.
(Reproduced with permission from Studio Ghibli)

because they remember acting like that as children (Abe, Oguro, and Kiritōshi 2001, 146). Nearly all of Miyazaki's films are endowed with this intuitively personal sense of past. Even *Princess Mononoke*, which is set in the Muromachi period, evokes a strong commonality of feeling. According to Kazuhiko Komatsu, "[t]he forest has already been conquered. Shishigami has been dead for a long time. . . . But, it is not that thoughts and history of the forest are lost and forgotten. People still have these feelings in their mind. . . . The forest is a holy place for human beings. The reason why Hayao Miyazaki's films appeal to people so much is, I assume, because they remind people of memories of such thoughts and history" (Komatsu 1997, 53).

Of Miyazaki's films set in Japan, *Spirited Away* is the one that synthesizes the historical and personal pasts. While *My Neighbor Totoro* and *Princess Mononoke* appeal to their audience's unconscious memories of an ancient Asian evergreen forest culture, they are very different in the pasts they recreate. *My Neighbor Totoro* is based on Miyazaki's personal recollections of the Japanese countryside, while *Princess Mononoke* is set in a distant past. What makes *Spirited Away* distinctive among Miyazaki's *oeuvre* is that it fuses past, present, and future into a fictional whole. The past it recreates derives from Miyazaki's own personal memories, but it is also a fantasy world designed to showcase what he regards as quintessentially Japanese—a picture that turns out to be a pastiche of Japanese culture taken from various moments in its past, as Risaku Kiritōshi notes:

In *My Neighbor Totoro*, Mr. Miyazaki perfectly reconstructs Tokorozawa in the period around 1954 by assembling things that now only remain here and there. In

Spirited Away, on the other hand, each object gives a strong sense of déjà vu, but the way the past is regarded, or how memory of the past is depicted, is different. . . . The shadows in the train give an impression that different layers of time exist simultaneously, being mixed up. I thought that we were seeing different time periods existing outside the window, one on top of another, with some gaps. So maybe what happens is not time travel to one specific period depicted in the film. Instead, various time periods exist simultaneously in that world in the film. (Abe, Oguro, and Kiritōshi 2001, 145–146)

This fantasy world in *Spirited Away* is also fused with personal memories, particularly those associated with buildings from the Meiji and early Taishō eras. As Miyazaki tells us, "I feel that those buildings built of wood and mortar, which I have seen since after the war, will someday disappear. Then I realized that such a landscape, which I thought was really shabby—I myself actually lived there, though—is a product of a really limited period of time in terms of history. Regardless of their value in architectural or artistic history, I just wanted to preserve such houses somewhere, so that's what I did in *Spirited Away*" (Yōrō 2002, 139).

Like Kunio Yanagita, who avidly collected folktales that were rapidly disappearing, Miyazaki is motivated to save the past because it contains the heart of Japaneseness. What Miyazaki does, however, is not literal or cinematic preservation so much as a novel artistic *recreation* of the past. Although the buildings originate from the Meiji/Taishō period, Miyazaki is attempting to create an imaginary past that affects his audience sentimentally.

Reimagining the Past—Miyazaki's Nostalgia

The interwar years, especially the Taishō period, are a popular setting in anime and manga.[8] That era has a strange power to evoke nostalgia. It contains images of modernity and cosmopolitanism. The phrase *Taishō roman* conjures up the eclectic atmosphere of the 1920s in which the "modern girl" swings to the rhythm of jazz. This idealization of cities like Tokyo and Osaka, as H.D. Harootunian has noted, "more than reflecting a historical reality already in place in the 1920s, figured a fantasy life that demanded to be filled" (Harootunian 2001, 14). Often, manga and anime envisage the *Taishō roman* nostalgically. As Fredric Jameson has observed, such works never try to capture the history accurately, but reenvision it "through stylistic connotation, conveying 'pastness' by the glossy qualities of the images" (Jameson 1992, 19). Famous works like *There Goes Miss Haikara* and *The Tale of Tokyo* do refer to historical events, such as the women's rights movement or the colonization of China. But they do so to create an exotic backdrop against which the plot can unfold. The Taishō period here is a fantasy world, more ideal than real.[9]

Miyazaki's fascination for this period dates back at least ten years before he made *Spirited Away*. In 1990, he drew up a proposal for an anime to be titled *Dai Tokyo monogatari* (The Tale of Great Tokyo)[10]:

We must not call the early Shōwa period the "good old days." . . .
If we call the war experience the base for postwar politics and economic growth, the base for our mind can be found in those days just before the war. In those days, there were heroes who definitely existed as objects of our longing:
—a boy, believing in justice and good will, trying to live a straight life; a generous young man who does not show off his ability; a girl who represents love and freshness; a story of their encounter, friendship, and adventure.
The Tale of Great Tokyo—
Now, having lost sight of the path ahead of us, looking for our origin, we set out on a trip to a world that existed only briefly between the earthquake and the war. (Miyazaki 1996, 409–410)

Although it is unclear how Miyazaki intended to adapt his script into an anime, we do know that he wanted to include architectural images. In his essay on the Takei Sanseidō, a stationary shop from early Shōwa preserved at the museum, Miyazaki vividly imagines what life would have been like back then by recalling experiences from his own childhood. The *tatami* mats in the shop remind him of a small hardware shop in Saitama, where the shopkeeper would take out a cushion, ask the customer to sit down, and serve some tea. He also fondly recalls when the employees had a feast there, linking it to his own recollections of the foods he used to eat and the outside bath he used. He concludes by noting, "Life changed before we knew it, and the style of life that once flourished in buildings like Takei Sanseidō is now somehow lost. . . . 'Know what you really need'—there was a time when this motto was still a virtue. . . . [T]he Takei Sanseidō for me is a building from those days in which such virtues, even if only barely, were still alive in Tokyo" (Miyazaki 1996, 317).

This is a blending of fragmentary childhood memories with an evanescent moment of history. Miyazaki does not see his work, even *My Neighbor Totoro*, as nostalgic. Rather, he hopes that *Totoro* will evoke that playful spirit in the heart of children. He hopes the movie will inspire them "to run around in a meadow, or pick up some acorns, or look at the space underneath the floor of their houses and feel excited. That's what I am looking forward to" (Miyazaki 1996, 490). Miyazaki wants to create a child's fantasy world that can emerge within a "real" or mimetic world that serves to ground the plot.

Spirited Away, however, deals with two different worlds—the "real" world of contemporary Japan and the fantasy world, which remains ambiguous. One is left unsure whether or not it is anchored in the Japanese past.

Before *Spirited Away*, the fantasy and "real" worlds of Miyazaki's films are not directly linked to his audience's world. *Totoro* and *Princess Mononoke* take place in the past, and their fantasy familiarizes an unfamiliar past. For example, the youngest daughter Mei's overactive imagination in *Totoro* is, as Miyazaki has observed, something that relates to the child within us, whether or not we know anything about rural Japan of the 1950s. This historical distancing keeps the audience from identifying too closely with the characters. The temporality of these films forces the audience to watch the action unfold from a third-person vantage point. This is reminiscent of science fiction films, which keep the audience at a distance because the action unfolds on alien worlds or in outer space. Miyazaki's fantasy worlds are also remote because they exist as a kind of alternate universe behind the screen. When the fantasies touch reality, that reality is still remote from our own, whether it is *Totoro*'s "real" Japan of the 1950s or *Princess Mononoke*'s ancient Muromachi period. In other words, fantasy is framed within the "reality" of each film. Fantasy is not juxtaposed directly with the contemporary world to mount a critique. Rather, Miyazaki tries to create a world that has a depth and life of its own that are only partially captured by the movie (Miyazaki and Yamaguchi 1997, 34).

The "real" world that frames the fantasy is suggested by each film's setting. In *Totoro*, this is Tokorozawa in the mid-1950s, a part of the Japan that was about to experience an economic "miracle" after a devastating war. In *Princess Mononoke*, this is the forest and an iron works, part of the wider world from which Jiko-bō and all the soldiers eventually come. This also seems true for *Spirited Away*. Its setting is a fantasy town; its place in a wider world is hinted at by the various places the train runs through in the film. For example, Chihiro's train trip to Zeniiba's house gives us a glimpse of the scale of this fantasy world. But what relationship does this fantasy world have with the "real" Japan? One possibility is that this "real" outside world is just an extension of the fantastical other. Miyazaki suggests that the complex fantasy world in *Spirited Away* is also connected to the real world:

> The world itself is not an isolated world that suddenly appears as we go through fog but some corner of the world [that] is connected to another one of our own world. I created the [fantastic] world imagining that it has its own complex structure. . . .
> When you create a world just by your imagination, the product is very often shabby. Rather than only creating a world that is framed [as a background of the film], I wanted to create a world that is a part of a much larger world. I made [the fantastic world in *Spirited Away*] that way. (Miyazaki 2001a, 138)

How, then, does the "real" world of the audience on "this side" relate to the "real world" on "the other side" of the screen? *Spirited Away*, unlike Miyazaki's earlier films, creates a deeply familiar simulacrum. The audience can readily identify with Chihiro, experiencing no gap between her world and their own. And when she takes her otherworldly journey, the audience moves smoothly in step with her. In other words, Miyazaki blends the real world with the fantasy world in a way that makes it an extension of our reality. He ties viewers directly into his fantasy world and links them to his own imaginary take on the Japanese tradition, which he believes is vital.

In *Spirited Away*, Miyazaki illustrates how Japanese tradition has a diverse and rich heritage because it is part of a wider culture. While *Totoro* and especially *Princess Mononoke* use the primeval forest to show how Japan is deeply linked to an ancient Asian culture, material culture serves as the symbol for Japanese tradition in *Spirited Away*. Traditional Japanese design is a treasury of cultural riches. But Japanese artifacts are not stylistically "pure," static, or monotonous. Instead, they show the chaotic, dynamic, and diverse nature of Japanese culture.

> One thing that was really amusing when we were drawing Japanese style buildings is that our art staff showed such an extraordinary ability. They don't draw them like Western paintings. I can see, instead, say, *some memory of, or instinctive talent for Japanese paintings* in them [italics added]. . . . All of us actually have some sense of traditional design: it has kind of soaked into our skin. When we opened the tap to that sense, it just flooded out much more than I expected. That gave a huge variety to the film. That was so amusing. Although I've already made quite a few films set in Japan, I didn't realize this until now. . . .
>
> Thus, this film has many different kinds of art and styles that are actually so diverse that it's almost unbelievable that they are in one and the same film. Still, they are completely mixed up in the film, and comfortably find their own places. And, that is actually the modernity of Japan itself. (Miyazaki, quoted in Yōrō 2002, 141–142)

Miyazaki is comfortable with this hybridity even when it seems cheap, artificial, or kitschy. This is apparent in his notes on the production sketches. For example, the bridge leading from the town to the bathhouse is not a delicately arched wooden bridge that might grace a Zen rock garden or an *ukiyo-e* painting. Instead, we find that "surprisingly, the frame of the bridge is built of steel frames" (Miyazaki 2001b, 55). The entrance to Yubāba's office is "[t]he height of Japanese vulgarity. The entrance is an extravagant-mishmash-nouveau riche-East Asian style" (191). In the corridor leading from the elevator to Yubāba's office, there is "a gate lamp that is somehow not fully Westernized, even if it does not intend to be" (192). Risaku Kiritōshi points out that this hybridity is modeled after the Edo Tokyo Open Air Architectural Museum, which the movie's dilapidated theme park recalls (Abe, Oguro, and Kiritōshi 2001, 145). In some respect, Miyazaki believes that these "Japanese" artifacts and buildings create a sense of collective identity. In his essay on Takei Sanseidō, Miyazaki writes, "I often imagined that the feeling of nostalgia is not something I acquire as I grow up, but I have it as an inherent part of myself ever since I was born" (Miyazaki 1996, 314).

We obviously have no memory of what happened before we are born, nor can we recognize anything we have never seen. However, people can "remember" things they have not experienced personally and recognize things they think they have never seen. They simply have forgotten these memories. It is reminiscent of the famous scene at the beginning of Marcel Proust's *À la recherche du temps perdu*, in which the narrator suddenly remembers his past when he eats a madeleine dipped in tea.

This same process shows at the end of *Spirited Away*, when Chihiro tells Zeniiba she feels she and Haku met long ago. Zeniiba replies, "In that case, it's easy. Nothing that happens is ever forgotten, even if you can't remember it." According to Kashō Abe, this is a very deep theme, comparable to a Proustian unintended memory. But in *Spirited Away*, "it is used to transcend personal memory to an ethnic, collective memory that has a material feel to it. . . . For example, when a child sees the *namahage* (a folk custom in Akita, in which men dressed as the god Namahage visit houses) or Oshirasama (a deity worshipped in Tōhoku area) in the film, they don't know what they are intellectually, but they instantly realize that these are things that have been around [in Japan] for a long while" (Abe, Oguro, and Kiritōshi 2001, 147). Chihiro's sudden recollection of her meeting Haku when she was a child is an unintended memory. It lurked hidden in her unconscious until she suddenly realized Haku's true identity as the river dragon who had saved her from drowning long ago. What happens, then, to Chihiro's memories when she finally leaves the fantasy world at the end of the movie?

Miyazaki's notes in his production sketch state that Chihiro is stunned because her parents remember nothing when she is reunited with them (Miyazaki 2001c, 621). His directions for the final scene, when Chihiro looks at the entrance to the tunnel right before she gets into the car, are edifying: "Entrance to the tunnel, half buried under bushes, is in front of Chihiro. Inside is pitch-dark. The sun shines from above. Chihiro, *not knowing why, is gazing at the tunnel absent-mindedly* [italics added]. Her hair is tied with the band Zeniiba gave her" (Miyazaki 2001c, 624).

The implication here is that Chihiro is losing her memory of her fantasy world, just as she forgot her previous encounter with Haku. The fact that she still has the hair band, however, suggests that her "fantasy" is "real." This is precisely Miyazaki's point. Even if she forgets what happened, it still remains a part of her. It is important to note that these experiences are not necessarily of *physical* events; rather, they are essentially metaphysical. The hair band Zeniiba gives Chihiro is not simply a reminder of Chihiro's experience in the fantasy world; it symbolizes her metaphysical connection with Japanese tradition. Miyazaki believes this is the heart of Japaneseness.

This view of Japaneseness is not radically different from that of others. In the 1930s, Tetsurō Watsuji also noted how important a factor Japanese cultural diversity was for understanding Japanese identity. In a lecture entitled *Kokumin dōtoku ron* (A Discussion on National Morals, c.1930), Watsuji notes that although the Japanese life had become Westernized, the Japanese mind was not. Watsuji believed that would never happen because "the Japanese people have their own, unique spiritual culture" (1930, 78). While Watsuji's idea seems similar to Miyazaki's, their arguments diverge completely. Watsuji was so concerned about the future of Japanese culture that he offered his own solution:

After the Meiji period, Japan has assimilated Western civilization, but not enough of Western culture. . . . Chinese scholarship was the basis and had a strong influence until the Meiji period. However, in the contemporary industrial world, Chinese influence is negligible. Therefore, as the Japanese people take in more Western civilization, they also have to assimilate more of its base, Western culture. . . . Nonetheless, however much they assimilate Western culture, Japan will never be Westernized, but the Japanese spirit will be even more strongly realized and expressed. In other words, Japanese people understand themselves through [observation and assimilation of] others . . . *Japanese people are the only people in the world who can do this.* (1930, 79; italics added)

Watsuji clearly distinguishes Japanese culture from Western culture. No matter how much the Japanese borrow from the West, their "spirit" will not only remain unchanged, but become even stronger. By contrast, Miyazaki believes that all Japanese share collective, though unconscious, memories from their past. Chihiro's journey to the fantasy world of the spirit town and bathhouse is a journey deep into that unconsciousness. But Miyazaki does not distinguish a uniquely Japanese culture from Western culture.

I have tried to describe what *Spirited Away* is *about*, but I would like to examine what it *is* as part of Miyazaki's *ouevre*. Watsuji, Yanagita, and other prewar intellectuals were concerned about finding a uniquely Japanese spirit that "appealed to practices that they believed were created prior to the modern period and thus exempt from the corrosion inflicted by exchange value" (Harootunian 1998, 144). However, in the 1920s, Japan was not immune from modernity. Yanagita observed that "it had become virtually impossible to see . . . continuity" between Japan's past and its present (Hashimoto 1998, 140). The "true Japan" endures only "in the fragments of people's memories barely living on in the form of legends[;] only through the concept of the common or Japanese folk could it be revived as a phenomenon of the mind" (1998, 140). At first, Yanagita's point seems similar to Miyazaki's. However, Miyazaki locates points of *continuity* in the changing relationship of people's present with their past. This is different from Yanagita's focus on the unchanging traditions of rural folk. Moreover, for Miyazaki it is his eclectic and constantly reworked fantasy that evokes a powerful sense of collective identity. While Yanagita (and Watsuji) assume that the "true Japan" is static and somehow untouched by modernity, Miyazaki regards the essence of Japaneseness as dynamically protean. *Spirited Away* is an example of the Japanese "mosaic" that combines Asian and Western culture. Therefore, Miyazaki's Japaneseness is not absolute or objective. It also transcends temporal and territorial boundaries, tending toward inclusivity rather than exclusion, commonalities rather than uniqueness. Miyazaki's anime is a modern "folktale" fusing a pastiche of disparate fragments into a new story. *Spirited Away* is Miyazaki's best attempt to transmit the heart of Japaneseness to future generations.

Notes

The author would like to thank Professor M. William Steele for his help and advice.

1. In Japanese, Chihiro simply asks *"Otō-san, daijōbu?"* (Daddy, is everything okay?). She might be worried about whether they can get off the path safely, not simply about getting lost. All quotations from films are based on the English subtitles included in the DVD of the film.

2. Strictly speaking, the buildings in Edo Tokyo Open Air Architectural Museum after which Miyazaki apparently modeled the buildings in the film are called *kanban kenchiku* (billboard architecture). They are not as explicitly typical of the pseudo-Western building of

the Meiji period, but are still somewhat representative. For more discussion on the merger of Western-style architecture and Japanese craftsmanship, see Hatsuta (1994). For more about *kanban kenchiku* and some examples found in Tokyo (quite a few of them have long since been demolished), see Fujimori (1989).

3. Miyazaki's view here on Japanese rice and its connection with Asia is completely different from the conventional view, which is often based on the *difference* between Japanese and Asian rice. For a good example of this conventional view, see Ohnuki-Tierney (1993, chapters 6 and 7).

4. He is an author known for his manga on Japanese spirits (*yōkai*).

5. This is a famous television drama, an epic story of a woman born in the Meiji period. It was aired between April 1983 and March 1984, and achieved an average viewing rate of 52 percent.

6. Osorezan Mountain is one of Japan's three holy mountains. In folk tradition, it is believed that the souls of the dead stay there forever. Itako is a blind female shaman who conveys the words of the dead.

7. Otsu-e are works of folk art originated in the seventeenth century and also were sold to the travelers along the Tōkaidō as souvenirs.

8. Two famous examples include *Haikara-san ga tōru* (There Goes Miss Haikara), a manga by Waki Yamato, originally published in 1975 and adapted into anime for television in 1978, and into a live-action film in 1987, and *Sakura taisen* (Sakura Wars), originally a video game created by Hiroi Ōji, released in 1996, and adapted into anime for television as an OVA (original video anime, anime distributed solely as video program) and film, theater plays, manga, and a novel. These two are typical romance (*roman* in Japanese) fantasies of the Taishō period. The first manga edition of *Haikara-san go tōru* has the subtitle, "Great Romance in Tokyo, the City of Blossoms" (*Hana no Tokyo dai-roman*), and the "catch phrase" in *Sakura taisen* proclaims "Taishō cherry blossoms amidst a fanciful storm!" (*Taishō zakura ni roman no arashi*) (Kudo 2002).

9. For example, in *Sakura taisen*, Taishō is written with Chinese characters meaning "thick" and "righteous," instead of "large" and "righteous." The game continues into Taishō 16 and Taishō 17, whereas the "real" Taishō period ends in Taishō 15. In the game, Shōwa never arrives. That is possibly due to the stereotypical Japanese view on Taishō and Shōwa. In Shōwa before 1945, militarism and fascism ruled over Japan, paving the way to war. Taishō, on the other hand, is regarded as an era of peace, democracy, and cosmopolitanism. Thus, the game manages to create another Taishō period of its own that is nothing but a pastiche. The nature of the plot—so-called steam punk, in which the protagonists (pilots of robots powered by steam engines and their own supernatural power) fight against evil—makes it clear that it uses the image of the Taishō period only as a source of fantasy.

10. "The Tale of Great Tokyo" was not a Miyazaki original story script, but was based on a manga called *Tokyo Monogatari* (The Tale of Tokyo) by Keiko Fukuyama, first published in 1989. The manga, which was reprinted in 1997, was out of print until recently in a new paperback edition (Fukuyama 2004–2005). It is about a young journalist working for a small magazine and a young man from China (a Japanese, born in colonized China), who, as later revealed, has supernatural powers. Miyazaki's anime project never materialized.

13
National History as Otaku Fantasy
Satoshi Kon's *Millennium Actress*
MELEK ORTABASI

> *Interviewer: When you directed your first film,*
> *Perfect Blue, you were apparently annoyed when an*
> *interviewer asked you, "So why not live action?"*
>
> *Satoshi Kon: Really, there's nothing dumber than*
> *asking a painter why he painted an apple instead of*
> *a pear. People have very fixed ideas about anime.*
> —Chiyoko Tanaka, 2002 interview with Satoshi Kon

Satoshi Kon: Emerging Talent

Film reviewers introducing a foreign film director have a habit of comparing the artist in question to someone their readership will recognize. But this is a rather difficult task in the case of Satoshi Kon (1963–). As one U.S. critic succinctly put it, "If Mr. [Hayao] Miyazaki is Japan's Walt Disney . . . Mr. Kon has no obvious peers in American animation" (Kehr 2004, 8). Kon's adult-oriented anime is still anomalous in the United States, even despite increased availability of subtitled and dubbed Japanese anime and their growing popularity with children and young adults.[1] But even in the comparatively large and diverse Japanese animation industry, Kon, a relative newcomer to anime, is somewhat unusual. Because he has introduced new ideas to the medium, the blurb on the front cover of his 2002 memoir *Kon's Tone* describes him as "the spirited director who has pioneered a new generation of animation" (Kon 2002).

The Hokkaido-born graduate of Musashino Art University, like many of his peers, got his start as a manga artist. In 1985, while still in college, he won the Tetsuya Chiba Prize, an annual award for aspiring manga artists administered by the popular weekly *Young Magazine*. After this debut, it took some time (and putting up with a very low income) to establish his reputation, but his career eventually started gathering momentum. Through his growing circle of acquaintances, among them Katsuhiro Ōtomo of *Akira* fame,[2] he started doing some anime work: background design for

Rōjin Z (screenplay Katsuhiro Ōtomo 1991); art direction on an anime adaptation of a famous 1940 story by Osamu Dazai, *Hashire Merosu* (Run, Melos, 1992); and various other projects.[3] This animation work coincided with the publication of various manga in book form (*Kaikisen* or Return to the Sea, 1990; *Wārudo apātomento horā*, or World Apartment Horror, 1991);[4] and serially (*Serafimu*, or Seraphim, in *Animage* magazine, May 1995–November 1996, incomplete). Apparently, his storyboarding and animation work on *Jojo no kimyō na bōken* (Jojo's Bizarre Adventures) in 1993 caught the eye of the MADHOUSE anime production studio, which recruited Kon to join its stable of talented and diverse anime staff.[5] His first project as a MADHOUSE employee was writing the script and controlling art direction for the vignette "Kanojo no omoide" (Her Memories), one of a three-part omnibus entitled *Memories* (1995). This impressive short, in which one can clearly see Kon's artistic and narrative style, led to a stunning offer: the opportunity to direct a project that would turn out to be the full-length feature entitled *Pāfekuto burū* (*Perfect Blue*, 1998).

Kon's directorial debut, which centers on the aspiring actress Mima and her stalker, pushed the medium of anime to new heights with its surreal blend of reality and fantasy. While some questioned the use of animation rather than live action, probably because of the real-world storyline and Kon's realistic backgrounds and characters, the medium is put to good use because "it is harder to tell how much of 'what the camera shows' is real and how much is Mima's imagination, or what someone is trying to convince Mima is her imagination—or whether the camera is showing both" (Patten 2004, 368). The "violently beautiful and surprisingly cinematic aesthetic" (Sharp 2001) of the film was a success in Japan. In his online journal, Kon describes his shock at the size and enthusiasm of the crowd at a November 1997 preview screening and reluctantly realizes that he is something of a celebrity (Kon 2004). *Perfect Blue* attracted international attention as well. Kon was invited to screen his film at Germany's 1998 Berlin International Film Festival in the United States and elsewhere, and it became a limited market release in 1999.

MADHOUSE encouraged Kon to begin work on his next project immediately in order to cash in on the popular and critical success of *Perfect Blue*. The film that resulted in 2001 was *Sennen joyū* (*Millennium Actress*), the focus of this essay, which has gathered even more accolades. Since then, Kon has directed another feature film, a light (if a bit odd) Christmastime comedy entitled *Tokyo Goddofāzāzu* (*Tokyo Godfathers*, 2003). His more recent effort, also produced by MADHOUSE, is a television series first shown on Japan's WOWOW cable channel, *Mōsō dairinin* (*Paranoia Agent*, 2004), a nightmarish look into the contemporary Japanese psyche, and a new masterpiece, *Papurika* (*Paprika*, 2006), a disturbing science fiction feature film about the possibilities of psycho-terrorism.[6]

Despite disappointing results at the U.S. box office,[7] there is no question that Kon's works have won their place on the international stage as well. Like Hayao Miyazaki, the first Japanese animator to strike a big deal with a U.S. film company (Disney), Kon too is building U.S. connections: *Millennium Actress* was released under Dreamworks' specialty division, Go Fish Pictures; *Tokyo Godfathers* was distributed by

Destination/Samuel Goldwyn Films; and *Paranoia Agent* even had a run on Cartoon Network's showcase for adult-oriented animation, *Adult Swim*. All of these works, including *Memories*, are available dubbed or with English subtitles on Region 1 DVD. So, despite his self-deprecating attitude—he even depicts himself as a meek-looking, bespectacled rabbit on the cover of his recent memoir—Kon is now an artist to be reckoned with in the anime industry both at home and abroad.

Millennium Actress: **Not Your Usual Anime**

Despite the broad range of anime genres, *Millennium Actress* does not fit clearly into any single category, nor does it treat familiar anime themes. One will not find, as one reviewer puts it, "big eyed, big breasted young girls battling phallic demons from far-away necro worlds."(Abbott, n.d). For this reason, the film is not particularly popular with the majority of anime fans in Japan or overseas. It resists categorization mainly due to the cinematic theme that dominates the film, in which an amateur film director sets out to make a documentary of a legendary film actress's career. In fact, Kon himself remarks that as with his first film, he has often been asked whether he thought this "movie about movies" would have been better off as live action. It is precisely this examination of conventional film through the medium of anime, however, that makes *Millennium Actress* compelling not only as a film but as a cultural artifact.

The film's refined choice of topic may have prevented it from being a cult favorite, but the strategy attracted attention from other quarters: along with Hayao Miyazaki's *Sen to Chihiro no kamikakushi* (*Spirited Away*, 2001), *Millennium Actress* received the grand prize at the Fifth Media Arts Festival held by Japan's Agency of Cultural Affairs.[8] *Spirited Away* was a box office success, due in no small part to Miyazaki's loyal following and the fact that the film is directed at children and families. But economic success is not a factor in the Agency's decision. The films do share high production quality, but more importantly, they both stay in line with what the Agency seems to encourage: a fairly conservative sense of what constitutes "worthwhile" Japanese cultural production.[9] The whimsical (and to most Western viewers, pretty far-out) characters and environment of Miyazaki's film send a clear message to Japanese viewers: the urban young must not forget the "native" beliefs that suppos-edly tie the Japanese to the natural world. The moral of the story, in which a young girl forms deep friendships with various Shintoesque deities, can be read within the liberal discourse on environmentalism, but the nativist view of Japanese identity the film presents is hardly progressive.

What, then, does Kon's film about a film actress—a character remarkably similar to the protagonist of the dark and voyeuristic *Perfect Blue*—have that appeals to the Agency of Cultural Affairs? It is certainly more wholesome than his first film: no rape, nudity, or murder. But what undoubtedly caught the eye of the judges was a certain kind of nostalgia, as in the case of *Spirited Away*. While Miyazaki's film invokes premodern, rural beliefs, Kon excavates the past by putting on display one of Japan's proudest histories. The rich and varied references to nearly half a century of Japanese live action film make it easy to read *Millennium Actress* as "a headlong cartoon love letter" to that tradition (Scott 2003). The golden age of Japanese cinema stretching from the 1930s to the 1960s—realistically rendered, lovingly colored, and obsessively detailed—unfolds chronologically as the aging actress tells her story. The film is just as much a fantasy (and spectacle) as *Spirited Away*, and creates something the Agency could only endorse: a pageant of Japan's most well-loved and aesthetically pleasing moments on film.

In the face of such spectacle, it is too reductive to propose a feminist critique of the film, which unquestionably reflects the sexism of Kon's telling remark in a recent interview: that he finds it easier to write female characters because "I don't know them the way I know a male, [so] I can project my obsession onto the characters and expand the aspects I want to describe" (Mes 2001). *Millennium Actress*, on a certain level, is not about a woman, but, as Michael Arnold remarks, "about men who watch films on women." Viewers seeking a strong, well-characterized female character will be disappointed to find only "the empty vessel Laura Mulvey wrote about nearly thirty years ago" (Arnold 2002). Chiyoko, the actress, is a lyrical, symbolic presence like so many of her cinematic female predecessors. The nationalistic meaning she bears, which I will discuss further, is the layer of the narrative that likely won the approval of the Agency for Cultural Affairs.

Yet the film presents its palatable, gendered and apparently mainstream historical overview in a subversive narrative format not so different from *Perfect Blue*. I do not refer to the blurring of reality and fantasy, a quality both films share, though the technique clearly has more political meaning in *Millennium Actress* than in Kon's debut, where it was a commentary only on the wavering mental state of the protagonist, not history itself. Instead, I refer to the dynamic between the documentarian and his subject, which is simultaneously that between a fan and his idol. This may not seem particularly radical; in fact, the reduction of the actress to a beautiful object adored by a worshipful lackey is as hackneyed as the voyeuristic misogyny of *Perfect Blue*, even if it seems less offensive. What this sort of critique overlooks is that the male viewer/documentarian in this film is a "type," rather than a character, as well. Genya, the middle-aged documentarian who aspires to make Chiyoko's last film, is also a gendered cultural emblem, one of fairly recent origin. Defined in relation to the object of his obsession, he is the *otaku*. This chapter will examine *Millennium Actress* in the context of the otaku—and his evolving relationship to cultural production in contemporary Japan.

The Discourse on Otaku

For the uninitiated, the term otaku is commonly used to designate a rabid fan/hobbyist of anime, manga, computer games, and related genres. Fans overseas have even adopted the term for themselves, thereby creating a sort of international fellowship of "geeks" bound by their intense absorption in these popular media. Indeed, as a descriptive term, it is applied only too easily to those who seem to have a more than passing interest in such "nonintellectual" subjects. This is precisely the problem with the label, since it implies not only type and level of fandom but, from a mainstream point of view, a rejection of or challenge to society.

Every culture has its share of geeks and nerds who occupy particular niches on the "fringes" of society, but the widespread discourse that surrounds the Japanese version is driven by more than a mild ethnographic curiosity about a flourishing subculture. The steadily increasing amount of literature on the subject in recent years attests to the fact that otaku have become the focus of what Sharon Kinsella has aptly called a nationwide "panic" in Japan, mainly on the part of groups that are generally expected to monitor the state of the nation's youth: "academia, the mass media, the police, the PTA ... [and] government agencies" (Kinsella 1998, 290).

The event that precipitated this panic, and, importantly, caused the otaku to be gendered primarily male in the public imagination[10] was the horrifying series of child murders committed from 1988 to 1989 by Tsutomu Miyazaki, a young man who was portrayed by the press as having an obsessive penchant for anime and manga, particularly of the "Lolicom" (Lolita complex) type. This genre, which is written for men but features cute young girls as its weapon-wielding protagonists, is not covert about its pedophilic appeal. Miyazaki's asocial habits, which included collecting and archiving large numbers of bootleg anime videotapes and manga magazines in his tiny one-room apartment, seemed to prove that youth with similar interests, who were instantly "discovered" to constitute a surprisingly large demographic,[11] were out to undermine mainstream social values.

Social scientists, public intellectuals, and reporters concerned with the present state of Japanese identity descried otaku, now suddenly lumped together as a homogeneous, sinister group. "Otaku came to mean, in the first instance, Miyazaki; in the second instance, all amateur manga artists and fans; and in the third instance, all Japanese youth" (Kinsella 1998, 311). The public response to the Miyazaki case in the following years was, as Kinsella outlines in her article, a series of attempts on the part of the Tokyo metropolitan police to censor the production and distribution of amateur manga (311–312). The public debate that surrounded the affair, however, demonstrated that the otaku was now more than a demographic or a set of behaviors: it became a buzzword to designate all that was wrong with contemporary youth and, by extension, Japan itself.

This effort to curb or correct the "deviant" behavior of the otaku has been reflected more indirectly in mainstream fictional media as well, where defanged but socially undesirable otaku characters have cropped up in manga, anime, film and TV dramas. As recently as 2005, the otaku again captured the national imagination, though in this watered-down form. A supposedly real otaku identified by his online username "Densha otoko" ("Train Man") reportedly got the girl of his dreams by soliciting the advice of his "Internet friends" through a popular online bulletin board in Japan, 2-chan. This "true story" generated a buzz online, and the apparently authentic threads were compiled into a bestselling novel, which then spawned not only a manga series but a television series and a movie (Campbell 2005). In all these versions, "Train Man" is cast as a vulnerable figure—the underdog who strives, if inexpertly, to form a bond with others—not a threat to public safety.[12]

In order to clearly label the type of underdog in question, all interpretations of this geek Cinderella story make liberal and specific reference to the otaku subculture. Certainly, Train Man's age and gender, as well as his desire for a certain type of cute and unattainable woman (more on the object of worship later), mark him as a member of this "underground" population, especially to Japanese audiences. This association is achieved through more overt cultural references as well. For example, by preserving the "look" of the web forum exchanges, the novel suggests the insular, secluded realm of the otaku, instead of rendering it into a more normative style of prose. Even the TV drama, a very standard format, relies on more than the actor's appearance to communicate the otaku stereotype. The opening of the series makes reference to one of the most famous otaku events of all time: the DaiCon IV science fiction convention of 1983. More specifically, the first episode opens with an anime sequence replete with references to the well-known amateur anime short shown at the opening of that convention, which will be discussed in its cultural context below. And as if this were not obvious enough already, the series also makes prominent use of the song "Twilight," by the popular 1970s band Electric Light Orchestra, which provides the soundtrack to the 1983 short.

Nevertheless, despite these nods to the unique qualities of otaku culture, the further the narrative strays from its Internet origins, the more the otaku character seems to become a two-dimensional laughingstock whom "normal" viewers can ridicule. The TV series and the movie, especially, simply offer a superficial update of the "unlikely romance story" by employing the virtual environment to add interest to the hackneyed narrative—along the lines of *You've Got Mail* (1998, with Tom Hanks and Meg Ryan). The TV drama goes out of its way to make "Train Man" (Atsushi Itō) appear unattractive, unfashionable, and somewhat comical, especially in contrast with his tall, willowy love interest (Misaki Itō, no relation). In the film, a rather good-looking actor (Takayuki Yamada) is forced into a bad wig and glasses, which come off at the end to reveal Prince Charming. Additionally, while he has real friends and family in the TV series, the film initially presents Train Man as almost totally isolated, moving him from "eccentric to psychologically disordered, from different to flawed" (Campbell 2005). In the end, the protagonist is "cured" of his otaku lifestyle and wins the girl, thus reentering the fold of the respectable citizenry.

What *Train Man* and other popular mainstream portrayals of the otaku and "his culture" demonstrate is that when the media reinvented Miyazaki as the embodiment of a social phenomenon, they simultaneously made a place for the otaku as a leading *fictional* character in the public narrative on contemporary Japanese society. Overexposure has turned the otaku into a personification of anxiety about the nation's future and a cousin to other similar figures such as the *modan gāru* (modern girl) of the 1920s. As other essays in this collection have demonstrated, the "modern girl," more than being a faithful representation of the actual young women during this decade, was instead "a creation of the mass media" (Silverberg 1991, 240). We can say that the male-gendered otaku takes his place alongside the modern girl, since he too is defined as a "minority" identity in relation to the controlling social narrative. The otaku, like the modern girl, seems to have become a blank screen upon which critics and the public alike may project whatever meanings and definitions they desire.

The otaku character evolves, though, when his definers are otaku themselves. Though producers of otaku culture (who tend to be self-identified otaku) seem to have accepted the idea of the otaku as one metonym for (post)modern Japanese culture, they often reject the idea that he signifies "an emblem for threats to tradition" in the way discussed above (Silverberg 1991, 266). Instead, as feminists have done with the modern girl, many associated with the anime, manga, and video game industry have sought to reappropriate the otaku and infuse him with their own meanings. One of the most successful (and celebrated) of these has been Toshio Okada, who has given himself the tongue-in-cheek title of "Otaking" (i.e., king of the otaku).

Okada perhaps deserves the title, since he has parlayed his experience as an otaku into multiple careers. He was one of the founding members and the first CEO of GAINAX, an anime, video game, and character spinoff goods company most famous for the TV series *Shinseiki ebangerion* (*Neon Genesis Evangelion*, 1995–1996). The company, established in 1984, was the brainchild of a number of university students, Okada included, who were also anime fans. What sparked the corporate project was their shared love for anime and, much like the amateur manga artists that Kinsella discusses, a desire to take part in its production.

The venture that created the momentum to form the company was an animated short these student amateurs made themselves, which was shown at the opening of the Osaka science fiction convention DaiCon III in 1981, "an event by otaku for otaku" (Murakami 2005, 112). While rough in quality, the piece was remarkably successful considering the lack of staff and resources. The follow-up short they made for DaiCon IV in 1983 was regarded as a great achievement in amateur anime. Featuring appearances by numerous well-loved science fiction characters and gadgets, from Mr. Spock of the original *Star Trek* series (1966–1969) to the space battleship Yamato of the pathbreaking 1974–1975 animated TV series *Uchū senkan Yamato* (The Space Battleship Yamato, known in the United States as *Star Blazers*), this fanciful clip has become something of a landmark in otaku culture. Recent references include the opening to the Train Man TV drama series, discussed above, as well as Takashi Murakami's 2005 pop art exhibition "Little Boy: The Arts of Japan's Exploding Subculture," where the clip was played on an endless loop. In any case, it was now official: by producing rather than just consuming, Okada and his business colleagues had made the transition from amateur to professional otaku.

Okada participated in several influential projects at GAINAX, including the "classic" *Ōritsu no uchūgun Honneamisu no tsubasa* (*Royal Space Force— Wings of Honneamise*, 1987), for which he was executive producer. However, he started to shift roles again when he wrote the script for *Otaku no bideo* (Video for Otaku,1991). A mockumentary that intersperses live action interviews of "real" otaku with an animated tale of a young man who converts to "otakuism," the film is a (somewhat autobiographical) commentary on otaku culture. More importantly, the film humorously critiques the media's fetishization of 1980s otaku by playing into the paranoia that stemmed from the Miyazaki murders. The anime plot outlines the comical descent of an "average" youth into the very depths of otaku culture; each step he makes toward being the ultimate fan is another step away from an acceptable social identity. He neglects his studies, quits playing sports, becomes scruffy and somewhat overweight, scuttles his chances for a corporate career, and as a result loses his attractive, respectable girlfriend. The goals that society sets for young men are replaced with his megalomaniacal desire to become the "Otaking," which involves professionalizing and marketing otaku activities (such as anime character modeling kits), much in the way that GAINAX actually did. Because plot and characters are comical and stereotypical to the extreme, the protagonist's fall from grace seems to suggest how foolish it is to blame otaku culture for the corruption of Japan's youth.

Okada continued his role as commentator on and promoter of otaku culture after he left GAINAX in 1992 and turned "academic." Popular culture of the supposedly most deviant kind infiltrated Japan's premier institution of tertiary education, The University of Tokyo, in a 1996 course on what Okada dubbed "Otakugaku" (otaku studies). Okada comments on this unlikely setting for discussions of otaku culture in his introductory remarks to the lectures, which were edited and published in book form in 1997 as *Tōdai otakugaku kōza* (Course on Otaku Studies at The University of Tokyo) (Okada 1997). "Tōdai [The University of Tokyo] and otaku—they seem to have nothing in common," he begins (5).[13] What, then, is the reason for discussing otaku within these hallowed halls? In a turn away from the self-deprecating and ironic tone of *Otaku no bideo*, Okada makes a bold claim. Rather than being a label for a type of person, or a particular deviant subculture within Japan, Okada argues, otaku is actually a global cultural force and, indeed, "the only" type of cultural production in the world "of which Japan can call itself the core" (1997, 7). Instead of being the locus of anxiety about Japan's future, for Okada, otaku represents its positive future. He does not deny the dark side of otaku culture but compares it to the "ugliness" that is part of each and every individual's psyche. In a rather stunning rhetorical move, he overturns the standard otaku narrative on its head when he suggests that there is "a little bit of otaku in . . . everyone" (12). Perhaps gathering strength from his elite audience, Okada insists that instead of being a sociopathic subculture, otaku culture is instead a shared national resource, defining Japan culturally both at home and abroad.

However, as Okada argues, it is not simply that anime, manga, and video games have become so prevalent that one can no longer call them a niche market in Japan. Otaku is not just mass culture, but signifies a new mode of being. Okada explains in rather cartoonish Zen fashion: being an otaku is "not studying, but becoming" the object (1997, 9). Other defenders of otaku culture share his point of view. In conjunction with a nationalistic "attempt to inscribe 'Japaneseness' in otaku" (Steinberg 2004, 458), which will be further discussed in the context of *Millennium Actress*, there is a move to define the relationship between the otaku and his object of worship as a socially productive one. Miriam Silverberg, who seeks to give the "modern girl" the "full respect that is her due," points out that though she was primarily depicted as a flighty, fashion-conscious consumer, the social reality was in fact one where women were, increasingly, producers, entering the workforce in ever greater numbers (Silverberg 1991, 240, 256–258). Similarly, if the otaku of tabloid news is Tsutomu Miyazaki, portrayed as a voracious but passive consumer of manga and anime, the other side of the debate is, as Marc Steinberg describes it, an otaku who contributes to society by practicing "consumption as production" (Steinberg 2004, 452).

Eiji Ōtsuka, a veteran critic of manga, anime, and literature born in 1958, the same year as Okada, agrees that otaku blur the line between consumption and production. Based on his observations of amateur manga artists at the teeming Comic Market conventions (see Kinsella 1998, 294–300), who commonly do rewrites of famous comics and animation, Ōtsuka projects a future in which "the production and consumption of the product are unified. All that will be left will be a multitude of consumers who produce and consume products made by their own hands."[14] Ōtsuka's statement anticipates a similar debate about the Internet, which critics accuse of causing a sort of narrative entropy; supporters credit it with placing the production of narrative into the hands of its consumers. Ōtsuka certainly wishes to emphasize the latter argument, which stresses not only consumers' passionate identification with narrative(s) but also the resulting democratization of ideas. It is this notion of cultural "leveling" that is also the motivation behind Takashi Murakami's exhibition, "Little Boy: The Arts of Japan's Exploding Subculture," which is framed from the particular perspective of the otaku.

Murakami, famous for his punky-cute pop art and his media-savvy personality, might deny that he is an otaku in the strict sense,[15] but he is unquestionably indebted to the aesthetics of manga and anime. Little Boy, the third and last exhibition in the Superflat series, is specifically billed as an exploration of "otaku . . . and their influence on the artistic vanguard of the 1990s and today" (Murakami 2005, vi). Furthermore, as Murakami would have it, the pervasive *kawaii* (cute) culture that otaku adore is the essence of Japan's post–post–World War II identity. While Murakami knows there is something "wrong" about this—"[f]rom social mores to art to culture, everything is super two-dimensional"—Little Boy is still a manifesto in defense of otaku cultural production (2005, 100). The exhibition prominently and unapologetically features what Murakami's colleague Noi Sawaragi calls the "meaningless and unorganized junk aimlessly produced daily in Japan": popularly sold plush characters like TarePanda, a big-eyed, supine, drooping panda; cels from popular animation like the DaiCon clip; and manga magazine covers (cited in Murakami 2005, 161).

By taking otaku culture overseas, Murakami effectively elevated it to the artistic plane. Murakami successfully resituates this "junk" in a new context. He is fully aware that in the transition from Tokyo magazine stand to New York art gallery, "the meaning of the exhibition changed. Although Superflat may have carried the label of 'art' in Japan, it never escaped its subcultural identity. But in America, where the hierarchy of genres is well-established, the exhibition was immediately accepted into the critical discourse of art" (Murakami 2005, 157). Thus, the Superflat series did more than collapse the distinction between high art and popular culture (however ironically). It capitalized on what Okada suggested in 1996: that the *world* is starting to recognize otaku culture, which "compris[es] a colossal industry at the core of Japan's 'soft power'—the nation's global cultural influence of the past decade" (Murakami 2005, vi). Japan may not attract the attention of politicians and economists at the moment, but these spokespeople argue that otaku culture, if formally theorized, promises to let Japan rise to international prominence once again—on the cultural front.[16]

Cinema, History, and Otaku as Storyteller

Kon, another undisputed denizen of the otaku realm, participates in the same "main-streaming" and elevating of the otaku that has been modeled perfectly by Okada's career, theorized by Ōtsuka, and put on display internationally by Murakami. Just as we see a movement from apologetic geekiness to proud affirmation in the three cultural critics/artists discussed above, so too has Kon produced two embodiments of the otaku: one a dangerous social misfit, the other a model of cultural awareness and preservation. The first, from *Perfect Blue*, is a destructive, Miyazaki-like killer out of touch with reality; his later incarnation in *Millennium Actress* is a harmless but passionate amateur filmmaker on a mission to preserve Japanese history from his own perspective.

Kon's directorial debut, *Perfect Blue*, falls within the paranoid discourse on otaku described by Kinsella in that it seems to condemn those who too obsessively worship pop idols, if not the pop idol system itself.[17] A young pop music idol, Mima, "earns" herself a stalker by deciding to pursue a career in acting instead. The young man who shadows her is a marginal figure, differentiated clearly, even from the other "nerdy" otaku fans who attend Mima's concerts and publish amateur micromagazines (*dojinshi*) about her band, Cham. At Mima's last concert, where we first meet her stalker, he stands out from the crowd of other youths, dead-faced and almost monstrous look-ing. We understand his social alienation immediately in that he is subdued among the cheerful crowd; in a telling (and somewhat obvious) scene he holds up his hand in front of the stage so that a diminutive Mima appears to be dancing on his upturned palm. His objectification of her is complete when we notice that he never speaks directly to Mima, but instead writes messages to her via an online chat room, the unthreatening locale of choice for the painfully shy and socially inept.

Even though Mima's real stalker turns out to be her increasingly delusional female handler (a former idol herself), it doesn't erase the sinister presence of the male otaku, who is the older woman's willing accomplice in defending Mima's "innocence," even when it means committing murder. He is the one the viewer suspects throughout the film because of the now established iconography surrounding the reclusive otaku, holed up in his room with nothing but his obsession for company. Whether it is the newswire photograph of Tsutomu Miyazaki's unoccupied room, with its cluttered stacks of pornographic anime videos silently speaking of their owner's murderous tendencies, or the "Mimaniac," lurking in his tiny room, lit only by the flickering screen of the computer terminal, viewers know the drill: a man who lets his hobbies stand in for human relationships is not to be trusted. What is more, the viewer is made complicit with the otaku, since we too witness Mima's most private moments.

Despite the voyeuristic aspects (and sexism) that it undoubtedly shares with *Perfect Blue*, *Millennium Actress* offers a much more positive and productive image of the otaku as cultural emissary. As Kon remarked in an interview, "I had the intention of making the two films like sisters, through the depiction of the relationship between admirer and idol . . . they show the dark side and the light side of the same relationship" (Mes 2001). But unlike mainstream popular media, the film does not create a comical, submissive "Train Man" type character who is at the mercy of those who seek to define him. Instead, he is the one who does the defining—not so much of himself, but by taking an active role vis-à-vis the larger cultural narrative. Genya Tachibana, a middle-aged small-time video producer/director, is the otaku consumer as producer that Eiji Ōtsuka describes.

However, Genya's positive qualities and his creativity are not immediately clear. Playing with the audience's expectations, the film opens with an outer-space, science fiction setting, strongly reminiscent of the space dock scene in *2001: A Space Odyssey* (dir. Stanley Kubrick, 1968). We see a young woman in a spacesuit (whom we later find out is Chiyoko, the "millennium actress" of the title) getting into a rocket, alone. Suddenly, we realize that we are watching a movie within a movie when we find ourselves in a dark, cramped room, videotapes stacked floor to ceiling, focused instead on a middle-aged man gazing raptly at a flickering close-up of the beautiful young actress. The place turns out to be Genya's editing room, which we find out when his assistant abruptly turns on the lights, but at first it clearly recalls the press photo of Tsutomu Miyazaki's room and its suggestion of quiet madness.

Furthermore, Genya's adoration of Chiyoko is clearly in line with Hiroshi Aoyagi's description of standard "idol otaku" behavior. Genya has seen all of Chiyoko's movies many times and now wishes to make his own documentary of her life. The "ritualized act" of collecting paraphernalia associated with his particular idol (in this case, video footage) marks Genya as a typical idol otaku, who expresses his worship through fanatic consumption (Aoyagi 2005, 205–206). For this visually oriented otaku, the only way to possess his idol is to capture her on film himself, especially as she is clearly out of his league as a romantic or sexual partner. In this way, his project is perhaps not so very different from that of the pop-idol otaku who "publish their own newsletters and magazines as ways of exposing their knowledge about, and their dedication to, their idols" (Aoyagi 2005, 205).

As the film unfolds, it continues to flesh out the fan/idol relationship when the focus of the narrative shifts away from poking fun at Genya's obsession to worshipping Chiyoko from his point of view. There is no question that Chiyoko is the embodiment of the "other" side of the otaku equation: the ideal object of admiration, to be gazed at by a heterosexual male eye. First, her obvious charm and physical attractiveness, emphasized over that of all the other characters, make her resemble the other "cute" female figures popular in anime. Additionally, like any good idol, Chiyoko is predict-

A newspaper photo of Tsutomu Miyazaki's room. The original caption draws attention to the stacks of manga magazines and anime videotapes, suggesting they are connected to his crimes.
(Copyright Mainichi Photobank)

Genya in his darkened studio, which at first very much resembles Miyazaki's room.
(Copyright 2001 CHIYOKO COMMITTEE)

able, having only two affective modes: manic persistence or quiet desperation. Though she plays experienced women on film—even an Edo-period geisha at one point—she remains emotionally chaste, sacrificing all in her relentless pursuit of her long-lost lover. Her chase continues even onscreen (a perhaps unintentional commentary on the roles Japanese cinema has reserved for women). Parading her beauty on screen for all to consume, Chiyoko somehow always remains out of reach, just as an idol should. She embodies a nostalgic, unthreatening ideal of femininity, and this is nowhere clearer than the 1950s-era billboard in the background of one scene, which shows a larger-than-life Chiyoko in a cheerful, ladylike pose, the leading actress in the (fictional) film *Tokyo no madonna* (The Madonna of Tokyo). In fact, she preserves even into old age (and, on film, eternally) the stereotypical "cute ... traditional adolescent femininity" valued by so many idol otaku (Aoyagi 2005, 121).

The critics' complaints that she is not fully developed as a character are justified—but only if we see her as a real(istic) human being. As described just above, it is easy to read the film as a sort of "idol fetishism" performed in "an effort to preserve traditional Japanese femaleness" (Aoyagi 2005, 218). Nevertheless, though the otaku–idol relationship frames the film and certainly limits the possibility of serious character development, Genya's quest is more than the realization of a personal fantasy. This becomes obvious in a number of ways as the film unfolds, but is most clearly demonstrated in this otaku's choice of idol: a screen actress who seems to have starred in nearly all the important and/or popular Japanese films around the middle of the last century. If this film were a "the making of" a famous actress's biography, then it really would have been more credible as live action. But this is not really Chiyoko's personal story. Chiyoko has more historical meaning than we might assume of an idol. Much like the eponymous heroine of the wildly popular TV drama series *Oshin* (1983–1984), I would argue that she represents "Japan itself" (Morris-Suzuki 1998, 132). Oshin, born in 1901, experiences everything from the great Kantō earthquake of 1923 and the destruction of her family's business in wartime bombing raids, to postwar economic revival. Chiyoko's story also covers these seminal events—she is actually born during the great earthquake—and more. She is recruited as an actress in the militaristic late 1930s—in the name of national service. When Chiyoko's mother objects to her daughter entering the film business and insists that she will get married and inherit the family business instead, the studio director counters, "Does a sweetshop matter more than the nation?!"

However, where Oshin's narrative provides "a guided tour of the landmarks of twentieth-century Japanese history" (Morris-Suzuki 1998, 132), Chiyoko provides an explicitly visual mode of connecting with that same history. Like *Oshin*, a big attraction of *Millennium Actress* is the "lovingly recreated period settings" (Morris-Suzuki 1998, 131). But the unified narrative of *Oshin* is replaced with a repeating cycle of events. Whether as an actress or in real life, whether she is the wife of a feudal lord or a pre–World War II socialist, her story is always the same: she madly chases her lost love. The lack of a linear narrative underscores the fact that Chiyoko is ultimately a vehicle through which to explore the entirety of Japanese history—past, present, and future—the way it looks *on film*.

In *Millennium Actress*, cinema becomes inextricably linked with national history because of the blurring of Chiyoko's real life and her career as an actress, so on one level the film is undeniably nostalgic for a past as interpreted on film. Genya, in his role of cultural guardian, continually upbraids his young assistant for his blasé attitude about the past. At the same time, the film sums up significant events in Japanese history in aesthetically pleasing images divorced from political commentary: crowds of soldiers going off to war on trains; bomber planes in a glowing sky over Tokyo. The 1970s and 1980s, when Japanese film (and history) were less dramatic, are conveniently omitted since Chiyoko's career ends in the late 1960s. One could simply say that the film presents a heartwarming view of modern Japan (as the Agency of Cultural Affairs perhaps judged), or, if one wishes to critique its politics, that it is irresponsible like *Oshin*, which offers a vision of "a peace-loving, suffering Japan, which is in no way responsible for the mid-century disasters that befall it" (Morris-Suzuki 1998, 135). However, this would ignore the cyclical structure of the narrative, which implies that retelling actual history is not the primary focus of the film.

The film in fact actively obstructs a linear historical reading. At some point, the viewer must stop worrying about who the "real" Chiyoko is. In some of the earliest memories she recounts to Genya, her sixteen-year-old self confronts a policeman with a prominent scar on his cheek who asks whether she knows anything of the young man with whom, unbeknownst to the policeman, she has just had a chance meeting. She lies to protect the young man. The memory is in the form of a flashback, without

Chiyoko with the director and her costar on a postwar, domestic Ozu-like set.
(Copyright 2001 CHIYOKO COMMITTEE)

any sort of voiceover commentary, and we are directly back in the growing fascist climate of 1930s Japan. However, we continue to confront the same man who plays the role of policeman in this scene, always clearly identified by the scar on his face. Some of these memories are from movies, some from real life, but he always plays Chiyoko's character's adversary, regardless of the historical context. In every era portrayed, it seems there is an evil force (the scarred man, who always embodies a dictatorial authority, whether as a rebel-crusher or jailer of human rights activists) that must be combated by a force of good (Chiyoko, whose purity of intention never falters), helped along by loyal followers (Genya, who willingly gets in on the action, whether as feudal retainer or rickshaw man).

Since the narrative is intrinsically predictable and repetitive, the message of the film is more firmly located in its visual elements. Like its otaku character, the film too collects images, relying on its viewer's knowledge of Japanese film history in order to give those visual elements their meaning. More specifically, the film locates memory in the visual rather than in narrative, thus diverting the focus from history and toward a mode of communication driven primarily by image. This visual cuing is achieved most obviously through referencing actual movies and their social context simultane-ously (this of course results in a film that is less accessible internationally than, say, *Spirited Away*). For example, Chiyoko herself is an amalgam of real actresses, among them Hideko Takamine (1924–)[18] and Setsuko Hara (1920–). The latter was the muse of director Yasujirō Ozu (1903–1963), whose distinctive cinematography and domestic settings defined a whole generation of Japanese film. *Millennium Actress* reproduces the low-angle, muted Ozu "look," complete with a Chiyoko in Setsuko Hara–like

Chiyoko on a movie poster for the movie *Meguriai* (Chance Meeting). Several women in the foreground imitate the way she wears her scarf. (Copyright 2001 CHIYOKO COMMITTEE)

clothing and hairstyle, which instantly evokes both Ozu films and the growing postwar prosperity of the 1950s that they represent.[19]

The interrelatedness of cinema and history is sometimes more overt, as in the sequence where a poster for the film *Meguriai* (Chance Meeting) hangs from a post behind which a protest is taking place. While it is not clear what is being protested, one can imagine the Ampo demonstrations of 1959–1960, which protested the renewal of the United States–Japan Mutual Cooperation and Security Treaty (*anzen hoshō jōyaku*). Several women watching the protest in the foreground have scarves draped over their heads in the same fashion as Chiyoko does on the poster. This is a clear reference to the film *Kimi no na ha* (What Is Your Name?, 1953), in which the female lead created a national craze for wearing what came to be called the "Machiko wrap."[20] Here, the melodramatic film and its huge popularity contrast with, as well as comment on, the political turmoil that characterized the same era.

In addition to cinema, the film relies heavily on the meta-representation of other visual media to evoke different eras of history. Printed media feature prominently: we see posters advertising Chiyoko's films—near-perfect facsimiles of actual movie posters from various decades—on Chiyoko's coffee table, in the "Gin'ei" studios, at media events, and on the streets. Many sequences also reproduce photographs in a realistic fashion, such as the formal posed portraits from Chiyoko's childhood, but later there is a more obvious commentary on the link between photography and history. When production at Gin'ei resumes after the war, we see Chiyoko, the only character rendered in sepia, walk out of her spot in what is obviously a commemorative black-

Chiyoko in sepia, stepping out of the "photo" that commemorates the reopening of Gin'ei Studios after World War II. (Copyright 2001 CHIYOKO COMMITTEE)

and-white photo of the studio staff. Other sequences similarly acknowledge history as it appears in photographs or newsreel footage by showing Chiyoko, in full color, against a two-dimensional, black-and-white background, as in the scene where she scans the crowds of returning soldiers to see if her lover is among them.

Similarly, visual mass media from the premodern period deeply inform *Millennium Actress*'s portrayal of Japanese history prior to the advent of cinema and photography. Of course, the film contains references to many well-loved samurai films, such as *Kumo no su jō* (Throne of Blood, 1957), directed by Akira Kurosawa (1910–1998). References to actual events are placed in a more period-appropriate visual context during a montage that is one of the most dynamic and visually striking in the film. Chiyoko, her costume perpetually transforming, rides through a continually changing landscape on a horse; in a carriage; in a rickshaw (pulled by Genya); and finally on a bicycle. The passage of history is suggested as well by the changing color palette and style in which the background landscape is rendered. In the first part of the sequence, which portrays the armed conflicts of the Boshin War (1868–1869), the background coloring resembles the *ukiyo-e* (woodblock prints) of Hiroshige (1797–1858), known for his landscapes. Suddenly, Chiyoko sits in a horse-drawn carriage in Western dress, and we are in the Meiji period (1868–1912); the landscape around her depicts stone buildings set against a bright red sky. Even if Kon had not made his influences explicit in the companion volume to the movie (Kon and Oguro 2002, 126), the distinctive hues and the unusual architectural perspectives in this sequence are clearly based on the more modern sensibilities of Meiji period woodblock prints known as *aka-e* ("red pictures").

More than the biography of a great actress, *Millennium Actress* is a rapidly moving

Chiyoko in turn-of-the-century Western dress riding in a horse-drawn carriage against a Meiji-era woodblock-like background. (Copyright 2001 CHIYOKO COMMITTEE)

bricolage of iconic Japanese visual elements collected from various media and histori-cal periods. In this sense, the film's otaku-like technical strategy mimics Murakami's idea of the "superflat," as summarized by Thomas Looser: "multiple layers, consisting of mixed styles and mixed media each with their own particular orientations, brought together on a single plane without any one point of origin that would fix the relations between them" (Looser 2002, 310). Certainly, *Millennium Actress* brings together a number of disparate media onto a single plane, "flattening" them into a series of two-dimensional moving images. However, since the film presents something of a visual history of Japan through this pageantry of composite images, the erasure of origins implied by Looser's definition is more problematic to apply.

Marc Steinberg, in his analysis of how Murakami and other contemporary superflat artists reference Tokugawa period (1603-1868) woodblock prints and other visual genres, considers the same idea of layering/compositing described by Looser, but with respect to history. Rather than creating a linear narrative of heritage or a sense of origins, these superflat works demonstrate a "scant assertion of continuity between premodern and postmodern, but rather a process of consumption-production, selection-folding that speaks more about contemporary sensibilities than about Edo" (Steinberg 2004, 466). This assertion agrees with Looser's—that superflatness rejects the conventional teleologies—but also points to a new mode of establishing hierarchy. Despite the fact that elements are chosen from the past, superflat art denies the cultural hegemony of the past. Through selecting, re-sorting, and collapsing together normally disparate media and histories at will, *Millennium Actress* too performs this controlling mode of consumption as production.

It appears that the otaku has come a long way since his infamous debut onto the national stage in 1989. Though the stereotype is still regularly lampooned on TV variety shows (where self-identified otaku willingly put themselves on display as such), I would agree that otaku culture and its proponents have successfully transformed otaku into "veritable subcultural heroes, ones, moreover, who are unique to Japan" (Steinberg 2004, 453). I would argue that they have taken the debate beyond this fight for equality, so to speak, to a discussion on the future of Japanese cultural identity. Within what have arguably become "high culture" manifestations, such as Okada's University of Tokyo lectures and Murakami's Superflat, the otaku is no longer simply a character, but becomes a synonym for contemporary cultural production.

In the case of *Millennium Actress*, the tangible and active otaku protagonist who collects and collates (Genya) becomes just an impetus for a mode of visual and narrative control that is ultimately performed by the film itself. Ōtsuka contends that through producing their own metanarratives, otaku seek to appropriate the "grand narrative" that subtends the products they consume (Steinberg 2004, 452). This is undoubtedly the case with Genya, who sees himself as archivist and storyteller, eager to have the last word on Chiyoko's grand career. However, the middle-aged otaku character's conservative nostalgia for the past is recast and extended on a different level by the visual aspects of the film itself. By successfully redefining otakuism as artistic method, rather than as personal taste, *Millennium Actress* puts the emphasis on how national culture is produced, rather than nation itself.[21]

I would argue that *Millennium Actress* does seek to rewrite a "grand narrative" in the way that Ōtsuka suggests—but not that of national history. The discourse addressed by *Millennium Actress* is rather the traditional hierarchy of visual media and their roles in *representing* history. Looser, in his discussion of the transformational effects of new media in early and late twentieth-century Japan, argues that the two eras can be compared to each other "as a relation between filmic and 'anime-ic' conditions" (Looser 2002, 297). He contends that a shift is taking place and that we live in "a transitional moment defined by a new, mixed-media relation" between these two modes (2002, 298). Probably no other work of visual art currently demonstrates this hybridity as literally as *Millennium Actress*, which foregrounds the unique possibilities and flexibility inherent in the anime medium. In making *Millennium Actress*, Kon says he wanted to "honor the accretion of past Japanese culture by consciously forming connections with it" (Tanaka 2002, 76). By its otaku-like incorporation and reimagination of earlier visual media in Japan, especially cinema, I would argue that the film actually redefines the relationship of those media to the history they represent. *Millennium Actress* asserts that anime is no subcultural medium, subordinate to film, but is rather the rightful heir to that tradition of recording and (re)creating cultural and national history.

Notes

1. In a *Kinema junpō* interview, Michael Stradford, the vice-president of Columbia Tristar Home Entertainment who oversaw the U.S. release of Kon's 2003 feature, *Tokyo Godfathers*, remarks that youth on both U.S. coasts are quite aware of Japanese animation, though young people

in California tend to be more informed than their New York counterparts. "Outside the cities," however, "the image of anime as viewing for children is still pretty strong" (Harada 2003, 73).

2. The manga version of *Akira* had its first run in *Young Magazine* as well, during the 1980s.

3. This information is all available in Japanese on Kon's personal Web site, *Kon's Tone* (the site has much of the content also available in the book of the same title, see bibliography). The site is periodically updated; a filmography and list of works is also in Kon 2002, 248–251.

4. Katsuhiro Ōtomo made an early foray into live action cinema using the latter: the identically titled *Wārudo apātomento horā* (1991), starring Hiroyuki Tanaka.

5. MADHOUSE was established in 1972 and remains one of the largest and most innovative forces in anime. Several directors and various other artists work on their own projects under the aegis of the company and with the sizable support staff. Kon has remarked that the management style at MADHOUSE is rather loose, and that the powers that be tend to leave him mostly to his own devices, unlike most other production houses (Toki Studio 2001, 82). This laissez-faire attitude is reflected in the diverse range of anime (mostly movie and OVA, i.e., straight-to-video releases rather than TV series) released under the MADHOUSE name: everything from an adaptation of *The Diary of Anne Frank* (*Anne no nikki*, 1995) to the baroque adult fantasy *Bampaiā hantā D* (*Vampire Hunter D*, 2001).

6. Popular culture takes on a very different meaning in *Paranoia Agent* than it does in either *Perfect Blue* or *Millennium Actress*, and is probably the topic of another paper. Maromi, a plush character marketed by a small "cute goods" company, eventually becomes a monster who psychologically and then literally takes over the city. This seems to contrast markedly with Takashi Murakami's almost gleeful marketing of similar products overseas—it is perhaps no coincidence that Maromi closely resembles TarePanda, a famous panda doll who has been featured in a number of Murakami's exhibitions.

7. This lack of financial (if not critical) success is not unique to Kon. Miyazaki's *Sen to Chihiro no kamikakushi* (*Spirited Away*, 2001) won the 2003 Oscar for Animated Feature and still could not make much of a splash (Patten 2004, 367). It seems that in the United States, the combination of animation plus foreign film still only adds up to very small audiences.

8. Incidentally, the film also received a grant from the same agency during its production (Kon 2002, 16). *Millennium Actress* actually made the circuit of international film festivals even before it was released in Japan. The premiere was at Montreal's Fantasia 2001 festival, where it won "the Best Animation Film category, as well as the Fantasia Ground-Breaker Award." Patten lists this and the impressive list of other festivals attended and awards gained in his review of the film (Patten 2004, 366).

9. The official site of the festival does not precensor submissions by citing requirements; it states simply that "the goal of the festival is to encourage the media arts in our country," and emphasizes technological advance. This fostering of digitally based art is in and of itself rather progressive, of course, even if it reveals that the government realizes these cultural products have economic potential for the nation. Nevertheless, though content does not seem predetermined, and judges for the anime division are from within the animation business for the most part, past and present prizewinning works do not tend to be of the morally or culturally challenging variety. See *MAP: Japan Media Arts Plaza*, http://plaza.bunka.go.jp/festival/about/index.html. Accessed December 21, 2005.

10. In the interest of time, I have not examined in detail this gendering, which ignores the fact that there are significant, and growing, numbers of female otaku. Sharon Kinsella points out that in the late 1980s and early 1990s, the majority of amateur manga artists were young women. What is more, male amateur artists and fans started to adopt their style and even became readers of this "soft, feminine" girl-oriented manga. As Kinsella explains, "[t]his manga and those men became the unlucky focus of the otaku panic" (1998, 300).

11. Kinsella remarks that amateur manga conventions in Tokyo attracted over a quarter of a million young people in 1992 (1998, 289).

12. This is hardly new as a narrative ploy, in Japan or elsewhere. *Cyrano de Bergerac*—or *Animal House* for that matter—provide ready examples of the nerd as everyman, a harmless and somewhat wistful figure who deserves better than he usually gets—even if, objectively speaking, his behavior is not entirely ethical or, at the very least, a bit creepy.

13. Hiroshi Aoyagi was doing his fieldwork on idol otaku in Tokyo in 1996. Discussing Okada's lectures at Tōdai with his corporate and academic acquaintances, he found that they generally regarded otaku culture as "too 'trashy' . . . to be studied seriously in academic institutions" (Aoyagi 2005, 206).

14. Cited in Steinberg (2004, 452). I am indebted to Steinberg for pointing out that Okada, Ōtsuka, and Murakami share this "*otaku* as consumer/producer" attitude.

15. Murakami, in a conversation with none other than Toshio Okada, whom he recognizes as an authority on the subject, says he feels like he "could never keep up with the distinctive climate of the *otaku* world" (Murakami 2005, 169).

16. Developing this "soft power" is in fact what the Japanese government is actively encouraging right now. The Media Arts Festival itself represents one of these efforts (see note 8).

17. Kon has said that he is "embarrassed" if viewers think the film is a critique of the pop idol system or even a realistic portrayal of it (Mes 2001). Nevertheless, it is hard to imagine any young woman aspiring to Mima's career after watching how she is manipulated not only by her stalker but by everyone who manages her.

18. In addition to referencing several of Takamine's films, including *Nijūshi no hitomi* (*Twenty-four Eyes*, 1954), several lines of dialogue are apparently lifted directly from Takamine's recently republished memoir, *Watashi no tosei nikki*, originally published in 1965 by Asahi shimbunsha (Kon and Oguro 2002, 115).

19. Chiyoko's husband is more closely modeled on the less-well-known Keisuke Kinoshita (1912–1998), who directed a number of important films both pre and postwar.

20. The poster itself, incidentally, almost exactly reproduces a publicity shot for *What is Your Name?* where actress Keiko Kishi poses with her trench coat–clad lover, albeit minus the famous wrap.

21. One can apply to Kon equally well what Steinberg says of Takashi Murakami: "it would be a mistake to miss the ambivalence of [his] nationalism and to neglect the more prevalent cultural logic of consumption" that prevails in his film (2004, 468).

14
Considering Manga Discourse
Location, Ambiguity, Historicity
JAQUELINE BERNDT

In the past few years, manga has become quite popular as material for research and education about contemporary Japan. However, academic theses and papers often give the impression that while manga may serve as a mirror for various social and cultural discourses, neither the media-specific aspects of comics nor the Japanese discourse on comics need to be taken into account. This observation leads me to the discussion below.

As a starting point, I should like to note why I use the term "discourse." The concept of discourse draws attention to both contesting views and the contingency of notions like "manga," "tradition," and "art"; in other words, this concept allows for considering the changing power relations and historic conditions that set the framework for what can be said about comics in a specific culture and what is widely affirmed as a typical manga at a certain point in time. From such a perspective, manga discourse is not limited to manga criticism; it also includes the ways in which social institutions—the mass media and the educational system, among others—define manga and its social relevance. Such definitions of "manga" are, of course, also indebted to the variety of manga readers and the works most widely shared. Therefore, the goal of this essay is to explicate what foreign students of manga are missing when they ignore Japanese secondary sources.

My call to consider Japanese manga discourse is addressed primarily to scholars with a command of the Japanese language and, in a broader sense, to all those who make public statements about manga. Of course, a lack of direct access to sources in Japanese (as is the case with many comics experts) or a lack of expertise in regard to the comics medium (as is the case with many Japanologists) does not necessarily diminish the importance of these authors' writings. However, authors in both fields should be aware that their points of view are naturally limited and valuable precisely because they need broadening by others. A comics expert unfamiliar with Japan is expected to place manga in the context of his or her individual experiences with non-

Japanese comics rather than to provide an overall picture of manga history. A scholar of Japanese studies, on the other hand, is supposed to open up Japanese sources and voices to a non-Japanese audience. My own perspective is that of a German-born art scholar teaching in Japan, who has been observing Japanese manga discourse at close range for nearly two decades and is motivated by an interest in the aesthetics of comics.

The first section of this essay describes common methodological blind spots in writings on manga (and to some extent, anime), paying special attention to the field of Japanese studies. It illuminates the way in which authors often neglect the aesthetic and cultural ambiguity of manga, which comes in part from a tendency to overlook Japanese manga discourse. The second section provides a brief historical survey, focusing on recent tendencies to critically question the primacy of the so-called story-manga as allegedly originated and developed by Osamu Tezuka. The third and final section analyzes inclinations in manga discourse to trace manga back to a purely Japanese premodern pictorial art. The emphasis here lies on contesting views within Japanese manga discourse and on the historical ambiguity inherent in manga.

Blind Spots in the Study of Manga

In view of manga's contemporary prevalence, it does not come as a surprise that it also serves as a subject of academic study. In Japanese studies programs, both at select Japanese schools such as Ōsaka University and in other countries, manga (along with anime and other popular media) has increasingly become a topic of study with regard to issues such as gender, global media culture, neonationalism, and dystopian images of the future (Bachmayer 1986, 1997; Guden 1998; Phillipps 1996, 2000). However, an overview of the status quo reveals some striking issues with regard to how authors situate themselves in relation to Japan, to comics in general, and to Japanese comics in particular.

First, how manga is treated depends highly on the cultural context of the researcher and intended audience. Non-Japanese publications, particularly academic ones, are generally not read by Japanese manga creators, editors, and readers.[1] The majority of them do not have any command of foreign languages and, until recently, have not been much interested in areas other than their domestic markets. Therefore, publications in languages other than Japanese are specifically addressed to a non-Japanese audience, and their authors' inclination to "universal readings" may lead to serious shortcomings, yet this is rarely considered. Even those authors with a background in Japanese studies often fail to explain why particular examples of manga or anime are discussed and why the Japanese public and experts consider them important (see, for example, Napier 2001).[2]

A typical example is the general critical commentary on Hayao Miyazaki. Non-Japanese scholars tend to assume that his movies are typical of anime as a whole because of their mere presence in Japan; they frequently treat these animated movies as mirrors of Japanese culture, assuming the existence of a homogenous audience, and often implicitly comparing them to Disney products, but they rarely locate them within the history and present variety of animation in Japan.[3] Equally symptomatic of a decidedly foreign approach is the astonishingly small emphasis on comparing animated movies (or series) with their respective manga works, even in the case of *Nausicäa of the Valley of the Wind* or *Ghost in the Shell*. This arises from different ways of experiencing the works in the first place, but it also involves a widespread disregard for Japanese perspectives. Such perspectives are vital, however, as they call to mind that neither manga nor anime is consumed by an "average Japanese recipient." Both genres have long targeted specific ages, genders, and tastes,[4] and today the vast number of works produced ensures that even dedicated fans are not able to gain an overall view. Publications by Japanese manga and anime researchers allow glimpses into ways of consumption that otherwise could only be gained through painstaking audience research (Hosogaya 2002).

Foreign scholars also tend to concentrate on thematic interpretations of manga and anime. However, considering how they are consumed in Japan would shift the emphasis of criticism in this area. Without this context, authors may overlook that genres *within* manga are less centered on thematic content than in the United States and, furthermore, that many regular readers today are less attracted by narrative content than by technical craftsmanship, visual spectacle, intertextual references, or cute characters. To rephrase it, whereas scholars attempt to locate a certain work within their own cultural or social milieu, fans prefer to remain within the limited realm of their specific media culture. What should distinguish scholarly academic research from fan expertise (and thus justify such endeavors) is to acknowledge the existence of multiple readings and mediate between them. However, to do so effectively, scholars need to be open to the nonacademic field of expertise (like that of fan-expert knowledge) as well as to Japanese discourse on the subject.

The external or non-Japanese perspective discussed above includes, secondly, manga's being regarded as an "outsider" to comics. Students of manga within Japanese studies usually do not attempt comparisons with other sorts of comics or consult theoretical literature by authors not specializing in Japan who publish in periodicals like the *Comics Journal* and the *International Journal of Comic Art*.[5] This segregation between manga and the "rest" of comics can be traced back to two completely different motivations. In some circumstances, it comes from an exclusive interest in things Japanese, without a significant exposure to comics and their specific discourse; at other times, its genesis is the enthusiasm of manga fans, who usually refrain from consuming any other sorts of comics. As opposite as these positions seem, both focus on manga as a peculiarly Japanese cultural artifact and therefore tend to reinforce exoticism and neonationalism. However, instead of engaging the issue of "Japaneseness," I prefer to draw attention to the lack of familiarity with comics as a whole, including the range of variations within the medium. This lack is perhaps one reason why Japanologists often neglect manga's aesthetic and cultural particularities. But without considering comics on their own terms, it will not be possible to examine multiple perspectives on them. Yet, manga call for multiple perspectives in the form of considering Japanese as well as non-Japanese views of them, and also, in the form of a methodological vacillation between the realm of representational contents and that of its specific renderings. An examination of "adult manga," for example, cannot be limited just to an investigation of adult subject matter and themes, but equally has to question what adult forms of manga expression and reading would be and to whom.

Before proceeding with this discussion, I need to clarify briefly how comics are defined. In general, contemporary scholars, curators, and publicists hold two opposing ideas about comics. On the one hand, comics are seen as a comforting medium of simplification and redundancy that reduces complexities (Clark 2003). Contrarily, comics are also viewed as a highly challenging medium that unites the seemingly incompatible, for example, the acts of reading and watching (Frahm 2000). The first view is often taken by persons who have just "discovered" comics. Even if they do not mean to disparage the medium, they tend to treat it prejudicially by relying upon a procrustean bed of binary oppositions to which they cling. This oppositional framework reveals itself, for example, by their dichotomizing of a desired authenticity of hand-drawn lines with the impersonal-looking products of the culture industry, assessing of works in regard to what they understand as "escapism" versus "realism," and distinguishing between "children's" and "adult" comics. Foreign comics experts, by contrast, dismiss those who would denigrate the medium by emphasizing its complexity, and they often regard the fact that comics ask their readers to read and view at the same time as suggestive of their fundamentally avant-garde potential. However, they, too, have their limitations insofar as they overlook the fact that experienced comics readers have no trouble reading and viewing simultaneously. Nevertheless, focusing on comics' incompatibility and ambiguity appears to be crucial in discussing comics, including the aesthetic particularities of the medium.

An inexperienced person might easily capitulate to comics' blurring of verbal and pictorial elements, where pictorial signs function like language and verbal signs assume pictorial qualities. Comics also make readers shift their attention between sequential panels that suggest temporal succession and (double) pages, which present these parts simultaneously. This invites consideration of issues such as narrative progression and repetition, analysis and synthesis of movement, invention and confirmation, the serious and the funny, and last but not least, the materiality and representationality of symbols. Indeed, it may be noted that symbols in recent comics do not necessarily symbolize anything. While signs in mainstream comics often appear transparent, that does not necessarily mean that they should be "read" as having specific meanings; for example, words in a speech balloon may merely indicate the presence of a speaker. This ambiguous status of words in comics may make content-centered interpretations appear arbitrary. In order to avoid that, the fundamental aesthetic ambiguity of comics must be taken seriously, and it should be acknowledged not only as a general affirmation of equivocalness and polyphony, but also as a structural characteristic of the methods used for analyzing this ambiguous medium. In the broadest sense, the issue of ambiguity highlights the dissolution of modernist concepts of identity. This dissolution is probably one factor among others in comics' current popularity and specifically in the exceptional interest in manga, which is the offspring of a non-Euroamerican modernization.

The fundamental characteristics found in the aesthetic ambiguity of comics also apply to its cultural hybridity. This leads me to my third point, a call to reflect upon manga as Japanese comics. Today, manga form one of the three main comics cultures of the world, along with American comics and Franco-Belgian *bande dessinée*. Admittedly, only a few foreign comics are translated into Japanese, and even those that are available are not approved as "manga," as has been the case with Hergé's *Tintin* series, which has been marketed in Japan as children's or picture books (*ehon*) carefully segregated from manga publishers and manga shelves. Yet, favoring a certain "manga style" shows ignorance of manga's own history and its present variety. Unlike modern fine art or literature, comics in general have been a fundamentally impure, parasitic form of expression, borrowing more from existing sources than aiming at inventive modernist originality (Carrier 2000). Manga, in particular, has consistently appropriated such diverse pictorial sources as Chinese ink-painting, European tableau with its central perspective, European caricature, and American superhero comics. After World War II all this was mediated by photography and film. What is globally known today as "manga style" is, in fact, the result of intercultural exchange.

But hybridity is not only an issue that concerns foreign cultures; it also concerns various cultures within a single nation. With this in mind, it must be remarked that manga's proliferation has given rise to an enormous contemporary range of expressions and readings. There are bestseller series appearing in major weeklies like *Shōnen jampu*—which themselves offer the choice between "throwaway products" and more solidly crafted works republished in book format—next to alternative comics in minor magazines like *AX*, and there is also a multitude of fan creations (*dōjinshi*). Still, Japan's comics culture is not characterized by an opposition between radically alternative and unscrupulously commercial comics so much as by forms that hybridize various cultural levels and artists who publish at different locations. For example, what the French publisher Casterman is presenting under its label *sakka, l'autre manga* actually belongs not to the presumed category of European *auteurism* (*sakka shugi*), but to a third kind of comics, which is reader-friendly although not consumeristic, and challenging although not underground. Likewise, Casterman's catchphrase "manga grows up" (*manga wa otona ni naru*) addresses values of European comics readers in order to promote a certain kind of manga. Still, it is difficult to apply the opposition of "infantile" and "adult" to Japanese comics; manga that are generically labeled *seinen* (youth) often address the "child inside the man," while those for children take minors seriously and do not shy away from issues like sexuality and violence.

This raises the question of how specifically Japanese manga are. Without going into detail, I would like to point to an "economic Japaneseness" here, that is, manga as an extraordinarily successful culture industry. What distinguishes manga from other comics cultures is, above all, the crucial role of special magazines, which serialize comics before republishing them in book format, and their editors, who often produce and co-create manga series. This system of production, which has been evolving since the late 1950s, has had many aesthetic and cultural consequences. Some of these include the evolution of multivolume entertaining graphic novels, the emergence of manga creators willing to serve their readers without aiming for the status of *auteur*, the formation of readers' communities centered around "their" magazines, and the evaluation of manga works in regard to their qualities of mediating relations. These are specifically Japanese aspects that derive from particular historic conditions, and they should lead one to realize that "manga" and "comic books" connote completely different cultures of publishing, distributing, and consuming comics.

The explanations above are meant to recommend an awareness of one's own location, the comics medium, and the issues specific to Japan; this will help avoid inconsistencies, or even the breakdown of traditions of scholarship in the face of a new topic like manga. The academic world is seemingly not yet at ease with manga, as shown by the situation in Japan.

Not even a decade ago, professors at Japanese universities still refused to supervise students who intended to graduate with a thesis on manga—some out of disdain for this topic, others out of an awareness of their own ignorance. Under these conditions, an academic symposium on manga, like that held during the annual conference of the Japan Society for Art History (Nihon Bijutsushi Gakkai) in May 1998, could become a milestone since this had never been possible before (Berndt 2001, 358). But a transformation in this field has taken place within a period of time that may be too short for historians to notice. Japan's academic world has become more open to manga, although often at the expense of scholarship, while nonacademic manga experts are simultaneously calling for more reliable data, multidisciplinary research, and basic knowledge of the history of manga discourse.

At universities—and at junior high schools as of April 2002—manga is often embraced in the spirit of a sheer populism (Berndt 2002). Educators use manga to bring their classes closer to daily life, but they do so without reflecting upon its ordinary context or unusually critical approaches to the medium. From a foreign perspective, the majority of Japanese publications on manga seem too journalistic and too insular to be of great help in European or American scholarship. Therefore, non-Japanese scholars gravitate toward books by university professors, especially if they carry the word *gaku* (study) in their titles. Yet, such publications are often less reliable than may be expected, because they take manga criticism as well as historical research on the topic very lightly.[6] In addition, they rarely use their academic training and heritage to advocate approaches toward manga that might challenge established views. In other words, they do not attempt to mediate between different fields of knowledge. Japanese academics who are critical of the institutional context do discuss topics like manga, but all too often they merely play academism off against populism. This is evident from the slapdash way they frequently treat the topic, as though failing to exercise proper scholarly care were the same as a critique of academism.

The Nihon Manga Gakkai (Japan Society for Studies in Cartoon and Comics, JSSCC) is the most authoritative Japanese source of reliable data and thorough research. The society was founded in July 2001 after dispelling misgivings among critics in regard to the possible monopolization of manga discourse by intellectuals and academics. At present, nonacademic manga critics and collectors—some of whom do occasionally teach at the university level—are a more influential group within the society than academics. A second important group in the JSSCC consists of M.A. and Ph.D. students from diverse academic disciplines; through the society, they gain an audience that is sympathetic to the application of research in areas such as sociology, media studies, and pedagogy to comics. Many of them show interest in methodological problems ranging from the contextual differences between reading, researching, and teaching manga (in other words, issues of location) to the actual possibilities for negotiating between manga studies and theories not related to either comics or Japan. Occasionally, differences between data-oriented research and theoretical endeavors cause friction, as do the differences between nonacademic and academic members. Especially in the case of manga, however, such friction should be welcomed as a kind of productive uncertainty. When properly harnessed, such uncertainty can motivate researchers to attempt a dialogue with people at home in other contexts and to translate between the various expert cultures. It can provoke researchers to cope with manga as an ambiguous medium—to let themselves get challenged by it as an academic subject—and to question their conventional criteria of quality assessment: What makes a "good" manga is quite different from a "good" novel or a "good" film. This productive uncertainty, which comes from the fundamental characteristics of comics, might benefit the study of other arts and media with which manga is often compared, but it should be intrinsic to the study of manga within Japanese studies in order to avoid the blind spots discussed above.

Tezuka and Beyond: Recapitulating Manga Criticism in Japan

If asked why manga is so popular today, many people in Japan would give one of the two standard answers: "because Japan had an Osamu Tezuka" or "because Japan has a long artistic tradition that dates back to *Chōjū giga*," a monochrome handscroll work of the late twelfth century. I will focus on the latter in the third and final section of this chapter, but here I will use the former as my springboard into crucial issues of Japanese manga criticism.

Unlike the kind of manga that has been at the center of comics' globalization for the last decade, the work of Osamu Tezuka (1928–1989) is not equally popular at home and abroad; yet, to most Japanese manga critics, he set the standard. In Japan, Tezuka is often called the "god of manga," because of his achievements, starting in the late 1940s, in establishing story-manga, as distinct from one-panel cartoons and newspaper comic strips (*koma manga*). He influenced generations of manga creators and readers, including such critics and researchers as Osamu Takeuchi, originally a professor of children's literature, and "manga columnist" Fusanosuke Natsume (Natsume 1992b, 1995; Takeuchi 1992, 1995). In their analysis, Tezuka's comics for children appeared revolutionary because of their shift from didactics to entertainment, their establishment of long and exciting narratives, the efficient and complementary intertwining of verbal and pictorial elements, and—most importantly—their use of allegedly cinematic techniques such as montage and varying shots and angles. Taking Tezuka, across all his stylistic transformations, as a model results in a *temporal* conceptualization of manga. Straightforward dramatic narratives about human or human-like protagonists are favored, and the pictorial elements serve as a language that is supposed to be "read." This kind of manga is not to be assessed as a graphic art, but rather with regard to how well its graphic rendering advances the narrative. Since the story has become the main criterion for assessing "quality," the author and his "work" are of more interest to the critics than multiple and creative readings.

This standard of story-manga fostered by Tezuka and developed by the so-called *gekiga* (a kind of comics addressed to older readers and closely tied to the rental libraries of the early 1960s) culminated in boys' manga magazines with exceptionally high circulations, like *Shōnen jampu*. However, these have seen severe setbacks since the mid-1990s. Today's children often become familiar with media such as anime and video or computer games before reading their first manga, and teenagers who regularly consume manga demonstrate an increasing indifference to the priority of the story and the traditional gender-specific genres. In view of this situation, Gō Itō published a book provocatively titled *Tezuka Is Dead* (*Tezuka izu deddo,* 2005). Established critics had been complaining about the loss of manga's previous attraction, but Itō countered that the carriers of this attraction have simply changed. He notes, for instance, that cute characters have taken over from dramatic stories and that multiple readings and applications of the texts—including appropriation and creative copying of the characters—have supplanted an author-centered and story-centered reading. Itō further claims that in order to understand this transformation, the Tezuka model must be relegated to history in two main respects.

The first issue Itō discusses is the modernity of Tezuka's manga. In this respect, he highlights Tezuka's reliance on artificial characters, such as robots, half-humans, and animals, which clearly do not exist outside the narrative. Readers are drawn into the story through their empathy for these characters, but at the same time that lure, which is fundamental to comics, is veiled by a modern realism and the autonomy of the characters.[7] According to Itō, the ambiguity of comics characters, which vacillate between being just a bunch of strokes drawn on paper and giving the realistic impression of a human personality, has been suppressed not only by Tezuka, but also by those manga critics who took him as their standard.

In addition, there has been little discussion of the ambiguous status of the focal plane, that is, the plane of the picture that the reader focuses on visually in manga. Many Japanese comics provide the readers with an enjoyable uncertainty as to whether the single panel or the whole page is to be treated as the main visual frame; characters may clamber over panel frames, or full views of protagonists may appear right next to a succession of panels. It is precisely this ambiguity, which distinguishes comics from film, that was overlooked by manga critics when, around 1980, they began to praise Tezuka retrospectively for his "cinematic" style.

Itō's book is worthy of discussion from various angles, but it is not easily accessible to people unfamiliar with Japanese manga criticism. Its primary goal is to reflect upon the kind of manga that has been made the focus of critical attention and upon the methodological consequences of such choices. In particular, the emphasis on ambiguity as a characteristic peculiar to comics is innovative and stimulating. But Itō is not the first to foreground manga criticism. The first authoritative publications in the area appeared in the late 1980s (Kure 1986; Takeuchi and Murakami 1989), and since then it has become common to discuss four stages of manga criticism.

In the early 1960s, some essays about manga appeared in the journal *Shisō no kagaku* (The Science of Thought, 1946–1996). Cultural sociologist Shunsuke Tsurumi, along with Chisui Fujikawa and film critic Tadao Satō, first treated manga, from caricatures and newspaper strips to entertaining stories, as an object worthy of intellectual investigation. They also discussed it as part of a specifically Japanese popular culture. Previously story-manga had been mainly addressed by educators who were suspicious of comics as readings for children, but now the interest shifted from pedagogy to popular culture and from children to youth. Tsurumi and his collaborators illuminated the potential of manga to be a medium for adults and related it to social issues of their time. Their main focus was on prewar manga series, like *Norakuro*, and on the rental comics (*kashihon gekiga*),[8] which were influenced by *kamishibai* (the paper theater thriving between the 1930s and the 1950s) and distributed by rental libraries. They understood Japanese comics as an outgrowth of traditional folk culture, characterized by close ties between creators and consumers in small communities. For Tsurumi, manga did not belong to either "pure art" (*junsui geijutsu*) or "mass art" (*taishū geijutsu*), but rather to what he called "liminal art" (*genkai geijutsu*) (Tsurumi 1982, 1987).

The second stage began around the time Junzō Ishiko, Susumu Gondō, Jun Kajii, and Sadao Yamane (who wrote articles on comics under the name of Asajirō Kikuchi) founded the review journal *Mangashugi* (Manga-ism, 1967–1978). Like earlier critics, they were primarily interested in comics as a medium of communicating social experiences, and they favorably discussed "anti-authoritarian" comics like those by Sanpei Shirato and Yoshiharu Tsuge. In contrast to the critics from the early 1960s, these commentators did not believe that such comics were read by ordinary Japanese people, particularly by those with ties to the traditional organizations of the working class, like trade unions. Rather, they identified the genre's audience as socially weak and isolated young men who built cultural communities through rental libraries and the comics available there. In addition, Ishiko criticized Tsurumi and his group for grounding their analysis in literary criticism (*bungakushugi*). He thought that manga should be evaluated through a distinctive approach that would allow a grasp of its blending of verbal and pictorial arts and its particular methods of story-telling (Ishiko 1967, 1972, 1973).

In the 1970s, a generation of critics, born in the 1950s and the very first to be raised on manga, rejected Shunsuke Tsurumi and Junzō Ishiko alike. These new critics, who included Tomohiko Murakami, Azusa Nakajima, and Yoshihiro Yonezawa, argued that

Tsurumi and Ishiko paid too much attention to the societal roles of certain manga and to groups to which they did not belong, such as nonorganized proletarian youth. They claimed that the proper approach for critics was to question themselves as individual readers; in other words, to verbalize their own personal experience of reading manga (Nakajima 1986; Yonezawa 1987; Murakami, Takatori, and Yonezawa 1987). Therefore, they went down in the history of manga criticism as the "first-person narrators" (*boku-gatari*). In addition, they were the first to state that "only those who really love manga" had the authority to discuss manga. They further argued that those who loved manga would not discuss it with the vocabulary of areas such as literature or film studies, nor would they speak from a distant and analytical perspective (Takeuchi 1997).

This kind of manga criticism sprang from the readers' feelings. Unlike traditional literary or art criticism, it emphasized the exchange among kindred spirits and about emotions. The critics, posing simply as manga readers, were at the same level as their audiences, and their analyses, rather than being self-critical, functioned as an arbiter of taste and a means for the fan community's self-affirmation.This approach, coupled with a refusal to explain oneself to outsiders including society as a whole, has also been typical of women's writings on girls' comics (*shōjo manga*). Just as rental comics fostered a sense of community for their readers in the early 1960s, both shōjo manga and writings about them have created a sense of identity among female readers since the 1980s. Readers of shōjo manga have usually expected critics of the genre to be their equal partners, using the comics that they both read mainly to exchange and discuss gendered experiences (Takahashi 2001; Spies 2001, 2003). This world appears hermetic to outsiders, but it was that very insistence on subjectivity and emotional community that prepared the ground for the articulation of a distinct manga aesthetics.

In the early 1990s, the semiotic investigation of manga's representational conventions began to flourish under the rubric of studying manga as a medium of expression (*manga hyōgenron*). Inuhiko Yomota (1994) and Fusanosuke Natsume, who pioneered this movement, disdained the extremes of both politically motivated criticism and extremely subjective criticism. This allowed more readers, including an older population, to join in the discussions about manga (Natsume 1992a, 1997; Inoue 1995; *Manga* 1996). Yomota and Natsume conceived of the manga creator not as an outstanding artist, but rather as a talented craftsman who conveys meaning through drawing and through guiding the reader's gaze via panel arrangements. Their semiotic approach was intended to claim manga as an autonomous medium by explicating its unique means of expression from an internal perspective. Attention was paid to such areas as speech balloons, impact lines, pictograms, and lettering, as well as the possibilities for visually rendering invisible phenomena such as sounds and smells. Writers like Natsume wanted their audience to reenact the achievements of the creator and to become aware of the mechanisms of reading manga, but they did not show much interest in plural or idiosyncratic readings of familiar works. In an apparent attempt to justify their chosen subject, they took their examples not from the margins, but from the average "quality goods" of manga. This turned manga criticism into a reassuring, rather than disturbing, area of discourse. Unlike earlier critics, the authors of the fourth wave veered away from discussing manga in terms of content or politically sensitive issues (be it pornography or neonationalism), but they affirmed commercialism as an indispensable condition for manga. While such tendencies of an apolitical approach to manga still prevail in Japanese manga criticism and research as the recent publications by Natsume, Miyamoto, and even Itō show, it is wrong to presume that the four stages sketched in this section replaced each other in the course of time; fragments of all of them can be found in current writings. At a symposium entitled Possibilities and Requirements of Academic Manga Studies (Gakujutsuteki Manga Kenkyū no Kanōsei to Kadai, Ritsumeikan University Kyōto) in 2000, Natsume stated that his interest in manga expression had been triggered by his aversion to Ishiko's political and content oriented approach, which he believed treated manga as a mere mirror (*han'eiron*). He went on to say, however, that he had come to realize the importance of opening the field to the perspectives of sociology, media studies, and foreign comics cultures (Natsume 2000).

Dis/continuity with Premodern Painting: On Recurring Assumptions About Manga's "Origins"

As I mentioned earlier, few people in Japan would link manga's astonishing international popularity to the unique system used to produce and distribute the works. It is more likely that they would give the credit to Japanese culture—not only to Osamu Tezuka, the "god of manga," but also to Japanese artistic traditions such as the *Chōjū giga* scrolls.[9]

Tracing contemporary manga back to their origin in medieval picture scrolls is a discursive act that in itself establishes traditions. This has served various purposes in modern Japan, from justification for seriously studying the field to sheer fashionable populism (that is, nowadays, it is much more often utilized with the connotation that high art is "out"). In any arena, status claims like these work most effectively by claiming national particularity; in the case of manga, the argument for "Japaneseness" in the medium is made by assuming a continuity between medieval arts and contemporary comics. However, from a foreign perspective it is easy to repeat this position without realizing its essential conservatism, and to overlook that the agents of such claims have changed since the 1990s. Recently, Japanese manga historians emphasize discontinuity as a basis for manga and admit its foreign origins. Too often, however, these historians disregard the mixture of continuity and discontinuity that has given rise to manga, and they therefore deprive the form of its historical complexity. I argue here that manga is historically (as well as aesthetically and culturally) ambiguous. It therefore seems much more appropriate, not to say manga-like, to pursue this ambiguity rather than settling for, or rejecting outright, modernist claims of national purity based on an alleged continuity.[10]

Manga experts, media figures, and art scholars have all claimed manga's cultural value by linking it to old Japanese art, most often medieval picture scrolls like *Chōjū giga* and famous printed works like *ukiyo-e* artist Katsushika Hokusai's *Hokusai manga*

(1814–1878). In the case of the manga experts, this lineage originally allowed them to elevate their field in the eyes of the public. In the early 1990s, when manga started to gain international attention, manga critics also used this link to highlight the "Japanese-ness" of the medium. Their arguments did often play into the agendas of ideologues, but by focusing on an uninterrupted Japanese art, they also made subcultural issues visible to the society in general. While some assume that manga critics' emphasis on the "Japaneseness" of manga was a calculated political decision (Kinsella 2000, 97), it more likely sprang from their ignorance of both Japanese art history and of foreign comics cultures. It is easy to stress the national uniqueness of manga, if you are the frog in the well; that is: if you are not familiar with artworks other than *Chōjū giga*, it is easy to believe in continuity. Moreover, if you do not know many American or Franco-Belgian comics, it is easy to claim Japanese uniqueness. This changed when Japanese critics went abroad and got in touch with foreign comics experts beginning in the late 1990s.

References to traditional fine arts were once used to elevate manga culturally, but in the early twenty-first century, manga is much more often used to popularize fine art. This is evident in some introductions to Japanese art history, which trace the "origins of manga" back to three specific phenomena. The first of these is *hakubyō*, the monochrome drawings characteristic of *Chōjū giga* as well as some narrative *yamato-e* paintings of the Kamakura era, the second is the pictorial expression of movement in scrolls of the twelfth century like *Bandainagon* (Illustrated Stories of the Courtier Bandainagon), and the third is the integration of script into picture planes (Hidaka 2003, 40–43). Some publications place segments of *Chōjū giga* side by side with a panel from Tezuka's *Tetsuwan Atomu* (*Astro Boy*), using speed-lines (lines which indicate actions such as running or jumping) to suggest an uninterrupted continuity of Japanese pictorial traditions (*Shūkan Nihon* 2002, 19).

However, claiming *Chōjū giga* as the direct ancestor of modern manga lacks historical accuracy. This artwork, which has been considered a national treasure since 1899 and was placed in the Imperial Museum in 1906, differs fundamentally from manga. *Chōjū giga* was painted by hand, and, since it resided originally in the Kōzanji temple, it was accessible only to certain people under restricted conditions. Moreover, it lacks a written narrative text (*kotobagaki*) and a clearly identifiable, coherent narrative (Köhn 2005).

These differences raise doubts about whether *Chōjū giga* can actually be called manga's ancestor. Nonetheless, many people in Japan cling to this notion regardless of researchers' arguments to the contrary and their own awareness that the comparison is free of any substantial reference to the respective artworks. The Japanese mass media and the educational system promote such a view and emphasize purely *formal* semblances between manga and old art (see Berndt 2002), without ever considering whether manga creators actually knew any of the now-canonized artworks. Tezuka, for example, appreciated *Chōjū giga* and often discussed simplification, exaggeration, metamorphosis, and satirical representation as its manga-like features. He admitted, though, that he saw reproductions of the complete scrolls only in 1955,[11] eight years

A manga history illustration of *Astro Boy* juxtaposed with a detail from
Tanyū Kanō's reproduction of the *Kōzanji Chōjū giga*.
(Copyright Tezuka Productions and reproduced with permission from the Honolulu
Academy of Arts, Purchase, Robert Allerton Fund, 1954, Accession #1951.1)

after the publication of the groundbreaking work *Shin-takarajima* (New Treasure
Island), which first established his distinctive style of manga storytelling.

Modern analyses of manga and its origins tend to emphasize painting while ignoring areas such as literature and the performing arts.[12] Since the rise of European
Japonisme in the late nineteenth century, Japanese elites had favored painting as a
means of cultural self-assertion. As painting could easily cross language barriers, it was
believed to be a good vehicle for Japanese particularity, and it was also authorized by
European culture. Painting in the modern sense, which was brought to Japan through
Europe, foregrounds purely pictorial representations; this is completely different from
the intertwining of pictures and literature that was common to Japanese art before

modernization. According to manga historian Hirohito Miyamoto, manga became a subgenre of painting at the end of the nineteenth century, "when forms of artistic expression that combined text and image had to be identified either as 'literature' or 'painting'" (Miyamoto 2002, 44). In other words, the meaning of "manga" after modernization was narrower than the meaning it held in the Tokugawa period.

Today, the word "manga," which is used outside Japan to describe "Japanese comics," primarily means "story-manga." But this emphasis on narratives was not—as often presumed—inherited from Hokusai's pictorial encyclopedia *Hokusai manga*. When the encyclopedia's first volume appeared in 1814, "manga" signified an "entirety of acts by which all sorts of things are drawn in all sorts of styles, and a vast amount of pictures as its result" (Miyamoto 2003a, 322). (The word itself comes from the Chinese name for a heron that moves in a peculiar way.) But around 1900, the term came to mean "satirical and funny picture" (*fūshi kokkei no ga*), and thus signified a certain style of pictures.[13] Journalists and painters with a modern Western education, such as Yukichi Fukuzawa's nephew Shūtarō Imaizumi (or Ippyō)[14] and the Western-style painter Hakutei Ishii, considered modern manga as something to view individually rather than to read together with other people and, therefore, often aloud. Thus, they suppressed Tokugawa period traditions of entertaining literature that combined reading, watching, and talking, as well as transitional phenomena, like the early modern *ponchi-e* (literally *Punch* pictures), which came from these traditions. Whereas *ponchi-e* provided wordplays as well as verbal and pictorial allegories that depended on a shared collective knowledge of symbols and stories, "manga" in the early twentith century was based on pithy pictures rather than on verbal elements (Miyamoto 2003b).

Manga researchers and critics have emphasized this discontinuity since the mid-1990s. Fusanosuke Natsume has stated that "in the Meiji era, Japan's traditional aesthetics experienced a break with the past, collided with the completely different expression of modern Euroamerican comic strips, and was absorbed by it," and that "before long, a modern form, that is, the panel sequence of the Euroamerican comic-strip (in other words, the function of articulating discrete moments of time in the course of events) was imported" (Inoue 1995, 209; see also Yamamoto 2004). Experts like Natsume and Miyamoto understand manga as a fundamentally *modern* phenomenon, and they point out three characteristics in that regard: First, they refer to the imported concept of the panel or single frame, which rendered the previously ambiguous pictorial time and space unequivocal. (This was a break from traditional pictures scrolls, for example, in which the representation of time and space was often indefinite—several moments sequentially depicted on the same picture plane, and the space represented from more than one central perspective.) Second, they stress the emergence of newspapers and magazines as modern mass media, and third, they link manga to Japan's distinctive modernization, which took the form of Westernization.

This argument for discontinuity in the field, which results from thorough historical research, counters popular assertions of continuity. An absolute denial of continuity, however, ignores the complexities not only of manga itself,[15] but also of painting as a form of Japanese fine art. Unlike the term "manga," the term "fine art" (*bijitsu*) was imported from European languages, but that said, fine arts themselves were less modernized than literature; at least the traditionalist branch of Japanese painting (*nihonga*) embodied continuity. Indeed, at the beginning of the twentieth century, the term "manga," regardless of its new connotations, was considered by some to be an unwelcome Tokugawa era anachronism (see Miyamoto 2003a). Others, however, appreciated manga because it allowed for more freedom of expression than a "beautiful" painting. Seiki Hosokibara, already an experienced cartoonist and critic when he published Japan's first manga history in 1924, was a member of the latter camp. In the introduction to his book, he distinguished manga from painting because of its "anatomical" stance and its interest in impure things, while in the main chapters he highlighted manga-like paintings. It should be noted, however, that Hosokibara's notion of painting differed from modern Western ideas of painting as fine art. For example, he believed that the creator of *Chōjū giga* was "the pioneer of Japan's manga artists," because he worked in an era which recognized neither a division between painting and literature nor a distinction between beauty and "probing into the facts of life" (Hosokibara 1924, 8).

All this suggests an intertwining of continuity and discontinuity. From a nationalist perspective, what is important is only *whether* an artwork like *Chōjū giga* is a predecessor of manga—a claim that manga historians would categorically deny, as demonstrated above. The much more important questions regard *in what way* critics have related modern manga to pictorial traditions and *which artistic traditions* they have had in mind. Emphasizing formal semblances does make sense if it reveals historic differences within the similar. Reflecting upon such differences could be stimulating not only for manga researchers but also for contemporary readers. This is particularly true since manga readers seem to be more interested in parody of and self-reference to traditions of contemporary manga genres than they are in issues of cultural authorization or premodern artworks.

It should be clear that the definition of manga springs in part from references to certain traditions, and vice versa. For example, those who claim that manga is directly descended from premodern painting tend to think of manga as a graphic art rather than a form of pictorial storytelling; they refrain from reflecting upon the modernity of the medium that Natsume finds in the three characteristics mentioned above and Itō finds in a specific treatment of comics characters. In this essay, I have attempted to demonstrate that manga studies will have to deal with the ambiguity of the medium and, indeed, will need to bring out the uncertainties of the form, not only with regard to manga's alleged traditions but also in a more general sense, with regard to manga's present functioning and manga's potential to go beyond narrow identity politics.

Notes

1. This is especially apparent in Sharon Kinsella's *Adult Manga: Culture and Power in Contemporary Japanese Society* (2000). In this instance, the actual subjects—editors of major manga publishing houses and manga artists—are not allowed to speak for themselves. See

Tsuji (2001) as an example of affirming formal continuity, and Yiengpruksawan (2000) for a critical art historical stance.

2. The Japanese translation of Napier's first edition of her book was critically reviewed by Ogawa (2004). A revised edition of Napier's book in English was published in 2005 with a slightly different title *Anime from Akira to Howl's Moving Castle: Experiencing Contemporary Japanese Animation*. One of the rare considerations of Japanese discourse linked to critical reflections upon the treatment of animated movies within Japanese studies can be found in Lamarre (2004/2005).

3. It should be noted in this context that the term "anime," as it is used outside Japan, is mostly unrelated to its two basic meanings in Japanese. There, it signifies a television series in limited-animation style; this meaning is originally subcultural and does not apply to Miyazaki's fully animated movies of feature-film length shown in theaters. But the term also means Japanese cel animation, which is appreciated abroad, so that Miyazaki's movies are praised as "anime" on a national rather than a subcultural level. As an introduction, see Tsugata (2004).

4. This can be said only with the reservation that the existence of gender-specific genres in anime is not identical with that of manga and needs further examination.

5. In the *International Journal of Comic Art*, Japanese writers (mainly women) have recently been introducing sources and materials in English that are fundamental to the study of manga in Japan (Ōgi 2001; Onoda 2002).

6. Representative of this trend are Kusaka (2000) and Ogino and Miyahara (2001). For a critical review see Natsume (2003).

7. In this regard, Itō's argumentation is clearly indebted to Ōtsuka (1994).

8. There is some critical disagreement about whether *gekiga* is to be distinguished from manga. This depends on whether the historically specific term "gekiga" is applied universally and whether "manga" signifies "comics" in general or a certain kind of comics.

9. This four-scroll artwork from the twelfth century is now officially named *Chōjū jinbutsu giga* (Scrolls of Frolicking Animals and Men), but the general public still refers to it as *Chōjū giga*, the title under which it was first registered as a national treasure in modern Japan. Since comparisons with contemporary manga tend to concentrate on the first scroll with its mostly humorous representations of only animals while leaving out the others, it is not completely inappropriate to speak of *Chōjū giga*. Furthermore, the popular discourse takes it for a fact that *Chōjū giga* was created by the priest Sōjō Toba (or Kakuyū, 1053–1140), whereas art historians have already revealed this to be an Tokugawa era ascription.

10. For an example not primarily related to manga research, see Fukushima (2003). Although the author's attempt to relate theater and comics is innovative and highly stimulating, from a manga studies perspective her argument is diminished by two things. First, she equates manga with a particular "Japaneseness" (apart from the historic transformation of manga as comics), and second, she assumes the continuity of this kind of "manga-likeness" (in contrast to the interplay of continuity and discontinuity that she acknowledges for Japanese theater).

11. According to Tezuka (1982), this exposure came through a special issue of *Iwanami shashin bunko*.

12. Within Japanese manga research, the so-called paper theater (*kamishibai*) is an exception; its eminent influence on story-manga as gekiga has been mentioned in all manga histories since the 1960s.

13. Even today, "manga" is often translated as "funny, exaggerated pictures." But the Japanese character for "man" has a range of meanings, such as broad, scattered, and careless, which might connote humor but do not necessarily denote it.

14. Ippyō Imaizumi worked for Yukichi Fukuzawa's newspaper *Jiji shimpō* from 1890 until 1899. His successor there was Rakuten Kitazawa, whose *Jiji manga* comic strips, begun in 1902, have entered manga history and made their creator the alleged heir of *Hokusai manga*.

15. It is questionable, for example, in what way Tezuka's emphasis on storytelling instead of splendid pictures, or the dissolution of the geometrical panel layout in girls' comics of the 1970s, relates to premodern traditions, modernist achievements and postmodern relativizations.

Bibliography

Introduction

Adorno, Theodor. 1991. *The Culture Industry: Selected Essays on Mass Culture.* Edited by J.M. Bernstein. London: Routledge.

Agular, Bill. 2007. "Fred Gallagher and *Megatokyo* Vol. 5." *PW Comics Week,* May 15. www.publishersweekly.com/article/CA6442270.html. Accessed July 29, 2007.

Allen, Kate, and John Ingulsrud. 2003. "Manga Literacy: Popular Culture and the Reading Habits of Japanese College Students." *Journal of Adolescent and Adult Literacy* 46 (May): 674–683.

Allison, Anne. 2006. *Millennial Monsters: Japanese Toys and Global Imagination.* Berkeley: University of California Press.

Anime News Network. 2001. "Animage Top-100 Anime Listing." January 15. www.animenewsnetwork.com/news/2001-01-15/animage-top-100-anime-listing. Accessed June 1, 2007.

Appadurai, Arjun. 1996. *Modernity at Large: Cultural Dimensions of Globalization.* Minneapolis: University of Minnesota Press.

Berndt, Jaqueline. 2001. "Permeability and Othering: The Relevance of 'Art' in Contemporary Manga Discourse." In *Approches critiques de la penseé japonaise du XXe siècle,* ed. Livia Monnet, 349–375. Montréal: Les Presses de l'Université de Montréal.

Berndt, Jaqueline, and Steffi Richter, eds. 2006. *Reading Manga: Local and Global Perceptions of Japanese Comics.* Leipzig: Leipziger Universitätsverlag.

Bouissou, Jean Marie. 2006. "Japan's Growing Cultural Power: Manga in France." In *Reading Manga: Local and Global Perceptions of Japanese Comics,* ed. Jaqueline Berndt and Steffi Richter, 149–165. Leipzig: Leipziger Universitätsverlag.

Brown, Steven. T., ed. 2006. *Cinema Anime.* New York: Palgrave Macmillan.

Camper, Cathy. 2006. "Yaoi 101: Girls Love 'Boys' Love.'" *The Women's Review of Books* (May).

Carrier, David. 2000. *The Aesthetics of Comics.* University Park: Pennsylvania State University Press.

Carroll, Noël. 1998. *A Philosophy of Mass Art.* New York: Oxford University Press.

Certeau, Michel de. 1984. *The Practice of Everyday Life,* trans. Steven Rendall. Berkeley: University of California Press.

Cha, Kai-Ming. 2007. "Viz Media and Manga in the US." *PW Comics Week*, April 3. www. publishersweekly.com/article/CA6430330.html. Accessed Juy 29, 2007.

Cha, Kai-Ming and Calvin Reed. 2005. "Manga in Engish: Born in the USA—American Style Manga Challenges the Purists," *Publishers Weekly*, October 17.

Chisolm, Lawrence. 1963. *Fenollosa: The Far East and American Culture.* New Haven, CT: Yale University Press.

Comi Press. 2006. "*Shōnen Jump* and *Yaoi*/BL Fans," August 25. http: //comipress.com/ article/2006/08/24/624. Accessed October 30, 2006.

Craig, Timothy, ed. 2000. *Japan Pop! Inside the World of Japanese Popular Culture.* Armonk, NY: M.E. Sharpe.

The Daily Yomiuri. 2006a. "'Captain Tsubasa' to Aid Reconstruction in Iraq." *The Daily Yomiuri*, March 5.

————. 2006b "Anime Transcending Borders." *The Daily Yomiuri*, October 4.

Elliot, Stuart. 2007. "Subaru Turns to the Land of Forbidden Secrets." *The New York Times.* July 10.

Evans, Jessica, and Stuart Hall, eds. 1999. *Visual Culture: The Reader.* London: Sage.

Gilson, Mark. 1998. "A Brief History of Robophilia." *Leonardo* 51: 367–69.

Gordon, Ian. 1998. *Comic Strips and Consumer Culture, 1890–1945.* Washington, DC: Smithsonian Institution Press.

Grigsby, Mary. 1998. "Sailormoon: *Manga* (Comics) and *Anime* (Cartoon) Superheroine Meets Barbie: Global Entertainment Commodity Comes to the United States." *Journal of Popular Culture* 32: 59–80.

Hardach, Sophie. 2007. "Japanese Comic Boosts Wine Sales: Manga Series Spins Vino Mystery and Helps Readers Impress Their Friends." *Globe and Mail.* June 6.

Hongo, Jun. 2006. "Porn 'Anime' Boasts Big U.S. Beachhead." *Japan Times Online*, July 11. http: //search.japantimes.co.jp/member/member.html?appURL'nn20. Accessed October 30, 2006.

Hoover, Stuart. 2001. "Visual Religion in Media Culture." In *The Visual Culture of American Religions, eds.* David Morgan and Sally M. Promey, 146–159. Berkeley: University of California Press.

Isao, Shimizu. 2001. "Red Comic Books: The Origins of Modern Japanese Manga." In *Illustrating Asia: Comics, Humor Magazines and Picture Books*, ed. John Lent, 137–150. Honolulu: University of Hawai'i Press.

Ito, Mizuko. 2003–4. "Technologies of the Childhood Imagination: Media Mixes, Hypersociality, and Recombinant Cultural Form." *Items and Issues* 4 (Winter): 31–34.

Iwabuchi, Koichi. 2002. "'Soft' Nationalism and Narcissism: Japanese Popular Culture Goes Global." *Asian Studies Review* 26 (December): 447–469.

J-CAST Business News. 2006. "Comics on Mobiles? Enjoy Women's Popularity," May 9. http: //en.j-cast.com/2006/05/09001258.html. Accessed October 21, 2006.

Kinsella, Sharon. 1999. "Pro-Establishment Manga: Pop-culture and the Balance of Power in Japan." *Media, Culture, and Society* 21: 567–572.

————. 2000. *Adult Manga: Culture and Power in Contemporary Japanese Society.* Honolulu: University of Hawai'i Press.

Krikke, Jan. 2006. "Computer Graphics Advances the Art of Anime." *IEEE Computer Graphics and Applications* 26: 14–19.

Kumagai, Fumie. 1996. *The Impact of Traditional Values on Modern Japanese Society.* Westport, CT: Praeger.

Kuwahara, Yasue. 1997. "Japanese Culture and Popular Consciousness: Disney's *The Lion King* vs. Tezuka's *Jungle Emperor.*" *Journal of Popular Culture* 31 (Summer): 37–48.

Lee, William. 2000. "From *Sazae-san* to *Crayon Shin-chan:* Family Anime, Social Change, and Nostalgia in Japan." In *Japan Pop! Inside the World of Japanese Popular Culture,* ed. Timothy J. Craig, 186–206. Armonk, NY: M.E. Sharpe.

Lent, John A., ed. 1995. *Asian Popular Culture.* Boulder, CO: Westview.

_____, ed. 1999. *Themes and Issues in Asian Cartooning: Cute, Cheap, Mad and Sexy.* Bowling Green, OH: Bowling Green State University Popular Press.

_____, ed. 2001. *Illustrating Asia: Comics, Humor Magazines and Picture Books.* Honolulu: University of Hawai'i Press.

Mainichi Daily News. 2006. "*Death Note* Puts Life into Japanese Manga Scene," June 18.

Makino, Catherine. 2007. "Japanese Anime Fans Gain Economic Power." *Voice of America News.* January 17.

Mari. 2004. "A Happy Anime Makes Us Blue," August 2. http: //smt.blogs.com/mari_diary/2004/08/a_happy_anime_m.html. Accessed October 30, 2006.

Masangkay, May. 2006. "Pop Culture Takes Center Stage in Japanese Diplomacy." *Japan Today,* December 22.

Masuyama, Hiroshi and David d'Heilly. 1993. "Family Values in Japan," September–October. *Wired.* www.wired.com/wired/archive/1.04/eword.html?pg=10. Accessed October 30, 2006.

McCloud, Scott. 1993. *Understanding Comics: The Invisible Art.* Northampton, MA: Kitchen Sink Press.

McDonald, Keiko. 2006. *Reading a Japanese Film: Cinema in Context.* Honolulu: University of Hawai'i Press.

Memmott, Carol. 2005. "Japanese Manga Takes a Humongous Step." *USA Today,* July 5.

Moeran, Brian. 2004. "Soft Sell, Hard Cash: Marketing J-Cult in Asia." Working Paper #76, Copenhagen Business School.

Morton, Leith. 2003. *Modern Japanese Culture: The Insider's View.* Oxford: Oxford University Press.

Nakamura, Ichiya. 2003. "Japanese Pop Industry." Kyoto: Stanford Japan Center—Research.

Napier, Susan. 2005. "The Problem of Existence in Japanese Animation." *Proceedings of the American Philosophical Society* 149 (March): 72–79.

Nihon Zasshi Kyōkai. 2006. *JMPA Magajin dêta.* www.j-magazine.or.jp/data_001/index.html. Accessed February 8, 2007.

Ogi, Fusami. 2003. "Female Subjectivity and *Shoujo* (Girls') *Manga* (Japanese Comics): *Shoujo* in Ladies' Comics and Young Ladies' Comics." *Journal of Popular Culture* 36 (Spring): 780–803.

Okamoto, Rei. 2001. "Images of the Enemy in the Wartime *Manga* Magazine." In *Illustrating Asia: Comics, Humor Magazines and Picture Books,* ed. John Lent, 204–220. Honolulu: University of Hawai'i Press.

Osmond, Andrew. 2005. "Castles in the Sky." *Sight and Sound* 10 (October): 28–31.

Phillips, Matt. 2007. "Comics Court Girls Inspired by Japanese Manga." *The Wall Street Journal,* June 8.

Pickering, Michael, and Emily Keightley. 2006. "The Modalities of Nostalgia." *Current Sociology* 54 (November): 919–941.

Publishers Weekly. "Graphic Novels by the Numbers." March 5, 2007. www.publishersweekly.com/article/CA6421266.html. Accessed July 29, 2007.

Reed, Calvin. 2007a. "Fast Growth at Del Ray Manga." *Publishers Weekly.* February 12, 10.

_____. 2007b. "DC Invests in Japanese Manga Startup." *Publishers Weekly.* June 18. www.publisherswweekly.com/article/CA6452850.html. Accessed July 29, 2007.

Robertson, Jennifer. 1988. "*Furusato* Japan: The Culture and Politics of Nostalgia." *International Journal of Politics* 4: 494–518.

Rommens, Aarnoud. 2000. "Manga Story-telling/Showing." *Image and Narrative* 1 (August): 1–10. www.imageandnarrative.be/narratology/aanoudrommens.htm. Accessed October 21, 2006.

Sato, Ken'ichi. 2006. "Manga Migrating to New Medium: Will Pixels Pummel Paper?" *The Daily Yomiuri*, May 20.

Sato, Ken'ichi and Miho Sakanari. 2007. "In Steep Decline, Comic Magazine Biz Needs Overhaul." *The Daily Yomiuri*, June 10.

Schodt, Frederik L. 1983. *Manga! Manga!: The World of Japanese Comics*. New York: Kodansha International.

_____. 1996. *Dreamland Japan: Writings on Modern Manga*. Berkeley, CA: Stone Bridge Press.

_____. 2007. *Astro Boy Essays: Osamu Tezuka, Mighty Atom, and the Manga/Anime Revolution*. Berkeley, CA: Stone Bridge Press.

Shuppan shihyō nenpō 2005. 2005. "Komikku," 236–253.Tokyo: Zenkoku shuppan kyōkai/Shuppan kagaku kenkyūjo.

Sontag, Susan. 2003. "The Image World." In *Visual Culture: The Reader*, eds. Jessica Evans and Stuart Hall, 80–94. London: Sage.

Sturken, Marita, and Lisa Cartwright. 2001. *Practices of Looking: An Introduction to Visual Culture*. New York: Oxford University Press.

Taylor, Richard. 2006. "Japanese Comics Go Mobile." *BBC News International Version*, March 24. http: //news.bbc.co.uk/2hi/programmes/click_online/4840436.stm. Accessed October 21, 2006.

Thorn, Matt. 2004. "A History of Manga. Parts 1–3," October. www.matt-thorn.com/mangagaku/history1.html. Accessed October 30, 2006.

Trautlein, Steve. 2006. "Tokyo International Anime Fair Returns with Global Interest in Japanese Animation Soaring." *Japan Today*, March 16. www.japantoday.com/jp/feature/1068. Accessed October 30, 2006.

Treat, John. 1993."Yoshimoto Banana Writes Home: Shōjo Culture and the Nostalgic Subject." *Journal of Japanese Studies* 19 (Summer): 353–387.

_____, ed. 1996. *Contemporary Japan and Popular Culture*. Honolulu: University of Hawai'i Press.

TV Asahi. 2006. "Sukina anime rankingu 100." *Getsubara*. www.tv-asahi.co.jp/anime100/index_top.html. Accessed June 1, 2007.

Ueno, Toshiya. n.d. "Japanimation and Techno-Orientalism." www.t0.0r.at/ueno/japan.htm. Accessed October 30, 2006.

_____. 2002 "Japanimation and Techno-Orientalism, Media Tribes and Rave Culture." In *Aliens R Us: The Other in Science Fiction Cinema*, eds. Ziauddin Sardar and Sean Cubitt, 94–110. London: Pluto.

Webb, Martin. 2006. "Manga by Any Other Name Is . . ." *Japan Times Online*, May 28. http: //search.japantimes.co.jp/cgi-bin/f120060528x1.html. Accessed October 30, 2006.

Wired News. 2007. "Cell Phones Put to Novel Use," January 12. www.wired.com/news/gizmos/0,1452,66950,00.html. Accessed January 21, 2007.

Witkin, Robert W. 2003. *Adorno on Popular Culture*. New York: Routledge.

Chapter 1

Aihara, Koji, and Kentaro Takekuma. 2001. "Even a Monkey Can Draw Manga." *PULP* 5, no. 11: 40–54.

Akatsuka, Fujio. 2000. *Tensai Bakabon (The Genius Bakabon)*. Vol. 2. Tokyo: Kōdansha.

Amano, Masanao, ed. 2004. *MANGA*. Cologne, Germany: Taschen.

Asahi Shimbun. 1998. *Japan Almanac*. Tokyo.

Asahi Shimbun. 2006. "Denshi kommikku," February 19.

Clements, Jonathan, and Motoko Tamamuro. 2003. *The Dorama Encyclopedia: A Guide to Japanese TV Drama since 1953*. Berkeley: Stonebridge Press.

Erino, Miya. 1993. *Rediisu komikku no jōseigaku*. Tokyo: Kosaido shuppan.

Evers, Izumi. 2001. "Nakayoshi: Kodansha's Classic Shojo Manga Magazine." *PULP 5*, no. 9: 6–7.

Gravett, Paul. 2004. *Manga: Sixty Years of Japanese Comics*. London: Lawrence King.

Hirschmeier, Johannes, and Tsunehiko Yui. 1975. *The Development of Japanese Business: 1600–1973*. Cambridge, MA: Harvard University Press.

Ishinomori, Shotaro. 1998. *Mangaka nyūmon*. Tokyo: Akita shoten.

Ito, Kinko. 1994. "Images of Women in Weekly Male Comic Magazines in Japan." *Journal of Popular Culture* 27, no. 4: 81–95.

———. 1995. "Sexism in Japanese Weekly Comic Magazines for Men." In *Asian Popular Culture*, ed. John A. Lent, 127–137. Boulder, CO: Westview.

———. 2000. "The Manga Culture in Japan." *Japan Studies Review* 4: 1–16.

———. 2002. "The World of Japanese Ladies' Comics: From Romantic Fantasy to Lustful Perversion." In *Journal of Popular Culture* 36, no. 1: 68–85.

———. 2005. "A History of Manga in the Context of Japanese Culture and Society." *Journal of Popular Culture* 38, no. 3: 456–475.

Kawasaki Shimin Museum. 1996. *Nihon no manga 300 nen kaisetsu zuroku*. Kawasaki: Kawasaki Shimin Museum.

Kumamoto nichinichi shimbun. 1991. May 10, 24; July 5.

Mainichi shimbun. 2002. November 28.

Men's Walker. 1999. "Kono mangaka omoshiroi," October 12, 30–56.

Mizuno, Ryutaro. 1991. *Manga bunka no uchimaku*. Tokyo: Kawade shobō shinsha.

Ogi, Fusami. 2001. "Beyond *Shoujo*, Blending Gender: Subverting the Homogendered World in *Shoujo Manga* (Japanese Comics for Girls)." *International Journal of Comic Art* 3, no. 2: 151–161.

Ōtsuka, Eiji, and Go Sasakibara. 2001. *Kyōyō toshite no manga, anime*. Tokyo: Kōdansha.

Reischauer, Edwin O. 1990. *Japan: The Story of a Nation*. 4th ed. New York: McGraw-Hill.

Schilling, Mark. 1997. *The Encyclopedia of Japanese Pop Culture*. New York: Weatherhill.

Schodt, Frederik L. 1988. *Manga! Manga! The World of Japanese Comics*. Tokyo: Kōdansha International.

———. 1991. "Sex and Violence in Manga." *Mangajin* 10: 9.

Schou, Solvej. 2006. "Future of Japanese Anime and Manga Looking Bright in US." *The Associated Press State and Local Wire*, July 18.

Shimizu, Isao. 1991. *Manga no rekishi*. Tokyo: Iwanami Shoten.

———. 2002. "Edo nikuhitsu jigokue kō." *Manga kenkyū* 1: 86–93.

Shinmura, Izuru, ed. 1991. *Kojiten*. 4th ed. Tokyo: Iwanami Shoten.

Shirakura, Yoshihiko. 2002. *Edo no shunga*. Tokyo: Yōsensha.

Shuppan shihyō nenpō 2005. 2005. Tokyo: Zenkoku shuppan kyōkai/Shuppan kagaku kenkyūjo.

Tchiei, Go. 1998. "A History of Manga." www.dnco.jp/museum/nmp/nmp_i/articles/manga/manga1.html. July 12, 2006.

Thorn, Matt. 2007. "Welcome to Matt Thorn.com." www.matt-thorn.com. July 30, 2007.
Wilson, Glenn. 1989. *The Sensual Touch: A Guide to More Erotic Love Making.* New York: Carroll & Graf.
Yasuda, Motohisa. 1989. *Kiso kara yoku wakaru Nihonshi.* Tokyo: Ōbunsha.

Chapter 2

Anime News Network Encyclopedia. Anime News Network. 2007. www.animenewsnetwork.com/encyclopedia/index.php. Accessed August 7, 2007.
Baricordi, Andrea, Massimiliano de Giovanni, Andrea Pietroni, Barbara Rossi, and Sabrina Tunesi. 2000. *Anime: A Guide to Japanese Animation (1958–1988),* trans. Adeline D'Opera. Montreal: Protoculture.
Beveridge, Chris. 2003. "2003 Release Checklist." AnimeOnDVD.com. www.animeondvd.com/releases/checklist2003.php. Accessed November 4, 2005.
Clements, Jonathan, and Helen McCarthy. 2001. *The Anime Encyclopedia.* Berkeley, CA: Stone Bridge Press.
"Creator Profile: Satoshi Kon." 2004. *Newtype USA* 3, no. 11 (November): 78–81.
"Inside GONZO." 2003. *Newtype USA* 2, no. 3 (March): 20–23.
Japan Foundation. 2004a. "Outline of the Results of the '2003 Overseas Japanese-Language Education Organization Survey,'" July 7. www.jpf.go.jp/e/japan/news/0407/07_01.html. Accessed November 4, 2005.
_____. 2004b. "Appendix Table Number of Japanese-Language Education Institutions, Teachers, and Students, by Country (2003)," July 1. www.jpf.go.jp/e/japan/news/0407/research/total.pdf. Accessed November 4, 2005.
Japan External Trade Organization (JETRO). 2004. "Japanese Animation Goes Global," July 4. www.jetro.go.jp/en/market/trend/changing/docs/2004_07_anime.html. Accessed November 4, 2005.
Parker, Ginny. 2004. "Learning Japanese, Once About Resumes, Is Now About Cool; Business Major of '80s Yield to Kids Smitten by Anime; Up at 4 a.m. for Cartoons." *Wall Street Journal* (Eastern edition), August 5, A1.
Patten, Fred. 2004. *Watching Anime, Reading Manga: 25 Years of Essays and Reviews.* Berkeley, CA: Stone Bridge Press.
Takeda, Yasuhiro. 2005. *The Notenki Memoirs.* Houston: ADV Manga.
Welles, Elizabeth B. 2004. "Foreign Language Enrollment in United States Institutions of Higher Education, Fall 2002." *ADFL Bulletin* 35, nos. 2–3 (Winter–Spring). www.adfl.org/resources/enrollments.pdf. Accessed November 4, 2005.

Chapter 3

Ekman, Paul, and Wallace V. Friesen. 1975. *Unmasking the Face: A Guide to Recognizing Emotions from Facial Clues.* Englewood Cliffs, NJ: Prentice Hall.
_____. 1978. *Facial Action Coding System.* Palo Alto, CA: Consulting Psychologists Press.
Ishigami, Mitsutoshi. 1977. *Tezuka Osamu no kimyōna sekai.* Tokyo: Kisōtengaisha.
Kawai, Hayao. 1988. *The Japanese Psyche: Major Motifs in the Fairy Tales of Japan.* Dallas, TX: Spring Publications.
MacWilliams, Mark. 1999. "Revisioning Japanese Religiosity: Tezuka Osamu's *Hi no tori* (The Phoenix)." *Japanese Religions* 24 (January): 73–100.
Nakano, Haruyuki. 1993. *Tezuka Osamu to rojiura no mangatachi.* Tokyo: Chikuma shobō.

_____. 1994. *Tezuka Osamu no Takarazuka*. Tokyo: Chikuma shobō.

Natsume, Fusanosuke. 1992. *Tezuka Osamu wa doko ni iru*. Tokyo: Chikuma shobō (Chikuma raiburarii 75).

_____. 1995. *Tezuka Osamu no bōken. Sengo manga no kamigami*. Tokyo: Chikuma shobō.

Oki, Kōsei. 1996. *Tetsuwan Atomu daijiten*. Tokyo: Shōbunsha.

Phillipps, Susanne. 1996. *Erzählform Manga. Eine Analyse der Zeitstrukturen in Tezuka Osamus "Hi no tori"* ("Phönix"). Wiesbaden: Harrassowitz.

_____. 2000. *Tezuka Osamu. Figuren, Themen und Erzählstrukturen im Manga-Gesamtwerk*. München: Iudicium.

Robertson, Jennifer. 1998. *Takarazuka. Sexual Politics and Popular Culture in Modern Japan*. Berkeley: University of California Press.

Shimizu, Isao. 1989. *Manga shōnen to akahon manga. Sengo manga no tanjō*. Tokyo: Zōonsha.

_____. 1998. *Ōsaka manga shi. Manga bunka hasshin toshi no 300 nen*. Tokyo: Nyūton puresu.

Takeuchi, Osamu. 1992. *Tezuka Osamu ron*. Tokyo: Heibonsha.

Tezuka Production. 1994. *The Osamu Tezuka Manga Museum*. Takarazuka: Takarazuka Shiritsu Tezuka Osamu Kinenkan (Exhibition Catalog).

Tezuka Production and Hiroaki Ikeda. 1998. *Tezuka Osamu kyarakutā zukan* (6 volumes). Tokyo: Asahi shinbunsha.

Tezuka Production and Atsushi Yamamoto. 2001. *Black Jack 300 Stars' Encyclopedia*. Tokyo: Akita shoten.

Tōkyō Kokuritsu Kindai Bijutsukan/The National Museum of Modern Art, Tokyo, ed. 1990. *Tezuka Osamu ten/Osamu Tezuka Exhibition*. Tokyo: Asahi shinbunsha (Exhibition Catalog).

Chapter 4

"An Anime Metropolis: Japanese Animators Bring Distinctive Touch to a Classic Film." 2002. *Morning Edition*. National Public Radio, January 24. www.npr.org/programs/morning/features/2002/jan/metropolis/020124.metropolis.html. Accessed March 18, 2003.

Blackwell, Laura. 2002. "A Dangerous, but Rewarding, Journey into the Heart of Osamu Tezuka's *Metropolis*." *Strange Horizons*, April 22. www.strangehorizons.com/2002/20020422/metropolis.shtml. Accessed March 18, 2003.

Brio, Matthew. 1994. "The New Man as Cyborg: Figures of Technology in Weimar Visual Culture." *New German Critique* 62 (Spring–Summer): 71–110.

Brooks, Rodney A. 2003. *Flesh and Machines: How Robots Will Change Us*. New York: Vintage.

Clammer, John. 2000. "The Politics of Animism." *INTERculture* 138 (April): 21–41.

Flippo, Hyde. 1997a. "Universum Film AG: Ufa, Berlin, Babelsberg, and Hollywood." *The German Hollywood Connection*. www.germanhollywood.com/ufa.html. Accessed August 10, 2004.

_____. 1997b. "The 'Metropolis' Connection 2: Fritz Lang's *Metropolis*," *German Hollywood Connection*. www.germanhollywood.com/metrop_2.html. Accessed August 10, 2004.

Graham, Elaine L. 2002. *Representations of the Post/Human: Monsters, Aliens and Others in Popular Culture*. Piscataway, NJ: Rutgers University Press.

Harbou, Thea von. 1975. *Metropolis*. Boston: Greg Press. Reprint of the 1929 edition published by The Readers Library.
————. 1988. *Metropolis* (with illustrations by Michael W. Kaluta). Norfolk, VA: The Donning Company.
Kitamura, Tetsuo. 1990. *The Dolls of Japan: Shapes of Prayer, Embodiments of Love*. Tokyo: The Japan Foundation.
Kleine-Ahlbrandt, W. Laird. 1993. *Twentieth-Century European History*. New York: West Publishing.
Law, Jane Marie. 1995. "The Puppet as Body Substitute: *Ningyo* in the Japanese *Shiki Sanbaso* Performance." In *Religious Reflections on the Human Body*, ed. Jane Marie Law. 251–288. Bloomington: Indiana University Press.
Lowry, Nicholas D. 2003. "Metropolis: A Manhattan of the Mind." *International Auctioneers Magazine* (Spring): 24–25.
Lydon, Andrew. 2003a. "Smearing the Urban: The Politics of Metropolis." *Talking Pictures*. www.talkingpix.co.uk/Article_Metropolis.html. Accessed June 6, 2003.
————. 2003b. *The Metropolis Case*. Directed by Enno Patalas. In Fritz Lang's *Metropolis*. Restored DVD Authorized Edition. New York: KINO Video.
Perkowitz, Sidney. 2004. *Digital People: From Bionic Humans to Androids*. Washington, DC: Joseph Henry Press.
Rafferty, Terrence. 2003. "Why Asian Ghost Stories Are the Best." *New York Times*, June 8, Section 2, 13
————. 2004. "The Monster That Morphed into a Metaphor." *New York Times*, May 2, section 2, column 1, 26.
Rutsky, R.L. 1993. "The Mediation of Technology and Gender: Metropolis, Nazism, Modernism." *New German Critique* 60 (Autumn): 3–32.
Scheuer, Jeffrey. 1996."Fritz Lang." www.jscheuer.com/lang.htm. Accessed March 12, 2003.
Schodt, Frederik L. 1988. *Inside the Robot Kingdom: Japan, Mechatronics and the Coming Robotopia*. Toyo: Kodansha International.
Sony. 2000. "Sony Announces Sale of 2nd Generation Autonomous Entertainment Robot "AIBO" [ERS-210]." www.sony.net/SonyInfo/News/Press_Archive/200010/00-050A/ Accessed August 7,2007.
Tezuka, Osamu. 2003. *Metropolis*, trans. Sivasubramanian, Kumar. Milwaukie, OR: Dark Horse Comics.
————. 2003. "Afterword." In Osamu Tezuka, *Metropolis*, trans. Sivasubramanian, Kumar. Milwaukie, OR: Dark Horse Comics, 164–165.

Chapter 5

Akiyama, Satoko. 1981. "Sofia no namida: Shōjo manga no naiteki sekai." *Yuriika: Shi to hihyō*. 13 no. 19 (July): 8–19. Tokyo: Seidosha.
Aramata, Hiroshi. 1994. *Manga to jinsei*. Tokyo: Shūeisha.
Berndt, Jaqueline. 1994. *Manga no kuni Nippon*, trans. K. Sat and K. Mizuno. Tokyo: Kadensha.
Fujimoto, Yukari. 1998. *Watashi no ibasho wa doko ni aru no*. Tokyo: Gakuyō shobō.
Hanamura, Susumu. 1989. "Jojō no tabibito." In *Ai no jojō-ga shū* (Bessatsu Taiyō), Tokyo: Heibonsha, 121–129.
Hebdige, Dick. 1981. *Subculture, the Meaning of Style (New Accents)*. London: Routledge.

Honda, Masuko. 1990. *Jogakusei no keifu*. Tokyo: Seidosha.
_____. 1995. "Shōjo genshō." *Imago* 6–4 (April): 48–53.
Ina, Masato. 1999. *Subculture no shakaigaku*. Kyoto: Sekaishisousha.
Inoue, Shōichi. 1999. "Hitomi ha kōushite oritekita." In *Utsukushiku ikiru Nakahara Jun'ichi—sono bigaku to shigoto* (Bessatsu Taiyō), eds. Takahashi, Yōji and Sōji Nakahara, 30–32. Tokyo: Heibonsha.
Ishiko, Junzō. 1974. *Kitchu no sei to zoku*. Tokyo: Taihei shuppansha.
Iwaya, Kunio. 1980. "Hagio Moto: Okashi no ie ni tsuite." *Kokubungaku: kaishaku to kanshō* (April), 136–137. Tokyo: Shibundō.
Iwaya, Kunio, and Mogo Hagio. 1995. "Shōjo manga to iu souchi." *Imago* 6–4 (April): 20–47. Tokyo: Seidosha.
Kawamura, Kunimitsu. 1993. *Otome no inori*. Tokyo: Kinokuniya shoten.
_____. 1994. *Otome no shintai*. Tokyo: Kinokuniya shoten.
Kimura, Midori. 1996. "Shōnen no toki, shōjo no yume: 70 nendai shōjo manga to sonogo." *Bijutsu techō* (December): 61–69.
Kume, Yoriko. 1997. "Shōjo shōsetsu: Sai to kihan no gensetsu sōchi." In *Media, Hyōshō, ideology*, eds. Yōichi Komori, Kensuke Kureno, and Shū Takahashi, 195–222. Kyoto: Ozawa shoten.
Kurosawa, Ariko. 1998. "Ozaki Midori to shōjo shōsetsu." In *Teihon Ozaki Midori zenshū*, vol. 2, ed. Masami Inagaki, 439–453. Tokyo: Chikuma shobō.
Kuwahara, Noriko. 1998. "Taishū no kokoro, Takehisa Yumeiji." In *Nihon bijutsukan*, ed. Seiki Aoyagi, et al., 1036–1037. Tokyo: Shōgakukan.
Minagawa, Mieko. 1991. "Himawari to *Junia Soreiyu*." In *Shōjo zasshi ron*, ed. Eiji Ōtsuka, 47–84. Tokyo: Tokyo shoseki.
Miyamoto, Hirohito. 1998. "Manga no ibasho." *Bijutsu shi* 48, no. 1: 225.
Mochizuki, Noriko. 1981. "Ōshima Yumiko." *Yuriika: Shi to hihyō* 13, no. 9 (July): 148–158.
Murakami, Tomohiko. 1989a. "*Ribon no kishi*." *Asahi Journal* 31, no. 17 (April): 43–45.
_____. 1989b. "Sengo manga e no ikutsuka no shiza: manga shi to wa nanika." In *Manga no jidai*, ed. Kunio Yaguchi, 206–217. Tokyo: Museum of Contemporary Art, Tokyo and Hiroshima City Museum of Contemporary Art.
Nakajima, Azusa. 1991. "Mizō no jidai." *Shōjo manga no sekai II* (Bessatsu Taiyō), 88–89. Tokyo: Heibonsha.
Nakano, Haruyuki. 2004. *Manga sangyō ron*. Tokyo: Chikuma shobō.
Nakano, Osamu. 1981. "Shōjo manga no kō zō bunseki." *Yuriika: Shi to hihyō* 13, no. 9: 20–31.
Nakayama, Kimio. 1997. *Shōjo manga no sekai ten*. Tokyo: Yomiuri shimbunsha and Bijutsukan renraku kyōgikai.
Natsume, Fusanosuke, ed. 1995a. *Manga no yomikata*. Tokyo: Takarajimasha.
_____. 1995b. *Tezuka Osamu wa doko ni iru*. 2nd ed. Tokyo: Chikuma shobō.
_____. 1997. *Manga wa naze omoshiroi ka*. Tokyo: Nihon hōsō shuppan.
_____. 1998. *Tezuka Osamu no bōken: sengo manga no kamigami*. 2nd ed. Tokyo: Shōgakukan.
Nimiya, Kazuko. 1994. *Shōjo manga no ai no yukue*. Tokyo: Kōei shuppan.
Okamoto, Yoshie. 1998. "Shōjo manga no ōgon jidai." In *Manga no jidai Tezuka Osamu kara Evangerion made*, ed. Kunio Yaguchi, 134. Tokyo: Tokyo-to gendai bijutsukan.
Ōtsuka, Eiji. 1994. *Sengo manga no hyōgen kūkan*. Kyoto: Hōzōkan.
_____. 1997. *Shōjo minzoku gaku*. Tokyo: Kōbunsha.

_____. 2004. *Otaku no seishinshi: 1980 nendai ron*. Tokyo: Kōdansha.

Ōtsuka, Eiji, and Gō Sasakibara. 2001. *Kyōyō to shite no manga, anime*. Tokyo: Kōdansha.

Schilling, M. 1997. *Encyclopedia of Japanese Pop Culture*. Boston: Shambhara Publications.

Schodt, Fredrick. 1993. *Manga! Manga! The World of Japanese Comics*. Tokyo: Kōdansha International.

_____. 1996. *Dreamland Japan: Writings on Modern Manga*. Berkeley, CA: Stone Bridge Press.

Sudō, Takumi. 1984. *Ehon II* (Bessatsu Taiyō), ed. Yōji Takahashi. Tokyo: Heibonsha.

Takahashi, Makoto. 1999. *Shōjo romance*. Tokyo: PARCO shuppan.

Takahashi, Yōji, ed. 1984. *Ehon II* (Bessatsu Taiyō). Tokyo: Heibonsha.

_____. 1985. *Fukiya kōji: Ai no jojo gashu* (Bessatsu Taiyō). Tokyo: Heibonsha.

Takahashi, Yōji and Sōji Nakahara, eds. 1999. *Utsukushiku ikiru Nakahara Jun'ichi—sono bigaku to shigoto* (Bessatsu Taiyō). Tokyo: Heibonsha.

Takumi, Hideo. 1978. "Taishō no koseiha." In *Genshoku Nihon no bijutsu*, ed. Terakazu Akiyama, 185–192. Tokyo: Shōgakukan.

Treat, John W. 1996. "Yoshimoto Banana Writes Home: The Shōjo in Japanese Popular Culture." In *Culture in Contemporary Japan and Popular Culture*, ed. J.W. Treat, 265–274. Honolulu: University of Hawai'i Press.

Yokomori, Rika. 1996. *Ren'ai wa shōjo manga de osowatta—ai ni ikite koso, onna!?* Tokyo: Kuresuto sha.

Yomota, Inuhiko. 1994. *Manga genron*. Tokyo: Chikuma shobō.

Yonezawa, Yoshihiro. 1980. *Sengo shōjo manga shi*. Tokyo: Shinyōsha.

_____. 1991a. *Shōjo manga no sekai I* (Bessatsu Taiyō). Tokyo: Heibonsha.

_____. 1991b. *Shōjo manga no sekai II* (Bessatsu Taiyō). Tokyo: Heibonsha.

Chapter 6

Deluze, Gilles. 1993. *The Fold: Leibniz and the Baroque*, trans. Tom Conley. London: Athlone Press.

Endō, Hiroko. 2004. *Shōjo no tomo to sono jidai: Henshūsha no yuki Uchiyama Motoi*. Tokyo: Honnoizumi.

Foucault, Michel. 1990. *The History of Sexuality. Volume One: An Introduction*, trans. Robert Hurley. New York: Vintage Books.

Fredericks, Sarah Anne. 2000. "Housewives, Modern Girls, Feminists: Women's Magazines and Modernity in Japan." Unpublished dissertation, University of Chicago.

Frühstück, Sabine. 2003. *Colonizing Sex: Sexology and Social Control in Modern Japan*. Berkeley: University of California Press.

Fujimoto, Yukari. 1998. *Watashi no ibasho wa doko ni aru no? Shōjo manga ga utusu kokoro no katachi*. Tokyo: Gakuyō shobō.

Horie, Akiko. 2003. *Otome no romansu techō*. Kawade shobō.

Iida, Yumiko. 2002. "Between the Technique of Living an Endless Routine and the Madness of Absolute Degree Zero: Japanese Identity and the Crisis of Modernity in the 1990s." In *Positions* 8: 2 (Fall): 423–464.

Ikeda, Riyoko. 2004. *Bersaiyu no bara*. 5 vols. Tokyo: Shūeisha bunkō.

Kawamura, Kunimitsu. 1993. *Otome no inori: Kindai josei imeiji no tanjō*. Tokyo: Kinokuniya shoten.

Masuda, Nozomi. 2002. "Kakusan suru jiku: koma kōsei no hensen kara mieru 1990 nendai ikō no shōjo manga." In *Manga kenkyū* 2 (October): 108–120.

Matsui, Midori. 1993. "Little Girls Were Little Boys: Displaced Femininity in the Representation of Homosexuality in Japanese Girls' Comics." In *Feminism and the Politics of Difference,* ed. Sneja Gunew and Anna Yeatman, 177–196. New South Wales, Australia: Allen and Unwin.

McCloud, Scott. 1993. *Understanding Comics: The Invisible Art.* New York: HarperCollins.

Murakami, Takashi. 2000. *Superflat.* Tokyo: Madra.

Nananan, Kiriko. 1997. *blue.* Tokyo: Magazine House.

Natsume, Fusanosuke, and Takakuma Kentarō, eds. 1995. *Manga no yomikata.* Tokyo: Bessatsu Takarajima.

Ōtsuka, Eiji. 1994. *Sengo manga no hyōgen kukan: kigō-teki shintai no jubaku.* Tokyo: Hōzōkan.

Pflugfelder, Gregory. 1999. *Cartographies of Desire: Male-Male Sexuality in Japanese Discourse, 1600–1950.* Berkeley: University of California Press.

Robertson, Jennifer. 1998. *Takarazuka: Sexual Politics and Popular Culture in Modern Japan.* Berkeley: University of California Press.

Takemiya, Keiko. 1993. *Kaze to ki no shi.* Vol. 1. Tokyo: Chūō kōronsha.

Yonezawa, Yoshihiro. 1991. *Shōjo manga no sekai.* 2 vols. Bessatsu Taiyō. Tokyo: Heibonsha.

Yoshiya, Nobuko. 2003a. *Hana monogatari.* 3 vols. Tokyo: Kokushō.

———. 2003b. *Yaneura no ni shōjo.* Tokyo: Kokushō.

Chapter 7

Bijutsu techō 1956. "Zadankai. Meiji no shūkanshi 'fūzoku gahō' wo megutte." *Bijutsu techō* 113, no. 4: 109–118.

Edstrom, Bert, ed. 2000. *The Japanese and Europe: Images and Perceptions.* Richmond, VA: Japan Library, Curzon Press.

Fuzoku gahō. 1997. CD-ROM han. Tokyo: Yumani shobō.

Guth, Christine. 1993. *Art, Tea, and Industry: Masuda Takashi and the Mitsui Circle.* Princeton, NJ: Princeton University Press.

———. 1997. "Some Reflections on the Formation of the Meiji Artistic Canon." In *New Directions in the Study of Meiji Japan,* eds. Helen Hardacre and Adam Kern, 35–41. Leiden and New York: Brill.

Haga, Tōru, and Isao Shimizu. 1985. *Nichirō sensōki-no manga. Kindai manga IV.* Tokyo: Chikuma shobō.

Haga, Tōru, and Izumi Hosokawa, eds. 1994. *Kawanabe Kyōsai gashū.* Vols. 1–3. Tokyo: Rikuyōsha.

Hardacre, Helen, and Adam L. Kern. 1997. *New Directions in the Study of Meiji Japan.* Leiden and New York: Brill.

Hijiya-Kirschnereit, Irmela. 2000. "Introduction." In *Canon and Identity—Japanese Modernization Reconsidered: Trans-Cultural Perspectives,* ed. Irmela Hijiya-Kirschnereit, 7–24. Tokyo: Deutsches Institut für Japanstudien.

Huffman, James L. 1997. *Creating a Public. People and Press in Meiji Japan.* Honolulu: University of Hawai'i Press.

Iguchi, Kazuki. 1998. *Nichirō sensō-no jidai.* Tokyo: Yoshikawa kōbunkan.

Inagaki, Shinichi. 1988. *Edo-no asobie.* Tokyo: Tokyo shoseki insatsu.

Iriye, Akira. 1989. "Japan's Drive to Great Power Status." In *The Cambridge History of Japan.* Vol. 5. New York: Cambridge University Press.

Ishiko, Jun. 1979. *Nihon manga shi.* Vol. 1. Tokyo: Ōgetsu shoten.

Jaffe, Richard M. 2001. *Neither Monk nor Layman: Clerical Marriage in Modern Japanese Buddhism.* Princeton, NJ: Princeton University Press.

Johnson, Scott. 1994. "From Aesop to Isoppu: The Making of a Book." In Kawanabe Kyōsai gashū, eds. Toru Haga and Izumi Hasegawa, vol. 2, 199–203. Tokyo: Rikuyōsha.

Jordan, Brenda J. 1994. "Continuity in the Art of Kawanabe Kyōsai." In Kawanabe Kyōsai gashū, eds. Toru Haga and Rifu Nakagura, vol. 3, 92–95. Tokyo: Rikuyōsha.

Kikeriki. 1904. "The International Situation—Or: One Wants to Swallow the Other," January 14, no. 4. In "A Different View: The Russo-Japanese War in Austro–Hungarian Political Cartoons. On Construction of the 'Other' in Iconographic Manifestations," by Monika Lehner. Paper presented at the International Conference Russo-Japanese War and the 20th Century. Jerusalem/Haifa, February 8–14, 2004.

Kindai manga-no so. Kitazawa Rakuten zuroku. 1991. Omiya: Omiyashi kigakubu kokusai bunkakahen.

Komatsu, Shigemi, ed. 1993. *Nōe hoshi ekotoba. Fukutomi sōshi. Hyakki yagyō emaki.* Tokyo: Chūō kōronsha.

Komori, Yōichi, and Ryūichi Narita, eds. 2004. *Nichirō sensō sutadisu.* Tokyo: Kinokuniya.

Kowner, Rotem. 2000. "Japan's Enlightened War: Military Conduct and Attitudes to the Enemy During the Russo-Japanese War." In Edstrom, 2000, 134–51.

Mikhailova, Yulia. 2000. "Japan and Russia: Mutual Images, 1904–39." In *The Japanese and Europe: Images and Perceptions*, ed. Bert Edstrom, 152–171. Richmond, VA: Japan Library, Curzon Press.

————. 2001. "Laughter in Russo-Japanese Relations. Comic Pictures of the Russo-Japanese War." *Asian Cultural Studies. International Christian University* 27 (3-A): 59–76.

Minami, Kazuo. 1999. *Bakumatsu Ishin-no fushiga.* Tokyo: Yoshikawa kobunkan.

Narita, Ryūichi. 2000. "The World of *Shōnen Sekai.*" In *Canon and Identity—Japanese Modernization Reconsidered: Trans-Cultural Perspectives*, ed. Irmela Hijiya-Kirschnereit, 145–166. Tokyo: Deutsches Institut für Japanstudien.

Nihon no manga sanbyakunen. 1996. Kawasaki City: Kawasakishi shimin myuzeumu.

Nikolai, Abp. of Japan and Kennosuke Nakamura. 1994. *Dnevniki Sviatogo Nikolaya Iaponskogo* (Diaries of St. Nikolai Iaponskii). Sapporo: Hokkaido University Publishers.

Shimizu, Isao, ed. 1976. *Manga zasshi hakubutsukan, Meiji jidai hen.* Vol. 1. Tokyo: Kokusho kankōkai.

————. 1982. *Kobayashi Kiyochika. Fushimanga.* Tokyo: Iwasaki bijutsusha.

————. 1991. *Manga-no rekishi,* Tokyo: Iwanami shinsho.

Shimizu, Isao, and Kōichi Yumoto. 1989. *Meiji manyōshū.* Tokyo: Bungei shunju.

————. 1994. *Gaikoku manga ni egakareta Nihon.* Tokyo: Maruzen bukusu.

Sugiura, Yukio. 1978. *Manga de tsuduru. Meiji Taishō Shōwa.* Tokyo: Mangasha.

Suyama, Keiichi. 1968. *Nihon manga hyakunen.* Tokyo: Haga shoten.

————. 1972. *Manga hakubutsu shi.* Tokyo: Banchō shobō.

Suzuki, Keiko. 1997. "*Yokohama-e* and *Kaika-e* Prints: Japanese Interpretations of Self and Other from 1860 through the 1880s." In *New Directions in the Study of Meiji Japan*, eds. Helen Hardacre and Adam Kern, 676–681. Leiden and New York: Brill.

Ueda, Masaaki, et al. 2001. *Nihon jimei daijiten.* Tokyo: Kōdansha.

Wray, Harry, and Peter Duus. 1983. "The Russo-Japanese War: Turning Point in Japanese History." In *Japan Examined. Perspectives on Modern Japanese History*, eds. Harry Wray and Hillary Conroy, 150–157. Honolulu: University of Hawai'i Press.

Yoshino, Takao, ed. 1993–1994. *Kokkei shimbun*, vol. 4. Tokyo: Yumani shobō.

Yui, Kazuto. 1998. *Nijū seiki bukko Nihon gaka jiten.* Tokyo: Bijutsu nenkansha.

Chapter 8

Akiyama, Masami, ed. 1998. *Maboroshi no sensō manga no sekai.* Tokyo: Natsume shobō.

Asada, Sadao. 1997. "The Mushroom Cloud and National Psyches: Japanese and American Perceptions of the Atomic Bomb." In *Living With the Bomb: American and Japanese Cultural Conflicts in the Nuclear Age,* eds. Laura Hein and Mark Selden, 173–201. Armonk, NY: M.E. Sharpe.

Braw, Monica. 1997. "Hiroshima and Nagasaki: The Voluntary Silence." In *Living With the Bomb: American and Japanese Cultural Conflicts in the Nuclear Age,* eds. Laura Hein and Mark Selden, 155–172. Armonk, NY: M.E. Sharpe.

Dower, W. John. 1996. "The Bombed: Hiroshimas and Nagasakis in Japanese Memory." In *Hiroshima in History and Memory,* ed. Michael J. Hogan, 116–142. New York: Cambridge University Press.

_____. 1997. "Triumphal and Tragic Narratives of the War in Asia." In *Living With the Bomb: American and Japanese Cultural Conflicts in the Nuclear Age,* eds. Laura Hein and Mark Selden, 37–51. Armonk, NY: M.E. Sharpe.

Gluck, Carol. 1993. "The Past in the Present." In *Postwar Japan as History,* ed. Andrew Gordon, 64–95. Berkeley: University of California Press.

Halbwachs, Maurice. 1992. *On Collective Memory,* ed. and trans. Lewis A. Coser. Chicago: University of Chicago Press.

Hein, Laura, and Mark Selden, eds. 1997. *Living With the Bomb: American and Japanese Cultural Conflicts in the Nuclear Age.* Armonk, NY: M.E. Sharpe.

Hellfire: A Journey From Hiroshima. 1986. Directed by John Junkerman and John Dower. Brooklyn, NY: First Run Icarus Films.

Hicks, George. 1998. *Japan's War Memories—Amnesia or Concealment?* Sydney: Ashgate Publishing.

Hirabayashi, Shigeo. 2000. "Mizuki Shigeru to sensō manga." In *Mizuki Shigeru senki kessaku taizen—bessatsu,* ed. Shigeru Mizuki, 69–84. Tokyo: Jinrui bunkasha.

Igarashi, Yoshikuni. 2000. *Bodies of Memory: Narratives of War in Postwar Japanese Culture, 1945–1970.* Princeton, NJ: Princeton University Press.

Ishiko, Jun. 1983. *Manga ni miru sensō to heiwa 90 nen.* Tokyo: Horupu shuppan.

Morris, Ivan. 1975. *The Nobility of Failure: Tragic Heroes in the History of Japan.* New York: The Noonday Press.

Morton, W. Scott. 1994. *Japan: Its History and Culture.* Tokyo: McGraw-Hill.

Nakar, Eldad. 2003. "Memories of Pilots and Planes: World War II in Japanese Manga, 1957–1967." *Social Science Japan Journal* 6, no. 1 (April): 57–76.

Natsume, Fusanosuke. 1997. *Manga to sensō.* Japan: Kōdansha Gendai Shinsho.

Richie, Donald. 1990. *Japanese Cinema—An Introduction.* New York: Oxford University Press.

_____. 1996 (1961). "'Mono no aware': Hiroshima in Film." In *Hibakusha Cinema: Hiroshima, Nagasaki and the Nuclear Image in Japanese Film,* ed. Mick Broderick, 20–37. London: Kegan Paul International.

Schodt, Frederik L. 1983. *Manga! Manga! The World of Japanese Comics.* Tokyo: Kōdansha International.

Smith, Christian. 2003. *Moral, Believing Animals: Human Personhood and Culture.* New York: Oxford University Press.

Snow, David A., and Robert D. Benford. 1992. "Master Frames and Cycles of Protest." In *Frontiers in Social Movement Theory,* eds. A. Morris and C. Mueller, 133–155. New Haven, CT: Yale University Press.

Takahashi, Saburō. 1988. *Senki-mono o yomu–sensō taiken to sengo Nihon shakai.* Kyoto: Academia Shuppan-kai sha.
Takeuchi, Osamu. 1995. *Sengo manga 50 nenshi.* Tokyo: Chikuma shobō.
Tanikgawa, Akihide, ed. 1995. *Manga wa jidai o utsusu.* Tokyo: Tokyo shoseki.
Treat, John Whittier. 1995. *Writing Ground Zero: Japanese Literature and the Atomic Bomb.* Chicago: University of Chicago Press.
Tsurumi, Shunsuke. 1987. *A Cultural History of Post War Japan 1945–1980.* London: Kegan Paul International.
Vinitzky-Seroussi, Vered. 2002." Commemorating a Difficult Past: Yitzhak Rabin's Memorials." *American Sociological Review* 67 (February): 30–51.
Yonezawa, Yoshihiro, ed. 1996. *Shōnen manga no sekai–kodomo no shōwa shi 2* Bessatsu Taiyō. Tokyo: Heibonsha.
Yoshida, Yutaka. 1995. *Nihonjin no sensō-kan–sengoshi no naka no.* Tokyo: Iwanami shoten.

Chapter 9

Aoyama, Yoshinobu. 1991. *Shinri no bengoshi ganbaruzo!* Vol. 2: *Naze watashi wa taihō sarenakutewa naranakatta no ka.* Tokyo: Oumu shuppan.
———, ed. 1992. *Risō shakai: Die Ideal Welt.* No. 3. Tokyo: Oumu shuppan.
Asahara, Shōkō. 1992a. *Haiesuto danma.* Tokyo: Oumu shuppan.
———, ed. 1992b. *Risō shakai: Shambala.* Tokyo: Oumu shuppan.
———. 1993. *Asahara Shōkō, Senritsu no yogen.* Tokyo: Oumu shuppan.
———. 1995. *Hi izuru kuni, saiwai chikashi.* Tokyo: Oumu shuppan.
Asahi Shimbun Gakugeibu. 1995. "Oumu shinrikyō to ima." In *Nani ga Oumu o umidashita ka*, ed. Asahi Shimbunsha, 81–104. Tokyo: Asahi shimbun.
Asami, Sadao. 1995. "'New Religions' Tend to Thrive Amid Social Malaise." *Daily Yomiuri*, May 24.
Aum Editorial Board, ed. 1989. *Jinsei wo kiru: Kōfukuna jinsei o ikiru tame ni.* Tokyo: Oumu shuppan.
———. 1992. "Senritsu no seikimatsu daiyogen." *Vajrayāna Sacca*, no. 5 (April): 6–99.
———. 1995. "Akuma no maindo kontororu: jinrui sennō keikaku no zenbō o abaku." *Vajrayāna Sacca*, no. 7 (February): 6–112.
Fukuda, Kazuya. 1995. "Oumu Shinrikyō no kakyō," In *Ji Oumu: Sabukaruchā to Oumu*, ed. PLANK, 28–36. Tokyo: JBD.
Gardner, Richard A. 1999. "Lost in the Cosmos and the Need to Know." *Monumenta Nipponica* 54: 217–246.
———. 2001a. "Aum and the Media: Lost in the Cosmos and the Need to Know." In *Religion and Social Crisis in Japan: Understanding Japanese Society Through the Aum Affair*, eds. Robert Kisala and James Mullins, 133–163. New York: Palgrave.
———. 2001b. "Review of *Destroying the World to Save It: Aum Shinrikyō, Apocalyptic Violence, and the New Global Terrorism*, by Robert Jay Lifton and *Religious Violence in Contemporary Japan: The Case of Aum Shinrikyō*, by Ian Reader." *Monumenta Nipponica* 56 (2001): 125–128.
———. 2002a "'The Blessing of Living in a Country Where There Are *Senryū!*' Humor in the Response to Aum Shinrikyō." *Asian Folklore Studies* 61: 35–75.
———. 2002b. "A Revisited." *Monumenta Nipponica* 57: 339–348.
———. 2003. "Aum and Humor: More Blessings from the Land of *Senryū.*" *Sophia International Review* 25: 1–34.

_____. 2005. "Collective Memory, National Identity: Victims and Victimizers in Japan." In *Quoting God: How Media Shape Ideas About Religion and Culture*, ed. Claire H. Badaracco, 153–172. Waco, TX: Baylor University Press.

Goshima, Tsutsumu. 1973. *Nosutoradamusu no daiyōgen*. Tokyo: Shōdensha.

Haga, Manabu, and Robert J. Kisala. 1995. "Editors' Introduction: The New Age in Japan." *Japanese Journal of Religious Studies* 22: 235–48.

Hardacre, Helen. 1995. "Aum Shinrikyō and the Japanese Media: The Pied Piper Meets the Lamb of God." *Institute Reports* (November). East Asian Institute, Columbia University.

Hoffman, Michael. 2005. "*Otaku* Harassed as Sex-Crime Fears Mount." *Japan Times*, February 6.

Ichikawa, Shin'ichi. 1995. "Seigi no kamen o tsuketa wakamonotachi," *Asahi shimbun*, July 19.

Ihara, Keiko. 1995. "Kyōtsugo wa SF Anime da." *AERA*, April 24, 19–21.

Ikegami, Yoshimasu, and Hirochika Nakamaki, eds. 1996. *Jōhō jidai wa shūkyō o kaeru ka: Dentō shūkyō kara Oumu Shinrikyō made*. Tokyo: Kōbudō.

Inoue, Nobutaka. 1995a. "Manga ya anime ga eikyō o ataete ita." *AERA*, May 25, 33.

_____. 1995b. "Kore kara no shūkyō o kangaeru: jōhō hōshoku no jidai." *Tokyo shimbun*, June 5, evening edition.

_____. 1995c. "Kore kara no shūkyō: bācharu riariteï no yūwakū." *Tokyo shimbun*, June 6, evening edition.

_____. 1995d. "Jōhōka shakai no otoshiana." In *Nani ga Oumu o umidashita ka*, ed. Asahi Shimbunsha, 48–57. Tokyo: Asahi shimbun.

Inoue, Nobutaka, Michio Takeda, and Kiyoyasu Kitabatake. 1995. *Oumu Shinrikyō to wa naki ka: Gendai shakai ni toikakeru mono*. Tokyo: Asahi News Shop.

Ishii, Shinji, ed. 1989. *Otaku no hon*. Bessatsu Takarajima 104. Tokyo: JICC shuppankyoku.

Kagami, Ryūji. 1995. "Litoru gunōshïsu-tachi e." In *Are wan an datta no ka: Oumu kaidoku manyuaru*, ed. Tetsu Kitagawa, 26–32. Tokyo: Daimondo-sha.

Karasawa, Shun'ichi. 1995. "Oumu to taishū." In *Are wan nan datta no ka: Oumu kaidoku manyuaru*, ed. Tetsu Kitagawa, 150–157. Tokyo: Daimondo-sha.

Kawai, Hayao, Shin'ichi Nakazawa, and Hidetoshi Takahashi. 1995. "Kyomukan kara no dashuttsu." In *Oumu Shinrikyō no shinsō* (special issue of *Imago*), ed. Shin'ichi Nakazawa, 8–25.

Kiridōshi, Risaku. 1995a. "Omae ga jinrui o koroshitai nara." *Takarajima* (August): 45–54.

_____. 1995b. "Manga ka anime wa oya ni kakurete miru no ga tadashii'n desu," *Pureibo-i*, September 12, 58–61.

Kisala, Robert J., and Mark R. Mullins. 2001. *Religion and Social Crisis in Japan: Understanding Japanese Society Through the Aum Affair*. New York: Palgrave.

Kitagawa, Testu, ed. 1995. *Are wan an datta no ka: Oumu kaidoku manyuaru*. Tokyo: Daimondo-sha.

Kiyomizu, Arika. 1995. "'Subukaruchāteki akumu' to kakumeiteki sōsōzōryoku," In *Ji Oumu: Sabukaruchā to Oumu*, ed. PLANK, 98–103. Tokyo: JBD.

Kondō, Katsushige, ed. 1995. *Oumu kyōdan: yabō to hōkai*. Special issue of *Sandē mainichi*, June 3.

Kotani, Mari. 1995. "Karuto toshite no fukensei." In *Ji Oumu: Sabukaruchā to Oumu*, ed. PLANK, 128–137. Tokyo: JBD.

Markley, Robert. 1996. "Introduction: History, Theory, and Virtual Reality." In *Virtual Realities and Their Discontents*, ed. Robert Markley, 1–10. Baltimore, MD: Johns Hopkins University Press.

Miyadai, Shinji. 1993. *Sabukarucha shinwa katai.* Tokyo: Parco.
_____. 1994. *Seifuku shōjo-tachi no sentaku.* Tokyo: Kōdansha.
_____. 1995a. "Mou hitotsu no Oumu kokufuku manyuaru." In *Are wa nan data no ka: Oumu kaidoku manyuaru,* ed. Tetsu Kitagawa, 166–174. Tokyo: Daimondo-sha.
_____. 1995b. *Owari naki nichijō wo ikirō: Oumu kanzen kokufuku manyuaru.* Tokyo: Chikuma shobō.
_____. 1995c. "'Ryōshin' no hanzaisha." *Takarajima* 30 (July): 28–39.
Miyadai, Shinji, Hideki Ishihara, and Meiko Ōtsuka. 1993. *Sabukaruchā shinwa kaitai.* Tokyo: Paruko shuppan.
Miyadai, Shinji, and Rika Kayama. 1995. "Oumu shinrikyō to wakamono." In *Nani ga Oumu o umidashita ka,* ed. Asahi Shimbunsha, 122–138. Tokyo: Asahi shimbun.
Murakami, Takashi. 1995. "*Shōnen jyampu* no naka de ikiru teren: *Akira* no shūmatsu to Oumu." In *Ji Oumu: Sabukaruchā to Oumu,* ed. PLANK, 116–119. Tokyo: JBD.
Nagase, Tadashi. 1995. "Kisō kagaku to mōsō heiki ni mamireta Oumu tekunorojii," In *Ji Oumu: Sabukaruchā to Oumu,* ed. PLANK, 272–299. Tokyo: JBD.
Napier, Susan. 1993. "Panic Sites: The Japanese Imagination of Disaster from *Godzilla* to *Akira.*" *Journal of Japanese Studies* 19 (Summer): 327–351.
_____. 1996. *The Fantastic in Modern Japanese Literature: The Subversion of Modernity.* London: Routledge.
_____. 2000. *Anime from Akira to Princess Mononoke.* New York: Palgrave.
_____. 2003. "Point of View: 'Spirited Away' Presages Golden Age of Anime." *Asahi shimbun,* April 23, 22.
Nihon keizai shimbun. 1995a. "'Gēmu' jinsei," December 11–15, evening edition.
_____. 1995b. "The Creator God Virtual Reality," January 22–26, evening edition.
Ninagawa, Masao, ed. 1995. *Oumu mahō o toku.* AERA, May 5, special edition.
Ōizumi, Mitsunari. 1995. "Oumu Shinrikyō o kaidoku suru kīwādo wa 'seishin sekai' to 'otakusei.'" *Oumu hametsu.* Shūkan yomiuri, June 1, special edition.
Okada, Toshio. 1995. "Otaku no Ōsama, Oumu mondai o kataru." In *Ji Oumu: Sabukaruchā to Oumu,* ed. PLANK, 104–115. Tokyo: JBD.
Osawa, Masachi. 1996. *Kyokō no jidai no hate: Oumu to sekai saishū sensō.* Tokyo: Chikuma shobō.
Ōtsuka, Eiji. 1995. "Warera no jidai no Oumu Shinrikyō." *Shokun* (May): 48–57.
Oumu Shinrikyō no sekai. Directed by Aum Shinrikyo. Japan. Video. Aum Shinrikyo, n.d.
Oyamada, Shin'ichi. 1995. "Asahara Shōkō naze miryōkuteki na no ka." *Takurajima* (August): 35–40.
PLANK ed. 1995. *Ji Oumu: Sabukaruchā to Oumu.* Tokyo: JBD.
Reader, Ian. 1988. "The Rise of a Japanese 'New New Religion': Themes in the Development of Agonshū." *Japanese Journal of Religious Studies* 15: 235–261.
_____. 1996. *A Poisonous Cocktail? Aum Shinrikyō's Path to Violence.* Copenhagen: NIAS Books.
_____. 2000. *Religious Violence in Contemporary Japan: The Case of Aum Shinrikyō.* Richmond, UK: Curzon Books.
Ruisu, Dēna, and Tomoko Ugajin. 1995. "Shinjigatai koto o shinjiru jidai." *Newsweek.* Japanese edition, June 14, 50–53.
Schodt, Frederik L. 1983. *Manga! Manga! The World of Japanese Comics.* Tokyo: Kodansha International.
_____. 1996. *Dreamland Japan: Writings on Modern Manga.* Berkeley, CA: Stone Bridge Press.
Schrimpf, Monica. June 2004. "'This Is a Serious Story!' Religions and *Manga.*" *DIJ*

Newsletter. Tokyo: German Institute for Japanese Studies, 1–3.

Shikawa, Yoshio. 1995. "Oumu to sarin to haribote." In *Ji Oumu: Sabukaruchā to Oumu,* ed. PLANK, 72–85. Tokyo: JBD.

Shimazono, Susumu. 1986. "The Development of Millennialistic Thought in Japan's New Religions: From Tenrikyo to Honmichi." In *New Religious Movements and Rapid Social Change,* ed. James Beckford, 55–86. London: Sage.

———. 1992. *Shishūkyō to shūkyō būmu.* Tokyo: Iwanami shoten.

———. 1995. "In the Wake of Aum: The Formation and Transformation of a Universe of Belief." *Japanese Journal of Religious Studies* 22: 381–416.

———. 2001. "The Evolution of Aum Shinrikyō as a Religious Movement." In *Religion and Social Crisis in Japan: Understanding Japanese Society Through the Aum Affair,* eds. Robert J. Kisala and Mark R. Mullins, 19–52. New York: Palgrave.

Shūkan taishū. 1995. "Oumu 'Harumagedon' no netahon hakkutsu." June 12, 31–32.

Suzuki, Takuma. 1997. "*Ebangerion* to Oumu sedai no 'ayausa.'" *Sande mainichi,* April 6, 212–13.

Suzuki, Yukio ed. 1995. "Oumu jiken manyuaru." Special edition of *FLASH.* May 5.

Takahashi, Hidetoshi. 1996. *Oumu kara no kikan.* Tokyo: Sōshisha.

Tanizaki Tetora. 1995. "Taikō bunka toshite no Oumu." In *Ji Oumu: Sabukaruchā to Oumu,* ed. PLANK, 156–169. Tokyo: JBD.

Tomino, Yoshiyuki. 1995a. "Anime to riaru no kyōka kara nozokeru mono." In *Are wa nan datta no ka: Oumu kaidoku manyuaru,* ed. Tetsu Kitagawa, 34–40. Tokyo: Daimondo-sha.

———. 1995b. "SF anime to 'Oumu' kō." *Sande mainichi: Oumu kyōdan yabō to hōkai,* June 3, 52–53.

Wakano, Yukihiro. 1995. "Tantara yoga no komikuka: Agonshū to taihi kara mita Oumu Shinrikyō." In *Ji Oumu: Sabukaruchā to Oumu,* ed. PLANK, 182–191. Tokyo: JBD.

Yoshimi, Shun'ya. 1995. "Ware ware jishin no naka no Oumu." *Sekai* (July): 48–59.

Yū, Miri. 1995. "Karera o fukaku musubitsuketa 'kakumo nagaki chichi no fuzai,'" In *Are wa nan datta no ka: Oumu kaidoku manyuaru,* ed. Tetsu Kitagawa, 10–17. Tokyo: Daimondo-sha.

Chapter 10

Asahi jānaru. 1984. Tokyo: Asahi shinbunsha (25 May): 6–14.

Barthes, Roland. 1983. *The Empire of Signs,* trans. Richard Howard. New York: Hill and Wang.

Conrich, Ian. 2000. "Seducing the Subject: Freddy Krueger, Popular Culture and the *Nightmare on Elm Street* Films." In *Horror Film Reader,* eds. Alain Silver and James Ursini, 223–235. New York: Limelight Editions.

Doi, Takeo. 1973. *The Anatomy of Dependence.* Tokyo: Kōdansha International.

Douglas, Mary. 1967. *Purity and Danger.* London: Routledge and Kegan Paul.

Freiberg, Frieda. 1996. "Akira and the Postnuclear Sublime." In *Hibakusha Cinema: Hiroshima, Nagasaki and the Nuclear Image in Japanese Cinema,* ed. Mick Broderick, 91–102. London: Kegan Paul International.

Freud, Sigmund. 2003. *The Uncanny,* trans. Daid McLintock. New York: Penguin Books.

Hino, Hideshi. 1989. *Panorama of Hell,* trans. Screaming Mad George, Charles Schneider, and Yoko Umezawa. New York: Blast Books.

———. 1995a. "Hatsuka nezumi." In *Holy horā komikku hassakusen daiisshū,* 115–179. Tokyo: Kadokawa Shoten.

_____. 1995b. *Hell Baby*, trans. Hirō Yamagata. New York: Blast Books.

_____. 2004. *The Bug Boy 2*, trans. Clive Victor France. Tokyo: Dark Horse Publishing.

Ivy, Marilyn. 1989. "Critical Texts, Mass Artifacts: The Consumption of Knowledge in Postmodern Japan." In *Postmodernism and Japan*, eds. Masao Miyoshi and H.D. Harootunian, 21–47. Durham, NC: Duke University Press.

Jameson, Fredric. 1996. *Postmodernism or the Cultural Logic of Late Capitalism*. London: Verso.

Komatsu, Shigemi, ed. 1994. *Gaki zōshi, Jigoku zōshi, Yamai zōshi kusō shi emaki*. In *Nihon no emaki 7*: 2–37. Tokyo: Chūō kōronsha.

Kristeva, Julia. 1982. *Power of Horror: An Essay in Abjection*. New York: Columbia University Press.

LaFleur, William R. 1986. *The Karma of Words: Buddhism and the Literary Arts in Medieval Japan*. Berkeley: University of California Press.

Magliola, Robert. 1984. *Derrida on the Mend*. West Lafayette: IN: Purdue University Press.

McCarthy, Helen. 1999. *Hayao Miyazaki: Master of Japanese Animation*. Berkeley, CA: Stone Bridge Press.

Napier, Susan. 1993. "Panic Sites: The Japanese Imagination of Disaster from *Godzilla* to *Akira*." *Journal of Japanese Studies* 19, no. 2: 327–351.

The Path of Purity, Buddhaghosa's Visuddhimagga. 1971. Trans. Pe Maung Tin. London: Luzac.

Rhys Davids, Caroline A. F. 1980 (1909). *Psalms of the Early Buddhists*. Boston: Routledge & K. Paul.

Ruch, Barbara. 1992. "Coping with Death: Paradigms of Heaven and Hell and the Six Realms in Early Literature and Painting." In *Flowing Traces*, eds. James Sanford, William LaFleur, and Masatoshi Nagatomi, 93–130. Princeton, NJ: Princeton University Press.

Standish, Isolde. 1998. "Akira, Postmodernism and Resistance." In *The Worlds of Japanese Popular Culture: Gender, Shifting Boundaries and Global Cultures*, ed. D.P. Martinez, 56–75. Cambridge: Cambridge University Press.

Chapter 11

Adorno, Theodor. 1991. *The Culture Industry: Selected Essays on Mass Culture*. Edited by J.M. Bernstein. London: Routledge.

Bellah, Robert N. et al. 1985. *Habits of the Heart: Individualism and Commitment in American Life*. New York: Harper and Row.

Eliade, Mircea. 1971. *The Myth of the Eternal Return: or, Cosmos and History*, trans. Willard R. Trask. Princeton, NJ: Princeton University Press.

Hirashima, Natsuko. 1997. "Funtazii ga umareru kūkan." In *Miyazaki Hayao no sekai*. 164–169. Tokyo: Seido-sha.

Kasulis, Thomas P. 2004. *Shinto: The Way Home*. Honolulu: University of Hawai'i Press.

Katagiri, Keiko. 2003. "'Sen to Chihiro' ha kōtukurareta." *Aera* 31 (March): 51–56.

Leed, Eric. 1991. *The Mind of the Traveller: From Gilgamesh to Global Tourism*. New York: Basic Books.

Miyazaki, Hayao. 2001a. *Spirited Away* [Movie Pamphlet]. Tokyo: Tōhō Inc.

_____. 2001b. "The Purpose of the Film." In *Sen to Chihiro no kamikakushi: The Hayao Miyazki Web*, trans. Royoko Toyama. http: //nausicaa.net/miyazaki/sen/proposal.html. Accessed August 26, 2004.

————. 2002. *Shuppatsu ten 1979–1996*. Tokyo: Tokuma shoten.
————. 2000 "A Statement by Hayao Miyazaki." In "Princess Mononoke" (appendix) in *Ghibli*, ed. Studio Ghibli, 3–4. Tokyo: Tokuma shoten.
Murase, Hiromi. 1997, "Kumorinaki sunda manako de mitsumeru "sei no yami." *Pop Culture Critique* 1: 53–66.
Nakane, Chie. 1989. *Tateshakai no ningen kankei*. Tokyo: Kōdansha.
Napier, Susan J. 2002. *Gendai Nihon no anime*. Tokyo: Chūōkoron.
Sawada, Ayumu. 2003. "Akademīshō kōho unda Hayao Miyazaki he no cyokugen." *Asahi shimbun*, February 22, 1–2.
Studio Ghibli, ed. 2002. *Nausicca no "shimbun kōkoku" tte mita koto ga arimasu ka-Ghibli no shimbun kōkotu 18 nenshi*. Tokyo: Tokuma shoten.
Takemura, Tomoko. 1997. "Ikiro omae wa muchakucha da." *Pop Culture Critique* 1: 23.
Watt, Ian. 1996. *Myths of Modern Individualism: Faust, Don Quixote, Don Juan, Robinson Crusoe*. New York: Cambridge University Press.

Chapter 12

Abe, Kashō, Yuichirō Oguro, and Risaku Kiritōshi. 2001. "Eiga ga owatte mo bokura o oboete ite hoshii—*Sen to Chihiro no kamikakushi* ishu kakutō gi zadan kai." *Yuriika* (August): 136–153.
Figal, Gerald. 1999. *Civilization and Monsters: Spirits of Modernity in Meiji Japan*. Durham, NC: Duke University Press.
Fujimori, Terunobu. 1989. *Kenchiku tantei no bōken Tokyo hen*. Tokyo: Chikuma shobō.
Fukuyama, Keiko. 2004–2005. *Tokyo monogatari*. 3 vols. Tokyo: Hayakawa shobō.
Harootunian, H.D. 1998. "Figuring the Folk: History, Poetics, and Representation." In *Mirror of Modernity: Invented Traditions of Modern Japan*, ed. S. Vlastos, 144–159. Berkeley: University of California Press.
Hashimoto, Mitsuru. 1998. "*Chihō:* Yanagida Kunio's Japan." In *Mirror of Modernity: Invented Traditions of Modern Japan*, ed. S. Vlastos, 133–143. Berkeley: University of California Press.
Hatsuta, Toru. 1994. *Tokyo toshi no Meiji*. Tokyo: Chikuma shobō.
Jameson, Fredric. 1992. *Postmodernism, or the Cultural Logic of Late Capitalism*. Durham, NC: Duke University Press.
Komatsu, Kazuhiko. 1997. "Mori no kami goroshi to sono noroi." *Yuriika* (*rinji zokan, sō tokushū Miyazaki Hayao no sekai*) (November): 48–53.
Miyazaki, Hayao. 1996. *Shuppatsu ten 1979–1996*. Tokyo: Sutajio jiburi.
————. 1999. *Kaze no tani no Naushika*. Vol. 1. 7 vols. (Animage Comics Waido Ban). Tokyo: Tokuma shoten.
————. 2001. Miyazaki Hayao, long interview. In *Bessatsu komikku bokkusu Sen to Chihiro no kamikakushi: Chihiro no dai bōken*, 132–148.
————. 2001a. "Fushigi no machi no Chihiro: Kono eiga no nerai." In *Sen to Chihiro no kamikakushi o yomu 40 no me*, 18–19. Tokyo: Kinema junpō sha.
————. 2001b. "*Sen to Chihiro no kamikakushi* seisaku houkoku kai." In *Sen to Chihiro no kamikakushi o yomu 40 no me*, 52. Tokyo: Kinema junpō-sha.
————. 2001c. *Sen to Chihiro no kamikakushi*. Vol. 13. *Sutajio Jiburi e-konte shū*. Tokyo: Tokuma shoten.
————. 2002. *Kaze no kaeru basho: Naushika kara Chihiro made no kiseki*. Tokyo: Rokkinguon.

Miyazaki, Hayao, and Izumi Yamaguchi. 1997. "Hikisakare nagara ikite iku sonzai no tame ni." *Yuriika (rinji zokan, sō tokushū Miyazaki Hayao no sekai)* (November): 28–47.

Nakao, Sasuke. 1966. *Saibai shokubutsu to nōkō no kigen.* Tokyo: Iwanami shoten.

Napier, Susan J. 1990. *The Fantastic in Modern Japanese Literature.* London: Routledge.

———. 2001. *Gendai Nihon no anime,* trans. K. Kamiyama. Tokyo: Chūō kōronsha.

Ohnuki-Tierney, Emiko. 1993. *Rice as Self: Japanese Identities Through Time.* Princeton, NJ: Princeton University Press.

Saito, Ryōichi, Chizuko Imanishi, Chitaka Katō, Takashi Suzuki, and Yoshiharu Tokugi, eds. 2001. *Roman arubamu Sen to Chihiro no kamikakushi.* Tokyo: Tokuma shoten.

Sakura Wars: Return of Spirit Warriors. 2002. DVD. Directed by Susumu Kudō. Houston, TX: A.D. Vision, Inc.

Spirited Away. 2001. DVD. Directed by Hayao Miyazaki. Tokyo: Buena Vista Home Entertainment.

Tachibana, Takashi. 2001. Interview 1. In *Sen to chihiro o yomu 40 no me.* Tokyo: Kinema junpō-sha.

Watsuji, Tetsurō. 1989 (1935). *Zoku Nihon seishinshi kenkyū.* In *Watsuji Tetsurō zenshū,* vol. 4. Tokyo: Iwanami shoten.

———. 1961. *A Climate,* trans. G. Bowans. Tokyo: Printing Bureau, Japanese Government.

———. 1992. "Kokumin dōtoku ron." In *Watsuji Tetsurō zenshū,* vol. 2, annex 2. Tokyo: Iwanami shoten.

Yamato, Waki. 1975. *Haikara san ga tōru—hana no Tokyo dai roman.* Vol. 1, *Kōdansha komikku furendo.* Tokyo: Kōdansha.

Yōrō, Takeshi. 2002. *Mushi me to anime.* Tokyo: Tokuma shoten.

Chapter 13

Abbott, Spence (aka "Spence D."). "Review of *Millennium Actress.*" *Rotten Tomatoes.* www.rottentomatoes.com/click/movie1124128/reviews.php?critic=columns&sortby =author&page=3&rid=1197562. Accessed December 20, 2005.

Aoyagi, Hiroshi. 2005. *Islands of Eight Million Smiles: Idol Performance and Symbolic Production in Contemporary Japan.* Cambridge, MA: Harvard University Asian Center.

Arnold, Michael. 2002. "Review: *Millennium Actress.*" In *Midnight Eye: The Latest and Best in Japanese Cinema,* eds. Tom Mes and Jasper Sharp, August 26. www.midnighteye. com/reviews/millactr.shtml. Accessed December 14, 2005.

Campbell, Adam. 2005. "Review: *Train Man.*" In *Midnight Eye: The Latest and Best in Japanese Cinema,* eds. Tom Mes and Jasper Sharp, November 22. www.midnighteye. com/reviews/train-man.shtml. Accessed December 14, 2005.

Clements, Jonathan, and Helen McCarthy. 2001. *The Anime Encyclopedia: A Guide to Japanese Anime Since 1917.* Berkeley, CA: Stone Bridge Press.

Harada Maya. 2003. "Maikeru Sutoraddofōdo intabyū (Michael Stradford Interview)." *Kinema junpō,* no. 1393 (November): 73–74.

Kehr, Dave. 2004. "New Contender for the *Anime* Throne." *New York Times,* November 22, late edition.

Kinsella, Sharon. 1998. "Japanese Subculture in the 1990s: *Otaku* and the Amateur *Manga* Movement." *Journal of Japanese Studies* 24, no. 2 (Summer): 289–316.

Kitagawa Reiko. 2003. "Satoshi Kon kantoku intabyū." *Kinema junpō,* no. 1393 (November): 70–72.

Kon, Satoshi. 2002. *Kon's Tone: Sennen joyū e no michi*. Tokyo: Shobunsha.
_____, ed. 2004. *Kon's Tone*. November 11, 2004. www.parkcity.ne.jp/~s-kon/. Accessed December 1, 2005.
Kon, Satoshi, and Yūichirō Oguro. 2002. *Sennen joyū gahō /Chiyoko Millennium Actress Special Edition*. Tokyo: MADHOUSE.
Looser, Thomas. 2002. "From Edogawa to Miyazaki: Cinematic and *Anime*-ic Architectures of Early and Late Twentieth-Century Japan." *Japan Forum* 14, no. 2: 297–327.
Mes, Tom. 2001. "Interview: Satoshi Kon." In *Midnight Eye: The Latest and Best in Japanese Cinema*, eds. Tom Mes and Jasper Sharp, November 2. http: //midnighteye. com/interviews/satoshi_kon.shtml. Accessed December 14, 2005.
Morris-Suzuki, Tessa. 1998. *Re-Inventing Japan: Time, Space, Nation*. Armonk, NY: M.E. Sharpe.
Murakami, Takashi, ed. 2005. *Little Boy: The Arts of Japan's Exploding Subculture*. New Haven, CT: Yale University Press.
Okada, Toshio. 1992. *Otaku no bideo/Zoku otaku no bideo*. Screenplay. DVD. Directed by Mori Takeshi. 1992. Animeigo (2001).
_____. 1997. *Tōdai otakugaku kōza*. Tokyo: Kōdansha.
Pāfekuto burū [Perfect blue]. 1998. Directed by Satoshi Kon. DVD. Tokyo: MADHOUSE. Manga Entertainment.
Patten, Fred. 2004. *Watching Anime, Reading Manga: 25 Years of Essays and Reviews*. Berkeley, CA: Stone Bridge Press.
Scott, A.O. 2003. "To the Samurai and Godzilla, With Love." *New York Times*, September 12, late edition.
Sennen joyū [Millennium actress]. 2001. Directed by Satoshi Kon. DVD. MADHOUSE. Dreamworks Home Entertainment.
Sharp, Jasper. 2001. "Review: *Perfect Blue*." In *Midnight Eye: The Latest and Best in Japanese Cinema*, eds. Tom Mes and Jasper Sharp, March 20. http: //midnighteye. com/reviews/perfectb.shtml. Accessed May 12, 2005.
Silverberg, Miriam. 1991. "The Modern Girl as Militant." In *Recreating Japanese Women, 1600–1945*, ed. Gail Lee Bernstein, 239266. Berkeley: University of California Press.
Steinberg, Marc. 2004. "*Otaku* Consumption, Superflat Art and the Return to Edo." *Japan Forum* 16, no. 3: 449–471.
Tanaka, Chiyoko. 2002. "Satoshi Kon *Sennen joyū* kantoku: Hasso sae areba jitsugen suru shudan wa ikurademo aru." *Kinema junpō*, no. 1365 (October): 75–77.
Toki Studio (Sutajio Toki), ed. 2001. *Mad About MADHOUSE*. Tokyo: Ōkura shuppan.

Chapter 14

Bachmayer, Eva. 1986. "Gequälter Engel: Das Frauenbild in den erotischen Comics in Japan: Versuch einer psychoanalytischen und feministischen Interpretation." In *Aspekte japanischer Comics*, ed. Institut für Japanologie der Universität Wien, 95–223. Vienna.
Berndt, Jaqueline. 2001. "Permeability and Othering: The Relevance of 'Art' in Contemporary Japanese Manga Discourse." In *Approches critiques de la pensée japonaise du XX siécle*, ed. Livia Monnet, 349–375. Montréal: Les Presses de l'Université de Montréal.
_____. 2002. "Manga de arawasu": Manga ni fusawashii bigaku no hanmen kyōshi toshite no chūgakkō shin bijutsuka." In *Manga kenkyū* 1 (May 2002): 80–85.

Carrier, David. 2000. *The Aesthetics of Comics*. University Park: Pennsylvania State University Press.

Clark, Vicky A., ed. 2003. *Comic Release: Negotiating Identity for a New Generation*. New York: D.A.P.

Frahm, Ole. 2000. "Weird Signs. Comics as Means of Parody." In *Comics & Culture. Analytical and Theoretical Approaches to Comics*, eds. Anne Magnussen and Hans-Christian Christiansen, 177–191. Copenhagen: Museum Tusculanum Press.

Fukushima, Yoshiko. 2003. *Manga Discourse in Japanese Theater: The Location of Noda Hideki's Yume no Yuminsha*. London: Kegan Paul.

Guden, Mireille. 1998. "Tagawa Suihō's 'Norakuro': Eine Analyse unter Berücksichtigung der Entwicklung des Manga in der Taishō und frühen Shōwa-Zeit." Unpublished dissertation, Japanese Studies. Universität Trier.

Hidaka, Kaoru. 2003. *Nihon bijutsu no kotoba annai*. Tokyo: Shōgakukan.

Hosogaya, Atsushi, ed. 2002. *Nihon manga wo shiru tame no bukku gaido*. Tokyo: Ajia Manga samitto jikkō iinkai.

Hosokibara, Seiki. 1924. *Nihon mangashi*. Tokyo: Yūzankaku.

Inoue, Manabu, ed. 1995. *Manga no yomikata*. Tokyo: Takarajimasha.

Ishiko, Junzō. 1967. *Manga geijutsuron. Gendai Nihonjin no sensu to yūmoa no kōzai*. Tokyo: Fuji Shoin.

―――. 1972. *Sengo mangashi nōto*. Tokyo: Kinokuniya shoten.

―――. 1973. *Gekiga no shisō*. Tokyo: Taihei shuppansha.

Itō, Gō. 2005. *Tezuka izu deddo. Hirakareta manga hyōgenron e*. Tokyo: NTT shuppan.

Kinsella, Sharon. 2000. *Adult Manga. Culture and Power in Contemporary Japanese Society*. Honolulu: University of Hawai'i Press.

Köhn, Stephan. 2005. *Traditionen visuellen Erzählens in Japan. Eine paradigmatische Untersuchung der Entwicklungslinien vom Faltschirmbild zum narrativen Manga*. Wiesbaden: Harrassowitz Verlag.

Kure, Tomofusa. 1986. *Gendai manga no zentaizō*. Tokyo: Jōhō sentā shuppankyoku.

Kusaka, Midori. 2000. *Mangagaku no susume*. Tokyo: Hakuteisha.

Lamarre, Thomas. 2004/2005. "An Introduction to Otaku Movement." *EnterText* 4, no. 1 (Winter): 151–187. http://people.brunel.ac.uk/~acsrrrm/entertext/home.htr. December 20, 2005.

Manga wa naze omoshiroi no ka. 1996. Twelve-part television series. NHK Ningen daigaku/Human University.

Maderdonner, Megumi. 1986. Kinder-Comics als Spiegel der gesellschaftlichen Entwicklung in Japan." In *Aspekte japanischer Comics*, ed. Institut für Japanologie der Universität Wien, 1–94. Vienna.

―――. 1997. "Shōjo manga no sekai. Japanische Mädchen-Comics als Spiegel der Mädchenwelt." Unpublished dissertation. Universität Wien.

Miyamoto, Hirohito. 2002. "The Formation of an Impure Genre. On the Origins of *Manga*," trans. Jennifer Prough. In *Review of Japanese Culture and Society* 14 (December): 39–48.

―――. 2003a. "'Manga' gainen no jūsōka katei—Kinsei kara kindai ni okeru." In *Bijutsushi* 52, no. 2: 319–334.

―――. 2003b. "'Ponchi' to 'manga,' sono shimbun to no kakawari." In *Shimbun manga no me. Hito, seiji, shakai*, ed. Newspark (Nihon shimbun hakubutsukan), (exh. cat., Nov. 2003—Feb. 2004), 106–109. Yokohama: Newspark.

Murakami, Tomohiko, Ei Takatori, and Yoshihiro Yonezawa. 1987. *Mangaden. "Kyōjin no hoshi" kara "Oishinbo" made*. Tokyo: Heibonsha.

Nakajima, Azusa. 1986. *Manga seishunki*. Tokyo: Shūeisha.

Napier, Susan J. 2001. *Anime from Akira to Princess Mononoke: Experiencing Contemporary Japanese Animation*. New York: Palgrave.

Natsume, Fusanosuke. 1992a. *Natsume Fusanosuke no mangagaku*. Tokyo: Chikuma shobō.

―――. 1992b. *Tezuka Osamu wa doko ni iru*. Tokyo: Chikuma shobō.

―――. 1995. *Tezuka Osamu no bōken*. Tokyo: Chikuma shobō.

―――. 1997. *Manga wa naze omoshiroi no ka?* Tokyo: NHK shuppan kyōkai.

―――. 2000. "Manga hyōgenron no 'genkai' wo megutte." In *Man-bi-ken. Manga no bi/gakutekina jigen e no sekkin*, ed. Jaqueline Berndt, Kyōto: Daigo shobō, 2–22.

―――. 2003. "Manga no shakaigaku ni igi ari." In *Manga no ibasho*, ed. Fusanosuke Natsume, 242–243. Tokyo: NTT shuppan.

Ogawa, Toshiaki. 2004. "Gendai Nihon anime *Akira* kara *Sen to Chihiro no Kamikakushi* made" (review). In *Japanese Journal of Animation Studies* 5 (1A): 37.

Ōgi, Fusami. 2001. "Beyond *Shoujo*, Blending Gender: Subverting the Homogendered World in *Shoujo Manga* (Japanese Comics for Girls)." In *International Journal of Comic Art* (Fall): 151–161.

Ogino, Masahiro, and Kōjirō Miyahara, eds, 2001. *Manga no shakaigaku*. Kyōto: Sekai shisōsha.

Onoda, Natsu. 2002. "Drag Prince in Spotlight: Theatrical Cross-Dressing in Osamu Tezuka's Early *Shōjo Manga*." In *International Journal of Comic Art* 4 (2): 124–139.

Ōtsuka, Eiji. 1994. *Sengo manga no hyōgen kūkan: Kigōteki shintai no jubaku*. Tokyo: Hōzōkan.

Phillipps, Susanne. 1996. *Erzählform Manga. Eine Analyse der Zeitstrukturen in Tezuka Osamus "Hi no tori" ("Phönix")*. Wiesbaden: Harrassowitz (Iaponia Insula, Bd. 3).

―――. 2000. "Tezuka Osamu. Figuren, Themen und Erzählstrukturen im Manga-Gesamtwerk." Unpublished dissertation. Munich: Iudicium.

Shūkan Nihon no bi wo meguru: Anime no hajimari—Chōjū giga. 2002. no. 15, Shōgakukan (August 6).

Spies, Alwyn. 2001. "Kokoro o iyasu shōjo manga to josei no byōrika." In *Ritsumeikan gengo bunka kenkyū* 13, no. 1: 137–148.

―――. 2003. "Studying Shōjo Manga: Global Education, Narratives of the Self and the Pathologization of the Feminine." Unpublished dissertation, Asian Studies. Vancouver: University of British Columbia.

Takahashi, Mizuki. 2001. "Manga kenkyū ni kansuru ichi kōsatsu. Shōjo manga kenkyū no shiten kara." In *Ritsumeikan gengo bunka kenkyū* 13, no. 1: 149–154.

Takeuchi, Osamu. 1992. *Tezuka Osamu ron*. Tokyo: Heibonsha.

―――. 1995. *Sengo manga 50 nenshi*. Tokyo: Chikuma shobō.

―――. 1997. *Manga no hihyō to kenkyū + shiryō*. Privately published.

Takeuchi, Osamu, and Tomohiko Murakami, eds. 1989. *Manga hihyō taikei*, 4 vols. + 1. Tokyo: Heibonsha.

Tezuka, Osamu. 1982. "Watashi to Chōjū giga." *NHK Nichiyō bijutsukan*.

Tsugata, Nobuyuki. 2004. *Nihon animēshon no chikara. 85 nen no rekishi o tsuranuku futatsu no jiku*. Tokyo: NTT shuppan.

Tsuji, Nobuo. 2001. "Early Medieval Picture Scrolls as Ancestors of Anime and Manga." In *Births and Rebirths in Japanese Art*, ed. Nicole Coolidge Rousmaniere, 53–82. Leiden: Hotei Publishers.

Tsurumi, Shunsuke. 1982. *Genkai geijutsuron*. Tokyo: Keisō shobō.

―――. 1987. *A Cultural History of Postwar Japan 1945–1980*. London: Kegan Paul International.

Yamamoto, Yōko. 2004. "Manga izen no Nihon kaiga no jikan to kūkan hyōgen. Manga no koma to no taihi ni oite." In *Meisei daigaku kenkyū kiyō*, no. 12 (March): 113–126.

Yiengpruksawan, Mimi. 2000. "Monkey Magic: How the 'Animals' Scroll Makes Mischief with Art Historians." *Orientations* 31, no. 3 (March): 74–83.

Yomota, Inuhiko. 1994. *Manga genron.* Tokyo: Chikuma Shobō.

Yonezawa, Yoshihiro, ed. 1987. *Manga hihyō sengen.* Tokyo: Aki shobō.

About the Contributors

Jaqueline Berndt was granted her Ph.D. in aesthetics at Humboldt University Berlin in 1991, and is currently an associate professor (*jokyōju*) for Art and Media Studies, Yokohama National University. Her research interests are in the aesthetics of comics, modern art in Japan, and contemporary visual culture. Her manga-related publications include: *Phänomen Manga. Comic-Kultur in Japan* (edition q, 1995), *Man-bi-ken. Manga no bi/gakuteki jigen e no sekkin* (Daigo shobō 2002), "The Time of Comics. Reading a Post/Historical Art Form from the Perspective of Manga," in: *AESTHETICS* 11 (2004), "Permeability and Othering: The Relevance of 'Art' in Contemporary Japanese Manga Discourse," in *Critical Perspectives on Twentieth Century Japanese Thought* (Montreal University Press, 2001), and *Reading Manga from Multiple Perspectives: Japanese Comics and Globalisation* (Leipzig University Press, 2006).

Richard A. Gardner is a professor of religion and Dean of The Faculty of Liberal Arts at Sophia University in Tokyo. His recent publications include: "Humor and Religion: An Overview," in *Encyclopedia of Religion* (Macmillan Reference USA, 2005), "Collective Memory, National Identity: Victims and Victimizers in Japan," in *Quoting God: How Media Shape Ideas About Religion and Culture* (Baylor University Press, 2005), "The Blessing of Living in a Country Where There Are *Senryū!*: Humor in the Response to Aum Shinrikyō," in *Asian Folklore Studies* 61 (2002), and "Aum and the Media: Lost in the Cosmos and the Need to Know," in *Religion and Social Crisis in Japan: Understanding Japanese Society through the Aum Affair* (Palgrave, 2001).

Kinko Ito was granted her Ph.D. in sociology from Ohio State University in 1987, and is currently professor of sociology at University of Arkansas at Little Rock. Her manga-related publications include: "Images of Women in Weekly Male Comic Magazines in Japan," *Journal of Popular Culture* 27 (1994), "The Manga Culture in Japan," *Japanese Studies Review* (2000), "The World of Japanese Ladies' Comics: From Romantic Fantasy to Lustful Perversion," *Journal of Popular Culture* 36 (2002),

"Japanese Ladies' Comics as Agents of Socialization: The Lessons They Teach," *International Journal of Comic Art* (2003), "Growing Up Japanese Reading Manga," in *International Journal of Comic Art* (2004), and "A History of Manga in the Context of Japanese Culture and Society," in *Journal of Popular Culture* 38 (2005).

Mark MacWilliams is an associate professor of Religious Studies at St. Lawrence University, Canton, New York, where he teaches East Asian religions. His current area of research is religion and visual culture. MacWilliams's manga-related publications include: "Buddhist Pilgrim/Buddhist Exile: Old and New Images of Retired Emperor Kazan in the Saigoku Kannon Temple Guidebooks, *History of Religions* 34 (1995), "Japanese Comic Books (*Manga*) and Religion: Osamu Tezuka's Story of the Buddha," in *Japan Pop!: Inside the World of Japanese Popular Culture* (M.E. Sharpe, 2000), and "Revisioning Japanese Religiosity: Osamu Tezuka's *Hi no tori* (*The Phoenix*)," in *Global Goes Local: Popular Culture in Asia* (University of British Columbia Press, 2002).

Lee A. Makela is an associate professor of East Asian history, emeritus, at Cleveland State University. His research interests range from Tokugawa-era urban cultural history through contemporary popular culture, particularly as both are expressed through structural and visual means. He has served regularly as a study leader for the Smithsonian Institution in Washington, D.C., leading annual travel seminars to Japan. In 1996 and 2003, he conducted research and taught at the Japan Center for Michigan Universities in Hikone.

Yulia Mikhailova has held research and teaching positions at the Institute of Oriental Studies (St. Petersburg, Russia) and Griffith University (Australia). Presently she is a professor at the Faculty of International Studies of Hiroshima City University, Japan. Her publications include *Motoori Norinaga: His Life and Work* (Nauka, 1988), *Social and Political Perspectives in Japan, 1860s and 1880s* (Nauka, 1990), and, most recently, *Russo-Japanese Images and Representations through Visual Media—for Understanding of Russian-Japanese Relations* (Hiroshima City University, 2005).

Eldad Nakar received his Ph.D. in Sociology from the University of Tsukuba, Japan, in 2003. He is currently a visiting scholar at Keio University in Tokyo. His research involves popular and material culture, social memory, and Japanese manga. His recent publications include "Tasha no hana—sono shikakutekina hyōgen," *Gendai shakai riron kenkyū* 11 (2001), "Manga—from Center to Periphery, Back and Forth," *Tsukuba Annals of Sociology* 14 (2002), and "Nosing Around—Visual Representation of the Other in Japanese Society," *Anthropological Forum* 13 (2003). He is presently doing research on the social memory of the late Japanese diplomat, Chiune Sugihara.

Melek Ortabasi is an assistant professor of comparative literature at Hamilton College in New York State. Her publications include "Fictional Fantasy or Historical Fact? The Search for Japanese Identity in Miyazaki Hayao's *Mononoke-hime"* (2000), "Sketching Out the Critical Tradition: Kunio Yanagita and the Reappraisal of Realism" (2003), and *The Modern Murasaki: Writing by Women of Meiji Japan,* coedited with Rebecca Copeland (forthcoming). Her research interests include Japanese film and popular culture, modern Japanese literature and intellectual history, and translation theory. She is currently working on a book about ethnologist Kunio Yanagita (1875–1962).

Rajyashree Pandey is reader/associate professor in the Asian Studies Program at La Trobe University, Melbourne. She is a specialist in medieval Japanese literature and the author of *Writing and Renunciation: The Works of the Poet/Priest Kamo no Chōmei* (University of Michigan, Japanese Monograph Series, Ann Arbor, Michigan, 1998). She is currently working on a book on representations of the body and of female sexuality in medieval literature and art.

Susanne Phillipps majored in Japanese studies, studies of linguistics and semiotics in Frankfurt/Main and Berlin, completing her Ph.D. in 2000 after working as a research fellow at the Free University of Berlin, 1995–1997 and the Univesity of Trier. Her works include: *Erzählform Manga: Eine Analyse der Zeitstrukturen in Tezuka Osamus "Hi no tori" ("Phönix")* (Wiesbaden: Harrassowitz, 1996) and *Tezuka Osamu: Figuren, Themen und Erzählstrukturen im Manga-Gesamtwerk* (München: Iudicum, 2000).

Gilles Poitras is a librarian in the San Francisco area who publishes a monthly column on Japanese animation in *Newtype USA* entitled, "Below the Surface." He has published three books in the field of anime: *The Anime Companion: What's Japanese in Japanese Animation?* (Stone Bridge Press, 1998), *Anime Essentials: Everything a Fan Needs to Know* (Stone Bridge Press, 2000), and the *Anime Companion 2: More What's Japanese in Japanese Animation?* (Stone Bridge Press, 2005). He remains active doing numerous presentations and workshops for Japan–U.S. friendship groups, the Smithsonian Institution, Pixar, and others.

Deborah Shamoon is an assistant professor at the University of Notre Dame, Department of East Asian Languages and Literatures. Her research focuses on representations of teenage girls in modern Japanese literature, film, television, and manga. She is currently working on a book on the connection between prewar girls' magazines and postwar *shōjo manga*.

Frederik L. Schodt has written extensively on manga. He is the author of *Manga! Manga! The World of Japanese Comics* (Kodansha International, 1983) and *Dreamland Japan: Writings on Modern Manga* (Stone Bridge Press, 1996). In 2000 the *Asahi shimbun*'s Osamu Tezuka Culture Award committee gave him a special prize in recognition of his work in helping to popularize manga overseas.

Mizuki Takahashi completed a masters of philosophy at the University of London, School of Oriental and African Study in 2000. She is currently based in Japan working as a curator at the Contemporary Art Center, Art Tower Mito. She specializes in Japanese visual culture, especially the relationship between ideology and form in Japanese contemporary art and popular culture.

Hiroshi Yamanaka is a professor for religious studies at Tsukuba University in Japan. He is a former president of the Japanese Association for the Study of Religion and Society, and currently the editor of *Journal of Religious Studies*. He recently published *An Introduction to Religious Studies* (Mineruba shobō, 2005) and currently working on the relationship between pilgrimage and cultural tourism in Japan as well as spirituality in Japanese pop culture.

Shiro Yoshioka is a Ph.D candidate in the Division of Comparative Culture at International Christian University, Tokyo. He is currently completing his dissertation on Hayao Miyazaki's view of Japanese history and culture.

Index